Capital, Power, and
Inequality in Latin America

Latin American Perspectives Series

Ronald H. Chilcote, Series Editor

†Available in hardcover and paperback

Capital, Power, and Inequality in Latin America

EDITED BY

Sandor Halebsky
and Richard L. Harris

Westview Press

Boulder • San Francisco • Oxford

Latin American Perspectives Series, number 16

Published in 1995 in the United States of America by Westview Press, Inc., 5500 Central Avenue, Boulder, Colorado 80301-2877, and in the United Kingdom by Westview Press, 12 Hid's Copse Road, Cumnor Hill, Oxford OX2 9JJ

Library of Congress Cataloging-in-Publication Data
Capital, power, and inequality in Latin America / edited by Sandor Halebsky and Richard L. Harris.
    p.   cm. — (Latin American perspectives series; no. 16)
    Includes bibliographical references and index.
    ISBN 0-8133-2116-6 — ISBN 0-8133-2117-4 (pbk.)
    1. Latin America—Economic conditions—1982– 2. Latin America—
Social conditions—1982– 3. Latin America—Politics and
government—1980– 4. Power (Social sciences)—Latin America.
5. Equality—Latin America. I. Halebsky, Sandor. II. Harris,
Richard L. (Richard Legé), 1939– . III. Series.
HC125.C32   1995
330.98—dc20
                                                                95-2898
                                                                CIP

Printed and bound in the United States of America

The paper used in this publication meets the requirements of the American National Standard for Permanence of Paper for Printed Library Materials Z39.48-1984.

10   9   8   7   6   5   4   3   2   1

Contents

Introduction: Capital, Power, and Inequality in Latin America

SANDOR HALEBSKY AND RICHARD L. HARRIS

More than two decades ago two social scientists, Fernando Henrique Cardoso and Enzo Faletto, published what soon became a classic analysis of the economic, political, and social development of Latin America, *Dependency and Development in Latin America*. In the preface to the English edition, they stated:

> We seek a global and dynamic understanding of social structures instead of look-
> ing only at specific dimensions of the social process. We oppose the academic
> tradition which conceived of domination and socio-cultural relations as "dimen-
> sions," analytically independent of one another, and together independent of
> the economy, as if each one of these dimensions corresponded to separate
> spheres of reality. In that sense, we stress the socio-political nature of the eco-
> nomic relations of production, thus following the nineteenth century tradition
> of treating economy as political economy. This methodological approach, which
> found its highest expression in Marx, assumes the hierarchy that exists in society
> is the result of established ways of organizing the production of material and
> spiritual life. (1979:ix)

The present volume of comparative essays on contemporary Latin America follows in the same intellectual tradition. To analyze and make sense of the many complex and changing conditions in Latin America, we use a comparative, regional perspective similar to that employed by Cardoso and Faletto. Moreover, to provide an integrative framework that encompasses the diversity of conditions analyzed by the contributors in this volume, we have selected three key organizing concepts. These three concepts are capital, power, and inequality. They share important analytical qualities in that they are multidimensional, multilevel, comprehensive, and integrative. Theoretically powerful, these concepts also facilitate a comparative analysis of the many complex, dynamic, and interdependent societal structures, processes, and relations underlying contemporary Latin American affairs. In addition, capital, power, and inequality are compatible with the intellectual tradition mentioned above. As Cardoso and Faletto explain with regard to the concept of capital:

> First of all, it is necessary to propose concepts able to explain trends of change. This implies the recognition of opposing forces which drag history ahead. Second, it is necessary to relate these forces in a global way, characterizing the basic sources of their existence, continuity, and change by determining forms of domination and the forces opposed to them. *So, without the concept of capital as the result of the exploitation of one class by another it is not possible to explain the movement of capitalist society.* (1979:xiii) [emphasis supplied]

Like Cardoso and Faletto, we use the concept of capital to draw attention to the inequitable manner in which wealth is accumulated in Latin America through exploitative relations of production and exchange that are particular to capitalism. Like Cardoso and Faletto, and the many others who have contributed to the intellectual tradition followed in this volume, we use the concept of capital because it reveals the fundamental relations of exploitation underlying contemporary conditions not only in Latin America but also elsewhere in the world.

Power and inequality have the same conceptual and analytical properties that Cardoso and Faletto attribute to capital. Applied broadly to the analysis of social phenomena in Latin America, the concept of power encompasses all those conditions and circumstances involving subordination and domination and the use of force and coercion as well as empowerment and emancipation. Thus, power in this volume is not to be narrowly construed as "political" relations but instead encompasses subordination and empowerment, the use of force and emancipation. Power applies to the subordination of women as well as their empancipation; the coercion exercised by international organizations such as the International Monetary Fund (IMF) and transnational corporations; the use of force by military as well as revolutionary organizations; and the empowerment of communities and social movements that organize to promote their interests.

In a similar manner, the concept of inequality focuses attention on the various forms of social inequity, unjust privileges and social discrimination that exist in Latin America. At the micro-level this concept applies to gender inequalities within the family unit, at the middle level it encompasses racial and cultural discrimination as well as the unequal access of different categories of the population to the basic necessities of human existence, and at the global level the concept encompasses phenomena such as the unequal terms of trade that exist between the Latin American countries and the United States. In fact, the social, economic, and political disparities are so ubiquitous and extreme in Latin America, one could argue that inequality should be the main *explanandum* (focus of explanation) of any intellectual effort to analyze the historical development and contemporary conditions of the Latin American societies (Schuurman 1993:30–31).

An analysis of inequality in Latin America inevitably involves an examination of the exploitative relations of capitalist production and distribution, the hierarchical relations of power and forms of coercion, and the intra- and inter-elite networks of political and social influence that dominate the region. In analyzing "the system of production and institutions of appropriation" in Latin America, Cardoso and Faletto linked "the strong inequalities" and "processes of domination" to the extremely exploitative and inequitable character of capitalist relations of production, distribution, and accumulation in the region (1979:x). Thus, the interdependent linkages that connect different aspects of the social reality of Latin America can be revealed only if the concepts of capital, power, and inequality are applied in unison.

The authors of the chapters in this volume use many specific concepts and approaches to analyze and explain particular aspects of contemporary Latin American affairs. Their main themes and conclusions, however, can be organized and integrated by using the concepts of capital, power, and inequality.

Capitalism in Contemporary Latin America

In the past two decades nearly every major aspect of contemporary economic, political, and social life in Latin America has been transformed by the region's integration into the global capitalist system. As revealed in the chapters by John Weeks, Carlos M. Vilas, and Richard L. Harris, the debt crisis and economic recession experienced by the Latin American countries during the 1980s have made these societies extremely vulnerable to the pressures of the international lending agencies and other global actors such as the transnational corporations and the U.S. government. These global actors have pressured the Latin American governments into restructuring their economies and adopting neoliberal economic policies that have had profound effects on the economic, social, and political conditions of the general population.

Chapter 4, by John Weeks, explains how the shift to neoliberal policies has come about in Latin America and explores the implications for the region. Weeks's analysis reveals that "this policy shift in Latin America had little to do with the alleged 'exhaustion' of import substitution and still less with the theoretically suspect arguments for the efficiency gains from free markets," which are the standard justifications given by the advocates of neoliberal structural adjustments. Behind the neoliberal rhetoric about the virtues of free markets and the supposed failure of the previous attempts on the part of the Latin American states to promote national development through the substitution of domestically produced goods for imported products, Weeks concludes that, in fact, the "policy shift resulted directly from the pressure on Latin American governments to service their debts in the wake of the explosion of indebtedness that followed the oil price increases of the first half of the 1970s."

The debt crisis in Mexico, Bolivia, and Argentina prompted the IMF, the World Bank, and other international lending agencies such as the Inter-American Development Bank (IDB) to impose free market structural adjustment policies on the Latin American governments to ensure that they dedicated sufficient funds to the repayment of their international debts. These adjustment policies opened up Latin America's domestic markets to foreign capital, promoted so-called nontraditional exports (to earn as much foreign exchange as possible for debt payments), deregulated the local capital and commercial markets, adopted unpopular fiscal austerity measures to divert public funds to debt payments, and privatized the large state enterprises developed during the preceding period of national industrial development.

These policies have in general slowed the rate of economic growth, brought about a drastic reduction of government services and public employment, resulted in the wholesale denationalization of these countries' major utilities and public enterprises, and abolished the protective tariffs and other forms of support previously enjoyed by local industries. National currencies have also been devalued and pegged to the U.S. dollar, and exports (particularly nontraditional exports such as fruit, vegetables, flowers, and some manufactured goods) have been promoted at the expense of the production of food crops for domestic consumption. As a result, even though the upper classes and their government agents incurred the huge debt, the lower classes have been saddled with paying for it.

The "austerity measures" adopted by most governments in the region have cut into public expenditures on education, health, and other social services, adversely affecting the incomes and living standards of not only the lower classes but also important sectors of the middle class. The consequences of these policies, in tandem with the effects of the global economic recession of the 1980s and early 1990s, have been graphically described by Juan de Días Parra, head of the Latin American Association for Human Rights: "In Latin America today there are 70 million more hungry, 30 million more illiterate, 10 million more families without homes and 40 million more unemployed persons than there were 20 years ago. . . . There are 240 million human beings who lack the necessities of life and this when the region is richer and more stable than ever, according to the way the world sees it" (Press 1993:E20).

Neoliberal economic policies have also jeopardized the limited political democratization under way in Latin American societies. Chapter 3, by Jorge Nef, reveals that these unpopular policies were introduced in most cases by the repressive military regimes that held sway throughout Latin America in the 1970s and 1980s. He notes that the civilian governments that succeeded these regimes have continued these unpopular measures, which, along with other factors, has undermined their popular legitimacy.

These developments must be viewed in relation to the larger global context of transnational capitalist concentration, centralization, and technological innovation. Viewed from a global perspective, the Latin American economies, as well as other economies in the world, are being integrated into a rapidly more interdependent global capitalist economic system. Chapter 11, by Richard Harris, indicates that global capitalist integration has involved the expansion of the activities and influence of the transnational corporations and financial institutions that dominate the global capitalist system. The accelerated integration of the Latin American economies into the global capitalist system has been accompanied by an increase in the direct investments of transnational corporations in the region as well as increased control by the transnational financial institutions over local financial structures and services.

The analyses of both Harris and Weeks reveal that Latin American countries are more dependent than ever on external trade because their economies have been restructured around the export of nontraditional products, the repayment of their huge debts through the foreign exchange earned from these exports, and their adoption of free trade policies at the behest of the international lending agencies and the U.S. government. Efforts at regional economic integration and interdependence have also increased, as evidenced by the growth of binational trade pacts, multinational free trade areas, and stepped-up trade among Latin American nations (Brooke 1994:3). However, these developments have not strengthened the position of Latin America in world trade because they are designed to eliminate the barriers to the mobility of capital between Latin American countries and to transform their economies into the captive markets of a single trade bloc dominated by North American–based transnational corporations and their local business associates.

Chapter 1, by Cristóbal Kay, reveals the transformations in agricultural practices as a result of the integration of the Latin American economies into the global capitalist food system. Kay's analysis indicates that export-oriented modern capitalist farms and agroindustrial complexes, many of which are tied to transnational corporations, have replaced most of the former large estates and plantations that dominated the Latin American countryside for centuries. Kay also notes that the traditional peasant sector is declining as a result of the peasantry's increasing reliance on wage-earning sources of income and their massive migration to the cities. His research reveals that the integration of Latin American agriculture into the global capitalist economic system is benefiting only a privileged minority of the rural population and that the peasantry have been largely excluded from the benefits. According to Kay, the exclusionary nature of the capitalist modernization of Latin American agriculture has increased rural impoverishment and accelerated the migration of the rural poor to the cities.

The massive rural-to-urban migration is discussed by Sandor Halebsky. His analysis in Chapter 2 indicates that the concentration of wealth, employment, and services in Latin America's cities has historically attracted migrants from the rural areas. In the past fifty years, however, changes in the capitalist system have transformed most Latin American countries from predominantly rural to largely urban societies.

Halebsky's analysis focuses on the survival strategies of the urban poor—how they have adapted to the harsh conditions in Latin America's growing urban areas. He argues that the absorption of rural migrants and unemployed workers into the growing informal sector (comprising self-employed street vendors, hired hands, workers in small workshops, day laborers, repairmen, prostitutes, domestic servants, and the like) and the spreading shantytowns has contributed to the restructuring of contemporary capitalism. This large informal sector depresses wages and reduces the costs of reproducing the urban labor force for both the local businesses and the transnational corporations. The capitalists have thus been able to maximize their profits by paying low wages and offering few if any benefits.

The informal sector, according to Halebsky, provides cheap services and goods as well as a reserve army of labor for the formal sector corporations and businesses. In this regard it represents a type of informal subsidy for formal sector enterprises. However, Halebsky makes it clear that the restructuring of the economy has made this sector the only avenue of survival for an increasing proportion of the urban population. The restructuring of the Latin American economies in response to global influences and the harsh effects of the neoliberal economic policies carried out by the Latin American governments have forced a large proportion of the urban population into the informal sector and the shantytowns.

The global process of capitalist restructuring and concentration and the neoliberal reforms have reconfigured Latin America's labor market, increased the transfer of income from the lower classes to the upper classes, and vitiated the position of the working class. Carlos M. Vilas analyzes the impact of these changes on the working class as well as the self-employed, underemployed, and precariously employed members of the informal sector. Vilas and Weeks describe how the working class and other lower-class elements (i.e., the peasantry, lower-middle-class strata, the poor laborers in the informal sector, etc.) have been forced to bear the costs of the economic crisis of the

1980s and the global process of capitalist restructuring under way since the 1970s.

Real wages in most Latin American countries have deteriorated significantly since the 1970s. Moreover, labor turnover and temporary jobs have increased, and four out of every five new jobs created since the 1980s have been either in the informal sector or the sector of small workshops and businesses. As a result, a large proportion of the working class holds precarious jobs, and the labor unions in most cases have lost the bargaining positions they held in the 1960s and 1970s. In fact, most workers find themselves in extremely precarious situations since they lack union representation, access to welfare benefits, effective legal protection, and job security.

Chapter 10, by Elizabeth W. Dore, on the social ecology of capitalism in Latin America, makes it clear that the global capitalist system has jeopardized not only the working class but also the environment. Dore argues that capitalism tends to be incompatible with environmental sustainability because production for profits ignores the need to preserve the environment on which the continued expansion of capital depends.

Dore reveals that to repay their international debts and comply with the neoliberal dictates of the international lending agencies, Latin American countries have increased their exports of natural resources and agricultural products and followed economic development strategies that have been antithetical to the preservation of their environment. In fact, the pressure to export and the so-called free market strategies advocated by the World Bank and other international development agencies—despite their lip service to environmental protection—have accentuated environmental degradation in Latin America.

The emphasis on exports in order to service the international debt, the neoliberal efforts to deregulate economies, and the reduction of government expenditures on programs such as reforestation have contributed to the already well established pattern of environmental despoliation characteristic of capitalist agriculture, mining, and manufacturing. As Dore indicates, under the present conditions of deregulation and so-called free market economics, the transnational corporations are attracted to Latin America because they can pollute, dispose of wastes, and extract natural resources with little fear of state interference. Thus, the degradation of the Amazon Basin as well as other important environmental resources in the region are the direct result of the expansion of global capitalism.

In sum, global capitalism has wrought significant transformations in the productive base, natural environment, domestic markets, international trading relations, monetary and banking systems, distribution of income, management-labor relations, job structures and working conditions, the structures of rural society, the quality of life in the urban areas, as well as the direction of economic development in Latin America. The impact of these transformations has been felt in nearly all aspects of contemporary Latin American affairs—economic, political, and social.

The Structures and Relations of Power in Contemporary Latin America

Power is exercised in Latin America primarily through the use of force. Nef and several other contributors to this volume note that the historical origins of Latin America lie in military conquest, political oppression, and authoritarian domination. Thus, Nef argues that the contemporary politics and social life of the region are to a large extent the legacy of European colonial domination, the forced conversion to Christianity of the indigenous population, the ideological domination of the Catholic Church, a tradition of militarism and armed conflict, as well as the institutionalization of numerous class, gender, racial, and ethnic inequalities. As a result of these and subsequent historical developments, contemporary Latin Americans have inherited state structures based on political authoritarianism, the exclusion and disenfranchisement of large sectors of the population from the governmental process, and chronic political violence, military dictatorships, and popular insurrections.

Most Latin Americans since the European Conquest have been subordinated to one or another external center of power—Spain, Portugal, Great Britain, France, and, more recently, the United States. Nef contends that this subordination has been an intervening variable that has reinforced internal patterns of domination and oppression. The ruling elites in Latin America have generally served as intermediaries for the dominant external power in subordinating the local population. Paternalistic, authoritarian, and clientalistic relations of subordination at the national and subnational levels have gone hand in hand with the subordination of entire Latin American societies to external colonial or neocolonial elites interested in the exploitation of the natural resources, labor, and capital of these societies.

In a context of cascading levels of subordination, the militarization of political life has become a long-standing tradition. Military dictatorships, military repression of popular protests and insurrections, foreign military invasions, and the frequent intervention of the military in the governmental process have been a continuing and prominent feature of the political scene. In fact, as Nef indicates, the importance of the military and the use of military force have been the natural outgrowth of a system of social relations based largely on the subordination and exploitation of the majority of the population.

In contrast to the region's history of exploitation, political oppression, and militarism—the apparent demilitarization and democratization of Latin

American states in recent years have been viewed as a welcome sign that the region is overcoming its past and undergoing a democratic political transformation. However, the contributions in this volume by Nef, Halebsky, Vilas, Hellman, and Harris call into question the significance and the extent of this transformation.

According to Nef's analysis, the civilian regimes that replaced the military dictatorships "have been neither truly democratic nor sovereign." Although they possess the formal trappings of democracy and sovereignty, the civilian regimes exclude the popular classes from effective participation in the political process. Their decisions are also subject to the de facto veto of the military and the external dictates of the IMF, the World Bank, the U.S. government, and the transnational corporations.

Because the contemporary civilian governments in Latin America are saddled with huge foreign debts, they are preoccupied with servicing these debts and implementing the neoliberal structural adjustment policies imposed by the international lending agencies. Nef concludes, therefore, that the new civilian governments are weak and "find themselves straitjacketed by utter lack of effectiveness and eroding legitimacy." Moreover, he argues that limited democratization and neoliberal economics are not likely to lead to the development of stable and sustainable regimes. Despite the rhetoric about democratic transitions, there has been more continuity than change in the power structures of Latin America. As Nef reveals, the authoritarian state structures largely remain intact, these states remain subordinate to external interests, and the military are waiting in the wings for a return to center stage.

Judith Adler Hellman's analysis, in Chapter 6, of what have been called the "new social movements" in Latin America provides a cautious but somewhat more optimistic perspective on the contemporary scene. She notes that these new movements have arisen in response to both old and new forms of subordination, and their struggles have primarily focused on consumption issues rather than (as in the case of the traditional trade unions and working-class parties) with issues related primarily to the realm of production. In many ways, however, she finds that these new movements are similar to the old movements and parties and that there are important linkages between the two.

The variety and diversity of social movements that have developed since the late 1960s in Latin America almost defy categorization: There are issue-oriented movements that arise around specific demands, such as lowering the rates for public transportation; territorial movements have arisen in shanty-towns so that the residents can gain legal titles to their housing plots and obtain public services; human rights movements have formed to oppose human rights violations in general or the violation of the rights of specific groups such as political prisoners, gays and lesbians, indigenous peoples, and so on;

religious movements such as the grassroots ecclesiastical base communities (CEBs), formed by lay members and progressive clergy within the Catholic Church; women's organizations both among the lower and middle classes; environmental movements; independent workers' associations that oppose the official trade unions in league with the authorities and employers; *indigenista* movements that seek to protect the interests and/or restore the traditions of indigenous peoples; and a host of additional new movements and organizations.

Hellman notes that, like the more traditional political parties, trade unions, and peasant organizations, these new movements have established themselves as a force with which to be reckoned on the local and national levels. Moreover, many of these movements, like the more traditional structures of political and social action in Latin America, tend to be based on clientalistic relations and influenced by the larger environment of patronage and party politics. Thus, Hellman concludes that in most cases, the new social movements have not contributed as much as might be hoped to the construction of a more democratic social order.

Yet many of the new movements have adopted innovative new tactics and gained the support of international public opinion. As Hellman notes: "Human rights as a transnational concern in which domestic and foreign activists work together to influence international public opinion is not only new in its conception, but like the feminist, gay and green movements, relies to a large extent on a network of international communications that has become feasible only in the computer age." Hellman also observes that many of the new movements develop ties with progressive political parties, trade unions, international nongovernmental agencies, and religious organizations that are willing to promote their specific interests as well as the more general goals of social justice, economic redistribution, and political democratization.

John Kirk's chapter on the Catholic Church describes the important role played by progressive church members in supporting the new social movements. The conservative orientation of the Catholic hierarchy, Kirk writes, and Pope John Paul II's assault on liberation theology have severely diminished the reformist branch of the Catholic Church. At one time, the CEBs were the most important of the new social movements, regarded by some observers as the best hope for mobilizing the population to press for major political and social reforms. It is not clear whether progressive Catholic organizations will play an important role in the political process in the future.

Dore's analysis on the social ecology of capitalism focuses attention on some of the newest of the new social movements. Environmentalism has emerged as one of the main forms of oppositional politics in Latin America. Like most of the new social movements, however, the environmental movements in Latin America rarely focus on the capitalist system and class politics. Instead, they tend to concentrate on particular issues of environmental degradation. Nevertheless, most environmental issues and crises in Latin America involve conflicts over property relations, resource use, and social justice. One of the three cases Dore chooses to illustrate this situation is the Brazilian Amazon, where competing local, national, and international groups struggle over how the region's natural resources should be used. The integration of the Amazon into the global capitalist system reveals clearly how environmental issues are intertwined with class conflict.

One of the most significant aspects of the Amazon Basin is that the conflict has been "greened" by a constellation of local, national, and international forces led by none other than the local rubber tappers and indigenous tribes. As this case suggests, an increasing number of cases are combining the rights of indigenous peoples and environmental issues.

In Chapter 8, Michael Kearney and Stefano Varese call attention to this connection by showing that the human rights violations of *indígenas* and ecological issues are inextricably interwoven—as evidenced by the international protest against the assassination of Chico Mendez, leader of the Amazonian rubber tappers' union. Their analysis reveals that in response to the invasion of their territory and the destruction of their natural resources, indigenous groups throughout Latin America have mobilized to protect their territorial rights, cultural autonomy, and environment. They have formed new movements to defend the human, cultural, and environmental rights of their members, and like many of the other new social movements, they have established linkages with supporting organizations at the local, national, and international levels.

Kearney and Varese reveal that the *indigenista* movements have formed transnational organizations to advance their common interests. These movements understand that the economic and political forces that threaten their rights and identity involve transnational corporations, national governments, and international agencies. In fact, Kearney and Varese argue that "the strategy of internationalizing the defense of collective indigenous rights appears to be more successful than the exclusive exercise of conventional mobilizations at the national level." The authors cite several successful cases to illustrate this proposition.

They note that local groups tend to form regional alliances that then coalesce with other regional alliances to form overarching national or transnational confederations. These organizations have relied on the use of the international media and international support because of their relative powerlessness at the national level. They have compensated for their domestic powerlessness by using information politics and the global media to mobilize international support for their struggles.

Chapter 7, by Francesca Miller, on the conditions of Latin American women, also reveals another important area of struggle against traditional relations of domination and subordination in the region. Miller traces the history of women's activism in Latin America back to the colonial period and demonstrates that women have played a continuing role in the struggle for social, economic, and political justice in the region. Her analysis indicates that by the 1980s the women's movement in Latin America "had developed a stinging critique of the traditional Left within their own communities, challenged the 'First World' view of feminists from Europe and the United States, and contributed organizational models, political strategies, and a new understanding of grassroots social movements to global feminism."

Miller points out that the strategies adopted by Latin American feminists have been emulated throughout the world—such as organizing household workers, using international events to publicize women's issues at the local or national level, organizing protests against the violence women experience daily, and mobilizing mothers who have lost their loved ones as a result of political repression. The recent proliferation of women's organizations throughout Latin America has had an important international dimension in that many of these groups maintain cross-national communications with one another and with women's organizations outside the region.

New social movements in Latin America represent alternative structures of power; in some cases, they have developed alternative relations of power. These alternative structures and relations have developed in opposition to the existing hierarchy based on class, gender, racial, and ethnic divisions. By joining forces with progressive political parties and organizations and enlisting international support, these new social movements could transform the existing power structures in Latin America into a new social order based on genuinely democratic relations. They have the potential to do this if they develop the shared vision, strategy, and interorganizational structures that they need to achieve this type of fundamental transformation.

Inequality in Contemporary Latin America

One of the most disturbing realities of contemporary Latin America is the extreme economic, political, and social inequality found there. Vilas's chapter on the effects of neoliberal policies on the working class shows the highest 20 percent of income earners accounted for 48 to 67 percent of the total annual income earned in thirteen Latin American countries in 1992, while the lowest 40 percent of income earners accounted for only 7 to 16 percent of the total income earned in these countries. Moreover, the polarization of the population between the haves and the have-nots is increasing in most parts of Latin America.

A concomitant feature of such income disparity is the fact that 40 percent of all Latin American households live below the poverty line—defined in terms of the income required to satisfy basic needs for food, housing, and clothing. In fact, half this group does not have an income sufficient to satisfy even their basic food needs (Cardoso and Helwege 1992:Chap. 9).

Nef reports that between 1980 and 1990 the number of poor people in Latin America increased from 120 to 200 million and that in Central America 80 percent of the population lives below the poverty line. He also reports that between 1990 and 1993 the poverty rate in Honduras increased from 68 to 78 percent, while in postrevolutionary Nicaragua more than 70 percent of the workforce is unemployed. Nef attributes these depressing statistics to the economic restructuring and observes that although the rural and urban poor have suffered the most from the structural adjustments, the middle class is disintegrating as the gap between the super-rich and the super-poor grows.

Halebsky examines the growing spatial and social polarization in urban Latin America, which stems from the increasing concentration of wealth in the hands of the privileged elites (who reside in the cities) as well as from the continuing rural-to-urban migration of impoverished elements of the population. He notes that 60 percent of the rural population in Latin America is poor, and more than one-third of the urban population lives in poverty. Halebsky also indicates that the extent of poverty has increased in the largest cities as a result of recent wage declines, the restructuring of the labor force (see Vilas's chapter), downsizing in the private sector, the reduction of the public sector workforce, and the drop in public services and subsidies.

Moreover, rates of illiteracy and infant mortality, although they have improved somewhat over the past several decades, are still unacceptably high—particularly in the rural areas. The rural population generally exhibits rates of illiteracy that are 50 percent to 75 percent greater than the population in the urban areas (Wilkie and Contreras 1992:Table 900). And somewhat more than one out of every twenty children who are born in Latin America die within a year of their birth, a rate six times as great as that in the advanced industrial nations (U.N. 1992:Table 15). For most of the population, access to doctors, medicine, and hospitals is severely limited. Disparities are especially striking between the rural and urban areas. Basic services such as running water, sewage, and electricity are unavailable for much of the rural population (see Grindle 1986:Tables 6.5, 6.6.).

Another striking condition of inequality in Latin America is the sharp disparity in land holdings, a deeply rooted historical inequity aggravated by the expansion of capitalist market relations, the widespread commercialization of agriculture, the development of agroindustries, and the concomitant displacement of large numbers of small farmers and poor peasants from the land. The general picture is one of a very small number of landholders who possess a very large proportion of the land. For example, one study on seven Latin American countries reports that less than 1 percent of the landowners (all with landholdings of one thousand hectares or more) owned 42 percent of the land, whereas 62 percent of the landowners (with landholdings of ten hectares or less) owned only 4 percent of the land (Cardoso and Helwege 1992:App. D).

Most landholders therefore cultivate acreage that is insufficient for the purposes of subsistence. As Kay notes in his chapter on rural Latin America, small landowners are often forced to seek additional, often quite meager, sources of income. They add their labor to the growing pool of underemployed rural workers that have either been displaced from their land by commercial agriculture or are the product of the rapid growth of the rural population. At the root of rural poverty is lack of sufficient arable land, the meager size of peasant farms, inadequate sources of financial and technical support, low crop prices, the displacement of basic food crops by export crops, the limited sources of permanent employment in the countryside, and rapid population growth (that has not been offset by the massive migrations to the cities or other countries).

Many Latin American states have enacted some type of agricultural reform program, principally during the 1960s and 1970s, but very few members of the rural population have benefited from these reforms. Even in those countries (such as Bolivia and Peru) where an extensive land reform took place, only a limited amount of land was distributed to poor and landless peasants, and the rural population's limited access to arable land remains a serious problem. Moreover, little or no government support (i.e., credit, technical assistance, the organization of cooperatives, etc.) was provided to help them improve the cultivation and marketing of their crops.

Kay also calls attention to the fact that women tend to be employed in the temporary and seasonal jobs within agriculture, while men are given the permanent positions. He notes that the rapid expansion of new export crops such as fruit and flowers has opened up seasonal employment opportunities for women, but the few permanent employment opportunities associated with these crops tend to be the preserve of men. In agroindustry and light manufacturing (e.g., the *maquiladoras* along the Mexican border with the United States), women are often hired instead of men because they will accept lower wages, are less inclined to join unions, and are considered to be more suited to tasks that require careful handling. In spite of inequalities in working conditions, however, the increasing numbers of women in the workforce—both in the urban and rural areas—have begun to give them greater influence in workplace and community organizations.

Halebsky notes that a disproportionate number of the members of the informal sector's workforce are women. He also reveals that those who are self-employed or employed in this sector work long hours, have low hourly earnings, and are not covered by state regulations on working conditions, pay, and labor benefits. Whether self-employed or working in small plants, they tend to operate outside of state regulations. For many lower-class women, their involvement in the informal sector is the only alternative because their arduous domestic duties and child-rearing responsibilities prevent them from finding other types of employment.

Apart from the inequities and abuses suffered by women in the lower classes, probably no other sector of the Latin American population has suffered more discrimination and injustice than the indigenous peoples of the region. For the past five centuries, the native peoples of Latin America have suffered every indignity and abuse imaginable. Kearney and Varese argue that since the Conquest, Latin American society has been based on the maximization of labor exploitation along ethnic lines and that the differential treatment of ethnic groups by both capital and the state has created a complex "ethno-class" structure. The indigenous peoples have generally occupied the lowest rung of this structure of extreme economic and social inequality, and until very recently they have been excluded or marginalized from the political process.

In sum, economic and social inequality is extreme throughout Latin America, and recent transformations in the global capitalist system as well as in the economies of the Latin American states have for the most part contributed to the already polarized structure of class, gender, racial, and ethnic differentiation in these states. In spite of unfavorable economic conditions, however, there is opposition and resistance to the existing ethno-class structure on the part of growing numbers of social groups and organizations—including the new social movements organized by women, indigenous peoples, the residents of the urban shantytowns, gays and lesbians, workers opposed to the traditional clientalistic trade unions, and middle-class environmentalists.

Contemporary Conditions in Latin America

Although centralized state power and an authoritarian governmental bureaucracy are pronounced features in all the Latin American countries, the role of the state in the economy has greatly diminished as a result of the privatization of state assets, deregulation of economic activities, and the drastic reduction of government expenditures and public employment. The elected civilian governments have restored the formal aspects of political democracy and freed civil society from most of the repressive restrictions of the former military regimes, but the military remains a threatening and powerful force in Latin American politics.

In general, political parties have regained the center of the political stage, and there has been a notable decline in the level and extent of political violence. Governmental stability has apparently begun to take hold—although deviations from this pattern have occurred with disturbing frequency. One of the most distressing features of the contemporary political scene is the government's unresponsiveness to the needs of the majority of the population even though the formal mechanisms of democratic politics have been established throughout most of the region.

The majority of the population continues to be for all intents and purposes excluded from the political process because their interests are not effectively represented by the state. In most countries the urban working class, the peasantry, rural workers, the lower sectors of the salaried middle class, and the large informal sector have been largely excluded or marginalized from the center of the political arena. Taken together, these various classes and sectors represent anywhere from two-thirds to three-quarters of the population, depending on the demographic profile of each country.

Past efforts to organize and unite these classes for the purposes of representing their interests in the centers of state power have proved politically difficult and/or dangerous. In addition to the violent reaction of the military and right-wing paramilitary groups, the political mobilization of these sectors of the population has been obstructed by traditional forms of political co-optation—such as clientalism, patronage, and corporatism—which the political elite has used to subordinate and divide the members of these sectors.

Many of the former radical and progressive members of the intelligentsia in Latin America have in recent years assumed a moderate political position, distancing themselves from the popular classes to secure positions in the public and private sectors, often accommodating their views to the prevailing neoliberal orthodoxy (Petras and Morley 1992:145–175). Many of the political parties and organizations (such as the unions) on the Left have assumed a low profile on the political scene (although there are notable exceptions such as the Workers' Party in Brazil), while others have fallen into organizational and ideological disarray.

The revolutionary movements and popular insurgencies in Nicaragua and El Salvador have been forced to give up their revolutionary projects and have been incorporated into the conventional political process. The revolutionary regime in Cuba has endured the collapse of the Soviet bloc and the continued U.S. economic and political embargo, but it has been forced by the end of the cold war and the "triumph" of Western capitalism to seek increasing accommodation with the global capitalist system.

The working class and peasant movements of the 1960s and 1970s, ruthlessly repressed by the military during the 1970s and 1980s, have not returned with the same militancy and popular support to the contemporary political scene. Yet the grassroots social movements that arose in the 1970s and early 1980s (in spite of the repressive nature of the military dictatorships then in power) continue to play an important role in contemporary social and political life. They have not, however, formed alliances with progressive parties and political organizations. The alliance of these movements with progressive political parties, such as the Workers' Party in Brazil or the PRD (Party of the Democratic Revolution) in Mexico, could change the balance of political forces and the course of development in these countries and perhaps the region.

Latin America's direction in the coming decades of the twenty-first century is not clear. There are indications that the region will continue on the current course of development under the influence of neoliberal economics and moderate-conservative civilian regimes. Yet there are also indications of growing discontent with these regimes, both among the popular classes who have received few if any benefits from these regimes as well as among the right-wing critics of these regimes and their allies in the armed forces, who fear that even the region's limited democratization has gone too far.

The Left and other progressive forces in Latin America have been weakened and disoriented by major developments at the global level, the demise of the revolutionary movements in Central America and other parts of Latin America, as well as their own failure to develop an effective strategy for mobilizing the population against the neoliberal project of the right-of-center civilian regimes throughout the region. The unsuccessful outcome of the Nicaraguan Revolution and the revolutionary movements in Central America during the 1980s appears to have foreclosed, at least for the time being, a leftist strategy based on popular insurrection. However, the leftist political forces in the region could change Latin America's current neoliberal course if they could devise an effective strategy for mobilizing the majority of the population.

Most of the progressive parties and movements in Latin America recognize that they are seriously handicapped by their failure to offer an effective alternative to the reigning neoliberal project. As a result, they have established an ongoing cross-national dialogue aimed at developing a new identity and strategy for the contemporary era. The main impetus for this dialogue has been the São Paulo Forum formed in July 1990 by representatives from more than forty leftist political parties and organizations (Robinson 1992). These representatives came from all over Latin America to a conference in São Paulo organized by the Workers' Party of Brazil for the purpose of exchanging ideas and developing an effective leftist strategy for the 1990s.

At the first meeting in São Paulo and at subsequent meetings in other parts of Latin America, the forum provided clear evidence that a New Left is developing in Latin America. The basic precepts for a general strategy are:

- The aspirations of most Latin Americans for a decent standard of living, genuine popular democracy, and social justice can be achieved only if the progressive forces in each country organize a broad-based multi-class political movement that represents the interests of a large majority of the population (not just the workers and peasants).

- The interests of this popular majority must be reflected in all the state's agencies and activities, and this can come to pass only if the state is democratized to the fullest extent possible.
- The autonomy of the many social movements in Latin America must be respected by the progressive political forces that coordinate the mobilization of the popular majority and secure popular control over the state.
- In the interests of the majority of the population, the state should regulate investments, production, distribution, and accumulation through the creation of a mixed economy that is based on various forms of property (private, state, mixed, and cooperative).
- In the interests of the popular majority, the state should promote the development of the domestic market, local industries, and small as well as medium producers.
- The integration of the Latin American countries should take place on a regional rather than a hemispheric basis to prevent U.S. domination of the process and to ensure that the needs of the Latin American peoples are served by this integration.
- Latin America's participation in the global economy should be based primarily on redressing the inequalities in the global economic system, particularly in the economic relations between Latin America and the advanced capitalist countries.

On the basis of these propositions, the progressive forces involved in this cross-national dialogue hope to develop and implement a strategy that will bring to an end the neoliberal project of the centrist and right-wing parties in power throughout most of the region. This subject is discussed in further detail in the final chapter of this volume by Richard Harris.

In the following pages, the conditions and trends briefly touched on in this introduction will be examined in depth by the contributors. They will describe and analyze the major institutions and forces that have shaped and are shaping the course of political, economic, and social development in contemporary Latin America. They will also identify and examine the relationships between basic structures and processes, current developments and issues, the effects of past events on contemporary realities, and the influence of international conditions on local forces.

The critical perspectives provided by the authors will reveal the exploitative relationships, social inequalities, and relations of dominance and subordination that predominate in Latin America. They will also provide insights into the forces of progressive change that could bring about a democratic transformation of the existing structures and relations of capital, power, and inequality in Latin America.

References

Brooke, James. "The New South Americans: Friends and Partners." *New York Times,* April 8, 1994:3.

Burns, E. Bradford. "The Continuity of the National Period," in Jan Knippers Black, ed., *Latin America: Its Problems and Its Promise.* Boulder, CO: Westview Press, 1991.

Cardoso, Fernando Henrique, and Enzo Falleto. *Dependency and Development in Latin America.* Berkeley: University of California Press, 1979.

Cardoso, Fliana, and Ann Helwege. *Latin America's Economy: Diversity, Trends, and Conflicts.* Cambridge: MIT Press, 1992.

Chilcote, Ronald, and Joel Edelstein. *Latin America: Capitalist and Socialist Perspectives of Development and Underdevelopment.* Boulder, CO: Westview Press, 1986.

Grindle, Merilee S. *State and Countryside: Development Policy and Agrarian Politics in Latin America.* Baltimore: The Johns Hopkins University Press, 1986.

Lindquist, Sven. *Land and Power in South America.* New York: Penguin Books, 1979.

MacEwan, Arthur. "Notes on U.S. Foreign Investment and Latin America." *Monthly Review,* January 1994:15–26.

Petras, James, and Morris Morley. *Latin America in the Time of Cholera.* New York: Routledge, 1992.

Press, Eyal. "Free-Market Misery for Latin America." *New York Times,* December 5, 1993: E20.

Robinson, William. "The São Paulo Forum: Is There a New Left in Latin America?" *Monthly Review* (December 1992):1–12.

Schuurman, Frans J. *Beyond the Impasse: New Directions in Development Theory.* London: Zed Books, 1993.

Stein, Stanley J., and Barbara H. Stein. *The Colonial History of Latin America.* New York: Oxford University Press, 1970.

Thiesenhusen, William C., ed. *Searching for Agrarian Reform in Latin America.* Boulder, CO: Westview Press, 1989.

U.N. (United Nations). *United Nations Demographic Handbook, 1991.* New York: United Nations, 1992.

Wiarda, Howard J., and Harvey F. Kline, eds. "The Latin American Tradition and Process of Development," in Howard J. Wiarda and Harvey F. Kline, eds., *Latin American Politics and Development,* 3d ed. Boulder, CO: Westview Press, 1990.

Wilkie, John W., and Carlos Alberto Contreras, eds. *Statistical Abstract of Latin America* 29. Latin America Center Publications, UCLA, 1992.

1

Rural Latin America: Exclusionary and Uneven Agricultural Development

CRISTÓBAL KAY

Since 1945 Latin America's rural economy and society have been transformed: External pressures have integrated the region's agriculture into the global agroindustrial food regime, while internal state policies have introduced agrarian reform and liberalization. By the 1990s the once-dominant hacienda had largely vanished. Instead, modern, capitalist farms and agroindustrial complexes—many of them linked to or owned by transnational corporations—hold sway over the countryside, greatly altering agrarian social and technical relations of production. In the 1960s and 1970s debate raged over whether the hacienda, or latifundio (large landed estate), was best characterized as feudal or capitalist (Kay 1977a); current debate focuses on whether the peasants' distinctive household-farm economy will survive.

Latin America's rural economy and society no longer play the primary role that they did historically. More than half the Latin American population was rural in 1960; by the 1990s only one-quarter were (IDB 1993:262). During this same period agriculture's share in the total value of Latin American exports declined from approximately one-half to one-fifth (ECLAC 1993:81), and its contribution to the gross domestic product (GDP) fell from 17 percent in 1960 (IDB 1986:397) to less than 10 percent (ECLAC 1993:77).

In this chapter, I will argue that an exclusionary modernization has transformed the social actors and their relationships in the rural sector. Landlords have been subordinated to the forces of both national and global capitalism. The peasant economy, although still an important provider of employment and staple foods, is a declining sector, and many peasants have been marginalized as producers and consigned to a subsistence level and/or wage employment.

The impact of globalization and modernization on the Latin American agricultural sector has varied from country to country. Shifts in the world market have changed national economic fortunes. Modernization and globalization have also brought uneven consequences for social groups within the individual Latin American economies, accentuating old forms and creating new forms of socioeconomic differentiation in the rural sector.

Latin American Agriculture in the World Economy

The relative position of Latin American agriculture in the world economy has undergone a striking decline since World War II. The drop-off can be partly attributed to the import-substitution industrialization (ISI) strategy pursued by most Latin American countries until the 1980s (Krueger et al. 1991). Yet the protectionist measures adopted by the industrial nations to safeguard their own agricultural sectors from imports are largely responsible for Latin America's declining share of international trade in agricultural commodities (Di Girolamo 1993; IDB 1986:145ff). In addition, both the United States and the European Community (now the European Union, or EU) have heavily subsidized their agricultural production and agricultural exports (Friedmann 1982). As a result, the industrial countries supply more than half the world's internationally traded agricultural commodities (GIA and CLACSO 1991:16).

Since the 1980s Latin America's shift away from import-substituting industrialization toward a new, outward-oriented development strategy has further integrated the region's agricultural sector into the world economy. Latin America's debt crisis of the 1980s and the subsequent adoption by most Latin American countries of "structural adjustment programs" sponsored by the World Bank, the International Monetary Fund (IMF), as well as the international banking system have stimulated agricultural exports in the hope that these would alleviate the region's debt and foreign exchange problems.

As a result of the export drive, agricultural exports have been growing much faster than production for the domestic market. Falling international prices, however, have meant that even though the volume of agricultural exports has risen considerably, the amount of foreign exchange so earned has not kept pace (Twomey 1989:549).

Agricultural transnational corporations (TNCs), or agribusinesses, have been key in shaping Latin American agriculture and linking it more closely to the requirements of the advanced industrial countries (Sanderson 1985, Gómez 1992). The TNCs have spearheaded changes in consumption patterns as well as changes in the production, processing, and marketing of

Latin America's agricultural sector (Arroyo et al. 1985). Advances in biotechnology and genetic engineering have further enhanced the power that agribusiness has over farmers and peasants (Goodman et al. 1987).

Land use has also been affected by the advent of the TNCs. Production has shifted away from staple foods grown for domestic consumption to exports, particularly products such as soybeans and sorghum, which are used mainly for animal feed in the industrial countries. In addition, technological developments in storage, processing, refrigerated transport, industrial organization, and communications have enabled the TNCs to take advantage of hemispheric seasonal differences by exporting vegetables, fruit, and flowers to the rich markets of the North, particularly during the winter months. This trend is evident in the rapid growth of Mexico's exports of winter vegetables to the United States; in Colombia's emergence as one of the world's leading flower exporters, again largely to the U.S. market; in the fortyfold increase of Chilean fruit exports since 1970; and in Brazil's burgeoning soybean and soya oil exports as well as its position as the world's leading exporter of concentrated orange juice.

The growth of the fast-food industry worldwide has meant that land previously dedicated to food crops for local consumption has been converted to pastures for livestock or for animal feeds (Barkin et al. 1991; Edelman 1992). In addition, land recently colonized through the expansion of the agricultural frontier is being devoted to livestock rearing (Goodman and Hall 1990). These patterns of production are supported not only by international agencies such as the World Bank, the IMF, and the Inter-American Development Bank (IDB) but also by the Latin American governments themselves as part of their export drive to repay debts (Reynolds et al. 1993). Because such practices are detrimental to staple food production, they have harmed the peasant economy, which has been, and to some extent still is, a major producer of food crops. The switch from food crops to livestock and forestry exports has also led to the destruction of tropical and native forests as farmers seek to create arable land (Goodman and Redclift 1991).

These shifting production patterns have modified the rural social structure in Latin America. The capitalist farmers have been the main beneficiaries of the new opportunities inasmuch as the financial, organizational, and technological requirements of the new export products are beyond the reach of most peasants. Nevertheless, agribusiness contract farming has enabled some smallholders to produce agroindustrial products for export or for high-income domestic urban consumers. As some peasants become integrated into the agrofood complex, the socioeconomic differentiations have become accentuated.

Some peasants have been able to accumulate capital to expand production, evolving into "capitalized family farmers" (Lehmann 1982; Llambí 1989), or "capitalist peasant farmers" (Llambí 1988; Brass 1990; Korovkin 1992). Others have become "proletarians in disguise" (i.e., formal owners of a smallholding but in effect dependent on an agribusiness, from which they earn an income similar to the average rural wage) or "semiproletarians" whose principal source of income no longer derives from their household plot but from selling their labor for a wage. Furthermore, a significant proportion of peasants have been fully "proletarianized," that is, forced to depend totally on wage-earning employment. They have been displaced from their former markets through the shift in consumer tastes, cheap and subsidized food imports, competition (often unfair) from agribusiness, and technological obsolescence, among other factors (Burbach and Flynn 1980; Teubal 1987).

Latin America's agricultural resource base is increasingly directed toward satisfying the demands of local high-income urban consumers as well as foreign markets. The emphasis placed by the TNCs on production for export and/or on crops for high-income consumers has created a new world food regime (Friedmann 1991; Teubal 1993). The ensuing neglect of staple crops has resulted in greater dependence on food imports from the industrial countries, particularly from the United States, thereby undermining Latin America's food security (Friedmann 1990).

Latin American governments and local industrial as well as commercial groups are willing partners in this process as it suits their interest in promoting a cheap food policy for the rapidly rising population, particularly in the urban sector. Concessional U.S. food aid, together with the dumping of EU food surpluses on the world market, has enabled Latin American governments to maintain low food prices through cheap food imports. They have also helped to manipulate the exchange rate, which has overvalued the local currency, as well as to impose internal price controls on basic foodstuffs. Such measures benefit urban consumers and the industrial bourgeoisie because lower food costs depress industrial wages.

There are opposing interpretations of the activities and impact of TNCs. Some argue that agribusinesses have led to a growing divergence between the agrarian production system and the consumption, employment, and income needs of the poor. They argue that the rapid modernization of Latin America's agriculture has done little to alleviate malnutrition and rural poverty. They also contend that the TNCs, by undermining the basic domestic foodstuff sector, have jeopardized Latin America's food security (Teubal 1992). Imports of foodstuffs have soared since the 1970s and have increased Latin America's dependence on the international food markets, making these countries more vulnerable to fluctuations there. Attempts by some governments to remedy this situation have all been short-lived, the most notable being Mexico's Sistema Alimentario Mexicano (SAM) program, which was implemented between 1980 and 1982 and continued on a modest scale for a further two years (Barkin 1987).

Others disagree with this analysis of the role of the TNCs. For example, Scott (1985:496) concludes that discriminatory government policies against domestic food agriculture, such as controlled prices and low public sector investment in rural areas, have contributed more to food insecurity in the region than have the activities of the TNCs. It is difficult to prove which factor is more important, but both government policies and the operations of TNCs have contributed to food insecurity.

Agriculture and the National Economy

Agriculture's share of the GDP in Latin America declined during the 1950s, 1960s, and 1970s but then stabilized during the 1980s. Agriculture contributed a quarter of the Latin American GDP in 1950, but by 1980 this figure had fallen to 9.7 percent. Thereafter, it increased slightly, reaching 10.5 percent in 1991 (ECLAC 1993:77).

Agriculture, which in the 1960s and 1970s had been the least dynamic sector, experienced a higher rate of growth than other economic activities in the 1980s, growing twice as fast as total GDP (see Table 1.1). These figures mask a crisis, however, as agriculture's performance in the 1980s was well below that of the previous two decades and below the average annual rate of population growth of 2.1 percent for the 1980s. Thus, the per capita rate of growth was practically nil. Significantly, for the first time in the postwar period, however, agriculture grew at a substantially higher rate than industry, which was particularly hard hit by the economic crisis of the early 1980s.

Although agriculture employs more than one-quarter of Latin America's total workforce, it contributes only about 10 percent to the GDP (FAO

TABLE 1.1 GDP Growth Rates by Economic Sector in Latin America, 1960–1992 (average annual growth rates in percentages)

	1960–1970	*1970–1980*	*1980–1990*	*1990–1992*
Agriculture	3.6	3.4	2.0	2.6
Industry	5.9	5.9	0.5	3.2
Services	5.5	6.1	1.2	3.8
Total GDP	5.4	5.8	1.0	3.3

SOURCES: Inter-American Development Bank, *Economic and Social Progress in Latin America: 1993 Report*. Baltimore: The Johns Hopkins University Press, 1993:264; and Eliana Cardoso and Ann Helwege, *Latin America's Economy: Diversity, Trends, and Conflicts*. Cambridge: MIT Press, 1992:14.

1992a:35). This reflects its low labor productivity, arising from its technological backwardness compared with other economic sectors. Thus, average
rural incomes lag way behind those in the urban sector. Agriculture continues to be a major contributor to Latin American foreign exchange earnings,
but its contribution has declined substantially. Agricultural exports, which
accounted for 44 percent of the total value of exports in 1970, declined to
29 and 24 percent in 1980 and 1990 respectively (ECLAC 1993:81).

Although Latin American agricultural exports grew at the substantial rate
of 10.4 percent per year (in current U.S. dollars) between 1970 and 1984
(IDB 1986:74), agricultural imports rose even faster at a yearly rate of 12.8
percent during the same period. This disparate rate of increase has meant
that for a number of years (since 1960 or even earlier) the value of agricultural imports represented an increasing proportion of what was earned
from agricultural exports. During the first half of the 1980s, however, food
imports declined because of the adjustment and austerity measures imposed
by the governments while the quantity of agricultural commodities exported
continued to grow (FAO 1992b:35).

Capitalization of Agriculture and
Modernization of the Hacienda

The modernization of agriculture based on the growth of the export sector
has followed earlier modernization strategies. Prior to the recent neoliberal
policies, the hacienda had already been substantially modified in many Latin
American countries. During the 1960s and 1970s a shift toward the intensification of Latin American agriculture took place. Many governments encouraged the modernization of the hacienda system through such measures
as subsidized credits for the purchase of agricultural machinery and equipment; better-quality livestock, fertilizers, and seed varieties; as well as technical assistance programs (Caballero 1990:112–115).

Consequently, large commercial farmers began to shift to higher value-
added crops to meet the growing demand of urban consumers and to capitalize their enterprises by making land improvements (for example, by increasing
the area under irrigation), upgrading infrastructure, introducing mechanization, and so forth. This process of modernization has been characterized as
the "landlord road" to agrarian capitalism since the landlords themselves
transform their large landed estates into profit-oriented farms (Kay 1974).

In addition, "green revolution" technologies involving improved seeds
were applied. Only 10.8 percent of Latin America's wheat-growing region
was sown with high-yield varieties in 1970. This figure rose to 82.5 percent
in 1983 (IDB 1986:111). The spread of the so-called green revolution also
meant that more fertilizers and pesticides were being used. Between 1950
and 1980 the use of pesticides multiplied more than fifteen times, fertilizers

by almost fifteen times, and the number of tractors increased by 600 percent (Ortega 1985:97). Fixed capital formation also expanded considerably as the irrigated land surface grew by 77 percent, while the land under permanent crops (fruit trees, coffee, bananas, and vines) and semipermanent crops (such as sugarcane) grew by 72 percent. Moreover, livestock numbers increased 75 percent during this period.

Prior to the 1980s the expansion of land under cultivation accounted for 60 percent of output growth (Ortega 1992:123). Although Latin America's arable land increased by 19 percent in the 1970s, it grew only 12 percent during the 1980s, with Brazil alone accounting for 68 and 86 percent of this increase respectively (ECLAC 1993:610). Agriculture continues to expand in Brazil primarily because of the colonization of the Amazonian frontier. Furthermore, capitalization within agriculture has been largely confined to the commercial farm sector, leaving peasant agriculture relatively unaffected, as will be seen in more detail later.

The Impact of Agrarian Reforms

While the hacienda was modernized and capitalized in the 1960s and 1970s, other important structural changes were taking place as a result of agrarian reforms. The impulse behind these reforms was as much political as economic. Some governments viewed the social and political conflicts arising from landlord-peasant relations as a source of instability. Haunted by the specter of socialism following the Cuban revolution of 1959, the U.S. and the Latin American governments launched the Alliance for Progress in the early 1960s. That effort, as well as the agrarian reforms, were regarded as a way of defusing peasant uprisings and preventing more fundamental political and economic change.

Agrarian reform policies sought to replace the hacienda system, which was widely perceived as inefficient. The agrarian structure in the 1950s and early 1960s was dominated by latifundios, which constituted roughly 5 percent of all farm units but possessed about four-fifths of the land; small farms, or minifundios, made up roughly four-fifths of the total farm units but controlled only 5 percent of the land (Barraclough 1973:16). The latifundios underutilized land, investing only modest resources over extensive tracts of land, leaving a significant proportion uncultivated. The minifundios, by contrast, used too much labor on too little land. Not surprisingly, labor productivity was much higher on latifundios than on minifundios, while the reverse was true regarding land productivity.

The dominant social relations of production were those of unpaid household labor working on the minifundia and on various kinds of small-scale tenancies. Peasant holdings employed about half the agricultural labor force, of which four-fifths were unpaid family workers, while large estates employed less than one-fifth of the agricultural labor force. Furthermore, an estimated one-quarter of agricultural workers were tenants or squatters and a further one-third were either landless or proletarians, that is, totally dependent on wage-earning employment (Barraclough 1973:19–23).

It was hoped that a new reformed sector would increase agricultural productivity and production and that by improving access to land, rural income and employment prospects would improve, thus contributing to political stability. Urban consumers were also expected to benefit from lower food prices, and industrial producers were to gain a wider market for their industrial goods. At their broadest, agrarian reforms were regarded as a way of overcoming the domestic market and foreign exchange constraints that accompanied Latin America's efforts to industrialize after the so-called easy phase of import-substitution industrialization (ISI) was exhausted.

The farthest-reaching agrarian reforms in Latin American have been the outcome of social revolutions—in Mexico (1917), Bolivia (1952), Cuba (1959), and Nicaragua (1979). However, Chile's agrarian reforms under the elected governments of Eduardo Frei Montalva (1964–1970) and Salvador Allende (1970–1973), and Peru's during the military regime of Velasco Alvarado (1969–1975), were also quite extensive, with large amounts of land expropriated and a great many peasant beneficiaries. Of lesser consequence were the agrarian reforms of Venezuela, Colombia, Costa Rica, Honduras, Dominican Republic, Ecuador, Panama, and El Salvador. To date, Argentina and Brazil have not implemented any agrarian reforms. In Paraguay and Uruguay, colonization programs have been instituted, but no significant agrarian reforms have taken place.

About four-fifths of agricultural land in Bolivia and Cuba was expropriated; almost one-half was taken in Mexico, Chile, Peru, and Nicaragua; and in Panama, El Salvador, and the Dominican Republic between 14 and 22 percent of agricultural land was expropriated (Deere 1985:1039; CEPAL-FAO 1986:22; IDB 1986:130; Ghai et al. 1988:10, 14; Thiesenhusen 1989; Wilkie 1990:52 ff; Cardoso and Helwege 1992:261; Dorner 1992:34). Although in Venezuela about one-fifth of the land was redistributed, almost three-quarters of it belonged to the state and was largely in areas to be colonized. In Cuba, Bolivia, and Mexico approximately one-half to three-quarters of farming households were peasant beneficiaries; in Nicaragua, Peru, and Venezuela peasants accounted for about one-third or more of the total number of beneficiaries. Between 5 and 20 percent of the peasant population benefited from these land expropriations in the remaining countries.

A variety of new farming arrangements were established on the expropriated estates. For the most part, cooperatives, collectives, and state farms took the place of the expropriated estates in Mexico, Cuba, Chile, Peru, and Nicaragua; only a small amount of expropriated land was set aside for family farms. In addition, the nonexpropriated sector was also affected by land reform as landlords subdivided, modernized, or sold part of their estates in an effort to avoid expropriation. Also, peasant access to land and pastures through sharecropping and other arrangements decreased.

The legacy of agrarian reforms has, however, diverged from their initial purposes and organizational structures. Many reforms modernized the hacienda system, transforming it into a capitalist farm rather than eliminating it altogether via the redistribution of hacienda lands to peasants. In this sense, many land reforms merely accelerated an already well-established landlord path to agrarian capitalism (de Janvry 1981; Kay 1978, 1988).

Agrarian reforms failed for a variety of reasons. In some cases, the political will or power to enforce them was lacking. Even though governments presented land reform as a panacea, they failed to provide the needed financial, technical, and institutional support. For example, in Peru, the continuation of ISI policies and the persistent discrimination against agriculture in terms of prices and credit made a viable agrarian reform sector almost impossible (Kay 1983).

Mistakes in design and implementation of agrarian reforms also contributed to their unraveling. In some cases, an inadequate organizational model for the reform sector succeeded in alienating peasants by limiting their participation in the decisionmaking process or excluded them from the benefits of the reform altogether.

The more radical agrarian reforms encountered opposition from landlords and other groups that modified or subverted their original aims. In some cases, the early gains of the agrarian reform were reversed following a counterrevolution or military coup d'état. In Chile, 30 percent of expropriated land was returned to former owners after the 1973 military coup; almost 20 percent of it was sold to private or institutional investors, while slightly more than half remained in the reformed sector, which was subdivided into parcels or family farms (Kay 1985:309; Jarvis 1992:192). In the end, most landlords stayed in business since they either retained some land or managed to reclaim part of their former property as a result of the counterreform (Silva 1991). The latifundios have not been restored, however, since the average size of the larger estates is far smaller than before and, more important, the relations of production have been transformed.

The "unraveling" of Peru's agrarian reform began under Victor Andrés Belaúnde (1980–1985) and intensified in the late 1980s and early 1990s. Hardly any expropriated land was returned to former owners but was instead redistributed to peasants. The coastal production cooperatives established by the agrarian reform were subdivided into individual parcels. In the highlands, part of the cooperative land was transferred to adjacent peasant communities and part was distributed among individual members of the cooperative.

In Nicaragua, peasant pressure and the war waged by the U.S.-backed contras led the Sandinista government to modify its emphasis on state farms

(Kaimovitz 1985). In the mid-1980s more emphasis was given to a peasant-oriented organization of the reform sector (Harris 1987). Thus, more individual land titles were awarded, reducing the relative importance of state farms and enhancing that of individual farms (Enríquez 1991; Martinez 1993). This trend intensified with the fall of the Sandinista government in 1990, and some landowners were able to reclaim their farms (de Groot 1993; Spoor 1995).

Last but not least, although over the years more and more of Mexico's collective *ejidos* have been farmed individually, the 1991 reform of Article 27 of Mexico's constitution permitted legal privatization and thus opened the gates for private investors to own *ejido* land. The consequences have not been favorable to the peasants (Bartra 1993:xiii).

The shift from collectivist organizations to peasant farms following the agrarian counterreforms has smoothed the peasants' road to agrarian capitalism. The neoliberal policies in fashion since the 1980s, however, have dampened peasant support for the government. These policies, compounded by the increased exposure to international competition and the emphasis on exports, have benefited those with access to capital, technical, and informational resources, as well as access to markets.

Those with little or no access to these resources are being marginalized. For example, in Chile about half of the *parceleros* (those who received parcels of land) have had to sell their land because they could not repay the debts they incurred when they purchased the land or because they lacked the capital and market experience to continue their farm operations (Crispi 1980). Thus, as Chile's agrarian reforms unraveled, only about 5 percent of the country's peasants were able to retain their family farms.

Only where peasant farmers have been able to link themselves to new technologies and markets—often through contracts with agribusinesses—has a successful peasant sector emerged. Organized into producer associations, peasants can enjoy an even greater likelihood of success by strengthening their bargaining power with respect to both the state and agribusiness.

The breakup of the reformed sector has led to a more complex agrarian structure. The main beneficiaries of the neoliberal policies are likely to be the commercial or large entrepreneurial farmers. Although one cannot say that the classical landlord road to agrarian capitalism has triumphed as a result of the counterreforms, the former landlords who retained land have been able to capitalize and prosper under neoliberalism. In addition, the strengthening of the land market has enabled new types of entrepreneurs (such as agribusinesses, agronomists, farm managers, and traders) to acquire land and invest in agriculture to a greater extent than in the past. Some capitalist farmers have acquired more land over time, but talk of "neolatifundism" is premature and inappropriate. Even where large farms have arisen (as in livestock and forestry plantations), their social and technical relations of production differ from those of the old latifundios.

Agrarian reform has therefore left a complex legacy. Certainly, the more radical agrarian reforms put an end to the dominance of the landed oligarchy in Latin America. In general, however, they contributed to capitalist development through institutional changes. By making land and labor markets more competitive and flexible, they enhanced agriculture's responsiveness to macroeconomic policy and market forces (Thiesenhusen 1989).

New Relations of Production

The quickening pace of the capitalist transformation of the countryside, together with the changes in the land tenure structure following agrarian reforms and counterreforms, has restructured both technical and social relations of production. In addition, the spread and dominance of agroindustries and the growth of export agriculture have helped to reshape rural labor markets and production relations throughout Latin America.

The technological transformation of agriculture discussed earlier has largely been confined to the capitalist farm sector, or "entrepreneurial agriculture" (a term that gained prominence with the publication in 1982 of Alexander Schejtman's influential book by CEPAL; it is synonymous with "capitalist farm sector"). Macroeconomic policy, favoring the development and diffusion of capital-intensive technologies, and the bias of extension services in favor of commercial farmers have widened the technological gap between entrepreneurial agriculture and the peasant economy.

It is difficult, if not impossible, for peasant farmers to adopt new technology. Besides being too risky and expensive, the new agricultural technologies are also not well suited to the small scale and inferior soils of peasant farming. In addition, the negative environmental consequences of fossil fuel–based technology are increasingly being called into question. The capital-intensive (and often import-intensive) nature of this technology is also held to be unsuitable for Latin American economies as it requires too many scarce capital resources (especially foreign exchange) and too few members of the abundant labor supply (Bebbington and Thiele 1993:60–73).

The modernization of the latifundio and its final transformation into a capitalist farm have been accompanied by a structural shift in the agricultural labor force. Unlike the old personalistic and clientalistic relations between landlords and peasants, relations between capitalist farmers and peasants are increasingly mediated by impersonal market forces and characterized by new forms of exploitation and subordination.

Four major changes in the composition of the labor force can be highlighted: (1) the replacement of tenant labor by wage labor; (2) within wage labor, the growth of temporary and seasonal labor; (3) the feminization of the agricultural labor force; and (4) the urbanization of rural workers.

Tenant labor used to supply most of the latifundios' permanent and temporary labor needs. But as landlords modernized their estates by raising their productivity, largely from the 1950s onward, tenant labor became increasingly more expensive than wage labor for them. The rent income received from tenants (sharecroppers, labor-service tenants, or others) became lower than the profit income landlords could earn by working the land directly with wage labor. Mechanization, which was attractive because of the often overvalued local currencies and the availability of government-subsidized credits, turned direct cultivation by landlords into a more profitable activity than tenancy. Thus, the higher opportunity costs of tenancies and tenant laborers resulted in their being transformed into proletarians or replaced by wage laborers.

Landlords also reduced the number of tenants and permanent laborers they employed for political reasons. In the changing political climate of the 1950s and 1960s, landlords responded to pressure from rural labor, especially among tenants for land or reduced rent payments, by introducing labor-displacing technology. In addition, landlords anticipated the implementation of agrarian reform legislation by subdividing their estates among family members or by selling part of their land, thereby lowering their labor requirements.

Within the shift to wage labor, there has been a marked increase in the proportion of temporary, often seasonal, wage employment. In many countries permanent wage labor has declined, even in absolute terms, although in almost all countries temporary labor has greatly increased. In Brazil it is estimated that in 1985 permanent wage labor had fallen to one-third of rural wage laborers, the remaining two-thirds being employed on a temporary basis (Grzybowsky 1990:21). In Chile the shift from permanent to temporary labor has also been dramatic. In the early 1970s approximately two-thirds of wage labor was permanent and one-third temporary, but by the late 1980s these proportions had been reversed (Falabella 1991).

This growth of temporary labor is related to the expansion of agroindustries that export seasonal fruit and vegetables and is therefore particularly evident in those Latin American countries that export these products. For example, in Chile about 60 percent of temporary wage laborers are employed in fruit cultivation for export (Stephen 1991). The labor requirements of many of these export products are restricted to a few months of the year. Thus, a striking feature of the current labor system is its marked seasonality.

The expansion of temporary employment has led to the increasingly precarious nature (*precarización*) of rural wage labor. Temporary workers are generally paid a piece rate, are not usually entitled to social security benefits, and have no employment protection. This shift toward more casual and flexible labor has enabled employers to increase their control over labor by reducing workers' rights and bargaining power. They have been facilitated by regressive changes in labor legislation, introduced by the military governments but continued by their neoliberal civilian successors.

The precariousness of rural employment has contributed to the fracturing of the peasant movement. Although seasonal laborers can be highly militant, they are notoriously difficult to organize given their varied background and shifting residence. Thus, the shift from permanent to seasonal labor in the countryside has generally weakened peasant organizations and hampered efforts to negotiate improvements in their working conditions either directly with their employers or indirectly by pressuring the state.

Associated with the expansion of temporary and/or seasonal wage labor is the marked increase in the participation of women in the labor force. In the past, rural women worked as day laborers, milkmaids, cooks, or domestic servants on the landlord's estate. They also found seasonal wage employment during the labor-intensive harvests on coffee, cotton, and tobacco farms. With the increasing commercialization of agriculture and the crisis of peasant agriculture (discussed below), more and more rural women have joined the labor force.

The rapid expansion of new export crops (fruit, vegetables, flowers) has opened up employment opportunities for women in agriculture. Agroindustries largely employ female labor since women are held to be more readily available, more willing to work on a seasonal basis and accept lower wages, are less organized, and, according to employers, are better suited for activities that require careful handling. Any permanent employment, however, tends to be the preserve of men. Although they are generally employed in low-skilled and low-paid jobs, for many young women these jobs provide an opportunity to earn an independent income and to escape (at least partially and temporarily) from the constraints of a patriarchal peasant-family household. As a result of their incorporation into the formal labor market, they have begun to exercise increasing influence in the affairs of peasant organizations and, in some instances, have even established their own organizations (Stephen 1993).

In Mexico, statistics for 1989 showed that women made up between one-third and one-half of the wage labor force in the countryside and more than one-third had temporary jobs (Lara 1992). It is estimated that between 80,000 and 90,000 women in Mexico were employed in cultivating garden produce for export and 100,000 women in growing strawberries. Women account for more than 70 percent of the labor in Colombia employed in the cultivation of flowers for exports and about 40 percent of coffee harvesters (ECLAC 1992a:103). In Chile, about 70 percent of temporary workers in the fruit-growing export sector are women, who are employed mainly in the fruit-packing plants (Stephen 1991).

An additional dimension to the growth of temporary wage labor concerns the geographical origins of the workers so employed. More and more temporary workers are coming from urban areas. About half of Brazil's temporary workers employed in agricultural activities are of urban origin. They are known as *bóias frias* (workers with a cold lunch) since they go to work with their lunch boxes containing cold food. They are also called *volantes* (fliers) because they reside on the periphery of cities or towns and float between rural and urban employment (Ibáñez 1990:57). For example, about three-quarters of female *volantes* are employed in the coffee-growing industry, and when there is no agricultural work they tend to look for employment in the urban areas largely as domestic employees (ECLAC 1992a:98).

The growing prevalence of labor contractors (*contratistas*), who hire gangs of laborers from small towns and cities for work in the fields, means that the farm owner or manager is often not the direct employer. Rural residents frequently have to compete with these urban laborers for agricultural work.

The expulsion of tenant farmers, who used to reside on the estates, and the growth in temporary employment have often resulted in the creation of new rural villages or the expansion of old ones into rural towns. Without the basic physical and social infrastructure, these villages provide few, if any, social services like schools and medical centers (Cruz 1992). In the past, shantytowns were associated mostly with the large cities of Latin America, but today they have spread to the smaller cities and even to rural towns. This spread of shantytowns is explained not only by the demise of the traditional hacienda system and the changes in the agricultural labor market noted above but also by the peasant economy's inability to absorb the growing population, as will be seen later.

The Future of the Peasantry

The internationalization of Latin America's agriculture, the demise of the hacienda system, and the increasing dominance of entrepreneurial agriculture are having a profound impact on the peasantry. As a result, the fate of the peasant economy and of Latin America's peasantry has been the subject of much debate. In the late 1970s the dominant view that the landlord road to capitalism was steamrolling ahead was challenged by those who emphasized the resilience, vitality, and relative importance of the peasant economy (Stavenhagen 1978; Warman 1979). The ensuing debate between the *campesinistas* and the *descampesinistas* has continued (Feder 1977a, 1977b, 1978; Paré 1977; Stavenhagen 1978; Esteva 1978, 1983; Warman 1979, 1980; Schejtman 1980; Bartra 1974, 1993).

The *campesinistas* believe peasant farming—seen by some as superior to capitalist farming—will endure (Harris 1978; Crouch and de Janvry 1979; Astori 1981, 1984; Heyning 1982; Hewitt de Alcántara 1984; Reinhardt 1988; Barsky 1990; Deere 1990). They reject the view that the wage relation is being generalized in the countryside and that the peasant is disappearing, arguing that the peasantry is persisting and even being reinforced. Characterizing peasants mainly as petty commodity producers who are able to compete successfully with capitalist farmers, *campesinistas* have certain affinities with the neopopulist tradition of Alexander Chayanov ([1923] 1966) and his contemporary followers like Teodor Shanin (1986, 1988).

By way of contrast, the *descampesinistas* argue that the peasant form of production is economically unviable in the long run and that peasants will eventually be eliminated as petty commodity producers. They argue that capitalist development increases differentiation among the peasantry and that, ultimately, most peasants will become proletarians; only a few will become capitalist farmers. The "depeasantization" approach (sometimes called "proletarianization") is influenced by classical Marxist writers on the agrarian question, such as V. I. Lenin ([1899] 1964) and Karl Kautsky ([1899] 1988).

The debate over the future of Latin America's peasant economy raises crucial issues about the characteristics of capitalist development in the countryside (Llambí 1991). Although theoretical differences continue to feed the debate, the changing reality and the availability of new statistical data also require an ongoing reinterpretation. The peasant economy will undoubtedly survive for some time to come in Latin America. The key question concerns the terms of this survival: prosperity or destitution?

In the past, the importance of the peasant economy in Latin America was often underestimated as national census data failed to record it accurately, especially the peasant tenant enterprises within the hacienda system. This past neglect of the peasant economy (largely predating the 1970s) has led scholars to underestimate the proletarianization of this group as well as to overestimate any subsequent peasantization resulting from land reform.

As for the present, the peasant household farm sector is still a significant sector of Latin America's rural economy and society. As we have seen, the peasant economy has not faced a unilinear decline. In particular, the parcelization of the reformed sector in Chile and Peru and, more recently, in Nicaragua has significantly expanded the peasant sector.

It is estimated that peasant agriculture in the 1980s in Latin America comprised four-fifths of all farm units and accounted for one-fifth of total agricultural land, over one-third of the cultivated land, and more than two-fifths of the harvested area (López Cordovez 1985:26). The peasant economy accounted for almost two-thirds of the total agricultural labor force, the remaining third being employed by entrepreneurial or capitalist farms.

Furthermore, peasant agriculture supplied two-fifths of production for the domestic market and one-third of the production for export. The contribution to food products for mass consumption is particularly important. At the beginning of the 1980s, the peasant economy provided an estimated 77 percent of the total production of beans, 61 percent of potatoes, and 51 percent of maize, as well as 41 percent of the share of such export products as coffee. In addition, the peasant economy owned an estimated 24 percent of the total number of cattle and 78 percent of pigs (López Cordovez, 1985:28). Other estimates, which use a wider definition of the peasant economy, show that peasant farming made a particularly large contribution to agricultural production in Bolivia

(80 percent), Peru (55 percent), Mexico (47 percent), Colombia (44 percent), Brazil (40 percent), and Chile (38 percent) (Jordán et al. 1989:225).

Although as a group peasants are far from disappearing, they are not thriving. Their relative importance as agricultural producers has declined. According to de Janvry and associates (1989b:396), Latin American peasants are experiencing a "double squeeze." First, they face a land squeeze. And because they fail to acquire additional land to match their increased numbers, the average size of peasant farms has decreased. This decline of the peasant sector mainly concerns the small peasantry (minifundistas), who account for about two-thirds of peasant farm households. Their average farm size decreased from 2.1 hectares in 1950 to 1.9 hectares in 1980. The remainder of the peasant sector retained an average farm size of 17 hectares, partly because of land reforms (de Janvry et al. 1989a:74). About 40 percent of minifundistas lack property titles to the land they farm, which underlines the precariousness of their status (Jordán et al. 1989:224). Moreover, peasants face an employment squeeze since employment opportunities have not kept pace with their population growth rate; they also face increased competition from urban-based workers for rural employment.

This double squeeze has led many peasants to migrate to urban areas, feeding the continuing and high rate of rural out-migration. High rural out-migration means that the rural population represents a declining share of total population, falling from 59 percent in 1950 to 28 percent in 1990 (Ortega 1992:121). Peasants have also responded by seeking off-farm sources of income (such as seasonal wage labor in agriculture) and/or nonfarm and nonagricultural sources of income (such as employment in small-scale rural enterprises and agroindustries).

In many Latin American countries, more than one-quarter of the economically active agricultural population currently resides in urban areas, and the proportion of the economically active rural population engaged in nonagricultural activities is rising—reaching more than 40 percent in Mexico and averaging about 25 percent in others (Ortega 1992:129). Thus, nonfarm employment is expanding faster than farm employment in rural Latin America. This shift reinforces the trend in which an increasing proportion of total peasant household income originates from wages, whereas income from on-farm activities often comes to less than half the total (de Janvry et al. 1989a:60, 141). This process, referred to as semiproletarianization, is the main tendency among the Latin American peasantry (de Janvry et al. 1989a, 1989b; Ortega 1982, 1986; ECLAC-FAO 1985).

In short, Latin America's peasantry appears to be trapped in a permanent process of semiproletarianization. Off-farm sources of income, generally seasonal wage labor, enables peasants to cling to the land, thereby blocking their full proletarianization. This process favors rural capitalists as it eliminates small peasants as competitors in agricultural production and transforms them into a source of cheap labor. Semiproletarianization is the only option open to those peasants who wish to retain access to land for reasons of security or survival because they cannot find alternative productive employment in either the rural or urban sectors.

One lucrative option open to poor peasants in some regions is the illegal cultivation of coca. The upper jungle regions and semitropical valleys of Peru and Bolivia are particularly well suited to growing coca, which thrives on poor soils, is labor intensive, and can be cropped five times a year. Production has expanded rapidly since the 1970s. Moreover, the adoption of market-oriented policies and stabilization programs by the governments of these countries have given a new, though unintended, boost to the coca economy. In Peru and Bolivia the rural poor have migrated to the jungle region in search of what is called "white gold," a migration that has had adverse ecological consequences: It is estimated that the cultivation of coca alone is responsible for about a tenth of this century's deforestation of the Peruvian Amazon region (Alvarez 1992).

It is extremely difficult to estimate the economic importance of coca production. The estimates given for Peru (Alvarez 1992) indicate that in 1988 the value of coca production ranged from 2 to 11 percent of GDP, that it generated between 14 to 35 percent of total value of exports, provided employment for about 4 percent of the total labor force, and accounted for 9 percent of the agricultural labor force. For Bolivia it is estimated that coca and cocaine exports were comparable to the value of all legal exports between 1987 and 1989 and that this activity employed between 2 and 6 percent of the total labor force (De Franco and Godoy 1992:376).

The paradox of coca is that although its production may enjoy a clear international comparative advantage, its expansion is highly undesirable because of its connection to drug abuse; the political instability, violence, and crime it promotes; the erosion of state and civic institutions it fosters; and the widespread corruption it creates (Zamosc 1990a). Although the social and political costs of coca production cannot be quantified in economic terms, they are dramatic enough to call for decisive action to contain, if not eliminate, its production. However, so far governments and international agencies have been unwilling to foot the bill involved in making alternative crops a more profitable proposition for the peasants who cultivate coca (Morales 1990; Léons 1993).

The Incidence of Rural Poverty

The form taken by agricultural modernization in Latin America, with its emphasis on capital-intensive farming and the double squeeze on the peasant economy, has made rural poverty a persistent and intractable problem. Estimates of the incidence of rural poverty in Latin America and the Caribbean for 1989 show that more than three-quarters of the rural population lived in poverty in Haiti, Bolivia, Guatemala, Honduras, Nicaragua, and El Salvador; between three-quarters and one-half of the rural population lived in poverty in the Dominican Republic, Brazil, Mexico, Peru, Panama, Colombia, Ecuador, Venezuela, Paraguay, Chile, and Jamaica; between one-half and one-quarter of the rural population lived in poverty in Trinidad and Tobago and Costa Rica; and less than one-quarter lived in poverty in Grenada, Argentina, and Uruguay (Ibáñez 1990:20).

The structural adjustment programs and stabilization policies of the 1980s are generally considered to have contributed to poverty. Both rural and urban poverty increased in the 1980s: rural poverty from 45 percent of the rural population in 1980 to 53 percent in 1989; urban poverty from 17 to 23 percent (*Economist* 1993b:43).

The adjustment policies exacerbated poverty since government expenditures on social welfare, subsidies for basic foods, and other essential commodities and services were severely cut back. However, some governments softened the negative impact by targeting welfare payments more closely and by introducing poverty alleviation programs. For example, in Chile the adjustment policies increased the number of poor families from an average of 38 percent in 1980–1981 to about 50 percent in 1982–1983. But by 1989–1990 rural poverty had declined to 40 percent (Larrañaga 1992:287), and it continued to fall thereafter because of the attempts of the new democratically elected government to reduce the level of extreme poverty. Extreme poverty or destitution in the countryside was 20 percent in 1987 and 18 percent in 1990, but it fell quite sharply to 11 percent in 1992 (*Economist* 1993b:44).

Approximately two-thirds of Peru's rural households were in poverty during the 1970s and 1980s, while urban poverty increased from 28 percent in 1970 to 45 percent in 1986. The proportion of families living in destitution is particularly higher in the rural sector as compared with the urban sector. In the countryside almost 40 percent of the households were destitute throughout the 1970s and 1980s, while in the urban areas, even though the level of destitution doubled from 8 percent to 16 percent, it was well below the rural proportion (Gonzales de Olarte 1992:373). In Brazil, rural poverty fell substantially during the years of economic expansion from a shockingly high level of 78 percent in 1970 to 50 percent in 1980, but rose to 61 percent by 1988 as a consequence of the economic crisis and adjustment measures (Nakano 1992:142).

The main cause of rural poverty is structural: unequal land distribution and increasing numbers of semiproletarian and landless peasants. Tackling the root causes of poverty will require major land redistribution and rural investments, increased employment opportunities, and greater agricultural productivity—particularly of smallholders. Only by a generalized assault on various fronts will it be possible to alleviate rural poverty significantly. Such an assault will depend on the organizational capacity of rural workers and peasants as well as their ability to forge alliances with other social groups to alter the balance of political power in their favor. Government efforts (if any) are likely to be directed toward tackling urban poverty, if only for short-term expedience.

Latin America's poverty is directly related to unresolved agrarian problems. How long massive rural out-migration and government neglect of the rural poor will continue remains an open question.

Future Perspectives

The future of Latin American agriculture has been the subject of extensive theoretical debate (Llambí 1990). In the early 1970s I argued that the landlord road was the main route to agrarian capitalism in Latin America, a view largely shared by Murmis (1980), de Janvry (1981), Zamosc (1990b), and others. Goodman and Redclift (1982), as well as the *campesinistas* in the debate mentioned earlier, criticized this view for underestimating the vitality of the peasantry. It was Lehmann (1982 and 1986), however, whose work on Ecuador first clearly identified a viable peasant path to rural development. But this path was confined to a section of the peasantry that he conceptualized as "capitalized peasant farmers." Many other researchers subsequently discovered a "capitalized peasantry" in other areas of Latin America. However, I never denied the possibility that there might be a peasant path to agrarian capitalism. I saw this course of development as either subordinated to the dominant landlord path or the possible result of a shift in the class struggle in favor of the peasantry, resulting in major redistributive land reforms and/or beneficial macroeconomic policies (Kay 1971, 1979, 1988).

In my view, the landlord road to agrarian capitalism was dominant in the past. However, today a multiplicity of paths can be observed. Compared with the previous bimodal structure of latifundio-minifundio, the Latin American countryside is now more complex and heterogeneous (CEPAL-FAO 1986). A large proportion of former haciendas or latifundios have successfully been, or are being, converted into medium-sized, modern capitalist enterprises that rely mainly on wage labor, advanced technology, and that are integrated into the domestic and international markets. In addition, in those countries where the reformed sector was subdivided into parcels, the peasant farm sector grew significantly.

A proportion of *parceleros* might eventually join the capitalized-peasant farmers by exploiting new market opportunities, new products, improved links with agroindustries, propeasant government policies, the support of nongovernmental organizations (NGOs), and other possibilities. Yet, at the same time, the modernization of the latifundio has increased the proletarianization

of the peasantry, especially the tenant farmers. Meanwhile, the semiproletarianization of many small peasants is a significant and persistent trend (López
Cordovez 1985:20–22), as is the increase of landless peasants (Barraclough
1991:55). Consequently, today's agrarian structure is both more complex and
fluid than it was forty years ago. Rather than speaking of a "new dualism," as
Grindle (1986) and many others do, one might more appropriately characterize this new agrarian structure as "polarization with heterogeneity."

The modernized capitalist farmers, often linked to agroindustrial and international capital, are undoubtedly setting the pace and controlling the direction of Latin America's agrarian developments—within the limits imposed
by the relative decline of agriculture in the economy and its subordination to
the penetrating processes of trade liberalization and globalization. What then
are the prospects for a peasant path to rural development? It is well known
that access to capital, technology, and domestic and foreign markets, as well
as knowledge and information systems, is becoming increasingly important
relative to access to land in determining the success of an agricultural enterprise. Even though in recent decades some peasants managed to gain access
to land through agrarian reforms, this by no means guarantees their success
(Carter and Mesbah 1993). Indeed, peasants in general are in an increasingly
disadvantageous position relative to capitalist farmers, and this does not
augur well for their future prospects.

For example, the widening technological gap between the capitalist and
peasant farm sectors has prompted those concerned about the latter to urge
international agencies, governments, and NGOs to adapt existing modern
technologies to the needs of the peasant sector and to create more "peasant-
friendly," appropriate, and sustainable technologies (Echenique and Rolando
1989; Bebbington and Thiele 1993:60–73). Such a policy, however, runs
the danger of relying exclusively on a technological fix, while the sustainability of peasant agriculture depends on broader social and political conditions,
particularly a favorable macroeconomic context (Figueroa 1993). A viable
peasant road to rural development raises questions about development strategy and ultimately about the political power of the peasantry and their allies
(Miró and Rodríguez 1982:16).

A successful peasant path to rural development requires a major shift in development strategy, land redistribution, and a major transfer of resources toward the peasant economy to ensure its capitalization on a scale broad and
deep enough for it to compete both in domestic and international markets.
However, the widespread adoption and intensification of liberalization policies in Latin America and the decline of developmentalist state policies do
not encourage such a possibility.

In recent years, concerned scholars and institutions have become increasingly vociferous in pointing out the adverse impact on the peasantry of the
particular type of "selective" agricultural modernization taking place in Latin

America. As opposed to the concentrating and exclusive nature of agricultural modernization, they call for a strategy that includes peasants in the modernization process (Calderón et al. 1992; Murmis 1993). Such an "inclusive" strategy of modernization is seen as part of the democratization of rural society (Fox 1990), and some authors speak of the need for "democratic modernization" to highlight this link (Chiriboga 1992). This type of change would require production patterns based on social equity and the "reconversion" of agricultural production so as to meet the challenges of an increasingly internationalized and global world economy in the new millennium (ECLAC 1990, 1992b). To forward these aims, special government policies in favor of the peasantry would be needed to reverse the past bias in favor of landlords and rural capitalists.

It is unlikely that in the current neoliberal climate these kinds of policies will be adopted. But the neoliberal project has not gone unchallenged by peasants. The peasant rebellion in Chiapas, the most southern and indigenous region of Mexico, at the beginning of 1994, was fueled by the exclusionary impact of Mexico's agricultural modernization on the peasantry and by fears that the negative consequences of trade liberalization on peasant agriculture will increase following the implementation of the North American Free Trade Agreement (Bulmer-Thomas 1994). Mexico's peasant economy cannot compete with the large-scale mechanized cereal farmers from North America unless special protective and developmental measures are adopted in their favor (Calva 1991; Carton de Grammont 1991; *Economist* 1993a).

Conclusion

Latin America's rural economy and society have been transformed in the past few decades as a consequence of the increasing capitalist development of agriculture and its integration into the world economy. Latin American agriculture is now integral to the new world food regime. Agroindustrial modernization and globalization have profoundly changed the technical and social relations of production in the countryside. The neoliberal era is reminiscent of the pre-1930 era of outward-oriented growth and involves a structural transformation in this direction.

This form of exclusive modernization has benefited only a minority of the rural population and excluded the vast majority of the peasantry. The beneficiaries are a heterogeneous group, including agroindustrialists, capitalist farmers, some capitalized peasant households, and the more skilled workforce. The losers are the semi- and fully proletarianized peasants—the majority of rural laborers whose employment conditions have become temporary, precarious, and "flexible." Some landlords have also lost out, especially in countries where more radical agrarian reforms were implemented or where they have succumbed to competition following the liberalization of the country's trade by opening their domestic markets to food imports.

Agriculture and the rural sector are increasingly being subordinated to industry and the urban sector with the growth of agroindustries. The dynamism of agriculture is increasingly dependent on the stimulus it receives from the urban-industrial economy. This situation is accompanied by the rising importance of nonagricultural employment in the rural areas as well as off-farm activities.

With the increasing integration of Latin America's rural sector into the urban sector, the boundaries between the rural and urban sectors have become ambiguous. The massive rural out-migration has partly "ruralized" the urban areas, while the countryside is becoming increasingly urbanized. Urban and rural labor markets have become more closely interlinked. The land market has become more open and competitive, enabling urban investors and international capital to gain greater access to agricultural land. Competition among agricultural producers has intensified because of a more fluid situation in the land, capital, and labor markets. The survival of large landlords, let alone peasant farmers, is no longer guaranteed unless they keep up with technological advances, make innovations, and adjust their output patterns and production structures to the changing market conditions.

Although the rural economy and society is less important today than in the past, it still retains critical significance in most Latin American countries. The "lost decade" of the 1980s revealed the strength of the rural economy in confronting the debt crisis, economic recession, and the new emphasis on export agriculture. Moreover, to ignore agrarian problems is ill-advised. In countries such as Brazil (De Souza Leite 1994) and Guatemala (Brocket 1988), the land redistribution issue has not yet been addressed, while in many others it remains unresolved. Rural poverty remains widespread and discrimination against indigenous communities is still pervasive. Last but not least, new ecological problems have arisen in the rural areas.

The shift from a state-centered and inward-directed development process to a neoliberal open market and export-oriented model of development has weakened the power of traditional peasant organizations because this shift has fractured the rural labor force. Many social conflicts, however, will continue to erupt in the countryside. New grassroots organizations have emerged in the rural areas, and it will be politically difficult to continue to impose the neoliberal model on peasants, especially in those countries where the transition to civilian government has occurred.

It is possible that rural conflicts might become even more violent because the state's capacity for mediating and co-opting opposition has decreased. Also, political parties, NGOs, churches, and other intermediary organizations have been unable to ameliorate the effects of unequal and exclusive rural modernization. Neoliberal economic policies have greatly increased the number of semiproletarian peasants and landless workers, and they could become a major force in future social struggles in the countryside.

References

Alvarez, Elena. "Illegal Export-led Growth in the Andes: A Preliminary Economic and Socio-political Assessment." A report prepared for the U.N. Research Institute for Social Development (UNRISD). Geneva: United Nations, 1992.

Arroyo, Gonzalo, Ruth Rama, and Fernando Rello. *Agricultura y Alimentos en América Latina. El Poder de las Transnacionales.* Mexico City: UNAM, 1985.

Astori, Danilo. "Campesinado y Expansión Capitalista en la Agricultura Latinoamericana." *Comercio Exterior* 31 (12) (1981):1357–1368.

———. *Controversias sobre el Agro Latinoamericano: Un Análisis Crítico.* Buenos Aires: CLACSO.

Barkin, David. "The End to Food Self-sufficiency in Mexico." *Latin American Perspectives* 14, 3 (1984):271–297.

Barkin, David, Rosemary L. Batt, and Billie R. DeWalt. "The Substitution among Grains in Latin America," in Michael J. Twomey and Ann Helwege, eds., *Modernization and Stagnation: Latin American Agriculture Into the 1990s.* New York: Greenwood Press, 1991, 13–53.

Barraclough, Solon. "Migrations and Development in Rural Latin America." *Economic and Industrial Democracy* 12 (1991):43–63.

———, ed. *Agrarian Structure in Latin America: A Resumé of the CIDA Land Tenure Studies.* Lexington, MA: D.C. Heath, 1973.

Barraclough, Solon, and Arthur Domike. "Agrarian Structure in Seven Latin American Countries." *Land Economics* 42, 4 (1966):391–424; Reprinted in *LTC Reprint Series,* no. 25, Land Tenure Center, University of Wisconsin–Madison, 1966.

Barsky, Osvaldo. *Políticas Agrarias en América Latina.* Santiago: CEDESCO/Ediciones Imago Mundi, 1990.

Bartra, Roger. *Estructura Agraria y Clases Sociales en México.* Mexico City: Era, 1974.

———. *Agrarian Structure and Political Power in Mexico.* Baltimore: The Johns Hopkins University Press, 1993.

Bebbington, Anthony, and Graham Thiele. *Non-Governmental Organizations and the State in Latin America: Rethinking Roles in Sustainable Agricultural Development.* London: Routledge, 1993.

Bradshaw, Sarah. "Women in Rural Chilean Society," in David E. Hojman, ed., *Neoliberal Agriculture in Chile.* London: Macmillan, 1990, 110–126.

Brass, Tom. "Peasant Essentialism and the Agrarian Question in the Colombian Andes." *Journal of Peasant Studies* 17, 3 (1990):444–456.

Brockett, Charles D. *Land, Power, and Poverty: Agrarian Transformations and Political Conflict in Rural Central America.* Boston: Unwin Hyman, 1989.

Bulmer-Thomas, Victor. "Chiapas Uprising Takes the Shine Off Mexico's Big Deal." *Guardian International,* 7 January 1994:15.

Burbach, Roger, and Patricia Flynn. *Agribusiness in the Americas.* New York: Monthly Review Press, 1980.

Caballero, José María. "La Agricultura de América Latina y el Caribe: Temas Actuales y Perspectivas." *Debate Agrario,* no. 8 (1990):103–136.

Calderón, Fernando, Manuel Chiriboga, and Diego Piñeiro. *Modernización Democrática e Incluyente de la Agricultura en América Latina y el Caribe,* Serie Documentos de Programas no. 28. San José, Costa Rica: IICA, 1992.

Calva, José Luis. "Posibles Efectos de un Tratado de Libre Comercio México–Estados Unidos Sobre el Sector Agropecuario." *Revista Mexicana de Sociología* 53, 3 (1991):111–124.

Cardoso, Eliana, and Ann Helwege. *Latin America's Economy: Diversity, Trends, and Conflicts.* Cambridge: MIT Press, 1992.

Carter, Michael R., and Dinah Mesbah. "Can Land Market Reform Mitigate the Exclusionary Aspects of Rapid Agro-export Growth?" *World Development* 21, 7 (1993):1085–1100.

Carton de Grammont, Hubert. *Economía Campesina y Agricultura Empresarial.* Mexico City: Siglo Veintiuno Editores, 1982.

———. "El Futuro del Campo Mexicano Frente al Tratado de Libre Comercio." *Revista Mexicana de Sociología* 53, 3 (1991):125–141.

CEPAL-FAO (Comisión Económico para America Latina y El Caribe–Food and Agricultural Organization). *El Crecimiento Productivo y la Heterogeneidad Agraria.* Santiago: División Agrícola Conjunta CEPAL/FAO, 1986.

Chayanov, Alexander V. *The Theory of Peasant Economy.* Edited by Daniel Thorner, Basile Kerblay, and R.E.F. Smith. Homewood, IL: Richard D. Irwin (1925) 1966.

Chiriboga, Manuel. "Modernización Democrática e Incluyente." *Revista Latinoamericana de Sociología Rural,* no. 1 (1992):27–37.

Crispi, Jaime. "El Agro Chileno Después de 1973: Expansión Capitalista y Campesinización Pauperizante," *Working Paper no. 71.* Washington, DC: Latin American Program. The Wilson Center, 1980.

Crouch, Luis A., and Alain de Janvry. "El Debate Sobre el Campesinado: Teoría y Significancia Política." *Estudios Rurales Latinoamericanos* 2, 3 (1979):282–295.

Cruz, María Elena. "From *Inquilino* to Temporary Worker; From Hacienda to Rural Settlement," in Cristóbal Kay and Patricio Silva, eds., *Development and Social Change in the Chilean Countryside: From the Pre–Land Reform Period to the Democratic Transition.* Amsterdam: CEDLA, 1992, 247–262.

De Franco, Mario, and Ricardo Godoy. "The Economic Consequences of Cocaine Production in Bolivia: Historical, Local, and Macroeconomic Perspectives." *Journal of Latin American Studies* 24, 2 (1992):375–406.

de Groot, Jan P. "Nicaragua: Reforma Agraria, una Actualización." Paper presented to the Annual Conference of ASERCCA, Maastricht, October 8–10, 1993.

de Janvry, Alain. *The Agrarian Question and Reformism in Latin America.* Baltimore: The Johns Hopkins University Press, 1981.

de Janvry, Alain, Robin Marsh, David Runsten, Elisabeth Sadoulet, and Carol Zabin. *Rural Development in Latin America: An Evaluation and a Proposal.* San José, Costa Rica: IICA, 1989a.

de Janvry, Alain, Elisabeth Sadoulet, and Linda Wilcox Young, "Land and Labour in Latin American Agriculture from the 1950s to the 1980s." *Journal of Peasant Studies* 16, 3 (1989b):396–424.

Deere, Carmen Diana. "Rural Women and State Policy: The Latin American Agrarian Reform Experience." *World Development* 13, 9 (1985):1037–1053.

————. *Household and Class Relations: Peasants and Landlords in Northern Peru.* Berkeley: University of California Press, 1990.

Deere, Carmen Diana, and Magdalena León, eds. *Rural Women and State Policy: Feminist Perspectives on Latin American Agricultural Development.* Boulder, CO: Westview Press, 1987.

De Souza Leite, Tasso. "Agrarian Reform and Development in Brazil: Re-opening a Debate in a Time of Crisis." *Working Paper Series.* The Hague: Institute of Social Studies, 1994.

Di Girolamo, Giovanni. "The World Agricultural Outlook in the 1990s." *CEPAL Review,* no. 47 (1992):95–114.

Dorner, Peter. *Latin American Land Reforms in Theory and Practice: A Retrospective Analysis.* Madison: University of Wisconsin Press, 1992.

Duncan, Kenneth, and Ian Rutledge, eds. *Land and Labour in Latin America: Essays on the Development of Agrarian Capitalism in the Nineteenth and Twentieth Centuries.* Cambridge: Cambridge University Press, 1977.

Echenique, Jorge, and Nelson Rolando. *La Pequeña Agricultura: Una Reserva de Potencialidades y una Deuda Social.* Santiago: Agraria, 1991.

ECLAC (United Nations Economic Commission for Latin America and the Caribbean). *Changing Production Patterns with Social Equity.* Santiago: ECLAC, 1990.

————. *Major Changes and Crisis: The Impact on Women in Latin America and the Caribbean.* Santiago: ECLAC, 1992a.

————. *Social Equity and Changing Production Patterns: An Integrated Approach.* Santiago: ECLAC, 1992b.

————. *Statistical Yearbook for Latin America and the Caribbean, 1992.* Santiago: ECLAC, 1993.

ECLAC-FAO. "The Agriculture of Latin America: Changes, Trends, and Outlines of Strategy." *CEPAL Review,* no. 27 (1985):117–129.

Economist. "Mexico Survey: Rural Revolution." *Economist* 13 February, 1993a: 10–12.

Economist. "Easing the Pain of Market Forces." *Economist* 329 (784), 11 December, 1993b: 43–44.

Edelman, Marc. *The Logic of the Latifundio: The Large Estates of Northwest Costa Rica Since the Late Nineteenth Century.* Stanford, CA: Stanford University Press, 1992.

Enríquez, Laura J. *Harvesting Change: Land and Agrarian Reform in Nicaragua, 1979–1990.* Chapel Hill: University of North Carolina Press, 1991.

Esteva, Gustavo. "¿Y si los Campesinos Existen?" *Comercio Exterior* 28 (6) (1978):699–713.

————. *The Struggle for Rural Mexico.* South Hadley, MA: Bergin and Garvey, 1983.

Falabella, Gonzalo. "Organizarse para Sobrevivir en Santa María. Democracia Social en un Sindicato de Temporeros y Temporeras." Paper presented at the forty-seventh International Congress of Americanists, New Orleans, July 7–11, 1991.

FAO. *FAO Production Yearbook, 1991,* vol. 45. Rome: FAO, 1992a.

————. *FAO Trade Yearbook, 1991,* vol. 45. Rome: FAO, 1992b.

Feder, Ernst. "Agribusiness and the Elimination of Latin America's Rural Proletariat." *World Development* 5, 5–7 (1977a):559–571.

————. "Campesinistas y Descampesinistas: Tres Enfoques Divergentes (No Incompatibles) sobre la Destrucción del Campesinado." (Primera parte), *Comercio Exterior* 27, 12 (1977b):1439–1446.

———. "Campesinistas y Descampesinistas: Tres Enfoques Divergentes (No Incompatibles) sobre la Destrucción del Campesinado." (Segunda parte), *Comercio Exterior* 28, 1 (1978):42–51.

Feres, Juan Carlos, and Arturo León. "The Magnitude of Poverty in Latin America." *CEPAL Review* 41 (1990):133–151.

Figueroa, Adolfo. "Agricultural Development in Latin America," in Osvaldo Sunkel, ed., *Development From Within: Toward a Neostructuralist Approach for Latin America.* Boulder, CO: Lynne Rienner Publishers, 1993, 287–314.

Flora, Cornelia Butler, and B. Santos. "Women and Farming Systems in Latin America," in June Nash and Helen Safa, eds., *Women and Change in Latin America.* South Hadley, MA: Bergin and Garvey, 1986.

Fox, Jonathan, ed. *The Challenge of Rural Democratisation: Perspectives from Latin America and the Philippines.* London: Frank Cass, 1990.

Friedmann, Harriet. "The Political Economy of Food: The Rise and Fall of the Postwar International Food Order." *American Journal of Sociology* 88 (supplement), edited by Michael Burawoy and Theda Skocpol, *Marxist Inquiries: Studies of Labor, Class, and States.* Chicago: University of Chicago Press, 1982.

———. "The Origins of Third World Food Dependence," in Henry Bernstein and Ben Crow, eds. *The Food Question: Profits versus People?* London: Earthscan Publications, 1990, 13–31.

———. "Changes in the International Division of Labor: Agri-food Complexes and Export Agriculture," in William H. Friedland, Larry Busch, Frederick H. Buttel, and A. P. Rudy, eds., *Towards a New Political Economy of Agriculture.* Boulder, CO: Westview Press, 1991, 65–93.

Ghai, Dharam, Kay Cristóbal, and Peter Peek. *Labour and Development in Rural Cuba.* London: Macmillan, 1988.

GIA and CLACSO (Grupo de Investigaciones Agrarias and Consejo Latin Americano de Ciencias Sociales), eds. *La Agricultura Latinoamericana: Crisis, Transformaciones, y Perspectivas.* Santiago: GIA, Universidad Academia de Humanismo Cristiano, 1991.

Gómez, Sergio. "Dilemas de la Sociología Rural Frente a la Agricultura y el Mundo Rural en la América Latina de Hoy." *Revista Latinoamericana de Sociología Rural (ALASRU)* 1 (1992):75–87.

Gonzales de Olarte, Efraín. "Impacto de las Políticas Macroeconómicas y Sectoriales sobre la Pobreza Rural en el Perú," in Rafael A. Trejos, ed., *Ajuste Macroeconómico y Pobreza en América Latina.* San José, Costa Rica: IICA, 1992, 353–400.

Goodman, David E., and Anthony L. Hall, eds. *The Future of Amazonia: Destruction or Sustainable Development?* London: Macmillan, 1990.

Goodman, David E., and Michael Redclift, eds. *Environment and Development in Latin America: The Politics of Sustainability.* Manchester: Manchester University Press, 1991.

Goodman, David, and Michael Redclift. *From Peasant to Proletarian: Capitalist Development and Agrarian Transitions.* Oxford: Basil Blackwell, 1982.

Goodman, David, Bernardo Sorj, and John Wilkinson. *From Farming to Biotechnology: A Theory of Agro-industrial Development.* Oxford: Basil Blackwell, 1987.

Grzybowski, Cândido. "Rural Workers and Democratisation in Brazil," in Jonathan Fox, ed., *The Challenge of Rural Democratisation: Perspectives from Latin America and the Philippines.* London: Frank Cass, 1990, 19–43.

Grindle, Merilee S. *State and Countryside: Development Policy and Agrarian Politics in Latin America.* Baltimore: The Johns Hopkins University Press, 1986.

Harris, Richard L. "Marxism and the Agrarian Question in Latin America." *Latin American Perspectives* 5, 4 (1978, issue 19):2–26.

———. "Evaluating Nicaragua's Agrarian Reform: Conflicting Perspectives on the Difference a Revolution Can Make." *Latin American Perspectives* 14, 1 (1987, issue 52):13–18.

Herrero, Fernando A., and Juan Diego Trejos. "El Impacto de las Reformas Políticas Macroeconómicas y Sectoriales en los Pobres Rurales de Siete Países Latinoamericanos," in Rafael A. Trejos, ed., *Ajuste Macroeconómico y Pobreza en América Latina.* San José, Costa Rica: IICA, 1992, 401–434.

Hewitt de Alcántara, Cynthia. *Anthropological Perspectives on Rural Mexico.* London: Routledge and Kegan Paul, 1984.

Heynig, Klaus. "The Principal Schools of Thought on the Peasant Economy." *CEPAL Review* 16 (1982):113–139.

Ibáñez, Gonzalo. *América Latina y el Caribe: Pobreza Rural Persistente,* Serie Documentos de Programas no. 17, San José, Costa Rica: IICA, 1990.

IDB (Inter-American Development Bank). *Economic and Social Progress in Latin America: 1986 Report.* Special Section: Agricultural Development. Washington, DC: IDB, 1986.

———. *Economic and Social Progress in Latin America: 1990 Report.* Special Section: Working Women in Latin America. Baltimore: The Johns Hopkins University Press/IDB, 1990.

———. *Economic and Social Progress in Latin America: 1993 Report.* Baltimore: The Johns Hopkins University Press/IDB, 1993.

Jarvis, Lovell S. "The Unravelling of the Agrarian Reform," in Cristóbal Kay and Patricio Silva, eds., *Development and Social Change in the Chilean Countryside: From the Pre–Land Reform Period to the Democratic Transition.* Amsterdam: CEDLA, 1992, 189–213.

Jordán, Fausto, Carlos De Miranda, William Reuben, and Sergio Sepúlveda. "La Economía Campesina en la Reactivación y el Desarrollo Agropecuario," in Fausto Jordán, ed., *La Economía Campesina: Crisis, Reactivación y Desarrollo.* San José, Costa Rica: IICA, 1989, 207–290.

Kaimovitz, David. "Nicaraguan Debates on Agrarian Structure and Their Implications for Agricultural Policy and the Rural Poor." *Journal of Peasant Studies* 14, 1 (1986):100–117.

Kautsky, Karl. *The Agrarian Question.* 2 vols. London: Zwan Publications (orig. 1899), 1988.

Kay, Cristóbal. "Comparative Development of the European Manorial System and the Latin American Hacienda System." D.Phil. diss., School of Arts and Social Studies, University of Sussex, 1971.

———. "Comparative Development of the European Manorial System and the Latin American Hacienda System." *Journal of Peasant Studies* 2, 1 (1974):69–98.

———. "The Latin American Hacienda System: Feudal or Capitalist?" *Jahrbuch für Geschichte von Staat, Wirtschaft und Gesellschaft Lateinamerikas* 14 (1977a): 369–377.

———. "The Development of the Chilean Hacienda System, 1850–1973," in Kenneth Duncan and Ian Rutledge, eds., *Land and Labour in Latin America: Essays on the Development of Agrarian Capitalism in the Nineteenth and Twentieth Centuries.* Cambridge: Cambridge University Press, 1977b, 103–139.

———. "Agrarian Reform and Class Struggle in Chile." *Latin American Perspectives* 3, 18 (1978):117–140.

———. "The Hacienda System, Proletarianization, and Agrarian Reform," in Maria Beatriz de Albuquerque and Mauricio Dias David, eds., *El Sector Agrario en América Latina.* Stockholm: Institute of Latin American Studies, University of Stockholm, 1979, 23–38.

———. "The Agrarian Reform in Peru: An Assessment," in Ajit Kumar Ghose, ed., *Agrarian Reform in Contemporary Developing Countries.* New York: St. Martin's Press, 1983, 185–239.

———. "The Monetarist Experiment in the Chilean Countryside." *Third World Quarterly* 7, 2 (1985):301–322.

———. "The Landlord Road and the Subordinate Peasant Road to Capitalism in Latin America." *Etudes rurales,* no. 77 (1988):5–20.

———. "The Agrarian Policy of the Aylwin Government: Continuity or Change?" in David E. Hojman, ed., *Change in the Chilean Countryside: From Pinochet to Aylwin and Beyond.* London: Macmillan, 1993, 19–39.

Kay, Cristóbal, and Patricio Silva, eds. *Development and Social Change in the Chilean Countryside: From the Pre–Land Reform Period to the Democratic Transition.* Amsterdam: CEDLA, 1992.

Korovkin, Tanya. "Peasants, Grapes, and Corporations: The Growth of Contract Farming in a Chilean Community." *Journal of Peasant Studies* 19, 2 (1992):228–254.

Krueger, Anne O., Maurice Schiff, and Alberto Valdés, eds. *The Political Economy of Agricultural Pricing Policy.* Vol. 1: *Latin America.* Baltimore: The Johns Hopkins University Press/World Bank, 1991.

Lago, María Soledad. "Rural Women and the Neo-liberal Model," in Cristóbal Kay and Patricio Silva, eds., *Development and Social Change in the Chilean Countryside: From the Pre–Land Reform Period to the Democratic Transition.* Amsterdam: CEDLA, 1992, 263–274.

Lara Flores, S. M. "La Flexibilidad del Mercado de Trabajo Rural: (Una Propuesta que Involucra a las Mujeres)." *Revista Mexicana de Sociología* 54, 1 (1992):29–48.

Larrañaga, Osvaldo J. "Ajuste Macroeconómico, Agricultura y Pobreza Rural: Chile en los Ochenta," in Rafael A. Trejos, ed., *Ajuste Macroeconómico y Pobreza en América Latina.* San José, Costa Rica: IICA, 1992, 259–307.

Lehmann, David. "After Lenin and Chayanov: New Paths of Agrarian Capitalism." *Journal of Development Economics* 11, 2 (1982):133–161.

———. "Two Paths of Agrarian Capitalism, or a Critique of Chayanovian Marxism." *Comparative Study of Society and History* 28, 4 (1986):601–627.

Lenin, Vladimir I. *The Development of Capitalism in Russia.* Moscow: Progress Publishers (orig. 1899), 1964.

Léons, Madeline Barbara. "Risk and Opportunity in the Coca/Cocaine Economy of the Bolivian Yungas." *Journal of Latin American Studies* 25, 1 (1993):121–157.

Llambí, Luis. "The Small Modern Farmers: Neither Peasants nor Fully-Fledged Capitalists?" *Journal of Peasant Studies* 15, 3 (1988):350–372.

———. "The Emergence of Capitalized Family Farms in Latin America." *Comparative Studies in Society and History* 31, 4 (1989):745–774.

————. "Transitions to and Within Capitalism: Agrarian Transitions in Latin America." *Sociologia Ruralis* 30, 2 (1990):174–196.

————. "Latin American Peasantries and Regimes of Accumulation," *European Review of Latin American and Caribbean Studies,* no. 51 (1991):27–50.

López Cordovez, Luis. "Transformaciones, Tendencias, y Perspectivas." *Pensamiento Iberoamericano,* no. 8 (1985):15–35.

Martínez, Philip R. "Peasant Policy within the Nicaraguan Agrarian Reform, 1979–89." *World Development* 21, 3 (1993):475–487.

Miró, Carmen A., and Daniel Rodríguez. "Capitalism and Population in Latin American Agriculture: Recent Trends and Problems." *CEPAL Review,* no. 16 (1982):51–71.

Morales, Edmundo. "The Political Economy of Cocaine Production: An Analysis of the Peruvian Case." *Latin American Perspectives* 17, 4 (1990, issue 67):91–109.

Murmis, Miguel. "El Agro Serrano y la Vía Prusiana de Desarrollo Capitalista," in Osvaldo Barsky and Miguel Murmis, eds., *Ecuador: Cambios en el Agro Serrano.* Quito: FLACSO and CEPLAES, 1980, 7–50.

————. "Algunos Temas para la Discusión en la Sociología Rural Latinoamericana: Reestructuración, Desestructuración y Problemas de Excluidos e Incluidos." Buenos Aires: CONICET in FLACSO, 1993. Mimeographed.

Nakano, Yoshiaki. "Impacto de los Programas de Ajuste y Estabilización sobre los Pobres Rurales: El Caso de Brasil," in Rafael A.Trejos, ed., *Ajuste Macroeconómico y Pobreza en América Latina.* San José, Costa Rica: IICA, 1992, 139–203.

Nash, June, and Helen I. Safa, eds. *Women and Change in Latin America.* South Hadley, MA: Bergin and Garvey, 1986.

Ortega, Emiliano. "Peasant Agriculture in Latin America: Situations and Trends." *CEPAL Review,* no. 16 (1982):75–111.

————. "La Opción Campesina en las Estrategias Agrícolas." *Pensamiento Iberoamericano,* no. 8 (1985):79–108.

————. "Políticas Agrícolas, Crecimiento Productivo y Desarrollo Rural," in CEPAL-FAO, *El Crecimiento Productivo y la Heterogeneidad Agraria.* Santiago: División Agrícola Conjunta CEPAL-FAO, 1986, 7–97.

————. "Evolution of the Rural Dimension in Latin America and the Caribbean." *CEPAL Review,* no. 47 (1992):115–136.

Paré, Luisa. *El Proletariado Agrícola en México: Campesinos sin Tierra o Proletarios Agrícolas?* Mexico City: Siglo XXI, 1977.

Reinhardt, Nola. *Our Daily Bread: The Peasant Question and Family Farming in the Colombian Andes.* Berkeley: University of California Press, 1988.

Reynolds, Laura T., David Myhre, Philip McMichael, Viviana Carro-Figueroa, and Frederick H. Buttel. "The 'New' Internationalization of Agriculture: A Reformulation." *World Development* 21, 7 (1993):1101–1121.

Rivera, Rigoberto, and Maria Elena Cruz. *Pobladores Rurales.* Santiago: GIA, Academia de Humanismo Cristiano, 1984.

Sanderson, Steven E. "The 'New' Internationalization of Agriculture in the Americas." In Steven E. Sanderson, ed., *The Americas in the New International Division of Labor.* New York: Holmes and Meier, 1985, 46–68.

Schejtman, Alexander. "The Peasant Economy: Internal Logic, Articulation, and Persistence." *CEPAL Review,* no. 11 (1980):114–134.

Scott, Christopher D. "Transnational Corporations, Comparative Advantage, and Food Security in Latin America," in Christopher Abel and Colin Lewis, eds., *Latin America, Economic Imperialism, and the State*. London: Athlone Press, 1985, 482–499.

Shanin, Teodor. "Chayanov's Message: Illuminations, Miscomprehensions, and the Contemporary 'Development Theory'," in Daniel Thorner, Basil Kerblay, and R.E.F. Smith, eds., *A. V. Chayanov on The Theory of Peasant Economy*. Madison: University of Wisconsin Press, 1986.

———. *Peasant and Peasant Societies*. Harmondsworth, England: Penguin, new ed., (orig. 1971), 1988.

Silva, Patricio. "The Military Regime and the Restructuring of Land Tenure." *Latin American Perspectives* 18, 1 68 (1991):15–32.

Spoor, Max. *The State and Domestic Agricultural Markets—Nicaragua: From Interventionism to Neo-Liberalism*. London: Macmillan, 1995.

Stavenhagen, Rodolfo. "Capitalism and the Peasantry in Mexico." *Latin American Perspectives* 5, 3 (1978, issue 18):27–37.

Stephen, Lynn. "The Gendered Dynamics of Rural Democratization: Brazil, Chile, and Mexico." Paper presented at the Forty-Seventh International Congress of Americanists, New Orleans, July 7–11, 1991.

———. "Challenging Gender Inequality: Grassroots Organizing Among Women Rural Workers in Brazil and Chile." *Critique of Anthropology* 13, 1 (1993):33–55.

Teubal, Miguel. "Internationalization of Capital and Agroindustrial Complexes: Their Impact on Latin American Agriculture." *Latin American Perspectives* 14, 3 (1987, issue 54):316–364.

———. "Food Security and 'Regimes of Accumulation': With Reference to the Case of Argentina." ISS Rural Development Studies Research Seminars, April 29. The Hague: Institute of Social Studies, 1992.

———. "Agroindustrial Modernization and Globalization: Towards a New World Food Regime." Working Paper Series No. 162. The Hague: Institute of Social Studies, 1993.

Thiesenhusen, William H., ed. *Searching for Agrarian Reform in Latin America*. Winchester, MA: Unwin Hyman, 1989.

Twomey, Michael J. "The Debt Crisis and Latin American Agriculture." *Journal of Developing Areas* 23, 4 (1989):545–566.

Twomey, Michael J., and Ann Helwege. *Modernization and Stagnation: Latin American Agriculture into the 1990s*. Westport, CT: Greenwood Press, 1991.

Warman, Arturo. "Desarrollo Capitalista o Campesino en el Campo Mexicano." *Comercio Exterior* 29, 4 (1979):399–403.

———. *Ensayos Sobre el Campesinado en México*. Mexico City: Nueva Imagen, 1980.

Wilkie, James W., Enrique C. Ochoa, and David E. Lorey, eds. *Statistical Abstract of Latin America*. vol. 28, Los Angeles: UCLA Latin American Center Publications, 1990.

Wilson, Fiona. "Women and Agricultural Change in Latin America: Some Concepts for Guiding Research." *World Development* 13, 9 (1985):1017–1035.

Zamosc, Leon. "The Political Crisis and the Prospects for Rural Democracy in Colombia," in Jonathan Fox, ed., *The Challenge of Rural Democratisation: Per-*

spectives from Latin America and the Philippines. London: Frank Cass, 1990, 79–96.

————. "Luchas Campesinas y Reforma Agraria: La Sierra Ecuatoriana y la Costa Atlántica Colombiana en Perspectiva Comparada." *Revista Mexicana de Sociología* 52, 2 (1990):125–180.

2

Urban Transformation and Survival Strategies

SANDOR HALEBSKY

For more than four centuries it has been customary to think of Latin America as a rural society. The plight in recent decades of peasant and indigenous people there and recent revolutionary struggles in the region sometimes still bring such images to mind. Yet in less than half a century the region has undergone sweeping and rapid transformation. In 1950, 41.5 percent of the population lived in cities; by 1995 the region's urban centers held 74.2 percent of the population. From 1960 to 1990, 94 percent of population growth was urban, and by the end of the twentieth century the actual number of rural residents may begin to decline. This rapid urban expansion has further exacerbated the historical Latin American pattern of primacy, where a single city is several times as large as the next largest city. Many are huge urban centers. In 1993, nine Latin American cities (three in Brazil) had populations of more than 4 million (UN 1993c). The world known by most Latin Americans has thus greatly changed, both for those with rural origins as well as for longtime urban dwellers.

I describe this growing urban world of Latin America by focusing primarily on the efforts of the low- and modest-income urban population to develop and sustain their lives in conditions of inequality and exploitation, with very little assistance from the state. I shall consider the principal features of urban life—the migration process, the effort to create a home and community, the role of family and personal networks, the informal sector, the effect of the economic crisis that developed after 1980, and the political behavior of the shantytown settlements. In effect, the efforts of the poor can be understood as survival strategies that one hopes will, over time, improve their circumstances.

Given the conditions experienced by the urban poor and the resources available to them over the past few decades, their accomplishments are a significant human achievement. I also hope to show how the urban poor are enmeshed in and frequently dependent on a wide and varied range of market, economic, and political circumstances or relationships that influence their behavior and shape and restrict their opportunities. They are often exploited while serving the needs of the prevailing institutional order and the groups dominant within it.

Migration: The Context and Process of Population Movement

For those not born in the urban centers, the prologue to urban adaptation and survival begins with migration. The concentration of resources and opportunity in the region's large urban centers has historically attracted rural migrants. This movement of people exploded, however, after 1940 and helped to transform Latin America from a rural to urban region in the postwar years. This migration from the countryside can be accounted for only within the context of a development model that undermined the economic conditions of livelihood in some regions while creating new yet restricted opportunities at a few limited points elsewhere. While import substitution industrialization concentrated economic opportunities within the large urban centers, a number of circumstances made rural life increasingly precarious. As Cristóbal Kay notes in Chapter 1, agroindustrial expansion and increased land concentration eviscerated Latin America's traditional production arrangements. Price policies and income transfers also disadvantaged rural areas, and the penetration of a rural consumer market by factory-produced items undermined local production. In contrast, the larger cities had a disproportionate share of opportunities and services. In addition, rapid population growth (from 159 million in 1950 to 437 million in 1990) further strained the limited economic opportunities in the countryside. At the same time, the prosperity created by the region's economic growth in the 1950s and 1960s was experienced mostly in the urban centers. One stark measure of this disparity is the poverty rate. In 1986, 60 percent of the rural population were poor compared with a poverty rate of 36 percent for those in the cities (Gilbert 1994:41). Even in more recent years the contribution of migration to urban growth has been considerable (Findley 1993).

A fine-grained analysis by Lourdes Arizpe (1982) brings to light diverse particulars that have induced the movement of people from their rural and small-town communities. Her study of "relay" migration in Toxi, Mexico, describes a number of changes in the countryside that increased economic pressures on the residents, even apart from agroindustrial expansion. She reports that:

The land rapidly lost its fertility, [there was] drastic soil erosion. . . . local sources of employment have decreased. . . . Traditional occupations also began to disappear. . . . Small local business and itinerant trading have also declined. They have been taken over by the large commercial enterprises in the regional cities. . . . At the same time the cash needs of families have increased for non-agricultural purposes. Electricity, the ever-more-frequent bus trips, . . . Drinking and irrigation water, are all new services that must be paid for. In addition, consumerism . . . has notably increased the acquisition of goods. (Arizpe 1982:26–27)

Thus, the undermining of the means of livelihood and the rising level of needs have fueled the rural exodus. Migration is therefore a strategy for meeting economic needs and improving life circumstances and opportunities. It is a "decision . . . based on a rational calculus of cost and benefits" (Grindle 1988:28) and is one of a number of household strategies to maximize total family income. It is determined by household not individual considerations.

Significant factors inducing migration include economic considerations, occupational mobility opportunities, and the availability of services. Browning and Feindt's (1971) Monterrey Mobility Study of the mid-1960s—the most extensive study carried out in Latin America on rural-to-urban migration—found that 70 percent of the respondents gave work as the major reason for migration to the rapidly growing industrial city of Monterrey; another 7 percent cited education. Family, the reason given by 17 percent of the respondents, partly reflects the earlier work-related decisions to migrate by other family members. Elizaga's findings for Santiago are similar (1966). Perlman's study of migrants to Río de Janeiro, however, suggests that the decision to migrate reflects a complex of reasons—especially economic (mentioned by 52 percent of the male respondents) and familial—essentially involving greater opportunities offered by the city (1976:67–69).

The significance of economics in accounting for the rural exodus has not meant, however, that either the poorest individuals (or families) or the most destitute regions show the highest rate of migration. That the poorest population sectors are *not* the most likely to move is explained by the fact that migration is greater where the risks and costs of moving are lower and the resources (personal and financial) greater. A move is more likely where the migrant has had previous urban experience or familiarity and possesses personal contacts in a city. The latter can offer assistance in housing and employment as well as social support. These conditions are more likely to be present for communities that are more, rather than less, fully integrated in the country's economic, social, communication, and transportation networks and are more likely to produce migrants; they are generally not the poorest or most isolated communities (Conning 1972; Graham 1970). Similarly, within such communities it is not the worst off who will at first migrate. Compared with "the more skilled and prosperous [migrants], . . . they will not have the contacts or resources to survive easily in the competitive job market of the big cities" (Roberts 1978:97).

Selectivity in regard to who is most likely to migrate also operates in regard to other personal properties. In brief, compared with nonmigrating members of a community, migrants tend to have a higher (even if modest) level of educational and occupational skills and to be younger and unattached (Browning and Feindt 1971; Roberts 1978:98–102; Butterworth and Chance 1981:51–63). However, over time this selectivity decreases as the remaining migrant pool becomes more homogeneous because of out-migration. Migration becomes less daunting an undertaking as the presence of earlier migrants means more contacts and greater means of assistance for even the less skilled and educated. The community is likely to develop a growing familiarity with larger urban centers through the visits of earlier migrants. This familiarity is likely to increase, and the obstacles or reluctance to move diminish, as the more isolated and poorer areas (from which the migrants are few at first) are increasingly incorporated into capitalist market relations and national communication and transportation channels. In addition, the education and occupational selectivity of the migrant stream into the larger urban centers will diminish over time.

A distinctive feature of Latin American migration, which differentiates it from migration in other developing regions, is that women outnumber men. In the five largest countries the sex ratio (number of men divided by number of women times 100) among rural-to-urban migrants for a portion of the years between 1960 and 1985 (the precise time period varied for each country) ranged from 94 for Colombia and 90 for Argentina to 93 for Mexico, 95 for Brazil, and 89 for Venezuela (UN 1993a:Table 7). The greater numbers of female migrants reflect economic and cultural circumstances in both rural and urban areas. Cultural restrictions and a gender-segregated labor market have meant limited economic possibilities in rural areas (Radcliffe 1992). Crummett notes that "men are relatively more privileged in terms of access to essential resources such as land, labor, cash, education, and know how" (1987:245) especially given the diminishing needs for labor in the wake of technological change. As the size and number of family farm holdings grow, women have fewer opportunities in agricultural production, while the weakening of domestic manufacturing has diminished their economic possibilities. With fewer prospects of finding paid employment than men, daughters are also more likely to leave the community to seek other prospects in the larger urban centers. Women have greater opportunities in urban communities, especially in the domestic, service, and the informal sectors. However, these sectors offer less income and mobility than male-dominated labor sectors. Some gender-specific opportunities have also appeared in recent years with the expansion of multinational assembly and other plants—for instance, the *maquiladoras,* and textile and sporting-goods plants.

The migration process involves considerably more, of course, than who migrates and why. Migration is a complex, multifaceted phenomenon involving a number of interlinked stages. Although it is characterized by rational decisionmaking, the psychological and geographic shift from rural to urban is not an abrupt transition. It develops and changes slowly over time. Migration takes place within a community and family context. Earlier moves by community members help to establish the appropriateness of the move, the preferred destination, and the assistance and contacts within the city that contribute to a successful entry. Many move as families or assist family members in making the move.

Migration occurs over time. Thus, it often takes place in stages that bring increasing contacts and familiarity with urban life; for example, visits, military service, moves to a small urban center and, and so forth. Its ongoing character is also exhibited in "chain" migration, whereby a family member moves to an urban center and, once established, then arranges for other family members to join him or her. Migration begets migration and is, in effect, self-perpetuating. The initial move leads not only to bringing along other family members but also to providing more information and assistance, which facilitates the moves of others.

The community of origin no less than the urban center is affected by migration. In Mexican peasant communities, a shortage of agricultural labor arising from the migration of men, for instance, has produced "a series of changes in farming practices," altering the type of crops farmed and adding to the burden of wives and children (Grindle 1988:46; Deere and León 1982). Collins contends that among the Peruvian Aymara families "the strain of seasonal absence . . . has begun to interfere with the system of labor mobilization in the highlands and has challenged continued subsistence production there" (1988:170). These absences have also begun a slow depopulation in some parts of the countryside. Nonetheless, the income received from migrant family members may make a significant contribution to rural household needs. Yet at the same time Grindle points to a dilemma: "Perhaps the most disturbing aspect of the migration process . . . is . . . that it . . . stimulates dependence on migratory income and thus requires further migration. . . . Migratory income serves as a crucial source of the household budget but is not generally used for investment capital in the local area" (1988:47). The selective character of permanent migration will also alter the demographic and psychological composition of the home community, leaving an older, more conservative, and perhaps more passive population.

For most of those who make the move, migration is experienced as an improvement in their circumstances and offers migrants a sense of control over their lives. Although migration has slowed in recent years, it is still a significant phenomenon given the economic downturn in the cities and the shrinking of the rural sector.

Adaptation and Survival in the City

Home, Community, and Social Networks

The migrant population's adaptation to and survival in the urban communities of Latin America attest to the immense resourcefulness, perseverance, and adaptibility of the poor. The magnitude of their accomplishments is particularly impressive given the absent or inadequate support society offers in housing, community, or jobs. The needs of migrants cannot be met by the prevailing economic system, development policies, or the resources and abilities of the state and the local municipalities. The disparities in terms of housing needs and housing created by the housing industry can be striking. A U.N. report on São Paulo states, for instance that "the number of two-bedroom apartments built every year decreased from about 12,500 units in 1980 to a little over 8,000 in 1989—at a time when three million people were added to the city's population" (U.N. 1993c:18). The very considerable achievement of the lower-income urban population has been their ability to create communities in the face of a great many impediments—something that neither the private nor public sector has been able to accomplish. They have built communities in material as well as in social and psychological terms and have rooted themselves firmly and effectively into the wider life of the metropolis.

The most visible aspects of the lives of low income populations in Latin American cities are their homes and the physical circumstances of their communities. Although some migrants still rent inner-city tenements that date back to the earliest periods of urban expansion, since World War II the poor have primarily lived in some form of unauthorized settlement, frequently at the urban periphery. Some settlements were a product of land invasions, usually of public land. Most prospective residents bought land, however, and constructed homes in illegal subdivisions (illegal in that they frequently failed to meet state zoning or service requirements, among other shortcomings). Such housing (referred to as self-help housing) "always begins as a rudimentary form of shelter," writes Gilbert, "lacking all kinds of services and is developed on land which either lacks planning permission or which has been invaded" (1994:80). It is estimated that 30–60 percent of the population in large urban centers lives in housing built and financed by low-income groups (Gilbert 1990a:65), which is several times the proportion of the 1950s and early 1960s (Gilbert 1994:82). This phenomenon reflects the explosion of the urban population as well as the inability and disinclination of the private and public sectors to meet the needs of those with modest resources. The rate of construction of self-help settlements has waxed and waned over time within particular cities and countries, principally reflecting the state's willingness to accept their formation.

Depending on topography and other particulars, some common problems with this sort of housing have been flooding, mud slides, dust or sand, open sewers, and the like. Major problems are the lack of adequate and potable water. For example, Hardoy and Satterthwaite describe the high-income Chapultepec zone of Mexico City, where the daily water consumption is nine times as great as that in the low-income Nezahualcoyotol settlement (1989:151). In 1980 roughly 20 percent of urban households in Latin America had no sewer hookup (Gilbert 1994:105). However, services and surroundings were slowly improved. The homes were upgraded through the diligent efforts of their owners. Public services were gradually installed by the municipality in response to the continuous demands by settlers, the trading of votes for services, and the occasional installation of populist or reformist regimes. Nonetheless, housing conditions in most urban areas are grossly inadequate. It is estimated, for instance, that two-thirds of São Paulo's population are living in substandard housing (U.N. 1993c:1). Conditions worsened in the economic crisis of the 1980s, and the modest government assistance grew even scarcer.

A major impediment to individual or government efforts to address the housing problem has been the lack of a sufficient and low-cost supply of legal land sites. Where the government has not permitted land invasions, the effort to secure land has been especially difficult. "Given [the] scarcity [of land], the result has been that the settlements have almost invariably occupied the cheapest and environmentally poorest land in the city. Distant hillsides, areas with difficult drainage, and land close to industrial areas have been the typical preserve of the poor in Latin American cities" (Gilbert 1990b:114). The lack of land, however, is less one of geography than of economics and politics (Portes 1976a:45–49). Land is a common form of speculative investment for the well-to-do, from which they have reaped great profit with little risk. In part, the profits on the sale of land arise through the services introduced into the area or from the development of nearby communities, both of which raise land values. In effect, the efforts of others reap the landowner a tidy return. Governments have done little to control the entrepreneurial market in land or to make reasonably priced land available. Housing policies have often been highly politicized; for example to secure electoral support, co-opt community elements, and develop or strengthen patron-client relationships (Connolly 1990; Kusnetzoff 1990; Shidlo 1990; Vélez-Ibañez 1983). As land speculation has driven the price of land beyond the reach of the poor, the search for cheaper land has led to ever-more-distant settlements. The commute to work becomes exceedingly long, urban sprawl grows, and the cost of services becomes more expensive than they need otherwise have been.

Shantytowns start as groups of makeshift houses, as noted above, yet they improve slowly over the years with great effort. Over time they develop into increasingly complex communities. Even a small settlement of a few dozen families may have some modest services and business ventures. The somewhat larger community will possess a diverse collection of small shops and services run out of the individual households, from those that sell soda pop and home-prepared snacks to tailoring, repair services, hairdresser services, and so forth. Some of these stores meet community needs; others serve a wider population—all are a means of earning additional money. More sizable businesses will also appear in the larger and older settlements. To varying degrees, the communities will also contain public facilities—a playing field (if there is space), a meeting hall, perhaps a rudimentary clinic, and even an elementary school after some period of time and growth. If not constrained by topography, the community will grow and there will appear an increasingly broad range of services, small businesses, and community facilities. From meager beginnings, homes, neighborhoods, and communities have been created. Not all succeed, but many do.

As the community grows, and as services and public facilities improve and security of tenure becomes less problematic, shantytowns develop a more diverse population—the result both of more varied migrant populations as well as the changing circumstances of longtime residents. Thus, in many communities residents will exhibit a fairly wide range of economic circumstances; occupations; levels of education; family stability, organization, and size; length of residence in the community; and the like. An increasing, though still minority, proportion of the population will be made up of renters instead of homeowners (Gilbert and Varlay 1991)—a mix that can make effective community action more difficult.

Shantytown residents are extensively integrated into and involved in the economic, political, social, and cultural institutions of the broader metropolis. They provide much of the construction, service, and unskilled labor on which the city and its economy rest. Many of the women labor as domestics or in petty trade, and children collect scrap to sell for reprocessing by large manufacturers. A diversity of small shops in the informal sector, many located within the shantytown, employ settlement residents. Purchases are also made from businesses in the metropolis. Individual and community needs involve the shantytown residents with local and municipal bureaucracies, officials, and politicians. Shantytown residents vote in local and national elections. The urban popular movements in which some are involved bring them in touch with other members elsewhere in the city. They are an audience for national television. They attend sports events, schools, cinemas, and seek medical care in the metropolis. They visit friends and family throughout the city. Thus, they are extensively connected with the broader society and its institutions. They are not, as some earlier theorists contended, marginal to urban life.

Shantytowns exhibit varying degrees of organization. Such organization is sufficiently extensive, however, to belie the image of the urban poor as unorganized nonparticipants. Small settlements generally contain a neighborhood council and one or two other more narrowly focused interest organizations. Social, political, and religious organizations exist in the larger communities. As noted later in this chapter, political action, community councils, and self-help organizations are usually most active at the early stages of community formation. It is at this point that the need is most pressing to prevent evictions and to pressure public authorities to provide at least some rudimentary services. Thus, for instance, in Cornelius's study (1973) of settlements in Mexico City, he found 87 percent of the residents in the recent squatter settlements participating in communal self-help activities and 70 percent participating politically—approximately twice the level of participation within the more established settlements. A similar pattern of heightened participation in young settlements is reported in research in Santiago, Lima, and Río de Janeiro, though the proportion is lower and varies considerably (Portes 1976b; Goldrich et al. 1970; Perlman 1976).

Settlements will also exhibit some cooperative action to deal with communal needs (e.g., laying sewer pipes, erecting a community hall). Yet action varies considerably among communities. A number of earlier studies suggest an impressive level of relationships of trust, reliance, and mutual helpfulness (Perlman 1976; Lobo 1982; Peattie 1968). The popular urban movements, discussed below in the section on political behavior, evidence a more recent expression of such relationships. However, it is not possible to draw any firm conclusions in this regard. On the one hand, it is clear that there is an active and well-organized minority of settlements with high levels of participation and organization. On the other hand, "no evidence . . . indicates that self-help practices and community relations are any stronger now than they were twenty or so years ago" (Roberts 1989a:242). Also, fewer settlements are now being formed, namely, the ones where organizational membership and interhousehold cooperation would be expected to be greatest. The effects of the recession of the past fifteen years unite some, as evidenced by the popular movements, yet they can also weaken cohesion. The struggle to survive absorbs much of one's attention and energy. Households are increasingly burdened. Families double up to save money. Family conflict and dissolution intensifies. These conditions are not conducive to community involvement and are discussed in greater detail below. Bryan Roberts, a longtime observer of Latin American urban life, concludes that supportive, cohesive shantytown communities "are not beacon lights of an alternative future, but tiny islands gradually being eroded" (Roberts 1989a:243).

Family and kinship ties have played a crucial role in helping many of the urban poor to survive and, in time, to improve their circumstances. At the same time, some families dissolve in the face of economic pressures. Whether the need is adapting to a new community, finding housing or work, locating needed services or goods, dealing with emergencies, securing funds for an economic venture or health care, celebrating special events, or the like, the urban poor rely on family and kin. Butterworth and Chance observe that "without exception studies show that the family and kinship networks play a crucial role in migrant adaptation to Latin American cities. . . . Far from becoming atrophied in the city, the extended family remains strong . . . and in some cases even increases in significance" (1981:94–95). And the same applies to nonmigrants. Family and kinship ties are a fundamental resource for meeting many of the principal tasks of survival as well as for sharing life's more joyous moments.

Assistance and emotional support are facilitated when family members settle nearby or in the same neighborhood. Close, nonfamily ties are also developed through *compadrazgo*, a "system of ritualized personal relations" (Kemper 1977:173) that is frequently established at significant occasions or points in the life cycle. *Compadrazgo* develops ties of responsibility and caring with other individuals or families.

Larrisa Lomnitz specifies more fully the normative basis of the mutual assistance that exists among families. She asks, "How do millions of Latin Americans manage to survive in shantytowns without savings or salable skills, largely disowned by organized systems of social security?" (1974:135). Her research on Cerrada del Cóndor, a squatter settlement in Mexico City, shows that they rely heavily on the mutual assistance of kin. "Networks of reciprocal exchange" develop among family members (related through consanguinal and marriage ties) who have established households within the same shantytown. Already-settled family members aid new migrants or families elsewhere in the city to settle in Cerrada del Cóndor. The reciprocal exchange of goods and services is extensive, involving general information and job assistance, loans, services, sharing of facilities, and moral and emotional support. It is reinforced by a number of mechanisms: *compadrazgo,* male friendships, drinking relations among the men, and an ideology of assistance. "The duty of assistance is endowed with every positive moral quality; it is the ethical justification for network relations" (Lomnitz 1977:151). Although few low-income urbanites achieve the reciprocity networks that are common in Cerrada del Cóndor, reliance on and assistance from family is evident among the poor throughout the region.

Thus, the poor survive a harsh urban environment by relying on the mutual support of personal networks to create housing and communities. The world of work and securing an income, however, takes much of their time and energy.

The Informal Sector

For those who live in poverty as well as for the somewhat more comfortable, securing a livelihood is an ongoing effort. Sizable rural-to-urban migration, the high birthrate after 1950 (which produced an increasing number of young people entering the labor force from the early 1970s to the end of the century), and the failure of the economy to generate commensurate employment opportunities produced a situation where the cities had an excess labor supply of 30 to 60 percent—even before the economic debacle of the early 1980s (Portes and Schauffler 1993:37–38). The 1980s witnessed a very rapid increase in the labor force of 34 percent (calculated from Table 5.9), which has contributed to the development of the informal sector. In 1990, according to the Regional Employment Programme (PREALC) of the International Labor Organization (ILO), at least 31 percent of the population made a living in the informal sector (see Table 5.7). This is a rock-bottom figure; other well-based assessments of the urban economically active population (EAP) place the figure as high as 56.3 percent in 1980. The difference arises out of the criteria used to define the informal sector (Portes and Schauffler 1993). A significant portion of the EAP struggled to survive the 1980s by laboring in the informal sector. Yet in spite of what some observers have judged to be growing numbers of workers in the informal sector, incomes still declined. Hakkert and Goza report that "in Costa Rica, Brazil, Argentina, and Peru, rapid informal sector growth during this period was associated with income declines of between 23.5 percent and 39.3 percent" (1989:74).

Although no clear-cut line divides the formal and informal sectors, the latter is generally not in compliance with state regulations. Informal sector labor and enterprises are also commonly characterized by their labor intensiveness, small scale, lower-than-minimum wage levels, lack of job benefits, reliance on kin and family, instability of enterprises, erratic employment, and the like. An impressive panoply of retail jobs and working conditions exists (Bromley and Gerry 1979). Petty retail is the most common area, followed by services and repair, small-scale manufacturing or assembly plants, instruction, domestic labor, and small-scale transportation. Many workers are self-employed, others work in small plants. With minimal capital and modest skills, one can seek to eke out a living. Or, with family and kin, households can pool their labor to work within their home or in a small repair, service, or industrial establishment. The informal sector and those who labor in it survive through long hours, low hourly earnings, and lower costs by ignoring state regulations regarding conditions, pay, and labor benefits. The sector is dominated by women because of economic need, the paucity of jobs in the formal sector, and cultural barriers to the employment of women. It is also true, however, as Corcoran-Nantes observes, that the "lack of infrastructure on the urban periphery, the arduous nature of domestic chores, . . . and the incompatibility of school hours with those of registered employment make the urban subsistence economy the only viable alternative for low-income women" (1990:253).

Although the informal sector is disproportionately a low-income labor force, it also exhibits a great deal of heterogeneity in education, occupational skills, and income. Its ability to offer opportunities for profit not equally available in the formal sector attracts a broad range of participants, from skilled artisans to knowledgeable and educated microentrepreneurs. Portes and Schauffler would, at a "minimum," distinguish between "informal microentrepreneurs with access to some capital and labor resources; and unprotected workers and the self-employed" (1993:45). Gilbert suggests as a third category a "marginal" group composed of street beggars, bootblacks, street entertainers, and so forth (1990b:108).

The informal sector is not a carryover from more traditional forms of production destined to disappear with economic modernization nor is it extraneous to the formal sector. There is a close interdependence with the formal economy, and it performs a number of important functions that serve the needs and interests of the large modern, national, and transnational corporations, as well as of local business. Production (usually assembly or components) and marketing is subcontracted out by formal sector plants to shops in the informal sector. The multinationals are connected to local entrepreneurs and labor by a chain of subordinate linkages that can be quite elaborate. Portes and Schauffler summarize the research of Benería and Roldan in Mexico City: "They were able to document a complex chain reaching from a United States multinational firm producing electrical appliances for the Mexican market to domestic formal suppliers, informal subcontractors, and home workers—generally women—who assembled certain parts for a piece rate. At each descending step of the ladder, work conditions became more precarious and wage levels lower (1993:49)." The advantages of subcontracting ultimately rest on the lower production costs arising, as noted above, from the low operating costs, low wages, and absence of benefits in the informal sector (Oliveira 1985) as well as on the sector's flexibility given the formal sector's fluctuating production needs. The practice of subcontracting is therefore "common throughout the assembly industries of Latin America" (Lawson 1992:7). Foreign corporations obtain lower-cost production and higher profits than would be secured at home (Portes and Walton 1981: Chapter 3).

The existence of a low-paid labor force in the informal sector serves as a "reserve army of labor" that creates downward pressure on wages that can weaken formal sector labor. In short, it increases the profitability of capital. By providing relatively cheap services and goods, the informal sector helps meet the needs of workers in the formal sector, thus reducing the reproductive cost of labor and the pressure on wages by workers in formal sector plants. The advantages offered by the informal sector to the formal sector suggest it will persist even under conditions of formal sector growth. Predictions of the informal sector's survival contradict modernization theorists' assumption that with economic growth the size of the informal sector would shrink. Of course, the role of the service sector and its consequent survival is not limited to the developing countries.

Since the early 1980s, Latin America has increasingly recognized the importance of the informal sector in job creation and economic growth. Through its Small Projects Program, the Inter-American Development Bank (IDB) has sought to channel modest grants to small enterprises through private nonprofit organizations. These grants provide training in business skills and access to credit, which is extremely difficult to obtain from private sector banks (IDB 1989). A much more extensive series of measures to support small enterprises has been proposed (Bromley 1993): technical and managerial training; preferences in allocating public services, credit, subsidized raw materials and equipment, and rents in an effort to link small enterprises to potential purchasers of goods and services (including the government); and research on appropriate technologies and organizational forms, among others.

Much can be said about the usefulness of aiding the informal sector. At the same time, any sizable effort is likely to encounter opposition from the established business sector if scarce funds are to be allocated for such purposes, especially to potential competitors—at least in some sectors. In addition, if these new enterprises are expected to comply with state regulations on wages, benefits, and working conditions, their economic viability might be threatened. Nonetheless, even with such impediments, aid to the informal sector might provide a measure of job creation and economic growth.

The informal sector exists because of the energy, imagination, and adaptability of the men and women who seek out and develop all possible means for survival. As in other spheres of life, these subsistence activities depend heavily on social networks of family and friends for information, resources and labor, contacts, financial assistance, and the like. With an economy and a state that offers them very little, many of the poor have created their own means of livelihood, as earlier I observed that many created their own homes and communities. Of course, their ability to find or develop work reflects a broader economic system that can utilize the labor and services they offer. Those who secure employment or are self-employed meet the needs of the formal economy, although they are being exploited in the process, for example, by accepting below-minimum wages. In many ways the system rests on such exploitation, one that Vilas points out later in this volume is growing as formal sector enterprises are restructuring the labor market and production process (Chapter 5). The close ties between the formal and informal sector have meant that the economic decline in the former restricts income opportunities in the latter, as noted below. Hence, the ability of the informal sector to provide even a very modest income for the poor is qualified, as suggested in the rise in unemployment figures and falling income at the height of the economic crisis.

As with the creation of their homes and communities, the popular sector's pursuit of informal sector work is part of their repertoire of survival strategies. It complements self-help housing and home-based subsistence activity, community soup kitchens and craft workshops (discussed later), the utilization of the income-generating ability of all household members, and, of course, the development and retention of personal and family networks. The severe economic downturn through which the majority of the urban population has been living has required all their resourcefulness.

The Economic Recession and Its Bitter Fruit

The precipitous decline of the Latin American economy in the 1980s began for most countries in the early years of the decade. In 1992 per capita gross domestic product (GDP) in Latin America was 7.5 percent below that of 1980. The workforce was restructured (see Chapter 5), the private sector was downsized, public sector workers were dismissed, public enterprises were privatized, and public services and subsidies declined. Urban life became exceedingly harsh for the low-income, working-class, and middle-class residents of urban centers. The shift to an export-oriented development model and the abandonment of import substitution industrialization aggravated the effect of the economic crisis in the cities.

Wages and income dropped and unemployment rose. The minimum wage declined 3 percent a year in the 1980s. The urban poor, who work in the informal sector outside the range of government regulations, fared even worse. The average real income in the informal sector declined 5 percent a year from 1980 to 1989, and stood at 58 percent of the value it had nine years earlier (see Chapter 5)—a truly horrific decline. Urban unemployment rates increased appreciably, from 6 percent in 1974 to 14 percent in 1984 (A. Portes et al. 1994:8). Given the absence of unemployment insurance, the unemployed of necessity seek some type of income through work in the informal sector. Hence, unemployment figures have ordinarily been low. During the recession, however, an increasing number of the urban poor failed to find work even in the informal sector, a failure that reveals the close links between the formal and informal sectors (Portes et al. 1994). During economic downturns, the formal sector will reduce its subcontracts with and its purchases of goods and services from the informal sector.

The profound reversals had far-ranging and onerous consequences for the urban poor and modest-income populations. Households have struggled to lower costs and maintain income with the limited repertoire of choices open to them. Expenditures are reduced by increasing household size. Young married couples move in with parents and families double up: "53 percent of the households among the *poblaciones* of Santiago, Chile, involve sharing . . . of this kind" (Rodriquez 1987, cited in Roberts 1989a:242). And some move to cheaper and less desirable quarters. In São Paulo during the 1980s "large numbers of middle-class households experienced downward mobility and were forced to abandon dwellings near the centre and to buy or rent cheaper accommodations on the periphery. At the same time, many of the city's poorest inhabitants could no longer afford housing on the periphery and crowded into *corticos* (multifamily tenements, literally, "beehives") in the city's central zones" (U.N. 1993c). Portes reports a similar phenomenon in other Latin American cities (1989).

More women have entered the workforce, particularly in the informal sector. Although not attributable to the debt crisis alone, their stepped-up participation has been notable during the austerity era and constitutes an important element in the family survival strategy (Hakkert and Goza 1989:72–73). Gilbert reports on research in Oaxaca (Selby et al. 1990:169), Guadalajara (Gonzáles 1991), and São Paulo (Hirata and Humphrey 1991:580) that provides evidence for this trend (1993:73). Hakkert and Goza suggest that reported figures may actually disguise the degree of change, as women are now also involved in "the domestic production of consumer goods that were previously acquired in the marketplace" (1989:73). Where the household family structure offers no opportunity for increasing the number of working members, the consequences can be severe. Escobar and Gonzáles report that "young, single-worker households with several small children . . . have reduced both the quality and quantity of their per capita food intake, milk excepted," and "not surprisingly, dysentery, malnutrition, and anemia have increased their contribution to infant mortality during the crisis" (1991:7). The number of street children and of children working the streets appears to have increased (Barker 1992:6). The struggle to survive affects economic, personal, and household conditions and has at times sorely strained the interpersonal fabric of the family. "There is evident tension within households, as husbands demand that wives fulfill their domestic chores and take in work for pay" (Roberts 1989b:683). Family disorganization appears to have increased. Men translate their unemployment and "failure" as providers into alcoholism and violence. In response, women and their children establish matrifocal households (Selby et al. 1990:175–177; Roberts 1989a).

If economic growth were to take hold in Latin America in the remaining years of this century, these conditions may undergo a moderate improvement. However, it is questionable that any considerable change will be forthcoming given the restructuring of the labor force.

The Politics of Low-Income Settlement Populations

The political behavior of the shantytown population is diverse and complex. Although the behavior of such populations has shown considerable continuity over the past half-century, it has also exhibited some intriguing changes during the past two decades. On the whole, the urban poor have belied the fears of the established order that they would erupt into violent protest against elite-dominated regimes. A major issue has been whether the shantytown residents would use institutionalized methods and channels of established elite parties and state agencies or engage in independent forms of action. As the following account suggests, they have generally felt that the former approach provided the greater probability of success in securing governmental assistance. In the discussion below, popular political behavior and attitudes are sketched out, as are the determinants of political behavior, the integration and subordination of the shantytown and its organizations into the dominant political order, and the development of urban social movements during the past two decades.

Wayne Cornelius concludes in his 1971 review of approximately three-score empirical research studies on rural-to-urban migrants that these are "politically moderate-to-conservative individuals seeking small-scale improvements in living and working conditions without recourse to violence or radical restructuring of the social order" (1971:106). No evidence suggests city-born individuals differ from migrant populations (Cornelius 1971:107). Even among the more politically conscious and informed low-income settlements of Chile in the late 1960s and early 1970s, less than 15 percent of the residents exhibited an unambiguously radical orientation (Portes 1971). A more recent sampling shows little change. In Stokes's research on some of Lima's poorest shantytowns in 1985 and 1986, her three-question index of radicalism finds less than 8 percent of respondents choosing a radical answer on all three questions, and less than 16 percent did so on two of the three questions (Stokes 1991).

The general circumstances and characteristics of lower-income populations help account for their political restraint. The struggle to survive absorbs much of one's attention, and their political weakness renders the urban poor vulnerable to sanctions by state authorities (Goldrich, Pratt, and Schuller 1970). Lower-class occupations also atomize the labor force, providing little contact with large concentrations of workers or with organized trade unionists and scant opportunity to develop either political sophistication or shared political identities. Their experience has generally been that survival and improvements in their lives have come through hard work, diligence, family ties, patronage, and luck, not from political or collective efforts. The urban poor do not generalize their hardships as the result of the organization and inequalities of the broader social and political order. It is also the case that, hard though life had been, times were improving during about half the postwar period; many of the urban poor had some hope that their lives would improve as well. They lack what Portes has labeled "structural blame," a cognitive framework for explaining personal difficulties in terms of social structural determinants. In his study of four lower-class settlements in Santiago, Portes shows that such a cognitive framework arises from political socialization. Where such socialization is present, the probability of radical political attitudes and voting is increased, and where it is not, radical attitudes tend to be absent (Portes 1971).

Collective political action is spurred, however, when communal needs (e.g., electricity, water, schools) go unmet or when tenure is not secure. Usually, demands for action are specific, narrowly focused, and peaceful. In addition, requests are not ordinarily made on behalf of a broader collectivity or envisioned as requiring an alteration of political or economic structures. The extent to which a settlement is securely established and the level of public services it has attained are predictive of community solidarity and participation in self-help organizations and neighborhood councils. Considerable research shows that they are inversely related (Portes 1976b), a connection noted earlier in this chapter. Thus, settlements established through land invasion or that lack, for other reasons, legal recognition of their tenure may have to struggle to prevent eviction. Such low-income urban settlements also require basic services, particularly in the beginning. Activism tends to increase as particular needs or issues arise. Thus, in spite of the fears of authorities and the hopes of the Left, the low-income urban settlements have not posed a basic threat to political authority or to the prevailing political and economic institutions.

The urgency of the ends sought by political action is, of course, only one determinant of community-based political activity. In his six-community study of migrants to Mexico City and a review of the literature of low-income urban communities, Cornelius has identified "a number of factors bearing importantly upon the development of a cooperative political ethos" (1973:38). In addition to the influence of housing and service needs noted above, he reports that a cooperative ethos is more common in small and densely populated communities because of the increased opportunity for face-to-face interaction and the greater pressures toward conformity; in socioeconomically homogeneous communities given the greater probability that residents will recognize a mutuality of interest; in communities characterized by instability of residence; in communities perceived as separate from the rest of the city; in communities where past political activity has been successful; where community leadership encourages participation; where formal voluntary associations are present; and where internal political cleavage and competition is low (Cornelius 1973:36–45).

In the context of Cornelius's summary review it is important to note that several of the conditions noted above become especially difficult to meet over time. Socioeconomic homogeneity declines with time as the life circumstances of the original population undergo differential rates of change, as new, more diverse migrants join the settlement, and as the proportion of renters increases. Also, in time, the number of residents in the community will grow, and the settlement itself will come to resemble the rest of the metropolis. Schneider's research on the wave of protests in the mid-1980s in the *poblaciones* of Santiago extends Cornelius's analysis. Prior political organization and activity, she writes, affect contemporary political behavior: "The protest movement erupted most forcefully in the same 'red' neighbourhoods that had been the center of the leftwing political activity years before the military coup" (1991:94). In effect, earlier events and organization provide the traditions, orientations to politics, and militant grassroots leadership crucial for protesting fifteen to twenty-five years after the initial appearance of those conditions.

The character of Latin American political institutions and processes constitutes the political context within which low-income neighborhoods seek to secure a governmental response to their needs. The political context, which shapes political behavior, is characterized by the dependency of low-income settlements on the state, given their needs for public service, and by the prevalence of clientalism and co-optation. Dependency exposes shantytown residents to patronizing relationships, in which dominant elites provide the modest means for their survival in return for using them as a basis for political support or legitimacy (Castells 1983:Chapters 19, 20). The result is usually the subordination of popular efforts and movements to the needs of the state and dominant interests.

Imbedded in Latin American political and social life are what Carlos Vélez-Ibañez has labeled the "rituals of marginality," whereby the relations between dominant elites and the popular sectors that are "expressed in repetitive forms such as patron-client relationships, brokerage, political friendships of convenience and other favor-producing exchanges" (1983:4). Clientalism is a major aspect of rituals of marginality and is defined as "a pattern of relationships in which goods and services are exchanged between people of unequal status" (Chalmers 1977:33). Votes and other forms of political support are exchanged for community and personal benefits. Thus, these emoluments are seen, not as a right inhering in citizenship, but as having been secured through an exchange of favors. Castells observes that it is "the squatters' lack of citizenry [that] provides the political system with an ultimate weapon for controlling and enforcing their political allegiance" (1983:211). Clientalist practices are often linked to co-optation wherein "an informal, loosely structured group is led by its leader to formally affiliate with a supra-local institution" (Eckstein 1988:107).

Clientalism occurs in various circumstances and is especially common where the low-income sectors lack political organization or effective representation through parties of the Left. The *favalatos* of Brazil have for many years traded votes for basic community needs. With no regular parties or other formal structures through which to press their demands, the *favalatos* use clientalism and paternalistic ties to seek some response to their needs in exchange for votes at election time (Leeds and Leeds 1976). In Lima, Peru, variously from the late 1940s to early 1960s, General Manuel A. Odria and then General Manuel Prado offered land and services for votes to create the popular political base they otherwise lacked (Collier 1976; Castells 1983:Chapter 19).

Mexico offers one of the most sophisticated cases of the use of co-optation, clientalism, and paternalism to control the population and retain power. Through the machinery of the Institutional Revolutionary Party (PRI) and government-affiliated organizations, Mexico has for decades successfully concentrated power in the hands of the president and a small group of advisers. Eckstein's study of three lower-class neighborhoods in Mexico City offers a broad sketch of how, even though the settlements had created interest-based organizations, these associations and their leaders became tied to either PRI or government-affiliated organizations. Initially, these ties may bring some modest benefits, but they offer no institutional power, that is, no sphere within which these neighborhoods can possess resources or make decisions in regard to settlement policy. At the same time, "local leaders are constrained to conform to the 'rules of the game'. . . . Otherwise they can neither advance in politics nor secure benefits for their constituents" (Eckstein 1988:87). Related to the above point, she also finds that "the structurally induced personalistic style of Mexican politics makes residents . . . feel dependent on and indebted to the government for material benefits they receive," and "their 'gifts' are officially 'given' to them at public rallies which often are attended by . . . high-ranking dignitaries" (1988:93). In effect, co-optation and clientalism in Mexico have served more as instruments of social and political control than to advance lower-class interests.

Governments do not necessarily just wait for low-income neighborhoods to press demands. They often actively develop links with these communities as a means of controlling settler political participation. Such channels for dealing with the communities are more formal and public than clientalism or co-optation, though these older practices are not abandoned. Gilbert and Ward's comparative study (1985) of community action programs in Bogotá, Mexico City, and Valencia, Venezuela, shows how effective these can be in

maintaining governmental control, depoliticizing demand making, and legit-
imizing the political system. They observe that "the truth seems to be that in
Bogotá, Mexico City, and Valencia the state has developed highly effective
methods of channeling and controlling participation" (1985:238). As they
point out, community organizations and community action programs have
been effective means of social control, with some but rather modest benefits
received by the communities. Their research, carried out in 1980, also
showed the continued validity of earlier studies, noted above, concerning the
nonradical behavior of the urban poor and relatively low levels of resident
participation in community affairs, as well as how participation varies with
the age of the settlement and its level of services.

Castells's comparative analysis of squatter movements in the late 1960s
and 1970s in Peru, Mexico, and Chile—the most prominent in Latin America—adds an additional note of complexity to squatter mobilization and the
various contexts within which it appears. His analysis of Chile and Mexico
are of special interest. In Chile the particular needs and strategies of the
major parties of the center and the Left—the Christian Democrats, Socialists,
and Communists—determined the form of mobilization taken by the *cam-
pamentos* that they dominated. Greater independence is exhibited by the
urban movements in Monterrey, which were able to exploit the differences
between the central government under Luis Escheverría and the more conservative business leadership in the city. And they did so while maintaining
their independence and seeking transformative change, an early and rare example of the new social movement phenomenon (Castells 1983:Chapter
19).

Much of what is described in the preceding discussion is still an important
part of contemporary shantytown politics in Latin America. Nonetheless, in
the last twenty years or so, a multiplicity of new organizations have sprung
up and reinvigorated civil society. Loosely and questionably labeled at times
as "new social movements," they give voice to interests poorly met by the
traditional political order as well as offer greater grassroots involvement in
and control over their organizations. Women, environmentalists, indigenous
peoples, students, and others have fueled such efforts. One of the more notable has been the popular urban movement. These neighborhood-based organizations are not an entirely new phenomenon, and they do not necessarily seek either social or individual transformation. They differ from earlier
such groups, however, in that they evidence greater grassroots participation
and more autonomy from parties and the state (Mainwaring 1989:189–
193). Instead of offering votes in exchange for favors, they are demanding
their rights as citizens. These groups have not, however, replaced more traditional forms of lower-class organization but have instead added to the range
of existing organizations.

Many popular urban movements arose in response to the extremely difficult economic times brought on by the recession and neoliberal economic policies. To an important degree, they represent a strategy for survival. The rise of these neighborhood-based organizations also partly reflects the repression of political parties and trade unions by the authoritarian regimes of the 1970s and early 1980s. In the bloody stillness imposed by the generals, neighborhood, consumption-oriented, and ostensibly non-class-based organizations could more readily survive. They have addressed themselves to self-help tasks as well as to forming pressure groups seeking state action on issues of collective consumption. They have generally focused on concrete needs and have sought specific, narrow policy responses. With some exceptions, these organizations have not sought societal transformation, nor have they, even when there has been active membership involvement, been fully autonomous or independent from outside parties and leaders.

A number of features of popular urban movements stand out. A particularly striking fact is that their members are predominantly female, an empowerment that may in time affect other areas (Alvarez 1990:Chapter 2; Logan 1990; Schild 1994). There has been a growth of coordinating organizational structures linking groups within metropolitan areas, elected decisionmaking assemblies, and a panoply of local- and district-level organizations (Leiva and Petras 1987; Bennett 1992). The popular movements in Mexico exhibit the most developed expression of this phenomenon. The second national congress of urban popular movements in 1981 had two thousand delegates representing six hundred organizations. By way of contrast, Mainwaring comments on "the highly fragmented character of urban popular movements" in Brazil (1989:169). Thus, the reality is quite diverse. As this suggests, some popular movements practice grassroots democracy and participation in collective decisionmaking, with leaders drawn from the local population. However, hierarchical structures and less-democratic practices are also in evidence (Hellman 1994; Oxhorn 1991). Outside leaders—from the church, students, health professionals, political groups, and the like—play a role (Bennett 1992; Alvarez 1990). Thus, the abstract concept of fully autonomous, nonhierarchical, democratic organizations is often not an accurate depiction of current reality.

In spite of vigorous growth, urban popular movements face a number of vexing problems. Maintaining commitments and cohesion over time can be extremely difficult; a continued high level of participation is too demanding for most settlement populations. When some community needs are satisfied, community residents lessen their involvement. The offer by the state of benefits independent of the popular organization may also attract residents and weaken the movement (Banck and Doimo 1989; Janssen 1978; Vellinga 1989). Also, as the community matures over time, heterogeneity, and thus the range of interests, are likely to increase; shared concerns decrease. A significant problem, especially during periods of rapid growth, is finding an organizational form that will accommodate diverse interests and actors, bridging the differences not only within sectors of the neighborhood population but also among the various outside political actors: for example, political parties that may be linked to the popular movement (Oxhorn 1991).

The attention lavished on popular urban movements in recent years reflects a number of factors. The movements have undergone enormous growth—broadening their ties, increasing coordination and developing links with major political parties (particularly in Brazil, Mexico, and Chile), achieving concrete accomplishments on meeting community needs, and raising hopes in their ability to raise consciousness and help redefine the identity of the urban poor. Nonetheless, urban movements appear to reach only a very small portion (a few percentage points in most instances) of the population within which they are situated. Thus, for the greater number of shantytown residents, political behavior and attitudes may not be much different from earlier years. The development of popular urban movements is a process, however; initial advances provide a base for future growth. The coming years should see an increase in numbers and the political importance of such movements. Their larger political importance will depend, though, on the extent to which they develop links with trade unions and parties of the Left. This union would provide an agenda that goes beyond the limits of collective consumption needs by tackling the governmental policies and structural bases of the disabilities that they experience. This would also provide a means of "articulat[ing] their demands with the political system" (Vilas 1993:42). Yet the need for broader links also carries risks for the autonomy of popular organizations and the continued vitality of grassroots participation. However, they are necessary risks if the movements are to play a part in bringing a more profound improvement of the circumstances of the popular sectors.

In sum, the shantytowns have, in most instances, been temperate in their politics. They have responded to the world as they have understood it and been guided by an assessment of what kind of behavior would most likely secure their immediate ends. This essentially moderate approach has certainly not succeeded in transforming their lives, but it has frequently provided a means of meeting some crucial needs. Inasmuch as political moderation has been less successful in recent years, a somewhat more vigorous and autonomous politics may be imminent among the urban poor.

Conclusion

The immense urban transformation of Latin America during the past half-century has had a profound impact on the lives of the people in the region. I have sought in this chapter to provide a sketch of some of the principal challenges facing the urban poor. The prevailing economic and political system clearly offers them very little. Yet through their diligent perseverance and resourcefulness, shantytown dwellers have succeeded in creating homes, communities, and work opportunities, though at times the extent of each of these may be quite modest. This success has often been accomplished through cooperation with family and community, though the latter can wane and be co-opted.

It is difficult to expect a marked change in the circumstances of the urban poor without some significant alteration in the economic policies being pursued or in the distribution of political power. The poor have usually been constrained to adapt their own economic and political efforts to the parameters of the broader system, and hence they have not fundamentally changed its character or its exploitativeness. An economic upturn (still uncertain) would lighten the burden of life in an unresponsive political context and harsh economic environment; more than that seems unlikely.

The popular sectors have tried to organize and press demands outside the formal channels of the prevailing order. Yet in spite of the considerable attention that they have received, these efforts are still relatively limited. The growing strength of progressive movements, such as in Mexico and Brazil, give reason for hope. Yet no hemisphere-wide resurgence of the Left or the labor movement appears imminent. And it will not be generated merely by the urban neighborhood, though it could be a useful component of such a broader movement. What does seem probable is that the vast and diverse populations in the shantytowns ringing the cities will continue to exercise the same fortitude and resourcefulness that have made survival possible—qualified and great at times as the costs have been.

References

Alvarez, Sonia E. "Women in the New Social Movements of Urban Brazil," in Sonia E. Alvarez, ed., *Engendering Democracy in Brazil.* Princeton, NJ: Princeton University Press, 1990, 37–56.

Arizpe, Lourdes. "Relay Migration and the Survival of the Peasant Household," in Helen I. Safa, ed., *Towards a Political Economy of Urbanization in the Third World Countries.* Delhi: Oxford University Press, 1982, 19–46.

Banck, Geert A., and Ana Maria Doimo. "Between Utopia and Strategy: A Case Study of a Brazilian Urban Social Movement," in Frans Schuurman and Ton Van Naerssen, eds., *Urban Social Movements in the Third World.* London: Routledge, 1989, 125–150.

Barker, Gary K. "More Than a Minor Problem." *Hemisfile* 3, 1 (January 1992):6–17.

Benería, Lourdes, and Marta I. Roldan. *The Crossroads of Class and Gender: Homework, Subcontracting, and Household Dynamics in Mexico City.* Chicago: University of Chicago Press, 1987.

Bennett, Vivian. "The Evolution of Urban Popular Movements in Mexico Between 1968 and 1988," in Arturo Escobar and Sonia E. Alvarez, eds., *The Making of Social Movements in Latin America*. Boulder, CO: Westview Press, 1992.

Bromley, Ray. "Small Enterprise Promotion as an Urban Development Strategy," in John D. Kasarda and Allan M. Parnell, eds., *Third World Cities: Problems, Policies, and Prospects*. Newbury Park, CA: Sage, 1993, 120–133.

Bromley, Ray, and Carl Gerry, eds. *Casual Work and Poverty in Third World Cities*. New York: John Wiley, 1979.

Browning, Harley L. "Recent Trends in Latin American Urbanization." *Annals of the American Academy of Political and Social Science* 316 (March 1958):111–120.

———. "Primacy Variation in Latin America During the Twentieth Century," in Instituto de Estudios Peruanos, ed., *Integración y Proceso Social en América*. Lima: Instituto de Estudios Peruanos, 1972.

Browning, Harley L., and Waltraut Feindt. "The Social and Economic Context of Migration in Monterrey, Mexico," in Francine F. Rabinovitz and Felicity M. Trueblood, eds., *Latin American Urban Research*, vol. 1. Beverly Hills, CA: Sage, 1971, 45–70.

Butterworth, Douglas, and John K. Chance. *Latin American Urbanization*. Cambridge: Cambridge University Press, 1981.

Castells, Manuel. *The City and the Grassroots*. London: Edward Arnold, 1983.

Chalmers, Douglas A. "The Politicized State in Latin America," in James M. Malloy, ed., *Authoritarianism and Corporation in Latin America*. Pittsburgh: University of Pittsburgh Press, 1977, 23–45.

Collier, David. *Squatters and Oligarchs*. Baltimore: The Johns Hopkins University Press, 1976.

Collins, Jane. *Unseasonal Migrations: The Effects of Rural Labor Scarcity*. Princeton, NJ: Princeton University Press, 1988.

Conning, Arthur. "Rural-Urban Destinations of Migrants and Community Differentiation in a Rural Region of Chile." *International Migration Review* 6, 2 (Summer 1972):148–157.

Connolly, Priscilla. "Housing and the State in Mexico," in Gil Shidlo, ed., *Housing Policy in Developing Countries*. London: Routledge, 1990, 5–32.

Corcoran-Nantes, Yvonne. "Women and Popular Urban Social Movements in São Paulo, Brazil." *Bulletin of Latin American Research* 9, 2 (1990):249–264.

Cornelius, Wayne A. "The Political Sociology of Cityward Migration in Latin America: Toward Empirical Theory," in Francine F. Rabinovitz and Felicity M. Trueblood, eds., *Latin American Urban Research*, vol. 1. Beverly Hills, CA: Sage, 1971.

———. *Political Learning Among the Migrant Poor: The Impact of Residential Context*. Sage Comparative Politics Series no. 01-036. Beverly Hills, CA: Sage, 1973.

———. *Politics and the Migrant Poor in Mexico City*. Stanford, CA: Stanford University Press. 1975.

Crummett, Maria de los Angeles. "Rural Women and Migration in Latin America," in Carmen Diana Deere and Magdalena León, eds., *Rural Women and State Policy*. Boulder, CO: Westview Press, 1987, 239–260.

Deere, Carmen Diana, and Magdalena Léon. *Women in Andean Agriculture*. Geneva: International Labor Organization, 1982.

Eckstein, Susan. *The Poverty of Revolution: The State and the Urban Poor in Mexico.* Princeton, NJ: Princeton University Press, 1988.

Elizaga, Juan C. "A Study of Migration to Greater Santiago." *Demography* 3, 2 (1966):352–377.

Escobar Latop, Agustin, and Mercedes Gonzáles de la Rocha. "Introduction," in Mercedes Gonzáles de la Rocha and Agustin Escobar Latop, eds., *Social Responses to Mexico's Economic Crisis of the 1980s.* San Diego: Center for U.S.-Mexican Studies, University of California–San Diego, 1991, 1–15.

Findley, Sally E. "The Third World City: Development Policy and Issues," in John D. Kasarda and Allan M. Parnell, eds., *Third World Cities: Problems, Policies, and Prospects.* Newbury Park, CA: Sage, 1993, 1–31.

Gilbert, Alan G. *Latin America.* London: Routledge. 1990a.

———. "Urbanization at the Periphery: Reflections on the Changing Dynamics of Housing and Employment in Latin American Cities," in David Drakakis-Smith, ed., *Economic Growth and Urbanization in Developing Areas.* London: Routledge, 1990b, 73–124.

———. "Third World Cities: The Changing National Settlement System." *Urban Studies* 30, 4/5 (1993):114–140.

———. *The Latin American City.* London: Latin America Bureau, 1994.

Gilbert, Alan G., and Ann Varley. *Landlord and Tenant: Housing the Poor in Urban Mexico.* London: Routledge, 1991.

Gilbert, Alan G., and Peter M. Ward. *Housing, the State, and the Poor: Policy and Practice in Three Latin American Cities.* Cambridge: Cambridge University Press, 1985.

Goldrich, Daniel M., Raymond B. Pratt, and C. R. Schuller. "The Political Integration of Lower-Class Urban Settlements in Chile and Peru," in Irving L. Horowitz, ed., *Masses in Latin America.* New York: Oxford University Press, 1970.

González de la Rocha, Mercedes. "Family Well-Being, Food Consumption, and Survival Strategies During Mexico's Economic Crisis," in Mercedes Gonzáles de la Rocha and Agustin Escobar Latop, eds., *Social Responses to Mexico's Economic Crisis of the 1980s.* San Diego: Center for U.S.-Mexican Studies, University of California–San Diego, 1991, 115–128.

González de la Rocha, Mercedes, and Agustin Escobar Latop, eds. *Social Responses to Mexico's Economic Crisis of the 1980s.* San Diego: Center for U.S.-Mexican Studies, University of California–San Diego, 1990.

Graham, Douglas H. "Divergent and Convergent Regional Economic Growth and Internal Migration in Brazil, 1940–1960." *Economic Development and Cultural Change* 18, 3 (April 1970):362–382.

Hakkert, Ralph, and Franklin W. Goza. "The Demographic Consequences of Austerity in Latin America," in William L. Canak, ed., *Lost Promises: Debt, Austerity, and Development in Latin America.* Boulder, CO: Westview Press, 1989, 69–97.

Hardoy, Jorgé E., and David Satterthwaite. *Squatter Citizen: Life in the Urban Third World.* London: Earthscan Publications, 1989.

Hellman, Judith. "Mexican Popular Movements, Clientelism, and the Process of Democratization." *Latin American Perspectives* 21, 2 (Spring 1994):124–142.

Hirata, H., and J. Humphrey. "Workers' Responses to Job Loss: Female and Male Industrial Workers in Brazil." *World Development* 19 (1991):671–682.

IDB (Inter-American Development Bank). "A Woman in the Service of the Microentrepreneurs." *IDB Journal* (March 1989):6–9.

Janssen, R. "Class Practices of Dwellers in *Barrios Populares:* The Struggle for the Right of the City." *International Journal of Urban and Regional Research* (1978):147–159.

Kemper, Robert, V. *Migration and Adaptation: Tzintzuntzam Peasants in Mexico City.* Beverly Hills, CA: Sage Publications, 1977.

Kusnetzoff, Fernando. "The State and Housing in Chile," in Gil Shidlo, ed., *Housing Policy in Developing Countries.* London: Routledge, 1990, 5–32.

Lawson, Virginia A. "Industrial Subcontracting and Employment Forms in Latin America: A Framework for Contextual Analysis." *Progress in Human Geography* 16 (1992):1–23.

Leeds, Anthony, and Elizabeth Leeds. "The Significant Variables Determining the Character of Squatter Settlements." *America Latina* 12 (1969):44–86.

———. "Accounting for Behavioral Differences: Three Political Systems and the Responses of Squatters in Brazil, Peru, and Chile," in John Walton and Louis Masotti, eds., *The City in Comparative Perspective.* Beverly Hills, CA: Sage, 1976.

Leiva, Fernando Ignacio, and James Petras. "Chile: New Urban Movements and the Transition to Democracy." *Monthly Review* 39, 3 (July–August 1987):109–124.

Lloyd, Peter. *Slums of Hope? Shantytowns of the Third World.* New York: Penguin Books, 1979.

Lobo, Susan. *A House of My Own: Serial Organization in the Squatter Settlements of Lima, Peru.* Tucson: University of Arizona Press, 1982.

Logan, Kathleen. "Women's Participation in Urban Protest," in Joe Foweraker and Ann L. Craig, eds., *Popular Movements and Political Change in Mexico.* Boulder, CO: Lynne Rienner, 1990, 150–159.

Lomnitz, Larissa. "The Social and Economic Organization of a Mexican Shantytown," in Wayne A. Cornelius and Felicity M. Trueblood, eds., *Latin American Urban Research,* vol. 4. Beverly Hills, CA: Sage, 1974, 135–155.

———. *Networks and Marginality: Life in a Mexican Shantytown.* Orlando, FL: Academic Press, 1977.

Mainwaring, Scott. "Grassroots Popular Movements and the Struggle for Democracy: Nova Iguacu," in Alfred Stepan, ed., *Democratizing Brazil: Problems of Transition and Consolidation.* New York: Oxford University Press, 1989, 168–204.

Mangin, William. "Latin American Squatter Settlements: A Problem and a Solution." *Latin American Research Review* 2, 3 (Summer 1967):65–98.

———. "The Role of Regional Associations in the Adaptation of Rural Migrants to Cities in Peru," in Dwight Heath and Richard N. Adams, eds., *Contemporary Cultures and Societies of Latin America.* New York: Random House, 1974.

Oliveira, Francisco de. "A Critique of Dualist Reason: The Brazilian Economy Since 1930," in Ray Bromley, ed., *Planning for Small Enterprises in Third World Cities.* New York: Pergamon Press, 1985, 65–95.

Oxhorn, Philip. "The Popular Sector Response to an Authoritarian Regime: Shantytown Organizations Since the Military Coup." *Latin American Perspectives* 18, 1 (Winter 1991):86–91.

Peattie, Lisa R. *The View from the Barrio.* Ann Arbor: University of Michigan Press, 1968.

Perlman, Janice E. *The Myth of Marginality: Urban Poverty and Politics in Río de Janeiro.* Berkeley: University of California Press, 1976.

Portes, Alejandro. "Political Primitivism, Differential Socialization and Lower Class Leftist Radicalism." *American Sociological Review* 36, 5 (October 1971):820–835.

———. "The Economy and Ecology of Urban Poverty," in Alejandro Portes and John Walton, eds., *Urban Latin America: The Political Conditions from Above and Below.* Austin: University of Texas Press, 1976a, 7–69.

———. "The Politics of Urban Poverty," in Alejandro Portes and John Walton, eds., *Urban Latin America: The Political Conditions from Above and Below.* Austin: University of Texas Press, 1976b, 70–110.

———. "Latin American Urbanization During the Years in the Crisis." *Latin American Research Review* 24, 3 (1989):37–44.

Portes, Alejandro, and Michael Johns. "The Polarization of Class and Space in the Contemporary Latin American City," in William L. Canak, ed., *Lost Promises.* Boulder, CO: Westview Press, 1989, 111–137.

Portes, Alejandro, and Richard Schauffler. "The Informal Economy of Latin America: Definition, Measurement, and Policies." *Population and Development Review* 19, 1 (March 1993):33–60.

Portes, Alejandro, and John Walton. *Urban Latin America: The Political Conditions from Above and Below.* Austin: University of Texas Press, 1976.

———. *Labor, Class, and the International System.* Orlando, FL: Academic Press, 1981.

Portes, Alejandro, José Itzigsohn, and Carlos Dore-Cabral. "Urbanization in the Caribbean Basin: Social Change During the Years of the Crisis." *Latin American Research Review* 29, 2 (1994):3–38.

Radcliffe, Sarah A. "Mountains, Maidens, and Migration: Gender, Poverty, and Population Movement on the Costa Rican Periphery," in Sylvia Chant, ed., *Gender Migration in Developing Countries.* London: Belhaven Press, 1992, 30–48.

Roberts, Bryan. "The Interrelationships of City and Provinces in Peru and Guatemala," in Wayne A. Cornelius and Felicity M. Trueblood, eds., *Latin American Urban Research,* vol. 4. Beverly Hills, CA: Sage, 1974, 207–235.

———. *Cities of Peasants: The Political Economy of Urbanization in the Third World.* Beverly Hills, CA: Sage, 1978.

———. "Comments on John Friedmann's 'The Dialectic of Reason.'" *International Journal of Urban and Regional Research* 13, 2 (June 1989a):241–244.

———. "Urbanization, Migration, and Development." *Sociological Forum* 4, 4 (1989b):665–691.

Roberts, Kenneth D. "Agrarian Structure and Labour Mobilization on Rural Mexico." *Population and Development Review* 8, 5 (June 1982):299–322.

Rodriquez, Daniel. "Agricultural Modernization and Labor Markets in Latin America: The Case of Front Protection in Central Chile." Ph.D. diss., Department of Sociology, University of Texas at Austin, 1987.

Schild, Veronica. "Recasting Popular Movements: Gender and Political Learning." *Latin American Perspectives* 21, 2 (Spring 1994):59–80.

———. "The Hidden Politics of Neighbourhood Organizations: Women and Local-Level Participation in the *Poblaciones* of Chile." *N/S Canadian Journal of Latin American and Caribbean Studies* 15, 30 (1990):137–158.

Schneider, Cathy. "Mobilization at the Grassroots: Shantytowns and Resistance in Authoritarian Chile." *Latin American Perspectives* 18, 1 (Winter 1991):92–112.

Selby, Henry A., Arthur D. Murphy, and Stephan A. Lorenzen. *The Mexican Urban Household: Organizing for Self-Defense.* Austin: University of Texas, 1990.

Shidlo, Gil. "Housing Policy in Brazil," in Gil Shidlo, ed., *Housing Policies in the Third World.* London: Routledge, 1990, 33–47.

Stokes, Susan C. "Politics and Latin America's Urban Poor." *Latin American Research Review* 2, 26 (1991):75–102.

U.N. (United Nations Department of Economics and Social Information and Policy Analysis). *World Population Trends and Policies: 1987 Monitoring Report Population Studies No. 103,* ST/ESTA/SER.A/103. New York: U.N., 1988.

———. *Internal Migration of Women in Developing Countries,* ST/ESTA/SER.R/127. New York: U.N., 1993a.

———. *Population Growth and Policies in Mega-Cities: Mexico City,* ST/ESTA/SER.R/105. New York: U.N., 1993b.

———. *Population Growth and Policies in Mega-Cities: São Paulo,* ST/ESTA/SER.R/122. New York: U.N., 1993c.

———. *World Urbanization Prospects: The 1992 Revision,* ST/ESTA/SER.A/136. New York: U.N., 1993d.

Vélez-Ibañez, Carlos E. *Rituals of Marginality: Politics, Processes, and Culture Change in Central Urban Mexico, 1969–74.* Berkeley: University of California Press, 1983.

Vellinga, Menno. "Power and Independence: The Struggle for Identity and Integrity in Urban Social Movements," in Frans Schuurman and Ton Van Naerssen, eds., *Urban Social Movements in the Third World.* London: Routledge, 1989, 151–176.

Vilas, Carlos M. "The Hour of Civil Society." *Report on the Americas* 27, 2 (September–October 1993):38–42.

Whiteford, Michael B. "Neighbors at a Distance: Life in a Low-Income Colombian Barrio," in Wayne A. Cornelius and Felicity M. Trueblood, eds., *Latin American Urban Research,* vol. 4. Beverly Hills, CA: Sage, 1974, 157–181.

Wilkie, James W., and Carlos Alberto Contreras, eds. *Statistical Abstract of Latin America, 1992,* vol. 29. Los Angeles: Latin American Center Publications, UCLA, 1993.

3

Demilitarization and
Democratic Transition
in Latin America

JORGE NEF

The term "democratic transition" has become a buzzword in official circles in the Americas. It has also generated a copious amount of scholarly literature (Nef 1988: 132; Di Palma and Whitehead 1986; Drake and Silva 1986; and O'Donnell et al. 1986). Democratization and redemocratization have been equated by mainstream thinkers and their followers with the change from military to civilian rule. For them, this trend is one of four global transformations that are associated with the triumph of American ideals. The second is the transition from economic nationalism to neoliberalism (Mouffe 1983; Offe 1981), construed as the proof of the inherent superiority of pragmatism and market forces. The third trend is a decline of populism (Costa-Pinto 1978; Raby 1983) and its replacement by "limited democracy" (Siat and Iriarte 1978). The latter entails a semicorporatist "pact of elites" that facilitates the governability of the state by reducing the scope of participation (Chomsky 1977). The fourth trend is international. After the collapse of eastern Europe, the reversal of the Sandinista Revolution in Nicaragua, and the isolation of Cuba, regional elites do not face the dangers of revolution, expropriation, and reduced profits. The sum total of these trends is seen by some as a vindication of modernization theory (Almond 1978), a surge of conservative triumphalism, and, most important, business confidence.

There is, of course, another point of view: Even without the menace of impending revolution, the region remains a ticking bomb. The profound social tensions brewing under the democratic surface have not disappeared (Crane 1989: D1). On the contrary, they have compounded over time. The vicious spiral of poverty and violence—repressive, institutional, and insurgent—has not been arrested. Politically, the weak and entangled civilian governments to emerge from two decades of authoritarianism find themselves straitjacketed by utter lack of effectiveness and eroding legitimacy. Despite the optimism among Western elites, a review of the literature and the mass of statistical data, both aggregate and at the national level, does not convey a rosy picture (Pollock 1989). "Confidence," therefore, has little to do with the state of economic, social, and even political democracy in the region, nor with actually existing security and stability for Latin Americans. Instead, it rests on the wishful ideological illusion that things are falling into place and that a felicitous correspondence between market politics and market economics has finally emerged. The main concerns of transition theory, like those of its predecessors, are the maintenance of the status quo and the prevention of revolution (Bodenheimer 1970).

The purpose of this chapter is to offer a critical interpretation of Latin America's democratization and its implications for human security in the hemisphere. Unlike the cold war term "national security," human security essentially involves an appraisal of the environmental, economic, social, political, and cultural risks and vulnerabilities affecting people. Two central theses are explored. The first is that the repressive military regimes of the 1970s and today's limited democracies are less discontinuous than the proponents of transition theory suggest. Despite political turmoil and persistent violence, the underlying social, economic, and international forces that have enjoyed extraterritorial power and privilege still prevail. The second thesis is that the long-run systemic consequences of the stability of these underlying forces have hindered sustainable, equitable, and democratic development. In fact, the current style of modernization increases, rather than decreases, mutual vulnerability, poverty, and insecurity for most people in both parts of the hemisphere.

The Genesis of the Crises: A Long-Range View

An appropriate historical analysis of the crises leading to the current transitions is beyond the scope of this essay. It would also be good to bear in mind that discussions about democratization and demilitarization in the "other" America call for overgeneralizations about a conglomerate of distinct national and subnational entities with specific characteristics. Nevertheless, a number of common and recurrent historical factors accounting for the serious shortcomings of the democratization process need to be spelled out. Without indulging in a debate about the merits of dependency theories, four important empirical observations about Latin American underdevelopment must be mentioned.

First, since the conquest, Latin America has been subordinated to one or another more highly developed parts of the world. Therefore, the structures and patterns of production, trade, and finance in the region have reflected an enduring satellite-metropole international division of labor. The insertion of the Latin American nations as commodity-producing states in the international economy, with its boom-and-bust cycles, was firmly ingrained by the latter part of the nineteenth century. This export economy was centered on the export of raw materials, the import of manufacture, and the superexploitation of laborers. Second, economic 'modernization' by colonial and neocolonial powers has often been antidevelopmental, as endogenous development has been undermined by decapitalization and marginalization. Third, nearly two centuries after the formal independence of Latin American nations, structural underdevelopment persists. Fourth, these structural circumstances have all been incorporated into the national and inter-American political regimes: the Latin American states and the system of inter-American relations. However, international factors can be understood only through their relation to the domestic political economy and its internal social processes. Far from being the single cause of underdevelopment, lack of autonomy has been a structurally persistent intervening variable that reinforces internal conflicts (Weaver 1976:17).

The social structures resting on these complex historical, political, and economic traits have also tended to endure. The ranch, the hacienda, the mining town, and the Central American plantation created conditions for the emergence and perpetuation of an outward-looking and parasitic commercial elite (Andreski 1967). These socioeconomic structures also gave rise to a highly exploitative and patrimonial system of labor relations based on indenture, paternalism, and servitude. In this highly hierarchical and rigid social structure, class and racial barriers were intertwined. The ruling groups have been fundamentally committed to this order, owing their very existence to being a linkage, or intermediary, between the national society and the dominant colonial or neocolonial power. The wars of independence (1808–1823), though violent and long, did little to alter the socioeconomic order. National consolidation unfolded without a revolutionary bourgeoisie, a revolutionary ideology, and, most important, without a radical national-capitalist transformation. On the contrary, authoritarian institutions inherited from the Iberian Peninsula, such as the Roman Catholic Church, a rigid class system, the practices of local bosses, clientelism, and familism put down deep roots in the New World and continued to shape the national period. Despite stereotypes to the contrary, Latin American societies have been distinctively unrevolutionary. The fragile economies, societies, and states have been subject to violent cyclical crises, yet true social revolutions have occurred in very few countries: Haiti (1803), Mexico (1910–1921), Bolivia (1952), Cuba

(1959), and Nicaragua (1979). Contemporary counterrevolutionary modernizations "from the top" have also been rare. If one discounts the foiled attempt in authoritarian Brazil (1964–1984), only Chile stands today as a thorough, albeit problematic, case of elite modernization.

Moreover, the destruction of the colonial order left a power vacuum, with regional fragmentation and warlordism. National armies came into being during this period of turmoil. As the founding fathers faded away, the postindependence period saw the emergence, in most countries, of partisan military establishments. Though some of the officer corps was the product of military academies, many armies evolved into predatory organizations under the domain of self-made chieftains, accountable to nobody and resistant to any constitutional order. With few exceptions, the frequent civil wars between so-called conservatives and liberals, unitarians and federalists, presidentialists and parliamentarists were more expressions of a crude struggle for booty and control than manifestations of clear class alliances or ideological agendas. The professionalization of the military, which started in the 1880s first along French and later German lines, brought men in uniform into the fold of the upper strata. This process took place in an era of sustained prosperity resulting from increased demand for raw materials, which facilitated intra-elite compromise and the gradual cessation of civil strife. But an expansion of the export economy also meant the sudden advent of manifest conflict between the elites and emerging working classes. Although military modernization reduced the chances of takeovers by caudillos operating outside gentlemen's rules, in most cases it created a severe imbalance within the state. The officer corps became stronger and more institutionalized than its civilian counterparts in the legislature, the bench, and the bureaucracy. Professionalization defined the prime directive of the armed forces as well: protecting the landed and commercial aristocracy from the lower strata and repressing labor unrest. With international and civil wars receding, the central task of the military was to act as an insurance policy against radical change.

Given the violence and polarization of political conflicts, militarization has been a long-standing feature of the Latin American state. With few exceptions, the military establishment has played a disproportionately large role in virtually all the countries, whether under civilian executives or not. Even in the exceptional cases, a careful examination reveals that direct military rule or militarized repression has always been present. For instance, Costa Rica, generally acclaimed as democratic and without a formal army (since 1948), had the de facto regime of Gen. Federico Tinoco between 1917 and 1919. Uruguay, another country with a democratic reputation before the 1973 coup, was ruled by "men on horseback" throughout the nineteenth century and had one coup in 1934. Chile, in addition to the civil wars of 1831 and 1891, and the seventeen-year Pinochet dictatorship (1973–1990), went through a period of intermittent dictatorships between 1924 and 1931. Before the revolution, Cuba was a military dictatorship. Colombia has a long history of civil wars and was ruled by a military dictator as recently as 1953–1958. In fact, Colombia has been under various forms of martial law ever since the civil war of 1948. Before 1958 Venezuela was governed by an almost uninterrupted succession of military dictators. As for Mexico, headed by civilian presidents since 1946, the one-party dictatorship of the Institutional Revolutionary Party (PRI) has constantly resorted to repression, civilian and military, to retain control.

The profound post–World War I recessions, culminating in the Great Depression of the 1930s, shattered the old export economy. With the collapse of its foundations, the tenuous system of elite accommodation that sustained the oligarchical republics began to crumble. As intra-elite tensions increased, so did the challenges to the existing order coming from labor, the peasantry, and the dispossessed. In the aftermath of economic collapse, the "dictator of the thirties" became a dominant feature practically everywhere. Yet the long-term effects of the crisis were quite diverse, depending on the previous modality of socioeconomic development and institutional consolidation.

Two notable patterns emerged in the region and resulted in sharply different socioeconomic and political arrangements between the 1930s and the 1950s and in equally dissimilar manifestations of state crisis in the decades that followed. One pattern, that of inclusive rule, emerged in the relatively more industrialized South American nations, where middle-class reformism had evolved in the previous decades and republican practices had become institutionalized. There, populist-oriented import substitution industrialization (ISI) became the dominant form. This ISI populism was an inclusive arrangement under middle-class, bureaucratic leadership in alliance with national entrepreneurs and unionized labor around a program of national development. Populism was also the trend in Mexico. The other pattern, exclusive rule, was characteristic of the lesser-developed societies in Central America and the Caribbean, where, with the exception of Costa Rica, a constitutional order had not emerged and a professional and bureaucratic middle class played no significant role. In these regimes, conflict-management precluded a populist alternative and was essentially exclusionary for the popular sectors. In these countries, for the next thirty or forty years dictatorial rule continued unabated.

These two patterns began to fall apart between the mid-1940s and early 1950s. Riots, revolts, and generalized political turmoil exploded in Colombia, Costa Rica, Guatemala, El Salvador, Argentina, Venezuela, Peru, Bolivia, Cuba, and Puerto Rico. U.S. administrations, mesmerized by the cold war, the Truman doctrine, and the newly established Río Treaty for the collective defense of the Americas (1947), responded to these domestic events in their backyard as threats to their "national security." Latin American oligarchies, besieged by social unrest and unable to withstand popular mobilization and pressures for democratization, took advantage of the new international environment by playing on the anticommunist fears of their American allies. Entangling transnational alliances between business, political, and military elites in the center and the periphery were built. The East-West conflict created the conditions for a new North-South confrontation. It also marked the return of an active U.S. interventionism reminiscent of the "big stick" and gunboat diplomacy approach that preceded the Good Neighbor policy, inaugurated by the administration of President Franklin D. Roosevelt in 1933. The rationale for interventionism was justified by a new and compelling ideological cloak: the struggle between the Free World and communism. The CIA-orchestrated overthrow of the elected government of Guatemala in 1954 was a harbinger of things to come. But U.S. interventionism was disastrous for the region's institutional and democratic development. The United States became the principal force for the preservation of an oppressive status quo and an unabashed supporter of military dictatorships.

U.S. interventions in Central America and the Caribbean proved insufficient to prevent the popular mobilizations that precipitated a crisis of domination in Venezuela and Cuba. Neither the Pérez Jiménez nor the Batista dictatorships and their external supporters were able to exercise effective control by force. The Venezuelan dictator, Col. Marcos Pérez Jiménez, was overthrown in 1958 and Fulgencio Batista fled Cuba shortly thereafter. The Cuban Revolution was the first of a wave of national revolutionary movements backed by a wide array of popular forces. The Cuban revolution was the most important development in the region since independence from Spain, highlighting the growing internationalization of domestic conflicts and setting the tone for a chain of events that became a major target for future U.S. responses.

Attempts by the United States to manipulate and subsequently undo the revolution culminated in both the calamitous Bay of Pigs invasion and President John F. Kennedy's Alliance for Progress, launched in 1961 (Levinson and de Onís 1970). Washington's main purpose was to prevent another Cuba by supporting social and economic reforms in the region. With it, U.S. policy moved away from the open support of dictators of the previous era. Instead, economic and social development was perceived as the prime directive and number-one antidote to insurgency. It was to be accomplished by propping up middle-class, progressive reformist, and anticommunist (Christian Democratic or Social Democratic) governments. But it was a case of too little too late. The economic impact of the alliance was quite limited. Import substitution industrialization had already come to a dead end, populism had run its course, social tensions were mounting, and a profound fiscal crisis had set in. The inability of the reformist governments to deliver and quell social unrest rendered the Alliance's progressive option virtually void and discredited.

The other side of the Alliance for Progress's strategy involved the isolation of Cuba as well as a massive effort to give new meaning to the collective defense of the Americas outlined in the Río Treaty by introducing counterinsurgency and civic action as the number-one preoccupation of the region's security forces (Barber and Ronning 1966). A radical reorganization of the Latin American military ensued. The change in military doctrine from the defense of territorial security with conventional forces to fighting the "internal enemy" with special forces was a final blow to the precarious sovereignty of the Latin American countries. It transformed the U.S. security establishment into the head of a vertically integrated regional counterrevolutionary system, giving the local military a new self-justifying and professional mission: fighting "subversion," however loosely defined. In a relatively brief period and with a modest expenditure, the United States, irrespective of its declared intentions, had turned the local military and police forces (the latter through the public safety programs of the U.S. Agency for International Development [USAID]) into the dominant internal linkage groups (Chalmers 1972: 11) and operators of its own hemispheric security regime. With the reformist and preventive side of the Alliance for Progress marred by internal and external inconsistencies, the counterinsurgency and containment elements took precedence over democratic considerations. This reorientation became manifest during the Johnson administration, with its encouragement and nurturing of Brazil's counterrevolution of 1964.

In the more institutionalized democracies, the exhaustion of import substitution and populism led to a crisis of legitimation: a breakdown of consensus and civic confidence (Habermas 1975). Import substitution with populism failed to bring long-term sustainable development and political stability. In the 1960s wage and price spirals had become a muted and protracted form of civil strife. Political deadlock eroded both the legitimacy and the effectiveness of these regimes. Labor practices inherited from the populist years reproduced and accelerated "the push-up effect" of the institutionalized social conflict. The rules of the democratic game slowly decomposed in the midst of rapid mass mobilization. In these countries, the existing socioeconomic order, both domestic and international, was maintained by resorting to naked, albeit highly bureaucratized, repression and by creating a new political alliance. The latter involved a coalition between the externally linked economic elites—which gave content to a neoliberal economic package—and the security establishments transnationalized by the ideological "professional" training of the cold war. The military, representing a unique U.S.-trained, -indoctrinated, and -financed fraction of the middle class, provided the force required to keep the population at bay. The concept of national security—defined in terms of an internal enemy and an external friend (the United States) and by ideological frontiers—eroded the very legitimacy of the local military institutions and decisively transnationalized the state. The explicit articulation of this emerging U.S. strategic doctrine for the Western Hemisphere was contained in the *Rockefeller Report* (Rockefeller 1969), a document that clearly showed a change in the normative American ideal for political development from democracy and participation to authoritarianism and order (O'Brien 1972). For the duration of the Nixon-Ford administrations, the number of military dictatorships climbed dramatically: ten in 1969, twelve in 1970, fourteen in 1972, and fifteen in 1973 (Nef 1986:43–55).

The authoritarian project rejected the nationalist and protectionist overtones of ISI policies. Instead, it saw economic growth as a function of a reinsertion of the countries' economies into the international division of labor as exporters of raw materials—a return to the export economy. With the exception of Brazil in the late 1960s and the 1970s, economic modernization, far from "deepening industrialization," meant increased reliance on the natural resource sector and heavy borrowing. The foreign debt, which in 1960 amounted to $2,213 million, or about one-third of the regional annual exports, had grown by 1970 to 1.7 times the total value of exports. Just before the oil crisis in 1973, it had climbed to 1.9 times the total value of regional exports. The strategy of accumulation also involved the creation of favorable conditions, through deregulation, denationalization, and the disarticulation of labor organizations, for transnational corporations to increase profits. The era of national security (Weil et al. 1978:36–72) was characterized by more than its extreme and persistent abuses of human rights: the neoliberal design implied the tearing down of the welfare state and ISI schemes dating from the 1930s. Instead, under the lead of repressive regimes, "authoritarian capitalism" (Bruneau and Faucher 1981:1–9) was established. The scheme rejected the demand-side implications of the early cold war liberalism of the Alliance for Progress and was more concerned with direct containment and the protection of the status quo than with development. Other than promising "economic miracles" financed by foreign investment, the orthodox policies imposed monetarism (later identified with the Chicago School) over the structuralist doctrine of the U.N. Economic Commission on Latin America (ECLA). These measures were far more successful as a shock therapy—by atomizing labor, freezing wages, letting prices float to world levels, and privatizing the economies—than in raising living standards. On the contrary, the long-term socioeconomic effects of these policies were, by and large, disastrous for the region. So were their environmental and financial implications. In fact, far from generating stability and bringing prosperity, the combination of dictatorial rule with unrestricted free-market policies created a serious governability problem in most countries. Moreover, the authoritarian capitalist formula set the conditions for the subsequent debt crisis and recession of the 1980s.

The bureaucratic-authoritarian states (Szymanski 1981:444–464) that emerged in South America—a forerunner of which was Brazil's "liberating revolution" of 1964—were in fact attempts at modernizations from the top as well as from the outside. The benefits of this new order accrued to a co-terie of domestic entrepreneurs and speculators, supported by a techno-cratic-military middle class and their business, political, and military associates in the United States (North 1978:79). The social cost for the majorities was high because living conditions declined and the gap between elites and masses widened dramatically. These regimes also failed to unleash real counterrevolutions. At best, the national security regimes provided a repressive brake on social mobilization, economic nationalism, regional integration, and a perceived socialist threat.

The neoliberal model required large amounts of international financing, which was facilitated in the 1970s and early 1980s by massive deposits of recycled petrodollars in private Western banks. A rapid process of indebtedness, fueled by the illusion of "economic miracles" ensued. As both the governments and, especially, the private sector in the region increased their financial obligations, the failure of production and exports to keep pace with borrowing and, most important, swelling interest rates resulted in staggering debt-burdens (Lefever 1987:2). In this regard, the hard-line military regimes in Brazil, Argentina, Chile, Uruguay, and Bolivia did not behave very differently from the more populist ones in Peru, Panama, or Ecuador or the civilian-controlled oil-producing countries, though the policy framework was quite different. In Mexico and Venezuela, heavy borrowing was part of a structural project of national development geared to economic self-reliance. However, irrespective of the intent of the policies, their effects were similar: a generalized debt crisis (see Table 3.1).

The crisis of the dictatorships in Brazil, Argentina, Uruguay, and Chile involved first and foremost the erosion of the political alliances that had permitted the implementation of the repressive socioeconomic projects. The

TABLE 3.1   Indebtedness: Selected Countries, 1970–1985 (in billion U.S.$s)

	1970	1982	1985	15-year Growth	Annual Growth
Argentina	1.9	15.8	50.8	2674.	1178.3
Brazil	13.2	47.6	107.3	3353.	223.5
Chile	2.1	5.2	21.0	1000.	66.7
Mexico	3.2	50.4	99.0	3094.	206.3
Venezuela	0.7	12.1	33.6	4800.	2320.0

SOURCE: Louis Lefever, "The Problem of Debt," *International Viewpoints,* supplement of the *York Gazette* (Toronto, Ontario). York University, March 2, 1987, 2.

main political limitation of the national security regimes was that government by fear is ultimately untenable. The Nicaraguan uprising of 1979 and
the long civil wars in El Salvador and Guatemala signaled another form of
transition: popular, radical, and potentially democratic in the broadest sense
of the word. From the optic of the American elites, these endogenous developments posed a more serious threat to the maintenance of the hemispheric
status quo than the erosion of the bureaucratic-authoritarian regimes in
South America. The combined impact of economic crises, a growing inability to manage conflict among internal factions, and a new political coalition
in Washington fearful of the long-run effects of authoritarian solutions created the conditions for military withdrawal. The transitional strategy was
outlined in 1975 by the Linowitz report (Linowitz 1975), which was heavily
influenced by the views of the Trilateral Commission (Wolfe 1975:561).
Critical of the Pentagon's influence on U.S. policy toward Latin America,
the report constituted the blueprint for President Jimmy Carter's initiative
on democratization in 1978.

Transition to democracy, however, had strict limits. Although authoritarian capitalism proved to be largely a failure as far as development was concerned, the radical restructuring of the economies along neoliberal lines by
means of political repression was profound enough to prevent a return to
economic nationalism. Likewise, the restructuring and transnationalization
of the security establishment made the pursuit of nationalist and nonaligned
foreign policies utterly impossible. In this sense, the political arrangements
that have emerged in Latin America as a result of redemocratization (although they possess the formal trappings of sovereignty and democracy)
have been neither truly democratic nor sovereign. They have produced weak
civilian regimes based on negotiations within the elites, with limited political
agendas and narrow support. In these countries, the popular sectors are effectively excluded from the political arena, while external actors, both economic and military, enjoy de facto veto power over the state (Stepan 1988).
In addition, they remain saddled with unmanageable foreign debts. The central role of the state has changed from at least symbolically promoting development and providing public services to that of manifestly servicing the foreign debt and implementing structural adjustment policies (SAPs) inspired
by the International Monetary Fund (IMF) (Feinberg and French-Davis,
1988:1–11). The ultimate effects of this condition of receivership, as far as
the society is concerned, are the perpetuation of dependence and underdevelopment. The latter effects express themselves in chronic vulnerability to
external economic and political influences, requiring ever-increasing doses of
external supports. This vulnerability can be dramatically illustrated by the inability of the countries to extricate themselves from chronic indebtedness
(the debt-trap), shown by the figures in Table 3.2 (Martínez 1993:65).

TABLE 3.2   Latin America: Foreign Debt, 1990

	Total in Million U.S.$	Per Capita	Debt/GDP Per Capita	Percent Annual Growth	Service as Percent of Exports
Argentina	61,144.	1,893.	79.9	2.73	4.1
Bolivia	4,276.	594.	94.3	6.2	39.8
Brazil	116,173.	772.	28.8	–1.0	20.8
Chile	19,114.	1,450.	74.7	–4.6	25.9
Colombia	17,241.	534.	42.4	1.4	38.9
Costa Rica	3,772.	1,347.	70.9	–0.1	24.5
Dominican Rep.	4,400.	620.	74.7	5.5	10.3
Ecuador	12,105.	1,175.	119.9	7.3	33.2
El Salvador	2,133.	410.	36.9	–6.1	17.1
Guatemala	2,777.	302.	33.6	–1.4	13.3
Haiti	874.	135.	37.0	4.2	9.5
Honduras	3,480.	682.	116.3	1.5	40.0
Mexico	96,810.	1,134.	44.5	–4.6	27.8
Nicaragua[a]	10,497.	2,693.	199.4	14.7	4.1
Panama	6,676.	2,782.	152.0	9.7	4.3
Paraguay	2,131.	496.	44.7	1.8	11.0
Peru	21,105.	973.	83.9	10.6	11.0
Uruguay	3,707.	1,196.	46.7	–19.3	41.8
Venezuela	33,305.	1,691.	66.1	–1.6	20.7

[a]Estimated on the basis of the 1987 figure and an average decline of 2.5 percent a year.

SOURCE: World Bank, *World Development Report, 1990, 1991, and 1992.* New York: Oxford University Press, 1990, 1991, 1992, tables 1, 21, 24, 26.

The Problems of Transition

The transition from dictatorship to limited democracy has to be seen in the context of the earlier transition to national security regimes, both in the bureaucratic-authoritarian context of the Southern Cone and in the less institutionalized setting of Central America, Paraguay, or Bolivia. Growing participation could coexist with dependent development only under conditions of economic expansion and for as long as such participation did not threaten the perceived interests of the local and U.S. elites. The military managed the crisis of legitimacy in the Southern Cone through strengthening the bourgeois-military alliance with U.S. support (military, business, political, and diplomatic) while forcibly demobilizing and excluding the bulk of the population. Dictatorship became a fundamental component of economic "freedom" (Letelier 1976:42). The end of the cycle of the national security regimes in the 1980s grew out of the insoluble contradictions in authoritarian capitalism, particularly the nature of the "reactionary coalition" in power and the centrality of external support for these regimes. On the one hand, there was the long-run impossibility of reconciling the interests of the national security bureaucracies with the interests of domestic and U.S. business, given limited resources. On the other hand, there was the additional difficulty emerging from the extreme vulnerability of authoritarian capitalism to external economic forces (e.g., the unmanageable debt burden, deteriorating terms of trade, and so on) and external constituencies (e.g., members of the U.S. administration, the U.S. Congress, and the transnational corporations). As the tensions between power contenders intensified in Washington in the post-Watergate era, the loss of crucial support from U.S. business and liberal political sectors compounded the internal erosion of power suffered by the Latin American dictatorships. "Democratic transition" became the alternative to popular revolt.

Despite the phasing out of the national security regimes, contemporary Latin America is not a region moving toward increased democratization, at least in the conventional sense. Demilitarization and the return to (limited) democracy are not synonymous with any alteration in the status quo. The current hegemonic discourse regarding democracy among the official intelligentsia in the United States and in Latin America involves combining a substantially tamed democracy with neoliberal economics (Montecinos and Markoff 1993:12–14). Although this type of "low-intensity democracy" (Gill et al. 1993:3–5) may appeal to many North Americans and to Latin America's consumption-intensive elites, it rests on flimsy and largely ideological assumptions. This elitist conception of democracy, based on the *Report on the Governability of Democracy* (Huntington et al. 1975) presented to the Trilateral Commission (Sklar 1980, 1–5), assumes a continuous expansion of the global economy led by the marriage of technology and finance capital. Furthermore, the followers of this doctrine posit no serious contradiction between national interests and the interests of transnational business. Low-intensity democracy relies heavily on the use of selective tactical repression to deter the organization of labor and mass mobilization—echoing the authoritarian development of Asia's new industrializing countries (NICs), South Korea, Taiwan, Singapore, and Hong Kong. Finally, it just entrenches under a legal façade the same economic, social, and political forces that sustained the former antidemocratic regimes.

The democratic transition in the hemisphere was largely the result of a negotiated pact among elites (O'Donnell et al., 1986) superintended by the United States. The orderly retreat of the national security regimes has preserved many of the basic features of the authoritarian past. The regressive socioeconomic policies implemented under authoritarian rule were enshrined both in the aforementioned pacts and in the constitutional frameworks of the new regimes. In addition, the new democracies are constrained by other factors. One is the weakness of the governing centrist political alliances because the transition arrangements effectively excluded left-of-center and populist political forces from holding power. A second factor is the crucial autonomous role played by the security forces as a parallel state to maintain the status quo and prevent the investigation of human rights abuses. A third factor is the already-mentioned odious and massive debt obligations incurred mostly under the previous repressive regimes. These obligations severely limit the rendering of services to those in need, while fiscal austerity measures inevitably lead to confrontation politics and repressive governmental responses. The impact of the debt service on limited fiscal resources is compounded by the strict conditionalities imposed by the international financial institutions (the IMF, the World Bank, and private banks). Structural adjustments resulting from such conditionalities have gravitated against demands for reform, equity, and social justice, already frozen by the long-lasting dictatorships.

Debt management has been the number-one political issue on the regional agenda (Inter-American Dialogue 1988:3–4) for more than a decade. Between 1979 and 1983 the total debt for Latin America rose from less than $175 billion to more than $375 billion. At the same time, the service, both principal and interest, grew from slightly over 40 percent of the total value of exports in 1979 to more than 65 percent of the same value in 1983. The total indebtedness figure for 1988 was more than $400 billion with the higher sums being those incurred by Brazil, Mexico, Argentina, Chile, Venezuela, and Peru. In 1990–1991, despite the fact that about one-half of the countries had reduced their liabilities, the overall debt had grown to $421 billion (a 5.2 percent increase). In fact, out of the seventeen most-indebted countries in the world in 1992, twelve were in Latin America and the Caribbean. Though the annual interest rates payments fell from 33 percent of all exports in 1987 to 22 percent in 1991 as the "lost decade" came to an end, comparatively speaking, Latin America was still more vulnerable and exposed than eastern Europe (Felpern and del Huerto 1991:93).

Under these circumstances, there emerged throughout the region a new type of state. Highly transnationalized and weak, this type of state acts in partnership with foreign creditors and international financial institutions as manager, executor, and liquidator of its own bankruptcy (Nef and Bensabat 1992). As mentioned earlier, the central function of this political arrangement has been the administration of the foreign debt combined with the implementation of SAPs geared to massive privatization and denationalization of the economy. This state reflects the nature of the transnationalized political alliances and the limited arenas for political participation. Economic policy has effectively been left out of the political debate. Upon close scrutiny, irrespective of the nature of the government in charge, it is evident that although these regimes have replaced the old authoritarian-capitalist systems, they continue to display many of the same characteristics.

All things considered, the present state arrangements, which I call a "receiver state," cannot be understood as just a transitional phase in elite domination leading to a new and more genuine democracy (i.e., the return to free and participatory politics). The main structural characteristics of the receiver state include transnationalization, corporatism, depoliticization, demobilization, privatization, structural adjustment, deindustrialization, limited democracy, conditional franchise, entrenchment of the status quo, and military guardianship (Nef and Bensabat 1992:171–173). The repressive state of the 1970s and the receiver state of the 1990s are two different manifestations of a similar cluster of interests.

The receiver state represents the consensus of the interests of a largely transnationalized, reactionary coalition. This consensus involves the prevention of (1) national self-determination and/or a nonaligned Latin America; (2) any challenges to the hemispheric or national orders; and (3) any real economic, social, and political democratization. Limited democracy, with its narrow mobility opportunities and exclusionary agendas, provides a thin cushion against the deep structural problems once controlled by repression. The current modality of conflict management, although reducing the most blatant and ugly human rights abuses, has left Latin America's pressing and fundamental socioeconomic and political problems largely unresolved. Stable governance cannot be created by combining a transnational integration of the Latin American elites (economic, military, and bureaucratic) with a continental strategy of political containment through the demobilization, marginalization, and alienation of the popular sectors. In the absence of tangible rewards to buy legitimacy, violence (insurgent, repressive, institutionalized, as well as criminal) has become the most common form of political interaction. Under the veneer of normality, violence itself—including banditry, terrorism, repression, official abuses by security forces, and generalized lawlessness—remains the region's dominant mode of conflict management.

On the surface, with the withering away of the cold war and despite widespread violence, the military is less conspicuously present in politics than in the recent past. A closer examination, however, reveals a more complex and nuanced picture. True, the ending of the civil wars in El Salvador and Nicaragua, declining insurgent threats in Colombia and Peru, as well as the effects of structural adjustment packages on defense budgets suggest a trend toward demilitarization. Between 1985 and 1991 the region's defense budgets declined on the average 24.6 percent, or 4.1 percent per year, and twelve out of twenty countries cut defense expenditures from 59 percent (Chile) to 4.8 percent (Honduras). By way of contrast, however, two rather large countries, Venezuela and Colombia, dramatically increased such expenditures by 23 percent and 275 percent respectively. When the number of troops are examined, the overall trend is a seemingly modest increase of 4.2 percent for the region, or 0.7 percent per year. The smallness of this average upturn is deceiving, though, as it is affected by the incidence of declines in personnel in countries with large establishments, such as Argentina (−39.8 percent), Chile (−9.1 percent), Nicaragua (−76.6 percent), and Peru (−12.5 percent). Twelve out of twenty of the countries actually increased the size of their defense establishments between 1985 and 1991. Colombia topped the list with 76.7 percent, followed by Venezuela (53.1 percent), Guatemala (40.7 percent), and Mexico (35.6 percent). The largest establishment, that of Brazil with nearly 270,000 troops, grew 7 percent (IISS 1987–1992). Table 3.3 reports on these and other particulars.

The size, cost, and influence of the security establishment remains extensive throughout Latin America. Not including some 760,000 members of

TABLE 3.3   The Military Balance in Latin America

	Defense as Percentage of GDP/GNP			Numbers in Armed Forces per 1000		
	1985	1991	Change	1985	1991	% Change
Argentina	2.9	1.7	−39.3	108.0	65.0	−39.8
Bolivia	2.0	2.0	0.0	27.6	31.5	14.1
Brazil	0.8	0.8	0.0	276.0	296.0	7.2
Chile	7.8	3.2	−59.0	101.0	91.8	−9.1
Colombia	0.8	3.0	275.0	66.2	116.9	76.7
Costa Rica	0.7	1.0	42.9	*	*	*
Cuba	9.6	5.0	−47.9	161.5	175.0	8.4
Dominican Rep.	1.1	0.5	−54.5	22.2	22.2	0.0
Ecuador	1.8	2.2	22.2	52.5	57.5	9.5
El Salvador	4.4	2.4	−45.5	41.7	43.7	4.8
Guatemala	1.8	1.2	−33.3	31.7	44.6	40.7
Haiti	1.5	11.1	−26.7	6.9	7.4	7.2
Honduras	2.1	2.0	−4.8	16.6	17.5	5.4
Mexico	0.7	0.5	−28.6	129.1	175.0	35.6
Nicaragua	14.2	9.1	−35.9	62.9	14.7	−76.6
Panama	2.0	1.4	−30.0	12.0	11.7	−2.5
Paraguay	1.3	n.k.	n.k.	14.4	16.0	11.1
Peru	4.5	3.8	−15.6	128.0	112.0	−12.5
Uruguay	2.5	2.7	8.0	31.9	24.7	−22.6
Venezuela	1.3	1.6	23.1	49.0	75.0	53.1

*The Costa Rican constitution abolished the military in the late 1940s.

SOURCE: International Institute of Strategic Studies (IISS), *World Military Expenditures,* 1987, 1990, 1991, 1992 (London: IISS).

paramilitary organizations and an indeterminate number of reserves, Latin America has more than 1.3 million men under arms and spends close to $9 billion on defense. Simply stated, the security sector still is a voracious competitor for the scarce resources needed for development and constitutes a persistent obstacle to the independence of, and the cooperation among, the Latin American nations. Most important, it continues to be the single most serious threat to political stability, sustainable democracy, and human rights. To put it bluntly, with the cold war over and the danger of insurgency significantly reduced, the fundamental security issue in Latin America is not so much protecting society from external and internal "enemies" but safeguarding the population from its own security forces.

In the socioeconomic realm, most of the Latin American population lives under extremely precarious and vulnerable conditions. Although the overall performance of the regional economy has shown signs of recovery in recent years, social, environmental, and (on the whole) political and human rights indicators reveal stagnation if not outright deterioration. As is the case throughout the globe, the slow economic recovery has failed to translate into employment. Nor are there signs of a fairer and more equitable distribution of income, power, and other, less tangible yet basic values such as respect for human life, honest government, and the reduction of discrimination and official abuse.

Between 1980 and 1990 the number of poor people in Latin America increased from 120 million to 200 million (Robinson 1994:5), nearly one-half the population. Central America has been the area most seriously affected by the double impact of the concentration of wealth and the spread of poverty—80 percent of its inhabitants live below the poverty line, and half of these are completely destitute (Robinson 1994:6). According to *NotiSur,* between 1977 and 1994 Guatemala witnessed an acceleration in the concentration of wealth and resources. Fewer than 2 percent of the landowners now own more than 65 percent of the total farmland. Between 1990 and 1993, after just two years of structural adjustment, the poverty rate in Honduras increased from 68 percent of the total population to 78 percent. In Nicaragua, as a result of the contra war and the implementation of President Violeta Barrios de Chamorro's austerity package, 71.3 percent of the economically active population were unemployed (*NotiSur,* 1/14/94:9). Illiteracy, which the Sandinista government had reduced to 12 percent of the population, increased to 30 percent under Chamorro. The same is the case with infant mortality, which stood at 50 per 1,000 in the 1980s, rising to 71 per 1,000 in 1991 and 83 per 1,000 in 1993 (Robinson 1994:6).

Even the much-hailed economic miracles did not produce lasting development. Entrenched elite interests, the neoliberal agendas, and the structural adjustment policies left a lingering legacy of poverty and despair. Since the end of the boom of the 1970s, Brazil's only enduring feature has been the most unequal income distribution in the Western Hemisphere. Chile's "success story" does not fare any better under close scrutiny. Between 1970 and 1987 the proportion of people living below the poverty line increased by an average yearly rate of 7.2 percent while real income per capita grew at an annual average rate of 0.3 percent. And widespread poverty persists in Brazil, despite an impeccably democratic government since 1990 that has arrested the velocity of impoverishment. The distributional profile is extremely skewed despite annual growth rates of about 10 percent.

Pauperization and expanding inequity are not limited to the cases documented above. They are present in Argentina, Uruguay, Paraguay, Venezuela, Colombia, Peru, Bolivia, Ecuador, Panama, Costa Rica, the Dominican Republic, Haiti, and particularly Mexico (Barkin, 1991; Boltvinik 1987: 305–317). Those most affected are the rural and urban poor, but white-collar, middle-class sectors have also seen their economic opportunities and social safety nets virtually disappear. In fact, in Latin America, as in North America today, their numbers are declining in the growing gap between the super-rich and the super-poor (*NotiSur,* 2/18/44:7).

Special mention should be made of Cuba's current predicament. Unlike the rest of Latin America, the Cuban economy experienced the fastest and most sustained growth in the region during the 1980s. Its average annual growth rate was 4.1 percent per capita versus a regional average of −8.3 percent (U.N. 1990:20), attributable largely to its trade relations with the former Soviet Union and its favorable access to east European markets. With the disintegration of the Eastern Bloc and especially its major supplier and market, the Soviet Union, Cuba came to a catastrophic standstill and its economy nearly collapsed. Structurally, Cuba remained tied to one commodity (sugar), one market (the former socialist countries), and a rigid, centrally planned economic model. As the basic supports of the model failed, so did production and consumption. Widespread scarcity and corruption were reportedly rampant. The rule of President Fidel Castro has been challenged, but by a new global and regional order where there is no place for Third World socialism.

Post-1990 political developments in Latin America, although conveying a more democratic picture (especially by contrast with its somber record), present at best mixed signs. On the positive side, most countries in the region are now ruled by governments installed through formally free, fair, and competitive elections. In some instances, some sort of democratic consolidation has taken place, as a second and even third generation of elected governments has been inaugurated. Sporadic yet significant attempts have also been made to hold governments accountable to the electorate. Instances of torture, disappearances, and state terrorism have, with notable exceptions, become less and less frequent.

However, there are also disturbing signs. One is the persistence, and even revival, of authoritarian and oligarchical traditions. Limited democracies, based on pacts among elites, are distinctly exclusionary. Despite their pervasiveness, the electoral processes are increasingly devoid of choice. The socioeconomic and institutional pillars of the former national security regimes are still paramount actors under the new democratic arrangements. Most of those who perpetrated heinous crimes against the people are still at large and have gone unpunished. Corruption is widespread and growing. Thus, it is hardly surprising that public apathy and cynicism are at an all-time high while governmental legitimacy is shrinking.

An examination of specific events illustrates the current predicament. These range from general and congressional elections and referenda in Paraguay, Costa Rica, Honduras, Venezuela, Guatemala, Peru, Chile, Colombia, Ecuador, and El Salvador to popular insurrections in Argentina and Mexico. Despite the contested presidential elections of 1993 and 1994 in Paraguay, Venezuela, Guatemala, Honduras, Chile, and El Salvador and the apparently normal constitutional reforms in Peru, Guatemala, Argentina, and Chile, these processes failed to provide real alternatives. The abovementioned alienation of the population from the political process—especially its limited representativeness and meaninglessness—has produced extremely high rates of electoral abstention. Twenty-five percent abstained in the Peruvian referendum, while 84 percent did so in Guatemala (*NotiSur*, 2/4/94: 8), and the abstention rate in El Salvador's general election of March 1994 was 50 percent. In the Colombian parliamentary elections of 1994, more than 70 percent did not vote, while in the Ecuadorean congressional competition the same year, spoiled ballots received the second-largest plurality. In addition, many of these contests were tainted by serious irregularities (*NotiSur*, 3/18/94:2–3).

The potential for greater political openness—created by the impeachments of the corrupt and discredited administrations of presidents Carlos Andrés Pérez of Venezuela, Fernando Collor de Mello in Brazil (Flynn 1993:351–371), and Jorge Serrano in Guatemala, resulted in stalemated arrangements where the same repudiated policies and forces persisted. Nor has corruption been stymied. In Panama the removal of Gen. Manuel Noriega's grip on the country by means of the bloody U.S. invasion in 1989 has failed to produce either democracy or socioeconomic development. The Endara administration, perceived as an American pawn, was unable to provide effective and legitimate rule. In Brazil the presidential scandal of 1992 was followed by the revelations of the existence of a "network of corrupt legislators, state governors, and federal government officials involved in many different forms of embezzlement and fraud" (*NotiSur*, 12/17/93:7). Beyond the ceremonial transfer of office by electoral means and the absence of direct military rule, democracy in Latin America has not been consolidated. It is suffering a continuous erosion. Political elites throughout the continent have shown a remarkable continuity. The old formula of presidential continuity has resurfaced, as with presidents Alberto Fujimori of Peru and Carlos Saúl Menem in Argentina and their efforts to push through constitutional reforms that would extend their tenure in office.

Thus, we must reconsider civil-military relations in the emerging inter-American order. Coups or the threat of coups and military intervention are still a political tactic in many places. Prior to the formal impeachment of President Pérez in Venezuela, two bloody coups were attempted. In Peru, President Fujimori dissolved the legislature, restructured the supreme court, and suspended the constitution in April 1992 in a self-administered coup. The country has also been living under the shadow of military intervention to prevent investigations of gross human rights violations.

A similar situation developed in Guatemala. There, President Serrano's Fujimori-style 1993 coup failed, leading to his impeachment and replacement by the country's human rights ombudsman, Ramiro de León. Despite expectations that real democracy would take hold, the new government became a virtual prisoner of the security forces, having to turn a blind eye to military impunity and human rights abuses. Murders, executions, disappearances, and torture once again reemerged, surpassing the dismal record of the previous government (*NotiSur*, 1/28/94:3–4). In 1993 popular mobilization in Honduras brought about a broad national consensus (as well as support from the Clinton administration) to curb the power of the armed forces and police. A comprehensive investigation of human rights violations was widely publicized, and the program of the newly elected Liberal Party government of President Carlos Roberto Reina was explicit about its intentions to control the armed forces. Some legislative measures have been passed to increase military accountability, improve hierarchical subordination to civilian authorities, overhaul the dreaded national security doctrine, and halt forceful conscription (*NotiSur*, 1/28/94:1–2 and 12/17/93:11–15). However, the implementation of these measures has met with minimal success.

In Chile, the election of Christian Democrat Eduardo Frei simply transferred the management from one democratically elected superstructure to another, while preserving the entrenched antidemocratic structure created and maintained by the forces that have controlled the country since the 1973 counterrevolution. The governing centrist coalition, as in 1989, was once again unable to obtain the two-thirds vote required by the 1980 constitution (created under military rule) to amend it. The resulting institutional logjam, carefully engineered by the dictatorship before it left office, gave the authoritarian neoliberal order, developed during the seventeen-year dictatorship, a new lease on life. Despite appearances, General Pinochet and his associates remain in firm control of the rules of the game, the autonomous (though downsized) military apparatus, key positions within the state (such as the supreme court, the constitutional tribunal, and numerous regulatory boards), not to mention the commanding heights of the economy and the media. The previous administration of President Patricio Aylwin, and through him most Chileans, was constantly reminded by military mobilizations, states of alert, and other saber-rattling machinations that investigations into or criticisms of the past and present conduct of Pinochet and his associates would not be tolerated. In Chile—as in Argentina, Uruguay, Brazil, Peru, Colombia, Bolivia, Paraguay, El Salvador, Honduras, and Guatemala—hardly any of the perpetrators of gross human rights violations have been punished. In fact, in Guatemala, El Salvador, Colombia, and Peru gruesome violations continue, while blank pardons, legislative forgiveness, and executive cover-ups in the name of national security are commonplace.

The institutionalized continuity of the national security regimes is present in other countries, too. In Brazil, the scandal-ridden government has to rely on the backing of the armed forces to compensate for a tarnished prestige and an expanding power vacuum. This growing influence is above and beyond the provisions that granted the security forces extraordinary autonomy after their return to the barracks in the late 1980s. In Paraguay, the slow phasing out of the Stroessner dictatorship culminated in 1993 with the election of Juan Carlos Wasmossy to the presidency. Although the product of the first truly transparent election in that country, President Wasmossy in fact represents the continuity of the former dictator's Colorado Party and the social, economic, and institutional forces that supported his regime.

Last but not least, we should consider the persistence of various old forms of resistance, rebellion, and insurgency and the emergence of new ones. Insurrections and various stages of civil war continue in Colombia, Guatemala, and Peru, ranging from the more traditional guerrilla activities of the Coordinadora Guerrillera Simón Bolívar (CGSB) in Colombia to the terrorism of Shining Path in Peru (McClintock 1983:19–34). Insurrectional movements and protorevolutionary situations exist in many countries. There are the latent wars accompanying the normalization processes in Guatemala, El Salvador, and Nicaragua. Low-intensity conflict is also present in practically all the tenuous democracies in the region, including Chile, Bolivia, and Ecuador. At times such conflict is hard to differentiate from generalized social violence of an anomic and criminal nature, as is the case with narcotraffickers. This multilayered violence is ubiquitous in Colombia, Peru, and Bolivia. In the midst of these complex patterns of conflict, official and semiprivate violence have reemerged. Death squads and state repression have not evaporated as a result of democratization but have instead mutated into new and less visible forms. In fact, in El Salvador, Guatemala, Colombia, and Brazil death squads continue to operate relatively unmolested (Sané 1993).

The most intriguing forms of contemporary violence, however, have been the popular insurrections in communities confronted with a threat to their livelihood. Two such events deserve special attention. One was the civil uprising in Santiago del Estero, Argentina, in December 1993. The other was the armed insurrection in Chiapas, Mexico, led one month later by the Zapatista National Liberation Army (EZLN). Despite formal differences, both rebellions have a number of things in common: (1) they both grew out of specific local grievances explicitly against neoliberal economic policies; (2) their discourse was at odds with the more traditional leftist ideological slogans associated with guerrilla movements (indeed, the end of the cold war and the effective isolation of Cuba make it more difficult to label these movements as threats to hemispheric security); and (3) the demands made by these insurgencies were quite negotiable and specific.

The Argentinean revolt was more spontaneous and middle-class in orientation, while the one in Chiapas was clearly a peasant and indigenous grassroots phenomenon. It presented an articulate grievance permeated with liberation theology, and the members were apparently well trained and organized. It also manifested itself in a military-political strategy that showed a remarkable degree of determination and success.

Regime responses also varied considerably: Argentine president Menem immediately dispatched a special envoy to address the grievances (mostly unpaid wages, rollbacks, and corruption), while the Salinas administration resorted to a two-pronged strategy of negotiation and repression, sending nearly one-tenth of the Mexican army to the affected zone. Of the two cases, the Chiapas insurrection has broader national and international implications because of the substantial support it has gotten all over the Americas from indigenous groups and the sympathetic portrayal it was given by the North American and European media largely on account of its native roots and its opposition to the North American Free Trade Agreement (NAFTA). The uprising highlights the profound malaise of the Mexican political system, underscored by the assassination of Salinas's handpicked successor, PRI presidential candidate Luis Colosio in March 1994. The rebellion in the south and Colosio's assassination on both point to the state's lack of legitimacy and fundamental democracy as well as the reversal of the social achievements attained since the 1917 revolution.

These developments have a twofold significance. First, they suggest that popular movements and rebellions have reemerged in the new regional order as political options and that more such events are likely in the near future. Second, by challenging the legitimacy of the new intra-elite and transnational arrangements, these insurrections reveal the intrinsic weakness of the current regimes.

Democratization and Human Insecurity in the Americas

Nicaragua's revolution, in 1979, might seem to many to be the region's final one. From a long-range structural and historical perspective, however, violent upheavals have not entirely vanished, although their manifestations have changed. For many, revolution is still seen as an alternative to the perpetual cycle of poverty, repression, dependency, and insecurity that has historically strangled the region's development. For others, repression offers a shortcut to stability and modernity. The end of the cold war and the collapse of communism do not automatically translate into the end of repression and rebellion in the hemisphere. Quite the contrary, compressed tensions and multiple conflicts could erupt at any moment. In this context, rebellion—though muted in the current conjuncture—could evolve into a self-fulfilling prophecy either as the perceived alternative to oppression and hopelessness or as a means for simple protection and survival. The constriction of political options tends to reduce the political process into a simple equation whereby force equals power. The prolonged civil wars in El Salvador, Guatemala, Peru, and Colombia provide evidence in support of this characterization.

An appraisal of contemporary Latin America over the past decade indicates that despite formal redemocratization, a tapering off of gross human rights violations, and diminished refugee flows, there has been a reduction of both real political arenas and alternatives for compromise. Consensus building is even more difficult when the debt-ridden Latin American economies do not have the capabilities necessary for stable governance. Between the early 1970s and the early 1980s, extreme political and social polarization, brutal repression, and exclusion became the regional trademarks of autocratic rule. Side by side with political repression there was also rapid, yet inequitable, economic growth. The "lost decade" between the mid-1980s to the 1990s produced a consolidation of basically the same exclusionary model, this time under civilian management. The difference is not the relative openness of the present formal political arrangements nor of civilian versus military rule. The difference is that redemocratization, irrespective of the commitment of those actors involved, unfolded in the middle of an economic recession and the restructuring of the world economy, which has made genuine democratic institutionalization nearly impossible.

The sovereignty of Latin American states has been undermined by their overreliance on transnational capital, international financial institutions, and Washington's support to maintain domestic equilibrium. This overreliance has reduced the internal legitimacy of the ruling elites, thus nurturing a vicious cycle of violence that leads to greater instability, power deflation, and ever-increasing dependency and intervention. This cycle, in turn, perpetuates and expands the contradictions between elites and masses, between transnational integration and national disintegration (Sunkel 1971), and between authoritarianism and democracy—discrepancies that are at the core of Latin American underdevelopment, instability, and insecurity.

The politics of limited democratization and neoliberal economics, although an improvement over the national security regimes, imposes built-in limitations on the realization of a truly stable and sustainable democratic project for and by Latin Americans. If economic recovery fails to produce a better standard of living for the majorities, or should the structural crisis deepen, it is likely that these weak and limited civilian regimes will be replaced, once again by equally weak, yet violently repressive, regimes. After all, the national security doctrine is still the ideological "software" of the hemispheric military establishments and a regular staple in the training of special forces in the United States. The notion of communist subversion is being replaced by a new internal enemy: terrorism, anarchy, or narcoterrorism.

In the context of power deflation, and as long as the benefits of modernization remain elusive for the majority of Latin Americans, no reformist development project will be viable. Democratization and development in Latin America remain largely meaningless unless their effects cease to be confined to the upper and middle sectors of society. Profound social conflicts, rooted in enduring inequities, cannot be circumvented by mere labeling. The use of terms such as "transition to democracy," "demilitarization," "competitiveness," and "macroeconomic equilibrium" is often an exercise in deconstructionism.

With Cuba effectively isolated, the Nicaraguan revolution defeated, and neoliberal policies imposed throughout the hemisphere, the regional superpower has moved to establish a largely unipolar and hegemonic inter-American system (Hakim 1992). A muffled inter-American dialogue has emerged between political elites who share a common agenda and accept the status quo as a given (Nef and Núñez 1994:113–115). The search for compatibility and consensus has been facilitated to a large extent by an opportunistic realignment of significant sectors of the political elites and the intelligentsia (Petras 1990:102), including the vast majority of the so-called independent research centers (IRCs) and nongovernmental organizations (NGOs) that depend on the generosity of Western governments and foundations. Even the United Nation's Economic Commission on Latin America (ECLA), once a voice of critical thinking, has been brought into the "pragmatic" fold (Hirschman 1990:117). It is in this political and intellectual context that President George Bush's "Enterprise of the Americas Initiative" of 1990 (Bush 1990:1) and President Bill Clinton's "guiding policies," advanced by Assistant Secretary of State for Inter-American Affairs, Alexander Watson, in 1994 have to be understood (*NotiSur,* 3/25/94: 11–21): "For the first time since the Monroe Doctrine was proclaimed we can define our relationships with Latin America and the Caribbean without the explicit threat of external aggression. Our policies can be driven not by fear, but by hope; not by threats to our security, but by the promise of a hemisphere of free nations living in harmony and sharing in a common prosperity" (*NotiSur,* 3/25/94: 12). These American initiatives, despite their seemingly diverse ideological bases, are specific reformulations of the Monroe Doctrine (1823), asserting U.S. hegemony in the region. On the one hand, they are conditional invitations for a partnership with the Latin American and the Caribbean regions (as well as Canada), which are invited to play a subordinate role in the post–cold war and post–Third World international division of labor. On the other hand, both initiatives represent a protective and multilateral American response to the challenge posed by the Asian and European trading blocs.

Latin America's options are extremely limited. As the hemisphere becomes more closely integrated, a potentially dysfunctional system of mutual vulnerability is beginning to take shape. Its impact on the lives of millions of people in both parts of the hemisphere could be dramatic. The present course points toward scenarios where unemployment, poverty, violence, criminality, health hazards, addiction, refugee flows, massive population displacements, repression, and environmental degradation feed on each other. Without profound changes in both Latin America and North America, the possibility of arresting or reversing threats to human security will remain minimal. Short of a radical reorganization in *both* parts of the Western Hemisphere, multiple and critical dysfunctions are likely to persist.

The end of the cold war for Latin America—as it is becoming painfully obvious elsewhere—has not automatically translated into a Fukuyama-type "end of history," ushering in global peace and democracy (Fukuyama 1989:3). Democratic transition in the region is not synonymous with either the consolidation of democratic practices or with substantive democracy. A great deal must be done to build and secure democracy in the Americas. Democracy cannot be the safe, meaningless, limited, or low-intensity commodity (Gill et al. 1993:3–5) peddled by transition theorists but, rather, a genuinely participatory system of governance based on justice and equality.

References

Almond, Gabriel. "The Development of Political Development," in Myron Weiner and Samuel Huntington, eds., *Understanding Political Development*. Boston: Little, Brown, 1978, 437–490.

Andreski, Stanislav. *Parasitism and Subversion: The Case of Latin America*. New York: Pantheon, 1967.

Barber, William, and Neale Ronning. *Internal Security and Military Power: Counterinsurgency and Civic Action in Latin America*. Columbus: Ohio State University Press, 1966, 217–245.

Barkin, David. *Un desarrollo distorsionado: La integración de México a la economía mundial*. Mexico City: Siglo Veintiuno Editores y UAM–Xochimilco, 1991.

Bodenheimer, Susanne. "The Ideology of Developmentalism: American Political Science Paradigm Surrogate for Latin American Studies." *Berkeley Journal of Sociology* 15 (1970):95–137.

Boltvinik, Julio. "Ciudadanos de la pobreza y la marginalización." *El Cotidiano* 19 (1987):305–317.

Bruneau, Thomas, and Philippe Faucher, eds. *Authoritarian Capitalism: Brazil's Contemporary Economic and Political Development*. Boulder, CO: Westview Press, 1981.

Bush, George. "Moves to Bolster Latin American and Caribbean Economies," East Room press conference. Washington, DC: The White House, June 7, 1990:1 (transcript).

Chalmers, Douglas. "Developing in the Periphery: External Factors in Latin American Politics," in Yale Ferguson, ed., *Contemporary Interamerican Relations: A Reader in Theory and Issues.* Englewood Cliffs, NJ: Prentice-Hall, 1972, 11–34.

Chomsky, Noam. "Trilateral's RX for Crisis: Governability Yes, Democracy No." *Seven Days* 1, 1 (February 14, 1977).

Costa-Pinto, Luis. *Pueblo y Populismo.* Madrid: Centro de Estudios Constitucionales, 1978.

Crane, David. "Debt: Latin America's Ticking Time-Bomb." *Toronto Star,* May 11, 1989:D1, D6.

Di Palma, Giuseppe, and Lawrence Whitehead, eds. *The Central American Impasse.* New York: St. Martin's Press, 1986.

Drake, Paul, and Eduardo Silva, eds. *Elections and Democratization in Latin America, 1980–85.* San Diego: Center for Iberian and Latin American Studies, Center for U.S.-Mexican Studies, Institute of the Americas, University of California–San Diego, 1986.

Feinberg, Richard E., and Ricardo French-Davis, eds. *Development and External Debt in Latin America.* Notre Dame, IN: University of Notre Dame Press, 1988.

Felpern, Myriam, and María del Huerto. "Democratización en América Latina y Europa del Este." *Política,* no. 28 (December 1991):93.

Flynn, Peter. "Collor, Corruption, and Crisis: Time for Reflection." *Journal of Latin American Studies* 25, pt. 2 (May 1993):351–371.

Fukuyama, Francis. "The End of History?" *National Interest,* no. 16 (Summer 1989):3–18.

Gill, Barry, Joel Rocamora, and Richard Wilson. *Low-Intensity Democracy: Political Power in the New World Order.* London: Pluto Press, 1993.

Habermas, Jürgen. *Legitimation Crisis.* Boston: Beacon Press, 1975.

Hakim, Peter. "Estados Unidos y América Latina en la década de 1990: ¿Buenos vecinos otra vez?" *América Latina/Internacional* 9, 33 (July–September 1992): 519–524.

Hirschman, Albert. "Es un desastre para el Tercer Mundo el Fin de la Guerra Fría?" *Pensamiento Iberoamericano,* no. 18 (1990):177.

Huntington, Samuel, Michel Crozier, and Joji Watanuki. *The Crisis of Democracy: Report on the Governability of Democracies to the Trilateral Commission.* Triangle Papers no. 8. New York: New York University Press, 1975.

IISS (International Institute of Strategic Studies). *World Military Expenditures,* for the years 1987, 1990, 1991, 1992. London: IISS.

Inter-American Dialogue. *The Americas in 1988: A Time for Choices—A Report of the Inter-American Dialogue.* Washington, DC: Aspen Institute for Humanistic Studies, 1988.

Lefever, Louis. "The Problem of Debt." *International Viewpoints.* Supplement of the *York Gazette* (Toronto, Ontario). York University, March 2, 1987, 2.

Letelier, Orlando. "The 'Chicago Boys' in Chile: Economic 'Freedom's' Awful Toll." *Nation,* August 28, 1976, 138, 142.

Levinson, Jerome, and Juan de Onís. *The Alliance That Lost Its Way: A Critical Report of the Alliance for Progress.* Chicago: Quadrangle Books, 1970.

Linowitz, Sol (Commission on United States–Latin American Relations). *The Americas in a Changing World*. New York: Quadrangle Books, 1975.

Martínez, Osvaldo. "Debt and Foreign Capital: The Origins of the Crisis." *Latin American Perspectives* 20, 1 (Winter 1993):65.

McClintock, Cynthia. "Sendero Luminoso—Peru's Maoist Guerrillas." *Problems of Communism* 23, 4 (1983):19–34.

Montecinos, Verónica, and John Markoff. "Democrats and Technocrats: Professional Economists and Regime Transition in Latin America." *Canadian Journal of Development Studies* 14, 1 (1993):7–22.

Mouffe, Chantal. "Democracia y nueva derecha," in Robert Green, ed., *Los mitos de Milton Friedman*. Mexico City: Nueva Imágen, 1983.

Nef, Jorge. "Redemocratization in Latin America or the Modernization of the Status Quo?" *Canadian Journal of Latin American and Caribbean Studies* 11, 21 (1986):43–55.

———. "The Trend Towards Democratization and Redemocratization in Latin America: Shadow and Substance." *Latin American Research Review* 23, 3 (Fall 1988):131–153.

Nef, Jorge, and Remonda Bensabat. "'Governability' and the Receiver State in Latin America: Analysis and Prospects," in Archibald Ritter, Maxwell Cameron, and David Pollock, eds., *Latin America to the Year 2000: Reactivating Growth, Improving Equity, Sustaining Democracy*. New York: Praeger, 1992, 161–176.

Nef, Jorge, and Ximena Núñez. *La relaciones interamericanas frente al siglo XXI*. Quito, Ecuador: FLACSO, 1994.

North, Liisa. "Development and Underdevelopment in Latin America," in Jorge Nef, ed., *Canada and the Latin American Challenge*. Guelph: Ontario Cooperative Program for Latin America and Caribbean Studies, 1978.

NotiSur. Vols. 3 and 4, December 17, 1993, to March 25, 1994.

Nylen, William. "Selling Neoliberalism: Brazil's Instituto Liberal." *Journal of Latin American Studies* 25, pt. 2 (May 1993):351–371.

O'Brien, Donal Cruise. "Modernization, Order, and the Erosion of a Democratic Ideal: American Political Science, 1960–1970." *Journal of Development Studies* 8 (July 1972):351–378.

O'Donnell, Guillermo, Philippe C. Schmitter, and Lawrence Whitehead, eds. *Transitions from Authoritarian Rule: Prospects for Democracy*. Baltimore: The Johns Hopkins University Press, 1986.

Offe, Clauss. "Ingobernabilidad: El renacimiento de las teorías conservadoras." *Revista Mexicana de Sociología* 42 (1981 special issue).

Petras, James. "The Metamorphosis of Latin America's Intellectuals." *Latin American Perspectives* 17, 2 (Spring 1990):102–112.

Pollock, David. "Debt, Development, and Democracy: Recent Trends in Latin America," in Peter Blanchard and Peter Landstreet, eds. *Human Rights in Latin America and the Caribbean*. Toronto: Canadian Scholars' Press, 1989, 119–125.

Raby, David. "Populism: A Marxist Analysis." *McGill Studies in International Development*, no. 32, Center for Developing Area Studies, McGill University, Montreal, 1979 (1983).

Robinson, William. "Central America: Which Way After the Cold War?" *NotiSur* 4, 8 (February 25, 1994):1–9.

Rockefeller, Nelson. *The Rockefeller Report of the United States' Presidential Mission for the Western Hemisphere* (*New York Times* edition). Chicago: Quadrangle Books, 1969.

Sané, Pierre. "Amnesty's Report Card from Hell." *Globe and Mail,* December 10, 1993.

Siat, Arturo, and Gregorio Iriarte. "De la Seguridad Nacional al Trilateralismo." *Cuadernos de Cristianismo y Sociedad.* Buenos Aires (May 1978):23–24.

Sklar, Holly. "Managing Dependence and Democracy—An Overview," in Holly Sklar, ed., *Trilateralism: The Trilateral Commission and Elite Planning for World Management.* Montreal: Black Rose, 1980, 1–55.

Stepan, Alfred. *Rethinking Military Politics: Brazil and the Southern Cone.* Princeton, NJ: Princeton University Press, 1988.

Sunkel, Osvaldo. "Capitalismo transnacional y desintegración nacional en América Latina." *Estudios Internacionales* 4, 16 (1971):3–61.

U.N. Economic Commission for Latin America and the Caribbean (ECLAC). *Changing Production Patterns with Social Equity.* Santiago: ECLAC, 1990.

Weaver, Frederick. "Capitalist Development, Empire, and Latin American Underdevelopment: An Interpretative Essay on Historical Change." *Latin American Perspectives* 3, 4 (Fall 1976):17–53.

Weil, Jean-Louis, Joseph Comblin, and Judge Senese. *The Repressive State: The Brazilian National Security Doctrine and Latin America.* LARU Studies, Document III. Toronto, Ontario: York University, 1979.

Wolfe, Alan. 1975. "Capitalism Shows Its Face." *Nation,* November 1975, 561.

World Bank. *World Debt Tables: External Debt of Developing Countries.* 1987–88 ed., vol. 2, Country Tables. Washington, DC: World Bank, 1988.

——. *World Development Report 1990.* New York: Oxford University Press, 1990.

——. *World Development Report 1991.* New York: Oxford University Press, 1991.

——. *World Development Report 1992.* New York: Oxford University Press, 1992.

4

The Contemporary Latin American Economies: Neoliberal Reconstruction

JOHN WEEKS

Looking Backward

During the years from the end of World War II until the late 1970s, broad agreement, if not consensus, emerged among Latin American governments with respect to the general orientation of economic policy. This broad agreement derived from two generally accepted propositions that (1) domestic markets in Latin American countries operated inefficiently, both with regard to the allocation of resources among alternative uses and the distribution of the gains from economic growth in an equitable manner throughout the population; and (2) the international trading system incorporated a bias against the major products that Latin American countries exported. These two propositions implied that state action was required to correct the failures of domestic markets and that governments needed to implement a broadly interventionist trade policy to transform the structure of exports and, by logical extension, domestic production. This combination of interventions in domestic markets and trade was encapsulated in the term "import substitution."

On the basis of this development strategy, during the 1950s and 1960s Latin American countries experienced moderate to strong growth performances. To a great extent this growth is attributable to a relatively favorable world economic environment. Although the terms of trade for many Latin American countries declined during the twenty-five years following World War II, flows of private and official capital tended to offset this. Overall,

Latin American countries benefited from a relatively stable world trading system of fixed exchange rates (overseen by the International Monetary Fund [IMF]), preferential trading agreements, and an increasing number of operative commodity agreements between producing and consuming countries.

So sustained was the growth performance of the Latin American countries that, toward the end of the 1960s, the distribution of the gains from growth received increasing emphasis, even to the point of making equity considerations integral to the definition of "economic development." Although earlier development theory had tended to stress the likelihood of a *positive* relationship between income inequality and growth, by the early 1970s quite the opposite perspective gained respectability. Inspired by innovative theoretical and empirical work, especially from the World Bank, a "basic needs" approach emerged whereby alleviation of poverty was placed at the center of economic policy in developing countries.

During the period in which a consensus emerged about the centrality of distribution to the development process, several shocks to the international system occurred that dramatically altered the world economic environment. At the outset of the 1970s the international trading system was shaken by the decision of the U.S. government to suspend the fixed-price convertibility of the dollar for gold, which ushered in a new set of international rules for trade and finance based on managed, but variable, exchange rates in the member countries of the Organization for Economic Cooperation and Development (OECD). This new exchange rate regime proved especially problematical for the Latin American countries due to the vulnerability of their economies to world market fluctuations and their lack of skilled people for the increased burden of economic management. The petroleum price increases of 1973–1974 followed quickly on the collapse of the postwar system of international regulation, generating large trade deficits for developing countries dependent on imports of oil. These deficits led to large-scale borrowing by Latin American governments from the world's major commercial banks.

The overwhelming consensus within the financial establishment in the 1970s was that growing indebtedness represented no long-term danger; on the contrary, in the absence of indebtedness the hard-currency surpluses of the oil-exporting countries would not have been recycled into the international expenditure stream. Further, world inflation during the 1970s resulted in buoyant primary product prices, which generated optimism about the ability of Latin American countries to service their debts.

However, the early 1980s brought new and unexpected shocks for developing countries. The most dramatic was the severe recession in the OECD countries, which resulted in a rapid decline in the rate of world inflation. Somewhat differently from previous postwar recessions, the downturn reflected in part the conscious policy of some developed-country governments, especially the U.S. government, to make control of inflation the first policy priority, at the cost of high unemployment. For the Latin American countries the recession generated high real international interest rates and falling primary product prices. At this point many Latin American countries, especially the heavily indebted, found themselves unable to service their debts and forced to turn to crisis borrowing on terms starkly unfavorable compared with those of the previous decade.

In 1982 Mexico announced it could no longer service its debt, which converted into an international financial crisis the difficulties created by the gathering pressure of Latin American country indebtedness, low primary product prices, and increased reluctance by commercial banks to make further loans. The alarm generated by the fear of the collapse of major commercial banks resulted in a dramatic change in the priorities of the international lending agencies, prompting them to move away from the previous emphasis on poverty reduction and equity-to-debt service. Debt service required immediate current-account surpluses, which would be achieved through import reduction and export expansion.

Closely associated with the financial crisis and the change in the policies of multilateral lending agencies, a radical shift occurred in economic policy by Latin American governments. By the end of the 1980s, almost all Latin American countries had adopted a neoliberal policy orientation. The altered agenda derived its theoretical justification from the mirror-image of the previously accepted import substitution strategy: namely, (1) that domestic markets were paragons of efficient operation, and (2) that the international trading system would provide producers throughout Latin America with the most appropriate "signals" on which to base their economic decisions. With this change of policy direction went a new language of discourse, deriving from the value-laden term "free" markets. This chapter explains how that change in policy came about, its consequences for the region, and its implications for development strategy.

The Ideology of Neoliberalism

The standard explanation for the policy shift toward neoliberalism in Latin America was that the strategy of import substitution had "failed." In response to this failure, governments had little choice but to embrace a new policy framework that would rescue their countries from crisis and correct the damage done to their economies by the misguided policies of the past. The failure of the strategy allegedly arose from two causes, the so-called exhaustion of the simple stage of import substitution (e.g., Gonzalez-Vega and Césepedes 1993:97ff), and the distortions generated by the state interventions to bring about a shift in production structures from primary products to industrial development (Rottenberg 1993). The first cause derives from the unsubstantiated theoretical and empirical proposition that replacing consumer imports with domestic production might somehow be less problematical than doing the same for intermediate and capital goods. One finds no serious defense of this oft-asserted opinion in the literature on industrialization.

More theoretically based is the concept of "distortions," a term that refers to any market outcome that differs from that which would be produced under conditions in which all state interventions were absent. For example, a tariff on textiles is said to produce a distortion by making the domestic production of this commodity more profitable than it would be in the absence of that tariff. As a result, more resources are drawn into the sector than would be the case without the tariff. To this point the argument is uncontroversial, for, indeed, the precise purpose of the tariff is to achieve this outcome. Orthodox ("neoclassical") economic theory judged such an outcome as inefficient and undesirable on the grounds that markets without interventions (i.e., the tariff) produce the optimal conceivable outcome. The free market outcome is optimal, or best, because it ensures that the country's resources are optimally employed.

Through propagandistic popularization, the free market advocates conveyed the impression that markets by their nature produced efficient results. But this conclusion is a priori theoretical, not empirically based on actual results of markets. Central to the force of the free market argument are three propositions that must be established theoretically; once established, they ensure the optimal efficiency conclusion as an abstract deduction from logic. First, it must be shown that all markets are perfectly competitive; second, that competitive markets through their interaction result in full employment of resources; and, third, that all economic variables assume values in the full-employment outcome that are unique (that there is one and only one full-employment outcome produced by unregulated markets). One need not be an economist to understand the necessity of each of these propositions. If unregulated markets are tainted by seller or buyer market power, then the result is *private sector regulation,* which in its effect on the orthodox concept of efficiency is strictly equivalent to state regulations. If one suspends disbelief and accepts that all markets are perfectly competitive, efficiency in each market requires full employment in all markets. If all labor and other resources are not in use, then by definition the outcome is not efficient, for it is undesirable compared with full resource use. The competitive and full employment outcome must be unique because if there were multiple outcomes, a social policy decision is required to select among them, which would require interventions and regulations.

Within orthodox, neoclassical economic theory, it is well established that (1) perfectly competitive markets result in full employment of resources only under extremely restrictive conditions, and (2) that even under these restrictive conditions there are in general multiple outcomes. One might think that excursion into this abstract and esoteric discourse would be unnecessary because to even the economically untutored eye it would be clear that markets, international and domestic, were not perfectly competitive in Latin America, that resources were certainly not fully employed in any country in the 1980s and 1990s, and that the theoretical question of uniqueness of outcomes is of no practical importance. But, on the contrary, so powerful was the free market ideology that it came to prevail in the 1980s notwithstanding all empirical evidence demonstrating its irrelevance. This ideological ascendancy resulted from the successful sale of a vulgarized popular version of the "high theory," in which powerful policy prescriptions were vended in the absence of their underlying analytical justification.

The Policy Debate in Latin America

The policy shift in Latin America had little to do with the alleged "exhaustion" of import substitution and still less with the theoretically suspect arguments for the efficiency gains from free markets. The shift resulted directly from the pressure on Latin American governments to service their debts in the wake of the explosion of indebtedness that followed the oil price increases of the first half of the 1970s. To understand why debt servicing came to dominate the policy agenda in Latin America, it is first necessary to consider why and how the Latin American governments came to be debtors and the industrial countries, especially the United States, to be creditors. The answers are not obvious, for the oil import requirements of the major industrial countries, the United States, (then) West Germany, and Japan were many times greater than for any Latin American country.

The descent into indebtedness by the Latin American governments fundamentally resulted from the institutional structure of the world economy. The monies of the major industrial countries served as de facto reserve currencies in the international system, the currencies in which other countries, especially the developing countries, conducted their trade and held in hoards to clear excesses of imports over exports. For example, when Brazil ran a persistent oil-induced balance-of-payments deficit, its government would sooner or later have to seek private bank financing or go to the International Monetary Fund in hopes of negotiating a short-term loan called a "standby agreement." When borrowing from a private bank in the United States, Brazil in effect partly financed the U.S. balance-of-payments deficit. The money borrowed by Brazil would not stay in that country but would, rather, be used to finance imports. Most of the nonoil imports of Brazil were from the advanced industrial countries, so the loans acted to finance advanced-country exports to Brazil. In the case of oil imports, the loans flowed out from Brazil to the petroleum-exporting countries, primarily Mexico and Venezuela in Latin America, and the countries of the Middle East. The governments of the latter countries, unable to spend all their oil revenues because of their small populations, deposited their surplus revenues in commercial banks in the industrial countries. These deposits then financed trade deficits of the advanced countries and, of course, provided the liquid capital for loans to Latin American governments.

This interactive relationship, in which the currencies of developed countries were sustained in part by the borrowing of governments of Latin America, involved the so-called recycling of petrodollars into the world economy. While the governments of Latin America found themselves increasingly burdened as debtors, the governments of the industrial countries could observe with satisfaction the accumulation of liquidity within their banking systems, such that they became lenders in this recycling process. In other words, petrodollars returned to the industrial countries as hoards held by oil-exporting governments and, to a lesser extent, direct investments in productive assets. While the Latin American governments experienced accumulating debt and a financial squeeze, in the industrial countries the oil price increases stimulated a financial boom. This asymmetrical pattern resulted directly from the system of reserve currencies, in which a minority of the industrial countries enjoyed the status of bankers for the rest of the world.

The method by which the current accounts of Latin American countries would be brought into surplus quickly became a subject of intense controversy. Reflecting in part the political changes in the major market economies, balance-of-payments adjustment became equated with policies of trade liberalization, market deregulation, fiscal austerity, and privatization. Unfortunately, these contentious policy packages provoked debate over abstract and generalized issues of economic philosophy instead of pragmatic discussion about policy options appropriate to each country's circumstance. Emphasis in the debate focused on justifying normative judgments rather than on the actual behavior of economies in Latin America.

The lead role in promoting the "free market" adjustment packages in Latin America was assumed by the IMF and the World Bank. These packages involved governments agreeing to major policy changes stipulated in a loan agreement ("conditionality") and were described by the generic term, "policy-based lending." Formally, there was a strict division of labor between the Fund and the Bank. Fund lending aimed at "stabilization," short-run reduction in inflation, and balance-of-payments correction. It fell to the Bank to fund "structural adjustment," medium- and long-term supply-side "reforms" to shift resources from domestic production to production of internationally competitive goods and services (from "nontradables" to "tradables"). Fund and Bank lending tended to go together, so the formal division of tasks proved difficult to distinguish in practice. By the early 1990s virtually every Latin American country but Cuba (and more than eighty developing countries in all) had accepted IMF and World Bank programs, and others introduced essentially similar policy frameworks in anticipation of such funding.

Although the World Bank previously made loans with policy conditionality attached to them, the scope and scale of structural adjustment lending represented a qualitative change in the institution's role. This was even more the case for the Inter-American Development Bank (IDB), which began policy-based lending somewhat later. The rapid expansion of conditional lending by the World Bank provoked controversy on several grounds. First, critics pointed out that structural adjustment loans, unlike the traditional project lending of the World Bank and IDB, created no asset. Governments, almost invariably already deeply in debt, incurred further debt that was not directed at creating any productive capacity that would generate a flow of foreign exchange to service that debt. As a result, a tremendous burden fell on the policy packages: If they proved unsuccessful in increasing export capacity via indirect means (i.e., market incentives), the borrowing government would find itself worse off than before it borrowed. Second, the predicted success of the packages in stimulating exports was based on the faith that deregulation of markets would increase allocative efficiency in resource use, not use of more resources.

Most economists agreed that under carefully specified assumptions, deregulation of markets would increase the *allocative* efficiency of economies. However, there was not agreement that the operation of markets in each Latin American country conformed to these assumptions. Third, and more important, economic theory provides little support for the view that increased allocative efficiency fosters faster growth, either of exports or national income. Indeed, critics pointed to a number of cases in which export growth had been spectacularly successful by governments allegedly violating the rules of static allocative efficiency, with the Republic of Korea being a frequently cited example. Critics maintained that it was an empirical question as to whether increased allocative efficiency would call forth dynamic growth and that no generalizations were possible. And, fourth, some evidence suggested that the presumption should not be made that export growth would translate into growth of national income. Latin America's experience seemed to support this criticism: According to data from the Inter-American Development Bank, its twenty-six Latin American and Caribbean members enjoyed a growth of exports in current prices of 5 percent per annum during the 1980s, but national income increased in real terms at barely 1 percent a year over the same period, a point to which we return below.

From the point of view of most Latin American governments, the debate over adjustment appeared all the more frustrating because of the asymmetry in pressures for policy change. While governments of developing countries came under heavy external pressure to liberalize trade, the OECD countries exhibited increasingly protectionist tendencies with respect to both agricultural products and labor-intensive manufactures from developing countries. Further, the policy changes demanded of Latin American governments by the multilateral agencies went far beyond what the industrial country governments practiced themselves. For example, it took the United States seven years to reduce its fiscal deficit from 6 percent to 4 percent of gross national product (GNP), while multilateral lending conditionality required Latin American governments to achieve much larger reductions over twelve months (Williamson 1990:15).

Criticism of structural adjustment programs has not been limited to academics in the North and Latin American progressives. In 1991 a Japanese aid agency, the Overseas Economic Cooperation Fund, issued a position paper taking issue with the market liberalization philosophy of the IMF and the World Bank. The paper argued that the experience of several Asian countries, especially the Republic of Korea and Japan itself, suggested that market interventions played an essential role in fostering an export-led development strategy. This was a particularly important commentary since Japan will probably be the single largest financial contributor to the World Bank in the 1990s.

In the mid-1980s the international financial establishment frequently referred to a "Washington consensus" on structural adjustment, the essence of which was the market liberalization philosophy of structural adjustment programs. Hans Singer, one of the world's leading development economists, suggests this was a narrow consensus—indeed, covering about four blocks along Pennsylvania Avenue in Washington, D.C. Consensual or not, the new policy orientation swept Latin America in the 1980s (see Table 4.1). Though the classification is to a certain extent arbitrary, by the end of the decade four countries had "highly liberalized" economies (Bolivia, Chile, Mexico, and Uruguay), and, excluding Cuba, only three maintained relatively unliberalized policy regimes (Brazil, Ecuador, and Venezuela).

Economic Decline in Latin America

By the early 1990s establishment sources heralded the recovery of Latin America from its long night of decline in the 1980s. However, it is necessary to place the "recovery" in longer-term perspective. The recovery story told by the "Washington consensus" went as follows: From the end of World War II until the early 1980s, Latin American governments tended to follow an import substitution policy regime that was inherently unsustainable; by the late 1970s the inherent limitations of this regime manifested themselves; there then followed a painful but necessary process of policy reform to correct the structural defects created by import substitution; and by the early 1990s the adoption of "realistic" policies produced the sweet fruit of recovery and growth.

TABLE 4.1   Policy Reform in Latin American Countries, 1980–1990

	Date of Reforms	*General Aspects of Reform*	*Characterization of Policy Regime*
Argentina	1983, 1987	Programs in 1983, 1987, and accelerated in 1989; tariffs replaced non-tariff barriers to trade (NTBT) on primary products and intermediates	Moderately liberalized during 1980s
Bolivia	1985	Elimination of NTBT, movement toward single uniform tariff of 10 percent	Highly liberalized after 1985
Brazil	1983 (1988)	In 1990 eliminated list of prohibited imports, as well as restrictions on national content for intermediate and capital goods	Not liberalized during 1980s
Chile	1973	Most NTBT (quotas) eliminated in 1970s, uniform tariff of 10 percent raised to 20 in 1983, then to 35 in 1984; subsequently reduced to 15 percent in 1988 and 11 percent in 1991	Highly liberalized after 1973
Colombia	1976	Most licenses for imports eliminated by 1990 and replaced by tariffs; abandonment of export subsidies; strong import controls in 1983–1984, followed by liberalization; crawling-peg exchange rate	Moderately liberalized during 1980s
Costa Rica	1982 (1986)	Conversion to flexible exchange rate with minidevaluations; gradual elimination of import licenses.	Moderately liberalized during 1980s
Ecuador	(1984) 1990	Program announced in 1984, little implementation until 1990; eliminated most NTBT, including deposits for imports	Not liberalized during 1980s
El Salvador	1989	Few NTBT in 1980s, imports financed by external aid; eliminated deposits on imports	War-affected (moderately liberalized) during 1980s
Guatemala	c. 1985	Fixed exchange rate until late 1980s when floated; substantial tariff reduction	Moderately liberalized during 1980s

(continues)

TABLE 4.1   (continued)

	Date of Reforms	General Aspects of Reform	Characterization of Policy Regime
Honduras	—	No formal liberalization program; multiple exchange rates	Moderately liberalized during 1980s
Mexico	1983	Introduced flexible exchange rate (conscious undervaluation); eliminated official import prices	Highly liberalized after 1985
Nicaragua	1989	Virtually complete import liberalization; dollarization of currency in 1990	War-affected (Not liberalized) during 1980s
Panama	1983	Liberalization conditionality in two World Bank loans	Moderately liberalized during 1980s
Paraguay	—	Low level of intervention in 1970s and 1980s	Moderately liberalized during 1980s
Peru	1978– 1984 1991	Import liberalization 1978–84 and sharp reduction in effective protection of manufacturing, followed by policy reversal; in 1991 eliminated import licenses and other controls; tariff reduction to 25 percent for consumer products and 15 percent for other commodities	Severe policy instability
Uruguay	1974	Abolished quotas and licenses in 1975; floated exchange rate after 1983 and established simplified tariff structure	Highly liberalized after 1974
Venezuela	1989	Unified and floated exchange rate; drastically reduced number of commodities subject to import controls	Not liberalized during 1980s

Notes: The criteria for characterizing the trade regimes are (in order of priority) (1) absence or presence of nontariff barriers to trade (NTBT); (2) exchange rate regime (including degree of convertibility); and (3) participation or nonparticipation in World Bank and IMF programs.

SOURCES: Balassa 1988; World Bank 1988; Bulmer-Thomas 1992; CEPAL 1992a; CEPAL 1992b; CEPAL 1992c; FAO 1992b; IDB 1992; Woodward 1992. By country: *Argentina:* World Bank 1985; Nogués 1986; World Bank 1987a; World Bank 1989a; Munlak et al. 1989. *Brazil:* World Bank 1990. *Colombia:* World Bank 1984; Ocampo and Lora, 1987. *Honduras:* World Bank 1987c. *Mexico:* Lustig and Ros 1987. *El Salvador:* World Bank 1989c. *Panama:* Zimbalist and Weeks 1991. *Peru:* Webb 1987; World Bank 1992. *Uruguay:* World Bank 1989b. *Venezuela:* World Bank 1993.

At least two elements of the "Washington consensus" story were beyond challenge: most Latin American governments implemented import substitution policies to some degree prior to the 1980s; and during the 1980s most governments shifted to a policy regime of market deregulation, privatization, and restriction of the size of the state. Very much open to challenge were the other two assertions of the story: (1) that import substitution led to its own demise, and (2) that the policy shifts in the 1980s promoted recovery. A few basic statistics suggest that it was not obvious that import substitution policies undermined the health of the Latin American economies. During the 1970s per capita growth of gross domestic product (GDP, or national income) far exceeded its rate in the 1980s; indeed, income per head declined, or did not rise, in all but two countries (Chile and Colombia) during the 1980s, while in the 1970s it *rose* in all but one (see Table 4.2). And that one country, Nicaragua, was the exception that proves the rule, for the decline is explained by armed conflict, not by economic factors as such. The armed conflict to overthrow the Somoza dictatorship led to a fall in GDP by more than 30 percent in 1978–1979, after a positive rate of growth from 1970 to 1977.

How, then, is one to sustain the argument that import substitution policies undermined economic growth when the statistics show that these policies coincided with quite rapid growth, especially in comparison with the decline coincident with the shift to liberalization regimes? Sustaining this hypothesis proves all the more difficult given the statistics on export performance. The stated purpose and alleged benefit of liberalization policies were to increase the rate of growth of exports. Yet if one averages across countries, export growth in terms of volume (constant prices) was slower in the 1980s than in the 1970s, and in only three of the eighteen countries did export growth increase in the 1980s (Argentina, Costa Rica, and Venezuela). Along with seeking to increase export growth in general, liberalization advocates claimed that the new policy regime would reduce Latin America's dependence on primary product exports by creating a favorable private sector environment for promoting exports of manufactures. This claim derived from the critique that import substitution policies had made production for the domestic market artificially profitable and had fostered inefficient industries. The evidence to support this claim was not overwhelming: Latin America's manufactured exports grew faster in the 1970s than the 1980s, 12.7 percent per annum compared to 9.1 respectively (IDB 1992:192). Although a neoliberal economist would find this a perverse result, it is in keeping with the theory of import substitution. Contrary to the neoliberal view, import substitution and export promotion are in theory quite compatible. Indeed, in its original conception, import substitution was put forth as the path to fostering manufactured exports. Benefiting from tariff and other protection, Latin American industry would acquire modern technologies and take advantage of economies of large-scale production as it expanded to fill the gap left by receding imports. As this occurred, costs would fall and at some point domestic industry would become internationally competitive. A strong case could be made that this process succeeded in Mexico and Brazil but was obscured in the former by the liberalization policies forced by the debt crisis.

In any case, export growth, in and of itself, should not be a policy goal, as Adam Smith so eloquently argued in his attack on mercantilism. Rather, promotion of exports would be a policy strategy to achieve other goals, such as economic growth and equity. The raison d'être of liberalization policy was that by fostering exports, economic growth would be increased. In any event, there was compelling evidence that faster export growth was associated with faster growth of national income in Latin America, but not in the manner predicted by the liberalization advocates. A simple statistical exercise relating the rate of growth of export volume to GDP growth shows quite a strong positive correlation for the 1970s when most of the eighteen countries pursued an import substitution regime and a much weaker one in the 1980s when liberalization dominated the policy approach. This disparity suggests that liberalization may or may not foster exports, but it apparently does not enhance the linkage between export growth and growth of the economy as a whole.

Were the advocates of liberalization to contain their claims within the bounds of neoclassical economic theory, evidence that trade deregulation may not foster growth would not be surprising. On the assumption of full employment of resources, standard international trade theory predicts once-and-for-all welfare gains from trade liberalization but is ambiguous with regard to the link between trade liberalization and growth. Simply put, in theory, trade liberalization has the effect of increasing exports (*and* imports) for a given level of national income, with no implication for the growth of national income.

The neoliberal economic story for Latin America in the 1980s strained credibility because it was essentially a tale of success when an explanation of failure was required; when confronted with failure, neoliberals could only fall back on the argument that the losers had not adopted appropriate (neoliberal) policies. With the exception of war-ravaged Nicaragua, every country grew more slowly in the 1980s than during the 1970s (see Table 4.2). It would seem to require a quantum leap of faith to conclude that such a uniform outcome could result from the policies pursued in each country. A much more plausible and obvious explanation for the so-called lost decade in Latin America was the burden of debt (see Table 4.3; the first column reports debt payments per capita for 1988, which were more than U.S.$100 for eight of the eighteen countries).

More indicative of the relative weight of the debt burden are the numbers in column two (Table 4.3), which show that for all but five countries debt ser-

TABLE 4.2 Economic Indicators by Country (annual rates of growth, constant prices of 1988)

	GDP Per Capita		Exports	
	1971–80	*1981–90*	*1971–80*	*1981–90*
Argentina	0.8	−2.8	4.8	6.0
Bolivia	1.4	−2.6	2.8	2.0
Brazil	6.3	−0.7	9.9	7.1
Chile	1.1	0.9	10.3	5.6
Colombia	3.1	1.4	6.3	6.0
Costa Rica	2.5	−0.5	5.9	6.6
Dom. Rep.	4.3	−0.6	8.1	3.4
Ecuador	5.7	−0.9	14.0	4.6
El Salvador	0.2	−1.9	5.1	−1.5
Guatemala	2.8	−2.0	6.5	−2.1
Honduras	2.2	−1.0	4.6	0.8
Mexico	3.7	−0.7	8.3	7.3
Nicaragua	−3.1	−5.2	1.0	−1.3
Panama	2.6	−1.5	7.0	0.8
Paraguay	5.5	0.0	10.1	6.6
Peru	0.9	−3.2	3.0	−0.8
Uruguay	2.6	−0.3	7.2	4.1
Venezuela	0.8	−2.2	−4.3	2.4
Latin America				
Weighted	3.4	−1.1	4.6	5.0
Unweighted	2.1	−1.1	6.1	3.2

Notes: For the average of Latin America as a whole, "weighted" refers to the GDP or exports of all countries taken together as a single number for the region. "Unweighted" is the simple average across the eighteen countries.

SOURCE: IDB 1992:286, 289.

vice consumed more than 5 percent of GDP. In three of the five cases—Nicaragua, Panama, and Peru—the low percentages resulted from a conscious policy of nonpayment, not the absence of a deadweight of debt. In the case of El Salvador, debt service was low because the country had been the dubious beneficiary of billions of dollars of U.S. grants to support that regime's war against a progressive and leftist insurrection. To put these numbers in perspective, the reparations paid by Germany to the victors of World War I averaged only 2.5 percent of GDP. Considered crushingly onerous at the time, Germany's reparations prompted John Maynard Keynes's famous polemical pamphlet, *The Economic Consequences of the Peace,* in which he predicted, and was proved correct in the event, that such a payments burden would destabilize the German economy. The average Latin American payment was more

TABLE 4.3   Measures of External Debt Service Burden by Country, 1988

	Debt Service	*As Percentage of*	
	Per Capita (in U.S.$)	*GDP*	*Exports*
Argentina	$161	5.5	55.4
Bolivia	49	5.5	62.4
Brazil	123	5.3	52.5
Chile	156	6.7	28.1
Colombia	98	7.0	58.0
Costa Rica	139	8.6	34.0
Dom. Rep.	50	6.9	38.8
Ecuador	106	8.3	48.5
El Salvador	41	3.9	33.2
Guatemala	43	4.9	35.0
Honduras	77	9.7	41.4
Mexico	199	9.1	75.2
Nicaragua	8	1.3	11.4
Panama	12	0.6	08.7
Paraguay	79	5.2	36.3
Peru	11	0.7	08.8
Uruguay	235	8.6	51.9
Venezuela	296	8.2	55.1
Latin America	$135	6.4	54.0

SOURCE: IDB 1992:285, 286, 311, 328.

than double the burden forced on a vanquished Germany after World War I (see Weeks 1989c).

Equally striking in Table 4.3 is the third column, which shows that in 1988 more than half of Latin America's export earnings were consumed by debt service. Such a burden of debt service could be achieved only by governments implementing policies to generate trade surpluses; that is, foreign exchange for debt service was foreign exchange that could not be used for imports. The extent to which this occurred could only be described as incredible. In 1981 the Latin American region imported U.S.$2.3 billion more than it exported; in the following year a trade surplus of U.S.$7.1 billion was achieved, despite a *fall in exports* of U.S.$9 billion; and for 1983–1985 the region's trade surplus averaged U.S.$33 billion (IDB 1992:8)! Contrary to the predictions and ideology of the neoliberal adjustment programs, these surpluses did not come from export expansion. In current prices, exports from 1983 to 1985 averaged about 5 percent below the level of 1981. Rather, the surplus resulted from a draconian compression of imports. In 1981 the Latin American region imported U.S.$101 billion, compared with an average U.S.$61 billion for 1983–1985. Not until 1991 did the region's current import value recover to the level of 1981. The method by which this improbable import compression was achieved can be inferred from Table 4.2: contraction of the region's economies. In 1983 imports had dropped by U.S.$40 billion from 1981 levels; per capita income in the region declined by 10 percent over the same two years.

Mismanaging the Debt Crisis

In the late 1970s, commentators warned of the dangers of Latin America's rapidly accumulating debt; by 1982 and the Mexican payments moratorium, no doubt remained that the debt had reached unmanageable proportions. Nonetheless, and in apparent rejection of all rationality, Latin America's debt continued to accumulate, not reaching its peak value until 1987, five years after the Mexican government sent panic through the financial establishment. Table 4.4 shows the changes in debt levels between the crisis year of 1982 and 1991, when the region's recovery was heralded. Ten years after the shock of 1982, total regional debt had increased by 28 percent. Further, for seven countries, debt in 1991 reached a level higher than for any previous year, and no country's debt in 1991 was below its level of 1982.

More than one commentator pointed out that it was a strange outcome, indeed, that a crisis brought on by too much debt would be managed by piling on more debt (e.g., Islam 1988). This perverse result loses its wondrous aspect when placed in the context of the goals of the most important players in the debt crisis, the world's major commercial banks. From the beginning of the crisis, the goal of the international financial establishment was to ensure that debts be paid (World Bank 1987b:x).

The goal of recovering in full interest and principal on loans from Latin America must be considered in light of standard financial practice. The accumulation of unmananageable debt in the private sector is common, and the legally sanctioned response is bankruptcy, or some form of devaluation of debt paper. If the former, bankruptcy, was not an option for Latin American governments, debt devaluation was. On the reasonable assumption that commercial banks treated loans to Latin America as having a degree of risk, it follows that the lending rate and terms of loans were set to incorporate the possibility of default. Several Latin American governments defaulted on loans during the 1930s and 1940s, and one presumes that banks in the 1970s were not ignorant of history. Once the debt crisis began, the "efficiently functioning markets" that the neoliberals so admire should have adjusted the face value of the outstanding loans. This would have been done through the creation of what is called a "secondary" market in debt, in which the original lender sells the claim on debt to others, with the sale price determined by buyer estimates of the likelihood and extent of repayment. By this

Table 4.4   External Debt by Country (in billion U.S.$, year end

	1982	Peak	1991	Percent Increase 1982–1991
Argentina	43.6	64.8	56.3	29.1
Bolivia	3.3	5.8	4.0	21.3
Brazil	92.9	123.7	118.1	27.1
Chile	17.3	21.4	19.3	11.6
Colombia	10.3	—	18.1	75.7
Costa Rica	3.6	4.7	4.0	8.9
Dom. Rep.	2.5	4.4	4.0	60.0
Ecuador	7.7	—	12.3	59.9
El Salvador	1.4	—	2.2	50.5
Guatemala	1.5	—	2.8	81.0
Honduras	1.8	—	3.6	96.2
Mexico	86.0	109.4	98.3	14.3
Nicaragua	2.9	—	10.7	266.5
Panama[a]	3.9	—	6.7	71.7
Paraguay	1.3	2.5	2.2	66.4
Peru	12.3	21.1	20.0	62.8
Uruguay	2.6	4.3	3.0	15.2
Venezuela	32.2	38.3	34.1	6.0
Latin America	327.3	na	419.7	28.2

[a]Because Panama uses the U.S. dollar as currency, the distiction between foreign and dosmetic debt is largely arbitrary.

Notes: "Peak" refers to the year end in which the debt was highest, 1982 through 1991. Dashes indicate that the debt was highest at the end of 1991. The percentage changes are calculated on debt figures prior to being rounded off to the nearest one hundred million.

SOURCE: IDB 1992: 324.

process Latin American governments would substantially reduce their debts, in part by repurchasing these debts at discounted prices. On the other side of the ledger, orthodox economic theory posits that bank collapses resulting from debt discounting are part of a process of market competition that sorts out the efficient from the inefficient. Once debt was discounted to a manageable level, debtors would again be creditworthy and competition among banks would bring forth new loans if these were demanded.

But secondary trading in Latin American debt did not develop on any scale in the 1980s because of the market power of the major international banks. In the 1930s Latin American governments borrowed from wealthy people and corporations in the advanced countries, with major banks serving only as intermediaries (salespeople). In consequence, default and secondary trading in debt in the 1930s did not affect banks. However, in the 1970s the banks lent directly to Latin American governments. It is not surprising that the major creditor banks sought to prevent the emergence of secondary trading apparently with the endorsement of the World Bank (1987b:xxxvi) and could do so easily since they held the vast bulk of Latin American debt.

Once the power of banks prevented a market-based solution to the debt crisis, the only alternative to general default was the addition of further debt, albeit of a particular type. From 1982 until 1987, when its peak was reached, Latin American debt increased by about one-third. The part of this increase from commercial banks was virtually all the consequence of debt rescheduling, a major aspect of which was the exchange of lower payments currently for a larger total debt. It was through this process of piling up more debt and stretching its repayment out over time that banks sought to recapture as much interest and principal as possible. Although this proved quite successful for banks, the result in Latin America was a phenomenal and debilitating drain of resources. CEPAL estimated that from 1982 to 1985 all net financial flows from Latin America to developed countries averaged U.S.$34 billion a year, or more than 6 percent of regional GDP.

The immense unrequited resource transfers out of Latin America resulted in a double immiserization of the region. First, the resource transfer itself reduced real national income annually for the region by 4 to 6 percent during the 1980s. Second, this resource transfer was achieved by a contraction of the region's economy. In other words, the populations as a whole reduced their incomes in order to reduce their incomes further through transferring a substantial percentage of the lower income abroad. This inversion of the development process prompted many authors to characterize the conflict over debt repayment in terms of the rich countries of the North exploiting the poor countries of the South (e.g., Roddick 1988). Although appealing for polemical purposes, analyzing the debt crisis in terms of countries fails to capture the political and social dynamics involved. If one stays at the country level, it is impossible to explain why the resource transfer occurred. From the outset of the debt crisis, Latin American governments had it within their power to force a solution that would have dramatically reduced the burden of debt. In 1982 many of the world's major banks faced collapse if debts were not serviced under prevailing arrangements; indeed, that was why the banks fought so vigorously to ensure payment. Had any two of the four major debtors—Argentina, Brazil, Mexico, and Venezuela—united in a payments moratorium, collapse would have moved from possibility to certainty. Concerted action by one of these four and a few smaller debtors would have had the same effect. Thus, relatively little solidarity would have been required to confront the international financial establishment with impending disaster. There could be little doubt that the consequence of debtor governments not putting the checks in the mail would have been the convening of an international conference on Third World debt. Such a conference might well have produced a package of debt reduction, changes in creditor country banking regulations, and complementary trade and investment policies that would have avoided the worst of the Latin American development disaster of the 1980s.

Far from showing solidarity with each other, the Latin American governments chose to cast their lot with the international financial establishment. When in 1985 President Alan Garcia of Peru announced that his government would limit its debt service to a proportion of export earnings, only the governments of Cuba and Nicaragua supported him; the other heads of state in the region treated him as a pariah. Even more important, on several occasions individual governments in Latin America worked in concert with the government of the United States to bring pressure on recalcitrant debt servicers in the region.

Might it have been that Latin American solidarity for debt relief foundered on the fear of each government that it might fall victim to retaliatory sanctions should it offend the major banks and creditor governments? This was not an argument to take seriously. Latin American governments defaulted in the 1930s and 1940s and suffered no significant barriers when they subsequently returned to international financial markets as borrowers (Bittermann 1973). Historically, changes of government and improved economic performance have proved sufficient to bring countries back into the good graces of commercial banks.

The passive acceptance of debt service by most Latin American governments requires a class analysis to be explained: the upper classes incurred the debt, while for the most part the lower classes paid it off. Private sector, largely corporate long-term loans and short-term government borrowing to finance imports accounted for more than half of Latin America's foreign debt. Most of the imports represented industrial or agroindustry inputs and elite consumption. Not a small portion of debts incurred went directly to private foreign bank accounts of wealthy Latin Americans in the form of capital flight. For example, it is estimated that almost half of the increase in Argentina's foreign debt during the 1980s became cash balances of the elite in the United States and western Europe.

In a laudable adherence to his ideology of free markets, the Chilean dictator Augusto Pinochet recognized the private sector responsibility for much of Chile's indebtedness and in the early 1980s announced that those who borrowed should pay; or if they could not pay, it was no concern of the government of Chile. The Chilean regime immediately came under tremendous pressure from the international financial community to reverse this shocking application of market principles. Within a few weeks the government reversed its position and socialized the private sector debt, a position eventually adopted in virtually every Latin American country. Once private sector debt came under state guarantee, debt service became part of fiscal expenditure. Thus, debts were paid by reducing other expenditures, frequently on health, education, and other social services. At the same time, the foreign exchange to pay the debt derived from the large trade surpluses discussed above. These trade surpluses derived from contraction of national income, which resulted in falling employment and sharply declining real wages (Canak and Levi 1989; Thomas 1993). To put the matter bluntly, the rich went into debt and the poor serviced it.

Looking for Recovery

From the previous discussion it should be clear that the economic decline of the 1980s in Latin America was not a natural process of adjustment to achieve a different growth trajectory, but rather a consciously managed period of economic contraction with the purpose of generating trade surpluses for debt service. A number of quite respectable mainstream economists pointed this out, drawing the conclusion that the process was considerably more draconian than circumstances warranted even to achieve creditworthiness in the eyes of the commercial banks (De Pinies 1989). The issue then arises, did the pain of contraction result in an adjustment that provided for future growth?

Table 4.5 provides several key indicators of Latin America's economic performance for the early 1990s. After the continuation of decline in GDP per capita in 1990, the eighteen Latin American countries enjoyed three consecutive years of positive growth of national income per head, at the quite modest rate of 1.7 on average. At this rate of growth forty years would be required for per capita income to double.

TABLE 4.5   Latin American Economic Indicators, 1990–1993

Indicator	1990	1991	1992	1993
Real GDP per capita (percentage rate of change)	−1.6	1.5	2.3	1.2
Exports (current value)	9.8	−0.8	5.1	4.5
Inflation	1,185	199	417	797
Terms of trade	−0.9	−8.7	−5.6	−4.9
Trade balance (U.S.$ billions)	27.3	9.1	−10.0	−14.8
Net resource transfer	−14.1	8.3	32.8	25.7

SOURCE: CEPAL 1993: "Tables & Figures" appendix.

Further, the rate was half that for the 1970s, when the Latin American economies allegedly suffered from the debilitating effects of import substitution policies. Further, only six of the eighteen countries grew faster from 1991 to 1993, after neoliberal medication, than during the 1970s. The best one could say was that after 1990 per capita growth was no longer negative. But considerable improvement would be necessary for the neoliberal model to demonstrate its superiority over the discredited import substitution policy regime.

This growth performance was all the less impressive in light of the considerable excess capacity that characterized the region's productive system at the start of the 1990s. Given the decline of the previous decade, plant and equipment fell idle in manufacturing, land went unused in agriculture, and unemployment rose for the economy as a whole. In these circumstances, what surprises is not that growth turned positive, but that it took so long to do so and proved so slow when it did. The economic performance of the early 1990s could be heralded as recovery in the limited sense, "I've been down so long, it all looks up to me." Questions about the sustainability of the recovery had to be raised. Key to sustainability would be the balance of external payments (capacity to import) and macroeconomic stability. With regard to the former, the signals were not favorable in the early 1990s. Export growth in current value proved quite feeble, averaging slightly over 4 percent per year, and the trade balance continually deteriorated, from +U.S.$27 billion in 1990 to almost −U.S.$15 billion in 1993. This deterioration could be sustained by the opposite reversal of the net resource transfer, from −$14 billion to +$26 billion. However, the net resource inflow declined sharply from 1992 to 1993, a shift that, if continued, will arrest import growth and recovery.

The characteristics of the recovery suggested that little had changed with regard to the constraints on Latin American growth, despite neoliberal market magic. Historically, the countries of the region had been balance-of-payments constrained; i.e., growth tended to draw in imports at a rapid rate, which export growth and capital flows could not match. The consequence, growth repeatedly foundering on a shortage of foreign exchange, was precisely what the neoliberal export-oriented model intended to change. The deterioration of the trade balance shown in Table 4.5 lends some support to the saying, "the more things change the more they remain the same." Part of the deterioration of the trade balance resulted from a severe fall in the terms of trade. The prices of Latin America's exports fell relative to its import prices during every year, 1990–1993, for a cumulative fall of about 20 percent, which came on top of a 22 percent fall during the 1980s (CEPAL 1993). As a result, the terms of trade index for Latin America in the early 1990s dropped to a level lower than for any time period during the twentieth century. The debilitating fall in trade occurred despite a substantial increase in manufactures as a share of total exports. Thus, the terms of trade losses could not be explained by primary product prices alone, which implied that the shift to manufactured exports might not prove the panacea predicted by the neoliberals.

With regard to macroeconomic stability, indicators were, if anything, worse. From 1989 the average inflation rate across countries decreased for three years but doubled in 1992, then almost doubled again in 1993, to 800 percent on an annual basis. Whatever else neoliberalism had achieved in Latin America, it had not arrested inflation. While in some countries neoliberal policies were associated with lower inflation, the record was quite mixed. Experience suggests that draconian monetarist policies could choke off inflation temporarily, but not slay the dragon. The deeply rooted nature of inflation in Latin America is suggested by Table 4.6. During the 1970s the highest average annual rates of inflation were found in Argentina, Brazil, Chile, Peru, and Uruguay.

During the first half of the next decade, Uruguay and Chile were replaced by Bolivia and Nicaragua. Then, in the second half of the 1980s Uruguay returned to the list, leaving only one change, Nicaragua for Chile. It could be argued for Brazil that little attempt had been made to reform the inflationary tendencies built into the society, but not for Argentina, Peru, and Uruguay. In 1983 an elected government replaced a military dictatorship in Argentina and entered into stabilization and structural adjustment programs with the IMF and the World Bank. The subsequent government also attempted to control inflation and in 1993 appeared to have succeeded. It remains to be seen if this success would be sustained or go the way of previous Argentinean stabilization programs. In the case of Peru, a neoliberal government took office at the end of the 1970s with the promise of eliminating inflation, only to preside over its acceleration. The next government, of Garcia, brought inflation down substantially for two years, only to watch it turn into hyperinflation at the end of the 1980s. The military dictatorship that seized power in

TABLE 4.6   The Five Countries with Highest Inflation, 1971–1990

1971–1980	1981–1985	1986–1990
Argentina (2)	Argentina (2)	Argentina (3)
Brazil (4)	Brazil (3)	Brazil (4)
Peru (5)	Peru (4)	Peru (2)
Uruguay (3)	Nicaragua (5)	Uruguay (5)
Chile (1)	Bolivia (1)	Nicaragua (1)

Notes: Number in parenthesis gives rank for the time period (i.e., "1" indicates the country with the highest rate of inflation).
SOURCE: IDB 1992:18.

Uruguay in the mid-1970s enjoyed brief success in restraining price increases but could not maintain a low-inflation economy.

The two countries in which the inflationary dynamics within society clearly changed were Chile and Nicaragua, which, again, are exceptions that prove the rule of the near-intractable nature of inflation in Latin America. These two countries underwent the most thorough social transformations in the region since the Cuban Revolution. In the case of Chile, the transformation was from a pluralistic society relatively balanced among Right, Center, and Left, to a neoliberal corporatist state in which all the important social institutions previously mediating income and wealth distribution were destroyed. In Nicaragua, a similar process of creative destruction occurred, but from the other direction: a dictatorship with a narrow base fell, replaced by a populist alliance that pursued policies of wealth and income redistribution (Dore and Weeks 1992). The lesson implied was that in most countries of Latin America, considerably more than economic policies, neoliberal or otherwise, were required to transform the social dynamics giving rise to inflation.

The Political Economy of Neoliberalism

The advent of neoliberal economic policy in Latin America produced a profound shift in development strategy. In its fundamental characteristic it represented a conscious decision by governments to denationalize economic policy and economies of the countries of the region. In all but extreme cases, every country must to some degree integrate itself into the world economy, and this necessity is the greater the smaller the country. Governments can choose alternative methods, however, by which this integration would occur, with the alternatives implying different degrees of policy autonomy. The choice is not between free trade integration into world markets, or "delinking," but among a range of options that determine the extent, both quantitatively and qualitatively, to which fluctuations in world markets will be transmitted to the domestic economy. The neoliberal project is an extreme one: To the extent possible, to remove all barriers that insulate domestic decisionmaking by the private sector and the state from the influence of world markets.

One obvious consequence of pursuing such a goal would be denationalization of the economy in the narrow sense of ownership of production, commerce, transport, and finance. Certainly this occurred with a vengeance in Latin America in the 1980s and 1990s through conscious and sometimes aggressive government policies. For example, privatization of state enterprises served as a vehicle of debt reduction through the sale of ownership claims to foreign investors. Also, governments removed restrictions on the degree of foreign ownership, most notably in Mexico. A key part of the

North American Free Trade Agreement (NAFTA) among Canada, the United States, and Mexico (extended to the latter in late 1993), involved eliminating the regulation that 51 percent of ownership must be national in a range of industrial and commercial activities.

An important vehicle for the denationalization of Latin American economies was the General Agreement on Tariffs and Trade (GATT), which most countries of the region did not join until the 1980s. Under the arrangements of the GATT, governments were required to eliminate all policy interventions that discriminate between domestic and foreign producers. This principle had far-reaching implications. For example, it meant that a government could not impose "domestic content" rules, in which a portion of the value of the materials in a product must come from local suppliers, which had been an important incentive to extend manufacturing production into intermediate and capital goods sectors. The nondiscrimination principle also implied that there could be no differential taxes on foreign and domestic companies. More generally, the GATT regulations prohibit any subsidies, direct or indirect, to domestically based producers, be they foreign or national. This restriction meant, among other things, that governments could not, under the GATT's rules, subsidize research and development of new technologies. These and other obligations placed on GATT members implied virtually no scope for an interventionist industrial policy.

Overall, liberalization of domestic markets and foreign trade resulted in a virtual elimination of the ability of all but the largest Latin American countries to pursue independent monetary and fiscal policies. Once governments deregulated capital markets, monetary policy in Latin America became derivative from the decisions of the U.S. Federal Reserve authorities. Prior to 1980 most Latin American currencies could be converted to other currencies only through the central banks of each country in question. This allowed for control of capital flows, essential for maintaining fixed exchange rates. With the elimination of state regulations on capital markets, currencies "floated"; that is, their values were determined by the purchases and sales of currency dealers, not just (or even most important) in the countries but also on the world's major currency exchanges in New York, London, and Zurich. In this context, if a Latin American government sought to implement an interest rate below the rate in international money markets, the probable result would be capital flight, as wealthy people and corporations sought the higher bond yields abroad. The capital flight would then confront the government with downward pressure on its currency. In the absence of the previous restrictions on capital movements, this pressure would require that domestic interest rates be brought back into line with international rates.

Closely related to the above, state deregulation of capital markets inevitably imposed on governments either a deflationary monetary policy or continuous devaluations of the national currency. If, for example, Costa Rica's rate of inflation exceeded the U.S. rate of inflation, the result with a fixed exchange rate would be lower real yields on interest-bearing national bonds and less competitive exports and domestic import substitutes. In the absence of price controls and import restrictions, the Costa Rican government would be forced either to restrict the growth of the money supply (to reduce inflation) or devalue the colón. The former policy measure would reduce output and employment, while the latter would increase the inflationary pressure that caused the problem in the first instance. In effect, capital market liberalization had the tendency to reduce the role of Latin America's central bankers to a close reading of the *Wall Street Journal* to keep up with the actions and pronouncements of the U.S. Federal Reserve.

Liberalization of markets implied analogous limitations to fiscal policy. As explained, membership in the GATT implied the prohibition of most forms of subsidies, either to consumers or producers. However, liberalization of trade and capital markets also restricted the tax policies a government might follow. For example, in the absence of capital controls, a government could impose taxes on corporations and wealthy persons that differed from its neighbors only at the threat of capital flight and relocation of production facilities abroad. Thus, the famous "business climate" placed strict limits on policy options, with the pressure on each government to conform to the policies of the most probusiness and least interventionist country in the region, whether these interventions affected the conditions of workers, regulation of capital, or exploitation of the environment. In this context, the deregulation of the capital market represented the most severe restriction on policy autonomy. The hint of increased regulation, taxation, or other interventionist measures could send currency speculators into a frenzy, resulting in devastating pressure on national currencies. In comparison with the financial resources of currency speculators in the developed countries, the central banks of Latin America were reduced to small players indeed.

Thus, the neoliberal policy package incorporated a long-term agenda considerably more profound in its implications than the impact on any particular market. It involved no less than the rendering of the Latin American state largely impotent in the making of economic policy. The prize held out for embracing the denationalization of policymaking was the promise of an export-led growth fueled by the growth of international trade. Yet in the early 1990s international trade grew at its slowest rate since the end of World War II. This slow growth implied that if Latin American countries would be export led, this could occur only by the region as a whole taking away export markets from other countries, especially the East and Southeast Asian countries. As the year 2000 draws closer, unfolding events will determine whether the neoliberal policy package will modernize and develop Latin America or leave it in the grips of its familiar maladies of inflation and stagnation.

References

Balassa, Bela. "Quantitative Appraisal of Adjustment Lending." *Policy, Planning and Research Working Papers, Development Economics, WPS 79*. Washington, DC: World Bank, August 1988.

Bittermann, Henry J. *The Refunding of International Debt*. Durham, NC: Duke University Press, 1973.

Branford, Susan, and Bernardo Kucinski. *The Debt Squads: The United States, the Banks, and Latin America*. London: Zed Books, 1988.

Bulmer-Thomas, Victor. "Life After Debt: The New Economic Trajectory in Latin America." Department of Economics Working Paper 225. London: Queen Mary and Westfield College, 1992.

Canak, William L., and Danilo Levi. "Social Costs of Adjustment in Latin America," in John Weeks, ed., *Debt Disaster: Banks, Governments, and Multilaterals Face the Crisis*. New York: New York University Press, 1989.

CEPAL (Comisión Económica para América Latina). *Economic Panorama of Latin America, 1992*. Santiago, Chile: CEPAL, 1992a.

————. *Estudio Económico de América Latina y el Caribe, 1990, vol. 2*. Santiago, Chile: CEPAL, 1992b.

————. *Estudio Económico de América Latina y el Caribe, 1991, vol. 1*. Santiago, Chile: CEPAL, 1992c.

————. *Preliminary Overview of the Economy of Latin America and the Caribbean, 1993*. Santiago: CEPAL, December 1993.

De Pinies, Jaime. "Debt Sustainability and Overadjustment." *World Development* 17, 1 (1989):29–43.

Dore, Elizabeth, and John Weeks. "The Red and the Black: The Sandinistas and the Nicaraguan Revolution." Institute of Latin American Studies Working Paper No. 28. London: Institute of Latin American Studies, 1992.

Eguren, Alberto. "Adjustment with Growth in Latin America." Economic Development Institute of the World Bank, Report 22. Washington, DC: World Bank, 1990.

FAO (Food and Agricultural Organization). *Informe sobre la agricultura en America Latina y el Caribe en los anos 80, Tomos 1 & 2*, Rome: FAO, 1992a.

————. *Políticas agrícolas y políticas macroeconómicas en América Latina*. Estudio FAO Desarrollo Economico y Social No. 108. Rome: FAO, 1992b.

González-Vega, Claudio and Víctor Hugo Céspedes. "Costa Rica," in Simon Rottenberg, ed., *The Political Economy of Poverty, Equity, and Growth: Costa Rica and Uruguay*. New York: Oxford University Press, 1993.

IDB (Inter-American Development Bank). *Economic and Social Progress in Latin America, 1992 Report*. Baltimore: The Johns Hopkins University Press, 1992.

Islam, Shafiqul. "Breaking the International Debt Deadlock." *Critical Issues 2*. Council on Foreign Relations Policy Paper. New York: Council on Foreign Relations, 1988.

Keynes, John Maynard. *The Economic Consequences of Peace*. New York: Harcourt Brace, 1920.

Lustig, Nora, and Jaime Ros. *Stabilization and Adjustment Policies and Programmes: Country Study 7, Mexico*. Helsinki: WIDER, 1987.

Munlak, Yair, Domingo Cavallo, and Roberto Domenech. *Agriculture and Economic Growth in Argentina, 1913-84.* International Food Policy Research Institute Research Report 76. Washington: IFPRI, 1989.

Nogués, Julio. "The Nature of Argentina's Policy Reforms During 1976–81." *World Bank Staff Working Papers Number 765.* Washington, DC: World Bank, 1986.

Ocampo, José Antonio, and Eduardo Lora. *Stabilization and Adjustment Policies and Programmes: Country Study 6, Colombia.* Helsinki: WIDER, 1987.

Pastor, Manuel. *The International Monetary Fund and Latin America: Stabilization and Class Conflict.* Boulder, CO: Westview, 1987.

Roddick, Jackie. *The Dance of the Millions: Latin America and the Debt Crisis.* London: Latin American Bureau, 1988.

Rodriguez F., Miguel A. "Consequences of Capital Flight for Latin American Debtor Countries," in Donald R. Lessard and John Williamson, eds., *Capital Flight and Third World Debt.* Washington, DC: Institute for International Economics, 1987.

Rottenberg, Simon, ed. *The Political Economy of Poverty, Equity, and Growth: Costa Rica and Uruguay.* New York: Oxford University Press, 1993.

Thomas, James J. "The Links Between Structural Adjustment and Poverty: Causal or Remedial?" PREALC Working Paper No. 373. Santiago: Programa del Empleo para America Latina y el Caribe, January 1993.

Thorp, Rosemary, and Lawrence Whitehead. *Latin American Debt and the Adjustment Crisis.* London: Macmillan, 1987.

Webb, Richard. *Stabilization and Adjustment Policies and Programmes: Country Study 8, Peru.* Helsinki: WIDER, 1987.

Weeks, John. *The Economies of Central America.* New York: Holmes and Meier, 1985.

———. *A Critique of Neoclassical Macroeconomics.* London and New York: Macmillan and St. Martin's, 1989a.

———, ed. *Debt Disaster: Banks, Governments, and Multilaterals Face the Crisis.* New York: New York University Press, 1989b.

———. "How the Third World Lost the Lending War," in John Weeks, ed., *Debt Disaster: Banks, Governments, and Multilaterals Face the Crisis.* New York: New York University Press, 1989c.

Williamson, Jeffrey, ed. *Latin American Adjustment: How Much Has Happened?* Washington, DC: Institute for International Economics, 1990.

Woodward, David. *Debt, Adjustment, and Poverty in Developing Countries,* vol. 1. London: Pinter Publishers, 1992.

World Bank. *Colombia: Economic Development and Policy Under Changing Conditions.* Washington, DC: World Bank, 1984.

———. *Argentina: Economic Memorandum.* Washington, DC: World Bank, 1985.

———. *Argentina: Economic Recovery and Growth.* Washington, DC: World Bank, 1987a.

———. *Developing Country Debt: Implementing the Consensus.* Washington, DC: World Bank, 1987b.

———. *Honduras: Country Economic Memorandum.* Washington, DC: World Bank, April 1987c.

———. *Report on Adjustment Lending.* World Bank Country Economics Department, Development Economics, Policy, Planning, and Research. Washington, DC: World Bank, August 1988.

———. *Argentina: Reforms for Price Stability and Growth.* 2 vols. Washington, DC: World Bank, September 1989a.

———. *Country Economic Memorandum on Uruguay.* Washington, DC: World Bank, January 1989b.

———. *El Salvador: Country Economic Memorandum.* Washington, DC: World Bank, August 1989c.

———. *Brazil: Agricultural Sector Review—Policies and Prospects.* 2 vols. Washington, DC: World Bank, July 1990.

———. *Peru: Agricultural Policies for Economic Efficiency.* Washington, DC: World Bank, September 1992.

———. *Venezuela: Structural and Macroeconomic Reforms—The New Regime.* Washington, DC: World Bank, March 1993.

Zimbalist, Andrew, and John Weeks. *Panama at the Crossroads.* Berkeley: University of California Press, 1991.

5

Economic Restructuring, Neoliberal Reforms, and the Working Class in Latin America

CARLOS M. VILAS

During the 1980s a number of economic and sociopolitical factors at both the international and domestic levels combined to introduce profound changes in the structure, physiognomy, and politics of Latin America's working class. The more important of these factors were the economic crisis triggered in August 1982 by the so-called foreign debt crisis; the restructuring of the international capitalist system; changes in the techniques of production, in financial and trade networks, as well as in labor processes; and the macroeconomic adjustment policies implemented by the Latin American governments in order to confront the economic crisis and adapt to changes in the international economy. These and related factors led to a drastic reconfiguration of the economy, the labor market, and state institutions in all the Latin American states. They also changed class relations and produced huge surplus transfers from the domestic to the international market and, within each national society, from the lower- and middle-income groups to the higher-income ones. Moreover, the existing patterns of wealth and power concentration increased in most countries, contributing to greater social inequality.

The impact of these changes on Latin American workers was severe. Employment grew at a very slow pace, lagging behind the rate of growth of both the economically active population (EAP) and the gross domestic product

(GDP). Union participation in shared management schemes with business associations and government agencies receded. Moreover, union representation of a broad array of social actors in addition to workers—such as retirees, low-income social groups, and others—received a drastic blow. On the whole, the economic crisis and capitalist restructuring contributed to a broad and accelerated deterioration of the class representatives of a large proportion of Latin American workers (Vilas 1993a, 1994).

In the pages that follow, I will discuss the effects of the restructuring and neoliberal governmental policies on the labor force, unions, and their strategies as well as on the overall configuration of the working class. On the basis of this analysis, I will then offer some hypotheses about the impact of current conditions on the strategies for collective action of Latin American workers.

From Populism to Neoliberalism

Latin America's working class developed between the 1870s and the 1920s during a period of export-led economic growth (see Furtado 1974). In Argentina, Mexico, and Brazil, export-oriented development created the preconditions for the expansion of the domestic market and for industrial growth through import substitution. These conditions improved after the crash of the world's major economies in 1929, since the Great Depression that followed reduced the supply of imported manufactured goods and provided a spontaneous impetus for the growth of domestic manufacturing in Latin America.

Starting in the 1930s the expansion of the internal market in conjunction with import substitution favored the growth of unions and their ability to improve workers' conditions. Prevailing industrial technologies in the region translated into extensive economic development. The growth of production was tied to the expansion of employment and the growth of the salaries and wages paid by the new industries and related firms.

There was an implied coincidence of interests between the industrialists and the unions regarding the goal of full employment: The growth of wages and salaries, derived from expanding employment, contributed to the expansion of the domestic market for industrial production, which in turn benefited from vigorous state protectionism, such as the imposition of high tariffs on competing industrial imports. This protectionism also benefited foreign firms that located in Latin America behind the protective trade tariffs, taxes, and other fiscal barriers in order to produce for the Latin American markets (Vilas 1992–1993).

The unions during this period played an important role in the configuration of the labor market not only by improving the employment and living conditions of workers and their families but also by facilitating the democratization of Latin American politics and society. The unions accomplished this by supporting the political enfranchisement of women and the aboriginal members of the population; promoting labor regulations that protected women and children; developing labor law as a specific branch of public law; sponsoring large programs of affordable and decent housing; and expanding education, health care, and welfare services. In fact, the enhanced institutional standing of unions in this period of Latin American history decisively shaped Latin American political culture and the character of the political regimes in power.

With ups and downs, this type of arrangement evolved over more than four decades, until the early 1970s. The overall situation was one in which the unions' participation in the institutional setting strengthened their dependence on state agencies. Increasingly, the unions subordinated their demands to their political dealings with state agencies and bureaucracies, and this jeopardized their autonomy.

In Argentina and Mexico, for example, the unions rapidly turned into institutional apparatuses of the corporatist and populist regimes there. The handling of large amounts of money frequently led to the bureaucratization of their organizations and to the generation of perks and privileges for their leaders. Union legitimacy in the eyes of their rank-and-file members became dependent on their ability to meet the demands of their members through access to resources that, in one way or the other, were administered by state agencies. Accordingly, fluent relations with state agencies and bureaucracies were considered to be an important asset, which the unions needed in order to achieve their specific goals. Therefore, the state, more than business, became the focal point for union activism.

It is important to note the ambiguity of this scheme. The unions were expected to represent the demands of their members and to improve their working and living conditions by increasing the share of global income going to wages. In doing so, unions reinforced their legitimacy vis-à-vis workers. Yet the unions also had to prevent their members' demands from exceeding the ability of the state agencies to meet them, which the agencies usually did by directly or indirectly transferring surplus from the entrepreneurial class to the workers without endangering the accumulation process or triggering inflationary pressures. That is to say, in order to preserve their legitimacy vis-à-vis the state and business associations, the populist unions had to hold up the corporatist side of the bargain. But they also had to organize the workers, mobilize them, and articulate their demands both to maintain the support of the rank-and-file and to exert pressure on the state and the business organizations in order to make sure the workers' demands were met.

From a structural perspective, the space that the unions had to maneuver in their relations with the state, business, and the workers was determined by the relations among mass consumption, the domestic market, and capital accumulation. From a political perspective, this relationship was conditioned by the goals and interests of the capitalist class. When capital accumulation shifted from meeting the consumer demands of the lower-income groups toward meeting the consumption patterns of the middle- and upper-income groups and reoriented its dynamism toward foreign markets and industrial exports, the unstable legitimacy of the populist unions collapsed.

Following the 1982 financial crisis, production for exports replaced the production of goods for the domestic market as the main locus of capital accumulation, which in turn led to profound changes in income distribution and political power sharing among the various social classes in Latin America. The reorientation of investment, production, and foreign trade policies had mixed results. Latin America's GDP grew by 18 percent between 1982 and 1990, but the quality of life deteriorated for large sectors of the population. During the same period per capita GDP declined by more than 7 percent. In fact, by 1992 Latin America's per capita GDP was 7.5 percent below the 1980 level (CEPAL 1992b). Industrial production stagnated due to currency devaluations, balance-of-payments and anti-inflationary policies, as well as credit shortages. As a result, the value added by manufacturing dropped from a 6.1 percent average annual growth rate during the 1971–1980 period to 0.4 percent in the 1981 to 1990 period (IDB 1992a).

The Latin American governments' handling of the crisis resulted in a clear-cut victory for capital and a defeat for labor, the peasantry, and vast segments of the middle class. Living standards plummeted. The population living below the poverty line grew by 44 percent between 1980 (when they represented about 135.9 million, or about 40 percent, of the entire Latin American population) and 1990 (when 196 million, or 46 percent, of total population were below the poverty line), in contrast to the 22 percent population growth rate for all of Latin America over the same period (CEPAL 1992b). Thus, Latin America produced poverty at twice the rate of its population growth. Moreover, throughout the 1980s urban poverty accounted for 80 percent of the poverty growth, and approximately 48 million new members of the urban poor were created.

In effect, an export-led strategy is also an import-oriented one. In this kind of strategy, domestic investment and consumption are no longer considered relevant inputs for growth, as in the previous (import substitution) economic scheme. Since the realization of surplus value is no longer tied to the domestic market, working- and middle-class wages are no longer considered positive instruments of capital accumulation but, rather, costs to be saved in order to enhance the country's or a firm's international competitiveness and capital accumulation. Moreover, domestic demands for investment and consumption tend to be met increasingly through imports, and the domestic market is redefined in terms of the higher-income groups that can afford these imports.

To a certain extent, this outward shift in economic strategy looks like a retreat to Latin America's linkage with the international market between the 1870s and 1930. However, the resemblance is just superficial, and it would be misleading to push it too far. The region's contemporary articulation with the international economy is basically through commodities produced in small plants that are linked to a transnational network combining high-tech attributes and relatively unskilled labor. Export-led growth is more a matter of increased trade than it is the development of new industries, a sophisticated service sector, or a highly efficient and modern economic and social infrastructure. Export-oriented manufacturing combines high-tech personnel with the de-skilling of certain kinds of work, which are transformed into simpler, less-skilled types of work in assembly plants located near cheap labor and weak unions. This also applies to agroexports, which over the past two decades have been experiencing dramatic changes linked to the development of new staples (such as flowers, fruits, and vegetables) as well as a heavy reliance on chemicals and other industrial inputs, mechanical irrigation, automated packing, and the like. All of which have introduced profound changes in both land-use patterns and the rural labor market, as well as in production schedules. Full employment and the growth of mass consumption are no longer policy goals. Collective labor contracting is bypassed in favor of individual dealings and subcontracting. In sum, all these economic transformations have resulted in what can be called a Latin American version of "post-Fordism" (Tironi and Lagos 1991).

Changes in the Labor Market

Labor's decline has been combined with major changes in its internal structure. Urbanization of employment has increased at a slower pace than in previous decades because the economic factors that fueled earlier labor migrations to cities have diminished. In El Salvador, Guatemala, Nicaragua, Colombia, and Peru, for example, political factors replaced economic conditions during the 1980s as the migration of people to cities took the form of refugees from rural violence. Because of the limitations of manufacturing to absorb the demand for employment of recently urbanized workers, people looking for jobs were forced into the already overpopulated service sector (see Table 5.1).

Technical changes in rural production compensated for a decline in the agrarian labor force. Table 5.2 presents the uneven cross-sectoral evolution of both EAP and GDP in seven countries that represent 80 percent of Latin America's labor force (Argentina, Brazil, Colombia, Costa Rica, Chile, Mexico, and Venezuela). Even more striking, however, than the increasing labor productivity suggested by these figures is the considerable disparity revealed between nonagricultural growth rates of EAP and GDP.

TABLE 5.1   A Comparison of Latin America's EAP by Economic Sectors, 1980 and 1990 (in percentages)

	1980	*1990*
Agriculture	32	26
Manufacturing	26	26
Services	42	48
Total	100	100

SOURCE: ECLAC (several years).

The estimated evolution of open urban unemployment from 1980 to 1992 is presented in Table 5.3. At the beginning of the 1990s open unemployment was at a similar level to that of the early 1980s (an average rate of 6 percent). For instance, in Chile, Mexico, Brazil, and Costa Rica, open unemployment in 1992 was lower than in 1980, while in other countries it had increased. However, it almost tripled in Argentina and Guatemala and grew by 70 percent in Panama, 50 percent in Ecuador, more than 30 percent in Venezuela and Paraguay, and 20 percent in Uruguay. As in other parts of the world, unemployment has hit the younger generations harder, particularly individuals looking for their first jobs.

Although open unemployment in Latin America is lower than in Europe or the United States, this does not mean that employment is better in Latin America than in the advanced industrial societies. The quality of jobs created in Latin America tends to deteriorate year after year, as will be seen in the discussion below. Latin America's unemployed either have no access to social welfare and unemployment benefits, or the existing programs are unsatisfactory. Moreover, the questionable manner in which statistics on labor markets are gathered in most Latin American countries makes the frontier between unemployment and underemployment unclear. Consequently, the underutilization of the labor force (open unemployment plus underemployment) is a

TABLE 5.2   Latin America's EAP and GDP, 1980–1989[a]

	EAP	*GDP[b]*
Total	2.8	1.2
Agriculture	0.6	2.1
Nonagriculture	3.7	1.1

[a]Average rates of annual growth (in percentages)
[b]Real rates
SOURCE: ECLAC (several years).

TABLE 5.3 Open Urban Unemployment in Latin America, 1980–1992 (annual average rates)

	1980	1981	1982	1983	1984	1985	1986	1987	1988	1989	1990	1991	1992[a]
Argentina	2.6	4.7	5.3	4.7	4.6	6.1	5.6	5.9	6.3	7.6	7.5	6.5	7.0
Bolivia	7.2	6.1	8.0	8.3	6.7	5.7	7.0	5.7	11.5	9.5	7.3	5.8	6.8
Brazil	6.2	7.9	6.3	6.7	7.1	5.3	3.6	3.7	3.8	3.3	4.3	4.8	4.9
Colombia	9.7	8.3	9.1	11.7	13.4	14.1	13.8	11.8	11.2	9.9	10.3	10.0	10.0
Costa Rica	6.0	9.1	9.9	8.5	6.6	6.7	6.7	5.9	6.3	3.7	5.4	6.0	4.3
Chile	11.7	9.0	20.0	19.0	18.5	17.0	13.1	11.9	10.0	7.2	6.5	7.3	4.9
Ecuador	5.7	6.0	6.3	6.7	10.5	10.4	10.7	7.2	7.4	7.9	6.1	8.5	8.7
El Salvador	—	—	—	—	—	—	—	—	9.4	8.4	10.0	7.1	6.8
Guatemala	2.2	1.5	6.0	9.9	9.1	12.0	14.0	11.4	8.8	6.2	6.4	6.7	6.1
Honduras	8.8	9.0	9.2	9.5	10.7	11.7	12.1	11.4	8.7	7.2	6.9	7.6	—
Mexico	4.5	4.2	4.2	6.6	5.7	4.4	4.3	3.9	3.5	2.9	2.9	2.6	2.9
Panama	10.4	10.7	10.1	11.7	12.4	15.7	12.7	14.1	21.1	20.4	20.0	19.0	18.0
Paraguay	3.9	2.2	5.6	8.3	7.3	5.1	6.1	5.5	4.7	6.1	6.6	5.1	5.3
Peru	7.1	6.8	6.6	9.0	8.9	10.1	5.4	4.8	7.1	7.9	8.3	5.9	—
Uruguay	7.4	6.7	11.9	15.5	14.0	13.1	10.7	9.3	9.1	8.6	9.3	8.9	9.0
Venezuela	6.6	6.8	7.8	11.2	14.3	14.3	12.1	9.9	7.9	9.7	10.5	10.1	8.8
Latin America	6.0	6.4	6.9	8.3	8.7	8.3	7.1	6.4	6.2	5.9	6.2	6.2	6.0

[a]Preliminary figures

SOURCE: PREALC, several years.

much better measure of insufficient employment. For example, when the underemployment rate is added to the rate of open unemployment, Mexico's 1993 rate of underutilization of the labor force climbs to 23 percent of the EAP—7.8 million out of an EAP of 33.7 million (Banco de México 1993).

The figures in Table 5.3 suggest that Latin America does not fit entirely into the pattern of "jobless development" referred to by some U.N. agencies (UNDP 1993). In recent years there has been some growth in employment, although it has lagged behind both EAP and GDP growth rates and, as will be seen in a moment, mild employment growth has been associated with the creation of precarious jobs and the segmentation of the labor market. Latin America is experiencing a breakdown of the traditional association between the growth of GDP and employment. The recent reactivation of the Latin American economies has not been coupled so far with an equivalent growth in employment to cover the sharp reduction of jobs during the recession of the 1980s. In other words, it appears that in the recessionary phases of the economic cycle, employment falls at a faster pace than the GDP, while in reactivating phases it grows slower than the GDP.

Throughout the 1980s a strong and protracted transfer of income from wage earners to capitalists and rentiers took place as part of the macroeconomic and financial adjustments and the related changes in employment (see Table 5.4). The transitions from military regimes to elected civilian govern-

TABLE 5.4   Share of Wages in GDP in Several Latin American Countries (in percentages)

	1970	1980	1985	1989	1990
Argentina	40.9	31.5	31.9	24.9	—
Bolivia	36.8	39.6	26.9[a]	—	—
Brazil	34.2	35.1	36.3	—	—
Colombia	42.1	46.2	45.3	42.6[b]	41.8
Costa Rica	52.7	56.1	53.9	56.7	57.8
Chile	47.7	43.4	37.8	—	—
Ecuador	34.4	34.8	23.6	16.0	15.8
Guatemala	32.3	33.6	30.8	30.6	—
Mexico	37.5	39.0	31.6	28.4	27.3
Panama	54.5	48.8	53.8	53.4	50.0
Paraguay	37.1	37.1	32.5	29.4	25.8
Peru	40.0	32.8	30.5	25.5	16.8[c]
Uruguay	52.9	35.7	36.3	39.7	48.4
Venezuela	40.3	42.7	37.6	34.6	31.1

[a]1986
[b]1988
[c]1991
SOURCE: CEPAL, several years.

ments did not have any relevant impact on either the magnitude or the class direction of this transfer. Despite their decisive role in ousting the military regimes in Argentina, Bolivia, Brazil, Chile, and Uruguay, the working class and other lower-income strata, as well as several segments of the middle classes, were now forced to bear the costs of the economic crisis and the restructuring of the capitalist economic system.

Table 5.5 shows the deterioration of real wages in several Latin American countries and compares it to the evolution of industrial labor productivity. By the end of the 1980s the share of wages in industrial value added in countries such as Argentina and Brazil was frozen at 1970 levels, although labor productivity (roughly measured through gross industrial product per worker) grew by four-fifths. In Mexico and Venezuela the share of wages declined 55 percent and 20 percent respectively, although labor productivity grew 53 percent and 7 percent respectively. And in Bolivia, the shrinking of the share of wages exceeded by almost 50 percent the decline in labor productivity.

Table 5.6 shows a drastic drop in urban real wages during the 1980s and early 1990s, with Paraguay, Costa Rica, and Colombia being the only exceptions to the trend. Real wages in Argentina grew during the first half of the 1980s to experience a sharp fall from thereafter. However, preliminary 1993 figures showed a mild recovery. It is difficult to assess whether this represents a turning point in a decade-long tendency or just a temporary modification.

Both rural and urban real wages were lower in the early 1990s than they were at the beginning of the 1980s. In spite of the incipient recovery of real

TABLE 5.5   Wage Earners' Income in Manufacturing, Several Countries, 1970–1989

	Income as Percentage of Value Added				Gross Product Per Worker (1980 = 100)			
	1970	1987	1988	1989	1970	1987	1988	1989
Argentina	29	29	27	28	—	—	—	—
Bolivia	43	26	27	27	65	44	41	59
Brazil	22	21	20	21	71	119	123	125
Chile	19	17	17	17	—	—	—	—
Ecuador	27	38	33	36	83	113	114	103
Mexico	44	20	20	20	77	112	113	128
Panama	32	32	37	38	67	88	81	79
Uruguay	—	26	26	26	—	110	109	110
Venezuela	31	25	28	21	118	132	139	121

SOURCE: World Bank 1992.

TABLE 5.6   Evolution of Real Urban Minimum Wages[a]

	1985	1988	1989	1990	1991	1992	1993[b]
Argentina	113.1	93.5	42.1	40.2	56.0	44.5	49.3
Brazil	88.9	68.7	72.1	53.4	59.9	55.4	56.2
Colombia	109.4	109.9	110.8	107.9	104.3	103.2	105.8
Costa Rica	112.2	114.6	119.4	120.5	111.8	111.5	112.8
Chile	76.4	73.9	79.8	87.5	95.6	100.0	104.6
Ecuador	60.4	53.4	46.5	36.2	30.4	29.5	21.4
Mexico	71.1	54.2	50.8	45.5	43.6	42.1	41.6
Paraguay	99.6	135.2	137.5	131.6	125.8	115.5	—
Peru	54.4	52.0	25.1	23.4	15.9	16.3	—
Uruguay	93.2	84.5	78.0	69.1	62.0	60.5	52.4
Venezuela	96.8	89.5	72.9	59.3	55.1	60.7	

[a]Index numbers, 1980 = 100
[b]Preliminary figures
SOURCE: CEPAL 1992b, 1993.

wages in manufacturing from 1990 to 1992, they were still 7 percent lower than the average industrial salary during the previous decade. This suggests that the decline in competitiveness in a number of Latin American economies starting in 1989 can be attributed not to a disproportionate improvement in wages but to the overvaluation of the exchange rate resorted to by the Latin American governments concerned with keeping inflation under control through making imports cheaper. In fact, labor costs in Latin American manufacturing remain at a lower level than those in Southeast Asia and amount to one-tenth of the labor costs in U.S. manufacturing.

The Informal Labor Market

What has variously been referred to as the informal labor market, urban informal sector (UIS), and informal economy encompasses a broad and variegated range of small-scale productive and nonproductive activities that have a number of common traits. The workers in these jobs operate out of household shops or ambulatory street posts; they rely on personal or family non-salaried labor and an occasional temporary hiring of nonfamily workers; the working conditions are poor, with no minimal wages, access to welfare benefits, or other legal provisions; income earned is usually very low although not necessarily below the subsistence level; and the activities are not directly taxed. Traditional examples of these informal activities are small repair shops, street vending, and various types of personal services.

Informal activities are not marginal to the formal economy. On the contrary, they are closely articulated with it, as in the case of subcontracting, small-scale transport, repair work, or some branches of small-scale manufacturing of furniture, food, garments, and the like. In all, informal activities contribute to the overall reproduction of the economic system and to the social fabric underlying the economy.

As such, the urban informal sector has been a traditional ingredient of the Latin American economies, particularly in some Andean and Central American countries. Economic crisis and the subsequent macroeconomic and financial adjustments have led to a huge expansion of both this informal economy and the labor market associated with it. By the early 1990s almost half of the Latin American workforce belonged either to the UIS or to the small firms sector of the economy, while in 1980 both categories accounted for one-third.

The UIS doubled its size from 1980 to 1992, lagging just behind the expansion of employment in small firms (see Table 5.7). Growth of employment in formal activities (large capitalist firms and the public sector) has been less than one-fifth of that in the informal sector and less than one-third of the overall economy. From 1980 to the early 1990s, four out of five new jobs created in the Latin American economy were to be found in either the informal or the small firms sectors.

A shift in the labor force has thus been going on from the formal sector to the informal. In cities such as Lima, Managua, and Guatemala City, the informal economy accounts for more than two-thirds of the urban EAP. In 1993, according to official estimates, the UIS generated one-third of Mexico's GDP. And within the formal sector, the labor force is being transferred from the larger to the smaller firms where working conditions tend to be

TABLE 5.7 The Structure of Latin America's Labor Market, 1980 and 1992: A Comparison

	1980		1992		Change
	Million	*Percentage*	*Million*	*Percentage*	*(in percentages)*
Large Firms	30.0	44.1	32.0	30.8	6.7
Small Firms[a]	10.0	14.6	24.0	22.5	140.0
Informal Sector	13.0	19.2	26.0	25.0	100.0
Domestic Services	4.0	6.4	7.0	6.8	75.0
Public Sector	11.0	15.7	16.0	14.9	45.4
Total	68.0	100.0	105.0	100.0	54.4

[a]Small firms: Up to 5 or 10 workers, according to country criteria.
SOURCE: PREALC, several years.

harsh. In fact, employment in small firms has more than doubled, while it has virtually stagnated in large and middle-sized firms.

Increased employment in the UIS goes hand in hand with decreasing income levels, even for similar occupational categories; this also holds true, though to a lesser degree, for employment in the formal sector of smaller firms (see Table 5.8). Wage levels in the larger firms within the formal sector show a milder deterioration than in the smaller firms sector. The figures are consistent with the wage policies of the larger firms, where wage levels are kept stable through progressively reduced employment. Moreover, unionization tends to be weaker in the smaller firms, which additionally reduces the bargaining space for negotiating labor contracts.

The rapid "informalization" of the labor market has been matched by the adoption in the formal sector of policies of "job flexibility," which enable firms to move workers from one position to another or to end the employment relationship without any special provision or compensation. It also involves the de-skilling of work processes and the use of individual labor contracts, which substitute for collective contracts and undermine union participation in the labor market. Even within the formal sector, there exists a great deal of what is referred to as precarious employment, such as in the case of seasonal agricultural laborers, most port workers, and many construction workers. Most of the workers in these branches of the labor market lack job stability, face hard and long working days, and have no access to health and welfare systems or to collective bargaining.

The expansion of subcontracting has also contributed to the creation of precarious employment in the formal sector, approaching that of the informal sector. Large firms in the formal economy subcontract for specific tasks

TABLE 5.8   Real Wages and Average Real Income in Latin America's Labor Markets, 1980–1989[a]

	Average Growth Rate (in percentages)	1989 Index (1980 = 100)
Real Average Income		
Private formal sector		
Large and middle firms	−0.8	93
Small firms	−3.9	70
Public sector	−3.1	70
Informal sector	−5.9	58
Minimum Wages		
Urban minimum wages	−3.0	76

[a]Argentina, Brazil, Colombia, Costa Rica, Chile, Mexico, and Venezuela
SOURCE: Vilas 1993a.

or processes with smaller firms, which in turn subcontract with household shops or self-employed workers. In small firms job stability is weak, sanitary conditions are unsatisfactory, and the workday often depends on production and delivery schedules. Work done at home is the most unstable; sanitary conditions are even worse, and the working day has no limits.

The rapid growth of informal employment coupled with the rapid deterioration of employment in the formal sector have given rise to an erosion of the frontiers between the formal and the informal labor markets. Precarious employment in both the formal and the informal sectors has become intimately linked to middle-sized and large firms in the formal economy. This process is also going on in the public, or government, sector. In recent years a number of Latin American governments as well as several multilateral agencies have sponsored emergency social programs that provide temporary employment and low-income jobs to segments of the unemployed EAP in projects aimed at building or repairing the economic and social infrastructure. Funded by agencies such as the Inter-American Development Bank (IDB) and the World Bank, these initiatives rely on hiring unskilled, mostly male labor for short periods of time to build or repair roads, bridges, ports, and the like. Salaries are low, not infrequently falling below the legal minimum, and there are no benefits. The rationale of these programs, as stated by the funding agencies, has been twofold: (1) to address the development of the infrastructure, which has been a much-delayed dimension in Latin America's economic development over the past decades, and (2) to provide a cheap method of reabsorbing workers previously expelled from the labor market by instituting programs addressed to people who are "willing to accept low wages" (IDB 1992b:9).

To put it in blunt terms: Workers are expelled from previous formal occupations, then reemployed to work in downgraded, lower-paying jobs with poorer working conditions. In sum, a new labor market is being developed that goes beyond the traditional formal/informal segmentation and combines the ingredients of both. State and international agencies together with capitalist corporations (i.e., the formal sector) now rely on forms of employment that conform to the standards of the informal sector such as no minimum wages, no welfare benefits, no unions, no legal protection, and no job stability.

The creation of precarious forms of employment is also the result of the privatization of state-owned firms, a development that has involved drastic cuts in employment and forced large numbers of state workers to search for alternative means of survival. Due to prevailing conditions in the formal economy and the already discussed linkages between the formal and informal labor markets, most of the expelled workers have had no other alternative but to accept downgraded working conditions mostly in informal activities. Privatization has also been coupled with severe cuts in social spending that have had a heavy impact on both the urban and rural working classes as well as other lower income groups—the traditional beneficiaries of welfare policies.

The Challenges Faced by the Labor Movement

Recent economic changes and policy shifts have dealt a strong blow to Latin American workers and their unions. Due to labor-saving technologies and the overall reshaping of productive processes, the aggregate demand for labor in the most dynamic, export-oriented sectors has tended to fall relative to the growth of the new waves of people entering the labor market; meanwhile, there has been an absolute decline in specific sectors of manufacturing and infrastructure. The need to raise productivity standards and to compete in the international market has resulted in pressures to lower labor costs through downgrading working conditions and freezing wages, to resort to subcontracting, to reduce the participation of unions in the settlement of labor disputes and in the definition of labor relations, and so on. Moreover, the restructuring of state-market relations has forged closer links between the public sector and the most globalized segments of the Latin American bourgeoisie, which have become the strategic point of reference, and the prime beneficiaries, of government policies.

Several countries (such as Uruguay, Argentina, and Chile) have emerged from years of military dictatorships that imposed severe hardships on the working class and debilitated the labor movement as well as other social and political actors who had been involved in labor activism—such as the student and squatters movements. Unions and political parties with a working-class appeal were outlawed and repressed, their members subjected to imprisonment, forced into exile, or victimized by death squads. This repression has been considered by scholars and observers to have been a strategic ingredient of the economic design implemented by these right-wing governments (Sheahan 1987; Pion-Berlin 1989; Figueroa Ibarra 1991).

There has also been a relative depoliticization of the new entrants into the labor market—apparently the combined effect of a repressive institutional setting, the failure of confrontational or populist union strategies, and the economic crisis and associated adjustment measures. Taken together, these factors have called into question the efficacy of class-oriented strategies and reinforced neoliberal and authoritarian claims for the supremacy of nonconfrontational and individualistic approaches to labor relations.

Additional factors have also forced the unions to take a defensive stance. The rapid expansion of the informal labor market since the 1980s, with its emphasis on occasional or self-employment, has threatened the very scope and efficacy of unions by undermining their representation and reducing their potential base. The adjustment programs have reduced employment in the formal sector, particularly in construction, manufacturing, health, and education, which over decades have been the traditional strongholds of the unions. Policies aimed at job flexibility have reduced several core aspects of union involvement in establishing working conditions and in shaping the labor market. Now it is capital and government that determine the basic conditions under which labor is hired, paid, and fired.

Individual labor contracts have increasingly been substituted for collective ones, and standard commercial law has replaced labor law in the overall regulation of labor relations. This is a regressive step because labor law develops a specific set of legal institutions intended to cope with the substantive inequality of workers vis-à-vis employers. Thus, it questions the principle of formal equality present in civil and mercantile law. Meanwhile, collective labor contracts have been increasingly contested by firms and the state. Working-class fragmentation has deepened as labor contracts have been negotiated at the level of specific firms rather than by sector or industry. This fragmentation usually reflects the uneven bargaining conditions of each union local with regard to each firm more than it reflects differences in technology or productivity among firms.

A combination of structural and institutional factors thus made for a weakened and disoriented labor opposition when the economic crisis exploded and the Latin American governments resorted to rearticulating their economies with the international economy and to the imposition of their economic adjustment policies. The obstacles to the unions taking a tough stance were greater in Argentina, Mexico, and Venezuela, where the larger unions have traditionally lacked political autonomy vis-à-vis the state and where the major political parties and labor's representational and redistributive efficacy have been subordinated to diverse types of corporatist arrangements. The unions have gone deeper into crisis as their allies of the past have concerned themselves with recovering from the impact of authoritarian rule and given up their prior commitment to promoting extensive development, greater social participation, and income distribution. Moreover, the evolution of the economic structure has called into question the feasibility of this kind of development and thrown large numbers of the economically active population out of the formal labor market.

Gender and Labor

In addition to the shortcomings stemming from or related to structural and policy changes, most of the Latin American labor movement has had difficulty meeting the demands of women in the labor forces—a segment of the labor force that has been growing at a fast pace in recent decades. Triggered by economic growth throughout the 1960s and 1970s, women's participation in the labor market grew substantially during this period, stabilizing after the 1980s crisis as women's share in the growth of employment decreased (see Tables 5.9 and 5.10). As the crisis deepened, gender stratification of working conditions was reinforced. Privatization has also had severe

TABLE 5.9   The Latin American Workforce by Gender, 1960–1990
(growth given in parentheses)

	1960	1970	1980	1990
Male	54,751	67,930 (13,179)	82,232 (14,302)	111,257 (29,025)
Female	12,976	18,846 (5,870)	30,873 (12,028)	40,329 (9,450)
Total	67,727	86,776	113,106 (26,330)	151,581 (38,475)

SOURCE: IDB 1990.

implications for women; women's wages and working conditions have been better on average in the public sector than in the private one, and gender-based wage differentials have also tended to be smaller in the public sector. Moreover, women are generally the first workers laid off when state enterprises are privatized, when there is a recession, or when the need to reduce production costs has resulted in labor cuts.

The rate of unionization of the female labor force has been lower than that of male workers (Godinho and Berenice 1990), which in turn has reinforced discrimination against women workers. The increased participation of women in the labor force has not produced concomitant changes in union structures, which need to adapt traditional organizational criteria to the new gender composition of rank-and-file. The recruitment of female union office holders has lagged behind female participation in the labor market. Inconvenient meeting schedules and traditional male chauvinism inside and outside the plant have obstructed women's participation in unions. Moreover, participation on the part of women in unions usually requires as many changes in their private life—such as the gender division of household work—as in the organization and culture of the unions themselves. These factors have favored female involvement in union affairs in plants where there is a majority of female workers. Finally, due to the twofold basis of gender bias (i.e., the reduced access of women to wage labor in the formal sector and the institutional and cultural obstacles to their participation in unions), women's participation has tended to develop outside the labor market in neighborhood and grassroots organizations, parents' associations, *clubs de madres* (mothers' associations), and the like.

TABLE 5.10   Women in the Latin American Workforce, 1960–1990
(in percentages)

	1960	1970	1980	1990
As Percentage of Total Workforce	19.2	21.7	26.1	26.6
Growth	—	31.0	46.0	24.0

The Restructuring of the Working Class

The interplay of the postcrisis increase in external links, structural changes, and state policies has given rise to far-reaching changes in the working population as well as in society as a whole. The sociodemographic dimensions of the working class have been redefined, due to the relative reduction of the formal labor market and subsequent growth of the informal labor force, together with the increasing diffusion of individual labor contracts and the depoliticization of the new generations of workers. The organizational dimensions as well as institutional projections of class identity have become feebler, particularly those dealing with the labor market. As government social spending has receded, the appeal of unions and wage employment in the formal sector has also declined. On the whole, an economic and social setting is being created whereby the modernization of capital and entrepreneurial activity is articulated along with the decline of the workforce's income, employment conditions, and quality of life.

The disciplining of most of the Latin American economies by the international financial system and the slow reactivation of these economies have coexisted with a sustained growth of the population living under the poverty line. The process of economic restructuring and "modernization" has involved the expulsion of large portions of the factors of production—capital, technology, and labor—from the productive system, elements that in the previous stage were dynamic factors in the process of accumulation.

The policy instruments the Latin American governments have resorted to have played a strategic function in the punishment of some social and economic actors and in the promotion of others. These policy instruments have included pricing, credit, and income policies; subsidies for private investment such as tax exemptions; and income transfers from productive to nonproductive sectors, from small and middle-sized firms to large ones, and from wage to nonwage earners.

Increased poverty has gone hand in hand with increased social inequality, as a vivid illustration of the uneven social distribution of gains and losses. Available information suggests that income polarization in Latin America is deeper than in new industrializing countries (NICs) or in the member states of the Association of Southeast Asian Nations (ASEAN) (see Table 5.11).

Extreme inequalities rose 23 percent in Brazil during the 1980s, and in Guatemala they tripled over the same period (see Table 5.12). In Mexico, extreme inequalities slightly diminished in 1992 vis-à-vis 1989 but remained deeper than in 1984. The exception is Costa Rica, where polarization decreased by 23 percent. Middle-income groups lost ground in Brazil and Guatemala, where widening social polarization transferred income to the richest groups; they gained in Costa Rica, where the redistribution of income benefited the middle groups much more than the poorer ones. Mexico's

TABLE 5.11   Household Income Shares

	Share of National Income Received by Each Household Income Category			Income Share of Highest 20% as a Multiple of Lowest 40% (col. 3 ÷ col. 1)
	Lowest 40%	Middle 40%	Highest 20%	
Brazil (1989)	7.0	25.7	67.5	9.6
Colombia (1988)	12.7	34.3	53.0	4.2
Chile (1989)	10.5	26.6	62.9	6.0
Costa Rica (1989)	13.1	36.1	50.8	3.9
Guatemala (1989)	7.9	29.1	63.0	8.0
Honduras (1989)	8.7	27.8	63.5	7.3
Jamaica (1990)	15.9	35.7	48.4	3.0
Mexico (1984)	11.9	32.2	55.9	4.7
Panama (1989)	8.3	31.9	59.8	7.2
Peru (1985–86)	14.1	34.0	51.9	3.7
Dominican Republic (1989)	12.1	32.3	55.6	4.6
Venezuela (1989)	14.3	36.2	49.5	3.5
Hong Kong (1980)	16.2	36.8	47.0	2.9
Indonesia (1990)	20.8	36.9	42.3	2.0
Philippines (1988)	16.6	35.6	47.8	2.9
Singapore (1982–83)	15.0	36.1	48.9	3.3
Thailand (1988)	15.5	33.8	50.7	3.3

SOURCE: World Bank 1993.

mild increase in the poorest 20 percent share illustrates the impact of government-sponsored programs to ameliorate extreme poverty (CEPAL-INEGI 1993). Sustained growth of the highest 20 percent of the income earners is additionally illustrated by the rapid growth in the numbers of Mexican billionaires: from two in 1991 to seven in 1992, and thirteen in 1993 (Rodríguez Castañeda 1993)—an 85 percent increase in three years in a country whose GDP grew by a mere 0.4 percent. In sum, these figures provide evidence of the ongoing production of poverty, inequality, and social degradation alongside the production of incredible wealth. Poverty is neither a given of nature nor a punishment of fate. It is instead the product of specific social relations, reinforced through public policies. Increased mass poverty—as a result of lower wages, higher unemployment, labor downgrading, reduction in welfare spending, and the like—can be interpreted as the counterparts of, and even as conditions for, the reconstitution of the profit rate.

TABLE 5.12   Changes in Household Income Polarization in the 1980s

		Share of National Income Received by Each Household Income Category				Income Share of Highest 20% as a Multiple of Lowest 40% (col. 3 ÷ col. 1)
		Lowest 20%	Middle 60%	Highest 20%	Top 10%	
Brazil	1983	2.4	35.0	62.6	46.2	26.1
	1989	2.1	30.4	67.5	51.3	32.1
Costa Rica	1986	3.3	42.2	54.5	38.8	16.5
	1989	4.0	45.2	50.8	34.1	12.7
Guatemala	1981	5.5	39.5	55.0	40.8	10.0
	1989	2.1	34.9	63.0	46.6	30.0
Mexico	1984	4.1	40.1	55.9	39.5	13.6
	1989	4.4	42.1	53.5	—	12.1
	1992	5.0	40.8	54.2	38.2	10.8

SOURCE: World Bank 1993, CEPAL-INEGI 1993.

Overwhelming urban poverty and the weakened organizational dimensions of working-class identity have brought about a regression among the working population from a *class position* to a *mass situation*. Together with a huge, rapid, and profound deterioration of living conditions, this regression involves the breakdown of solidarity based on collective values and a corresponding growth of particularistic allegiances. The regression of the workforce attenuates the concept of labor as a structural relation between collective actors and, instead, transforms it into a concept whereby an individual is linked to a particular firm or, as in self-employment, to just herself or himself. The decline of collective organizations such as unions—which have traditionally related jobholders to organized labor and linked organized labor to the working class (and therefore to the entire social structure and to the capitalist state)—has resulted in the disaggregation of vast portions of the working class into a mass of individuals competing with each other for survival.

At first glance, this disaggregation could be seen as a mere amplification of the well-known process of social marginalization intrinsic to the development of capitalist economies. From this perspective, recent structural and policy changes have merely accelerated and deepened a process that has been going on for several decades. However, the very concept of marginality was subjected to sharp criticism in the early 1970s (Oliveira 1972; Quijano 1973). According to this criticism, marginalized sectors of the population are neither alien nor "useless" to capitalist accumulation. Rather, they are functional to the accumulation process. They serve as an updated albeit perverted version of the classic "industrial reserve army" spoken of by Karl Marx and Friedrich Engels. The prevailing technological biases and the decreased demand for unskilled labor mean that the "marginalized" elements are no longer reabsorbed into the productive process, not even in times of economic recovery; they constitute a surplus population in an absolute sense, performing their traditional function by pulling down wage levels and labor conditions in those segments of the economy that still rely on unskilled employment—such as repair shops, personal services, public works, and the like.

It must be pointed out that these criticisms predate the contemporary process of global capitalist restructuring. Together with the international dispersal of the production cycle within many industries, the advent of what has been called "post-Fordism" involves the de-skilling of the labor process and, in so doing, increases labor turnover and the facile replacement of workers (job flexibility). This postadjustment restructuring also creates a new platform for labor and class relations. In the first place, both formal and informal labor markets are rearticulated according to the increasingly precarious condition of labor relations in the former and the subsequent downgrading of living standards. That is to say, there is now no job stability, less emphasis on labor skills, no unionization, and so forth. Although it may be true that today's workers in this new type of labor market resemble the former "marginals" in terms of their living standards—for example, their income, consumption patterns, and housing—they are not marginal, strictly speaking, to several of the most advanced and core branches of capital accumulation. Consequently, although the ongoing process is destroying the working class as it existed in previous stages of capital accumulation, the postadjustment restructuring admits smaller segments of this class back into the formal labor market.

There is a clear difference in the identity of those currently being pushed into poverty from those of the past. They do not hold much in common with the recently urbanized, predominantly illiterate Latin American masses that were active participants in the populist and developmentalist experiences of the 1940s and 1950s. Today's marginalized population holds citizenship rights and, up to a decade ago, was integrated into the formal labor market, participated in unions and other social organizations, entered the educational and health systems, and benefited from welfare and pension systems. Many of them joined the democratic mobilizations that forced the military dictatorships out of power and also participated in certain cases, as in Central America, in revolutionary attempts at social change. They tended to react to exploitation and oppression in a more aggressive, although not always collective, manner. They also tended to be an extremely volatile population, looking forward as much as backward, with hope and frustration, resentment and creativity.

This marginalized population poses social as well as political challenges to states and political organizations. The loss of collective allegiances usually leads to what Geertz (1973) has called a retreat to "primordial attachments," or what Bourdieu (1980) has termed the "retreat to the habitus" (i.e., the household, kinship, or ethnic group). Such retreats, or regressions, lead to increased social fragmentation as particularistic emotional ties substitute for collective identities based on notions of class and citizenship. This phenomenon may be understood as a transitional stage in the development of new social arrangements; it involves under any circumstances instability and uncertainty. As in any social transition, institutional links break down well before new ones can be substituted for them. As long as this process deals with devising new social foundations for the political system, the longer the transition lasts the higher the risk of uncertainty and the stronger the likelihood of renewed forms of authoritarian state control over the population.

Several scholars have recently pointed to the impact of the growing informal sector and increasing poverty on the growing electoral support for a new breed of political mavericks such as Alberto Fujimori in Peru, Carlos Menem in Argentina, and Fernando Collor de Mello in Brazil, who have combined representative democracy with the traditional personalistic politics of Latin American strongmen and the systematic use of the mass media (Cameron 1991, 1994; Panfichi 1994; Vilas 1993b). Preferences for personalistic, strong leaders may be an expression of voters' disillusionment with, or rejection of, conventional politicians who have failed to come to terms with the daily problems of insecurity, instability, and poverty. They are searching for something different, although it does not necessarily turn out to be, as in the above-mentioned cases, something better. In any case, the temptation to pour this new mass-politics wine into old populist bottles should be discouraged. Strong, personalistic populist leaders (caudillos) helped to integrate the urban masses into a system of expanded consumption, a system based on union organizing and political enfranchisement in an institutional environment that stressed popular mobilization. The contemporary version of caudillo politics, however, appears to propound the democratic principle of majority rule along with the neoliberal principle of profits for the few.

However, this does not mean a turn toward the Right, or a revival of authoritarianism, is inevitable. The increasing electoral successes of parties such as Brazil's PT, Venezuela's Causa R, and Argentina's Frente Grande suggest that there are a diversified and extremely creative series of political organizations capable of mobilizing popular support and developing new ways of bringing unions, social movements, and new types of political organizations together to press for progressive change.

The combined process of working-class restructuring and its political implications has been evolving throughout Latin America during the past decade, although it has had an uneven evolution from country to country and the results achieved to date have been subject to a variety of intervening factors that have led to disparate outcomes. The four most important of these factors have been: (1) the particular characteristics of the economic structure; (2) the type of political regime; (3) the nature of government commitments and policies; and (4) the particular experiences of the labor movement.

In the Brazilian case, union autonomy vis-à-vis the state and business has created conditions under which the workers have been able to take advantage of sustained economic growth—at least from the perspective of employment—and to prevent the full impact of crisis management policies from being imposed on them. Furthermore, autonomy and class perspectives have endowed the unions with a vast social and political representation going far beyond urban or industrial workers to include social movements, the urban poor, the peasantry, and broad segments of the middle sectors.

In both Chile and Mexico sustained growth has not been sufficient to support an equitable distribution of the gains and losses of the process of economic restructuring. This is particularly the case in Mexico, where the rank-and-file of corporatist unions, subordinated to state agencies and the governing party, has been depleted and where the population has been further marginalized from the power structure. To some extent, this is also the Argentine case. Although in Chile there was sustained growth during the second half of the 1980s and early 1990s, as well as labor autonomy to a certain extent, the absence of more active union strategies has forced the labor movement into a defensive stance.

In all four cases—Argentina, Brazil, Chile, and Mexico—union autonomy has been a central ingredient in the scope and orientation of the restructuring, either in an active or a passive way. Close links to the state in Mexico and Argentina—that is, the unions' lack of political autonomy—have prevented the populist corporatist labor movements from confronting the neoliberal restructuring, particularly its destructive effects on the working class. As a result, in both countries once-powerful populist unions have confronted a deep crisis as more and more workers have begun to search for independent alternatives. There is no danger of union subordination to corporatism in Chile, but large segments of the labor movement have apparently accepted the neoliberal socioeconomic project of the government and the role it assigns to the workers and unions—thereby abdicating their class autonomy. By way of contrast, the emphasis on autonomy has enabled the Brazilian labor movement to become a strategic actor in both the political arena and the economy, and labor leaders have neutralized the neoliberal attempts to reshape Brazilian society and created the prospects for progressive social and political change.

The 1980s crisis, subsequent socioeconomic restructuring, and government policy shifts changed both the structural and institutional environments for the working class and forced it to experience drastic transformations. To be a Latin American worker in the 1990s is quite different from being a worker twenty years earlier. The foregoing discussion conducted in this chapter does not provide a basis for concluding that the demise of the Latin American working class is at hand. However, its survival as something other than a sociodemographic aggregate and its further development as a political force, as well as its contribution to a more humane world, will depend on its ability to assess its autonomy vis-à-vis other classes and political actors while building broad alliances with social movements and other progressive actors, which in one way or another are pushing together for something better than the neoliberal vision.

Globalization and Labor Solidarity Across Borders

One of the most striking shortcomings of past working-class movements around the world was their emphasis on internationalist strategies and allegiances in a world dominated by nations and nationalism. Imperialism, as Hobson, Hilferding, Lenin, Bukharin, and Luxemburg have all pointed out so well, involves the international expansion of capital as well as the international displacement of labor, but not necessarily the internationalization of capitalist production relations. In reference to working-class politics, "internationalism" was usually the term pro-Soviet communist parties and unions used to label their subordination to the foreign policies of the Soviet Union. These may have been good or bad policies, but what is being stressed here is that, used in this sense, internationalism was no more than the international dimension of a national political strategy. Furthermore, tensions between international strategies and domestic political demands proved to be a source of shortcomings and confusion for both communist and noncommunist Marxist organizations, preventing many of them from building a stronghold among the Latin American working class (Caballero 1986). Internationalism was mostly an ideological device without any relevant articulation of the workers' problems, and it frequently required the subordination of labor demands and domestic political strategies to foreign policy concerns.

But, because of the increasing globalization of production and trade, internationalism may become a true ingredient of working class and people's struggles. From a working class and popular perspective, internationalism involves the quest for international projection and mutual support of worker's struggles at every point in the global economic network.

Freedom for the international circulation of goods and capital continues to be much greater than that of labor due to the severe national and international regulations that prevent its free movement. On the one hand, this discrepancy bears witness not only to the sharp inequalities in employment conditions among Latin American countries (as well as between them and the United States and Canada) but also to the way these inequalities help to reactivate the economies of the region in a manner that favors business rather than labor. On the other hand, the prohibition of the international migration of labor excludes workers from the institutional protection of the host country, enabling the generation of a labor rent for firms hiring illegal migrants.

The territorial anchorage of the labor force, articulated with the international homogenization of the other factors of production (capital and technology), creates a system of Northern Hemisphere prices and Southern Hemisphere wages. This system provides a subsidy that contributes to the international competitiveness of the firms that employ Southern workers while it creates precarious forms of employment for these workers. Due to the predominant export orientation of the firms, the impact of this system on the domestic market is considered to be irrelevant. Furthermore, in a context of mild economic reactivation without an equivalent growth in employment, state policies that prevent the free international circulation of the workforce contribute to a situation resembling that of the "unlimited supply of labor" in the well-known model by W. Arthur Lewis (1954).

Capital shifts from country to country in its search for better conditions for profit-making. The increasing relevance of technical improvements notwithstanding, cheap labor is the most strategic resource for profit-making. Moreover, since there is a trend toward the international equalization of technological levels, uneven labor conditions are what really account for differences in profit. The Latin American governments, as the governments of most other developing regions, have implemented public policies to lower labor costs in order to create favorable conditions for foreign investments. Workers in the globalized segments of the domestic economies might be well advised to respond by relying on coordinated strategies to confront these trends and policies and to improve labor conditions at all points in the global chain of production. Computerized networks linking each domestic node to the entire global matrix can project at an exponential rate any action conducted at any local branch. This endows unions at the domestic level with an extraordinary outreach capability. Certainly the task is not an easy one. Government agencies support and complement business opposition to the unionization of workers. In addition to this, their high reliance on unskilled workers enables transnational corporations to substitute nonunionized workers for unionized ones. To a lesser extent this has also been—and still is—the case in more traditional segments of the economy. The experience already gathered by unions in these branches will prove to be a valuable resource to advance labor organization in export-related sectors and to deal with high levels of labor turnover. The same holds true for ways to articulate unskilled and skilled wage labor demands. However, in both cases unions will have to refrain from their traditional dependence on corporatist strategies that no longer afford them either bread-and-butter gains or a voice in labor and social policies but, instead, reduce the unions' efficacy and appeal.

Since state agencies have become private instruments of the business elites, union independence should be emphasized.

Up to now, capital has operated across borders, but the labor force and people's organizations have remained enclosed within them. Supported by technological improvements and under the guise of state-sponsored policies of free trade and economic integration, working class and popular movements for democracy and social change must rely on increasing internationalization in order to be effective. The increased de-skilling of labor in globalized industries enables firms to establish semiautomated plants in developing countries and to take advantage of both their cheap labor and growing workers' productivity. This results in developing-country wages in exchange for industrial nation productivity. This is clearly the case with the North American Free Trade Agreement (NAFTA), where Mexican wages in export-led industries amount to an average of one-sixth to one-eighth of U.S. wages, while Mexico's labor productivity is growing at twice the rate of U.S. workers, a situation that threatens the chances of the working classes in both countries to improve their working conditions. MERCOSUR—the common market of Argentina, Brazil, Paraguay, and Uruguay—presents another case where the international coordination of labor movements is both possible and necessary.

Under the leadership of capitalist governments gathered in the Group of Seven (G-7), multilateral organizations such as the IMF and the World Bank have over the past decade promoted the true globalization of economic, trade, and financial policies. Any G-7 agreement on trade or interest rates may involve the difference between survival and starvation, life and death, for tens of millions of Latin American workers and their families. Therefore, there are no sound reasons for unions and social movements to restrict their struggles to national boundaries. Furthermore, issues such as the effective enactment of human rights or environmental protection call for international endorsement and greater international collaboration of popular organizations.

References

Banco de México. *Informe anual.* Mexico City: Banco de México, 1993.

Bourdieu, Pierre. *Questions de sociologie.* Paris: Minuit, 1980.

Caballero, Manuel. *Latin America and the Comintern, 1919–1943.* New York: Cambridge University Press, 1986.

Cameron, Maxwell. "The Politics of Urban Informal Sector in Peru: Populism, Class, and Redistributive Combines." *Canadian Journal of Latin American and Caribbean Studies* 16 (1991):79–104.

———. "Political Parties and the Informal Sector in Peru." Paper presented at the Conference on Inequality and New Forms of Popular Representation in Latin America, March 1994, New York, Columbia University.

CEPAL (Comisión Económica para América Latina y el Caribe). *El perfil de la pobreza en América Latina a comienzos de los años 90*. LC/L.716 (Conf.82/6) Santiago, Chile: CEPAL, November 1992a.

———. *Balance preliminar de la economía de América Latina y el Caribe 1992*. Santiago, Chile: CEPAL, December 1992b.

———. *Balance preliminar de la economía de América Latina y el Caribe 1993*. Santiago, Chile: December 1993.

CEPAL-INEGI (Comisión Económica para América Latina y el Caribe–Instituto Nacional de Estadística, Geografía, e Informático). *Informe sobre la magnitud y la evolución de la pobreza en México, 1984–1992*. Mexico City: CEPAL-INEGI, 1993.

Figueroa Ibarra, Carlos. *El recurso del miedo*. San José, Costa Rica: EDUCA, 1991.

Furtado, Celso. *Teoría y política del desarrollo económico*. Mexico City: Siglo XXI, 1974.

Geertz, Clifford. *The Interpretation of Cultures*. New York: Basic Books, 1973.

Godinho, Delgado, and Maria Berenice. "Sindicalismo, cosa de varones." *Nueva Sociedad* 110 (November/December 1990):119–127.

IDB (Inter-American Development Bank). *Progreso económico y social en América Latina: Informe 1990*. Washington, DC: IDB, 1992a.

———. *Políticas de desarrollo* 1, 4 (December 1992b).

International Labor Office (ILO). *Yearbook of Labor Statistics*. Geneva: ILO, several years.

Lewis, Arthur W. "Economic Development with Unlimited Supply of Labour." *Manchester School of Economics Studies* 22, 1 (1954):139-191.

Oliveira, Francisco de. "A economia brasileira: Crítica da razão dualista." *Estudos CEBRAP* 2 (October 1972): 3–82.

Panfichi, Aldo. "Los pobres de las ciudades latinoamericanas: Balance y perspectivas teóricas." *Revista de Sociología* (Lima) 9 (1994).

Pinto, Anibal. "Concentración del progreso técnico y de sus frutos en al desarrollo latinoamericano." *El Trimestre Económica* 125 (January–March 1965):3–69.

Pion-Berlin, David. *The Ideology of State Terror: Economic Doctrine and Political Repression in Argentina and Peru*. Boulder, CO: Lynne Rienner, 1989.

Programa Regional de Empleo de América Latina y el Caribe (PREALC). *PREALC Informa*. Santiago, Chile: PREALC, several years.

Quijano, Anibal. *Populismo, marginalización, y dependencia*. San José: EDUCA, 1973.

Rodríguez Castañeda, Rafael. "La élite empresarial de Salinas." *Proceso* 819, 13 (July 1993):6–7.

Sheahan, John. *Patterns of Development in Latin America*. Princeton, NJ: Princeton University Press, 1987.

Tironi, Eugenio, and Ricardo A. Lagos. "Actores sociales y ajuste estructural." *Revista de la CEPAL* 44 (August 1991):39–54.

UNDP (United Nations Development Program). *Human Development Report, 1991*. New York: UNDP, 1993.

Vilas, Carlos María. "Latin American Populism: A Structural Approach." *Science and Society* 56, 4 (Winter 1992–1993):389–420.

———. *Back to the "Dangerous Classes"? Capitalist Restructuring, State Reforms and the Working Class in Latin America*, ILAIS papers no. 34. New York: Columbia University, Spring 1993a.

————. "Partidos políticos, nuevos liderazgos y sociedad civil." Paper delivered at the conference on El fin de Siglo y los Partidos Políticos en América Latina, Mexico City: Instituto Mora, November 1993b.

————. "Política y poder en el nuevo orden mundial: Una perspectiva desde América Latina," in A. Triana Martínez, ed., *Democracia en América latina: Seis contribuciones al debate*. Mexico City: Triana Ediciones, 1994, 117–200.

Vuskovic, Pedro. "Distribución del ingreso y opciones de desarrollo." *Cuadernos de la Realidad Nacional* 5 (September 1970):41–60.

World Bank. *World Development Report 1992*. New York: Oxford University Press, 1992.

————. *World Development Report 1993*. New York: Oxford University Press, 1993.

6

The Riddle of New Social Movements: Who They Are and What They Do

JUDITH ADLER HELLMAN

It is astonishing to contemplate the number and variety of collective activities pursued by Latin Americans that have come to be grouped together under the general heading "new social movements." In the first comprehensive collection of writings on the topic, Tilman Evers (1985) provides a list of new social movements that includes squatters' groups, neighborhood councils, church-sponsored "ecclesiastical base communities" (CEBs), indigenist associations, women's organizations, human rights committees, youth groups, popular cultural and artistic activities, literacy groups, coalitions for the defense of regional traditions, environmental movements, and "a patchwork of self-help groupings among unemployed and poor people." Significantly, Evers also includes "workers' associations organizing independently and even in opposition to traditional trade union structures" (Evers 1985:43).

In the same volume Etienne Henry sketches a five-part typology of new social movements that substantially overlaps that of Evers. For Henry, the relevant categories are (1) "territorial movements," in which the residents of popular neighborhoods negotiate with authorities for control of an area of land; (2) "issue-oriented movements" that mobilize around the demand for public services (potable water, transportation, electric power, sewers, etc.); (3) "sectoral, or conjunctural, movements," in which groups of shantytown dwellers organized by territory support class-based struggles of teachers, municipal workers, street vendors, and public transport workers; (4) "urban revolts" such as bread riots and other spontaneous crisis responses; and (5) multiclass "regional and nationalist movements" (1985:127–145). According to Henry, these movements can be distinguished from traditional political organizations of the Left in that they "seem to be responding to crisis situations rather than acting as the bearers of a project of historical transformation" (1985:144).

In a more recent survey of new social movements, Calderón, Piscitelli, and Reyna (1992:19) insist that had they undertaken their study a quarter-century earlier, they would have focused on national liberation movements, national popular movements, and student, labor, and peasant struggles. They assert that in the contemporary period, "something different is unfolding. . . . The multiplicity of actors, themes, conflicts, and orientations is overwhelming" and that the questions raised by these new actors "have little to do with those we observed a quarter-century ago."

They go on to provide examples of the multiplicity of "new sociocultural actors who today produce our societies." These include Brazilian ecology activists, the Argentinean Mothers of the Plaza de Mayo, and the Chilean women who gained the recognition of civil society through their opposition to the authoritarian regime. The three authors also cite the Kataristas in the Bolivian *altiplano,* whom they characterize as "a peasant movement of an indigenous nature" that demands "ethnic autonomy, class transformation and affirmation of citizenship"; the São Paulo metalworkers who oppose "technocratic state policies" and critique the "effects of industrial automation . . . on workers' jobs and culture"; and the Rastafarians in the Caribbean, whose "political critique and cultural affirmation are expressed primarily through dance and music." Nor does this wide range of activities exhaust the authors' examples, which also include Mexicans and Peruvians struggling for the "democratization of micro-local urban territories," and even Sendero Luminoso, which they describe as a Peruvian mixture of millenarianism with authoritarian communism. This last movement is characterized by Calderón and associates as "absolute, cruel and disconcerting." However, they group Sendero among their examples of new social movements on the grounds that it "reflects the complex processes of exclusion and disintegration occurring in Peruvian society" (Calderón et al. 1992:20–23).

This brief survey of writings, which are themselves overviews of the subject, should give the reader an idea of the daunting task involved in establishing a broadly acceptable definition of new social movements. Confronted with the vast number and complexity of new movements, how are we to determine precisely which kinds of struggles are properly listed under this heading?

The widest area of agreement regarding these movements is expressed in the notion that they must be distinguished from what are generally referred to as traditional parties and unions. Moreover, it is usually assumed that the "new subjects" who participate in the new movements differ in some fundamental way from traditional political actors; either they are different people or they are the same people acting in different, more spontaneous, democratic, decentralized, and participatory ways. Furthermore, the activities of participants in new social movements are thought to unfold somewhere out in "civil society" or in the "realm of everyday life" rather than in what is normally conceived as the political arena (not to speak of the factory floor!). Movement activists are presumed to be responding in new ways to "new forms of subordination," and their struggles focus on the realm of consumption rather than production. "The common denominator of all the new social movements," writes Slater, citing Laclau and Mouffe, "would be their differentiation from workers' struggles, considered as 'class' struggles" (Slater 1985:3; Laclau and Mouffe 1985:159).

This much said, we can begin to appreciate the difficulty of squeezing all the movements listed by Evers, Henry, and Calderón and his coauthors into even the broadest definition of new social movements. Moreover, although the novelty of their approach and their distinction from traditional class-based struggles are widely accepted as two key characteristics of the new movements, we find students of the phenomenon constantly stretching the limits of even this loose definition. In fact, in the next section a more detailed look at specific cases will reveal that the new social movements are neither so new nor so isolated from class and partisan struggles as some have asserted.

The Link to Workers' and Party Struggles

Although there is almost perfect agreement among social movement theorists that such movements transcend traditional conflicts in the sphere of production and differ in some fundamental way from traditional interest groups and class-based organizations, some of the most interesting and significant struggles in recent times have taken place precisely at the point of intersection between trade unions and social movements. The Brazilian metalworkers are a case in point. Those who have analyzed this movement find a direct and logical link between the struggles of workers in the realm of production and those of neighborhood groups concerned with consumption issues. Lucio Kowarick (1985:86–89) argues that the "Brazilian miracle" was based on a strategy of exploiting labor in the factories and limiting the goods and services available to the urban poor. Thus, when Brazilian unions mobilize to fight the superexploitation of workers and the *bairro* associations protest the lack of social services, their activities can be said to "fuse" (Kowarick 1985:84). Collective action that brings together both forms of protest becomes, by definition, a common struggle on two fronts of the same battle against capitalist exploitation and the pauperization it requires (Kowarick 1985:88).

Likewise, the work of Maria Helena Moreira Alves (1984) focuses on the links forged between São Paulo's secular grassroots organizations, progressive Catholic ecclesiastical base communities, and independent trade unions. In her study of the mobilizations of the late 1970s and early 1980s, she shows that the neighborhood, or *favela,* associations often originated as part of the personalistic following of politicians intent on establishing clientalistic relations with the poor. Yet these organizations were transformed into genuine instruments for popular struggle when "the increased political consciousness of working-class members allowed slum dwellers to set up new associations and maintain a high degree of autonomous political action so as to escape the clientalistic ties of the past" (Moreira Alves 1984:77). In return, Moreira Alves finds that the social movements provided the workers with "a practical school for participatory democracy" that enabled them "to study the conditions that oppress them, to conduct and organize debates on matters that interest them, and come up with concrete alternative plans for development, for education, for health, and for union organization" (1984:100).

Yet another good example of a fruitful relationship between a trade union and a new social movement is the case of the Nineteenth of September Garment Workers Union, which developed out of the rubble of the 1985 Mexico City earthquakes that damaged or destroyed four hundred centers of garment production and left eight hundred workers dead and forty thousand unemployed. Teresa Carrillo (1990) shows how Mexican feminists managed to collaborate with female garment workers to build the first Mexican trade union (either independent or official party–linked) to be led by women: "In the garment workers' movement, feminist advisers have promoted a feminist discourse that attempts to move from 'female consciousness' to a type of popular feminism" (1990:231). Although the union has made only limited progress when measured in terms of contract negotiations, it has successfully developed a range of services including day care, health services, a job bank, a training center for women over forty, a popular education program, and some food distribution. Significantly, Carrillo notes that the union enjoys high visibility on a national and international level and "has taken a central role in initiating communication and collaboration among unionized women in Mexico," extending those linkages "to neighborhood associations and other independent organizations" (1990:231).

When we consider these experiences, the insistence of social movement purists that such movements are set outside the realm of class struggle begins to seem strained at best. The reality is that most social movements, like the traditional trade unions and parties from which they can be distinguished, respond to changing conditions in flexible ways. The movement that passionately eschews formal links with unions or political parties today may become engaged in enthusiastic campaign work if the right candidate were to appear tomorrow.

A case in point is the Asamblea de Barrios, a popular urban movement that grew out of the mobilization following the 1985 earthquakes in Mexico City. Initially formed by those left homeless in the disaster, the Asamblea outlived the emergency, expanded its membership, and began to organize poor urban people around the demand for affordable housing for slum dwellers in the center city and the extension of urban services—potable water, sewer lines, electricity, schools, clinics, and bus lines—to people living on the periphery of the Federal District. Although the Asamblea initially rejected any suggestion of involvement in partisan politics, once Cuauhtémoc Cárdenas emerged in 1988 as a progressive alternative to the continued rule of the official party (Institutional Revolutionary Party, or PRI), the Asamblea was quick to cast its lot with Cárdenas. Asamblea members campaigned for Cárdenas in the neighborhoods where the movement had painstakingly built support. Moreover, the opposition candidate was lent the prestige and support of Superbarrio, the Superman-like figure who has become the symbol of the struggle of the urban poor. Throughout the campaign, the masked man appeared with Cárdenas at major rallies around Mexico City, boosting the candidate's popular appeal. An observer of this process, Jaime Tamayo, writes: "The sudden politicization of these emergent social movements and their inclusion in Cardenismo's national project, has not so far affected their independence. Quite the contrary, it has allowed them to expand their intersectoral alliances without diminishing their autonomy" (1990:134).

The support lent to the Workers' Party (PT) by Brazilian social movements provides another clear example of an organic link between such movements and a party that has attracted a broad popular class base. Ilse Scherer-Warren describes the grassroots movements of São Paulo as a "transition" to expanded forms of popular expression or the "conquest of political space" (1987:48). For Scherer-Warren, the autonomy of new social movements from parties was a temporary situation. She argues that over the long run, grassroots movements in Brazil prepared their activists for political participation in the direct elections that were crucial in Brazil's transition from military rule to democracy. But the new parties of the Left retained the support of the new social movements they had won as electoral allies only by incorporating the movements' demands into their program for transformation. Scherer-Warren sees this process as the creation of a new political culture, a process through which the old pattern of authoritarianism could be broken.

These cases indicate that the situation of new social movements is more fluid than some theorists have appreciated. The deep distrust of unions, parties, and partisan politics that was often expressed by social movement activists in the late 1970s diminished, in many cases, by the end of the 1980s. To be sure, today many movements still fear absorption and demobilization when any kind of coalition with a political party is proposed (Hellman 1992:53–54). But the 1980s were marked by the steady immiserization of poor people under structural adjustment policies and also the weakening and marginalization of many parties of the Left throughout Latin America. Under these adverse circumstances, alliances between new movements and parties of the Left have come to look less sinister and problematic to the movements than was previously the case. Indeed, in Mexico, the fraud perpetrated by the official party in the 1988 elections brought even very independent, apolitical groups into a broad movement to protest the assumption of power by the PRI candidate, Carlos Salinas de Gortari. From that point on, most Mexican movements have, quite unproblematically, added electoral "transparency," that is, honesty in the conduct of elections, to their list of specific demands.

Moreover, even when new social movements remain aloof from partisan and union politics, they may, nonetheless, contain many characteristics that we might associate with class-based organizations. As we have noted, new social movements are generally defined as struggles that lie outside the realm of production. But the analyses, goals, and activities of some of these movements are, in fact, centered on the problem of access to, or control of, the means of production. This is particularly obvious in the case of rural mobilizations. For example, Calderón and his coauthors note that the Bolivian Katarista movement and the Union de Comuneros "Emiliano Zapata" based in Michoacán, Mexico, both call for communal autonomy and increased political participation, but also for "changes in the agricultural power structure" (Calderón et al.:21). What sorts of changes in the agricultural power structure are on the agenda of such movements? Normally they would include securing access to land and the means (water resources, agricultural credit, and technology) to work it productively. Surely these goals, central to virtually all peasant movements, correspond to the identity of the peasantry as a social class, even when they are combined with noneconomic, "cultural" demands the same people might make as an ethnically distinct, indigenous community.

Perhaps this point is most clearly illustrated by the problem of defining the 1994 rebellion in Chiapas, where the Zapatista Army of National Liberation (EZLN) burst on to the international scene on New Year's Day. The zapatistas' links to the progressive Catholic clergy and a broad range of national and international human and indigenous rights organizations have led many to view the EZLN as a new social movement. Moreover, the examination—if not to say deconstruction—of their published statements, in particular, the words of their principal spokesman, known as Subcomandante Marcos, have led many observers to underscore the distinction between the "discourse" of this group, and the "tired old rhetoric of the revolutionary Left." Citing the rebels' highly complex analysis and their sophisticated communication techniques, some have gone so far as to characterize the rebellion as the first "postmodern" peasant revolution. As a Mexican analyst, Gustavo Esteva, posed the question, "Is ours the last Central American guerrilla war, or has the new postmodern revolutionary era begun?" (Cockburn 1994:404).

Indeed, the zapatistas are careful to underscore their total autonomy from all existing political parties and organizations in Mexico; they call for cultural liberation as indigenous people and demand items like schools and health care facilities. In all these respects, the group seems to fit the definition of a new social movement. Yet the concentration of peasant land in the hands of large commercial owners lies at the heart of the struggle in Chiapas, and the movement grew directly from the alienation of the peasants of Chiapas from the means of production. Under the circumstances, if the *chiapanecos* constitute a new social movement in their concern with collective consumption, ethnic identity, and cultural survival, they must at the same time be seen as a class-based organization in which peasants are drawn together not only in ethnic solidarity but also in solidarity as a social class of agriculturists who have been despoiled of their lands.

It may be that June Nash (1989) is the analyst who has most clearly appreciated that culture and politics are often best understood as inextricably intertwined. In her study of the role of cultural resistance and class consciousness in Bolivian tin miners' communities, she writes, "The cultural roots of resistance to alien control can generate social movements that restructure the society, influencing the choice of timing for political acts of protest as well as the place and form in which rebellion arises." In the case of these industrial miners, Nash finds that beliefs and rituals surviving from precolonial periods "generate a sense of self that rejects subordination and repression" and that these historical ties are part and parcel of the class consciousness the miners develop as workers and trade unionists (1989:182).

How New Are the "New Movements"?

If the problem of determining which new social movements are genuinely social rather than political is considerable, even greater is the analytical challenge of determining which movements are really "new" and which are rooted in historical struggles of the past. As Frank and Fuentes (1989:179–180) note, "Social movements in the West, South and East that are commonly called 'new' are with few exceptions new forms of social movements which have existed through the ages." In his consideration of Mexican popular movements, Joe Foweraker writes:

> Deciding whether popular movements are a "new" political phenomenon is not merely a matter of weighing the historical evidence. The periodization of the movements is also an element of their definition. Thus, if the movements emerging after 1968 are new, then there has been some form of political rupture and things political are changing; if, on the other hand, they continue the popular political organization and practices of yesteryear, then politics itself is as usual. (1990:7)

In making this assessment, Foweraker has the good fortune to examine a case for which there is a clear cutoff date. The student movement of 1968, culminating in the regime's massacre of participants in the demonstration at the

Plaza of the Three Cultures on October 2, is widely understood to mark an indisputable watershed in Mexican history. As Foweraker argues, although every contemporary movement has historical forerunners, "the very accumulation of movements after 1968 works a qualitative change in the relationship between popular movements and the political system" (1990:7).

In the case of Mexico, the events of 1968 produced a generation of leaders who fanned out across the country and went on to organize new kinds of popular mobilizations in every corner of the republic. Thus, one way to recognize what is genuinely new in the Mexican context is to look for veterans of the 1968 movement in leadership roles. Another telltale sign is the presence of women, and Foweraker notes that "one specific indication of the novelty of the phenomenon is the important role played by women in the post-1968 popular movements" where the mass base is female, "even if their leadership is still mainly male" (1990:7).

But even in the case of Mexico, where the task is simplified by the existence of a broadly accepted periodization of movements, we still face the problem of whether we should label as novel movements that strive to construct "new identities" that are, in fact, rooted in the past. In particular, this dilemma arises with respect to indigenous movements that look to precolonial times to find the structures they propose as the framework for a new kind of community. Indeed, this can be said of *indigenista* movements everywhere in Latin America. And the Rastafarians enthusiastically cited by Calderón and his coauthors (1992) as an example of a new movement are, in fact, engaging in an exercise in identity politics that can be traced to the Back-to-Africa movement of Marcus Garvey in the 1920s, if not beyond to the slave rebellions and the Maroon communities of the seventeenth and eighteenth centuries.

In my own consideration of Mexican movements (Hellman 1994b), I have been struck more by the continuity rather than by the elements of rupture with the past. In comparing the independent peasant organizations I studied in the late 1960s with contemporary movements, I have noted that neither the fundamental goals nor the strategies and tactics of the rural movements have altered markedly and that this continuity undoubtedly reflects the agonizingly slow pace of change in the Mexican political system. The strategy of the old organizations—like that of the new—was to establish themselves as a force with which to be reckoned on the local and, eventually, the national scene, and ultimately to wrest concessions from the state. The techniques applied before 1968 were not so different from the mobilizational and pressure tactics used by movements today—although to hear all the excited talk about "new practices," a student of new movements could be forgiven for feeling some confusion on this point. Demonstrations, sit-ins, hunger marches to the capital, petitions, and letter-writing campaigns were the tactics the old movements employed. Then as now, group members were assembled, marched, or trucked (banners flying) to the Zócalo, the president's official residence, or the appropriate government agency. There they would remain—a public embarrassment to the regime—until they were received by some government functionary who promised to address, if not redress, their grievances.

To be sure, a whole new repertoire of protest (Tilly 1978, 1986; Tarrow 1991, 1994) has been added to the old, including the production of a countercultural pop-culture figure like Superbarrio, who embodies the goals of the have-nots of Mexican society, or the ski masks worn by the rebels in Chiapas, which have become an important symbol of resistance appearing on the heads of popular demonstrators throughout Mexico. Furthermore, today urban popular protesters outnumber those who arrive in the capital from the countryside, and contemporary protesters are more likely to address themselves to public opinion through the media—particularly the international media—than exclusively to the agents of the Mexican state. Indeed, referring to what he calls the "fabric of struggle," Harry Cleaver argues that "the most striking thing about the sequence of events set in motion on January 1, 1994, [was] the speed with which the news of the struggle circulated and the rapidity of the mobilization of support which resulted" (1994). The rapid diffusion of the zapatistas' demands and reports of their activities through computer communication networks like Peacenet or Usenet meant that information about the struggle was immediately "collected, sorted, compiled, and sometimes synthesized and rediffused," thus linking large numbers of potential supporters around the world.

However, notwithstanding the novelty of this repertoire of protest, on balance, at least for students of Mexico, it is far easier to discern signs of historical continuity with respect to the symbols and goals of protest than to find evidence of a clear break with the past (Knight 1990). After all, the Chiapan zapatistas, with their electronic linkups to world opinion, their skillful management of CNN and the *New York Times* correspondents, and their production of glossy, four-color pamphlets for distribution as press releases may be testing new approaches and new limits of protest in Mexico. But they are still zapatistas, articulating demands not much different from those voiced in 1915 by the original zapatistas as they rode through the mountains of Morelos behind their leader, Emiliano Zapata.

Still, if much of what goes on today in Mexico, or elsewhere in Latin America and the Caribbean, is rooted in past struggles, clearly there are also developments that can properly be seen as new. For example, women have long participated in popular mobilizations in Latin America, and the celebration of motherhood has always been part of Hispano-American culture. But the redefinition of motherhood as a political responsibility and the transfer of the mother's role from the private to the public sphere, where this identity may become a weapon of struggle, is unquestionably a new phenomenon.

This novel conception of women's role developed in the 1970s during the period of totalitarian military rule in the Southern Cone, and it subsequently spread throughout the region (Feijoo 1989; Perelli 1989; Schirmer 1993).

Moreover, some movements that have emerged in recent years have few or no historical precedents. To be sure, Jean Meyer (1973–1974) has argued that the activities of the ecclesiastical communities of the base in Mexico can be traced to the rabble-rousing priests of the Mexican independence movement or the "social Catholicism" of the immediate prerevolutionary and revolutionary period (cited in Knight 1990:88–89), and undoubtedly historians may uncover other links with the past in other Latin American countries. However, the CEBs, in their most democratic, participatory form, represent a genuinely novel experience that would not have been possible before Pope John XXIII, Vatican II, and liberation theology came on the scene. Likewise, the spread of feminism, gay rights, and ecology movements through Latin America marks a new chapter in the development of protest (Escobar and Alvarez 1992). Human rights as a transnational concern in which domestic and foreign activists work together to influence international public opinion is not only new in its conception but also, like the feminist, gay, and green movements, relies on a network of international communication that has become feasible only in the computer age. It is worth noting that on January 1, 1994, an estimated 260 Mexican and international nongovernmental organizations had some kind of presence in Chiapas, Mexico's most remote, communication-deprived region. Thus, the internationalization of social movement struggles in the form of the collaborative presence of foreign nongovernmental organizations in the *barriadas* of Lima, the backlands of Brazil, or the town squares of Chiapas has, for better or worse, transformed the way in which popular movements theorize, strategize, and carry out their activities.

Under the circumstances, the question of novelty turns out to be at least as complicated as the search for a clear, delimiting definition of new social movements. Perhaps the trickiest question of all, however, is not who or what new social movements are, but what it is they *do*. The final section, then, focuses on the knotty problem of assessing the goals and impact of the movements—or at least the claims that are made for them by their analysts.

What New Social Movements Do

The claims regarding the potential and the accomplishments of new social movements fall roughly into three categories: the first is that they transform the consciousness of participants; the second, that they win concrete concessions for movement activists; and the third, that they play a key role in the process of democratization that is supposed to be unfolding throughout Latin America.

The first assertion is perhaps the most difficult to argue persuasively because, abundant as the anecdotal evidence may be, there is no agreed-on way to demonstrate, let alone measure, the dimensions of the changes that are brought about in the participants' subjective feelings about themselves as political or social actors. I myself collected many such narratives in the course of my research among Mexican neighborhood activists (Hellman 1994a). More or less typical of the evidence provided in such interviews would be the statement made to me by an activist in the Asamblea de Barrios who described the changes she underwent in the course of her participation. She explained:

> I learned about politics. I even learned how to talk about sex without embarrassment. I learned so many things I never knew before. Most important, I learned how to deal with people, to talk to people. And now I know how to get more information out of the people who really know what's going on. I learned that only when we unite do we achieve anything. (Hellman 1994a:20)

The experience related to me by this woman is the kind of transformation generally described by other social movement analysts as "empowerment." Typically the term is used to refer to women who emerge from the private, isolated sphere of the home to participate in collective mobilizations around consumption issues. Nikki Craske (1993:112), for example, draws a comparison between Mexican women organized within the PRI's co-optive structures and others who are active in an independent neighborhood group. Craske finds that women in the latter "show greater knowledge of political institutions and the political system, and they are more confident regarding their ability to take on power positions, both personal and institutional; that is, they feel empowered by their experience."

From this statement, one may draw the inference that empowerment has to do with increased knowledge about politics combined in some way with growing personal confidence, and perhaps even a greater sense of control over one's life. However, although the literature on new movements is replete with references to empowerment, virtually no one has paused to define the concept, nor is there agreement on exactly how an empowered person differs from someone who has not undergone this transformative process. In short, although Marx provided some guiding principles to predict when a worker could be said to have acquired "worker's consciousness" (Miliband 1977: 31–33), nothing comparable exists in the world of social movement studies. Thus, although there is a broad consensus that important forms of learning and attitude change occur when the new subjects join the new movements, beyond these vague assertions, we have no intersubjective indicators of what those changes are, and Craske is one of the few analysts who has even attempted to establish a baseline from which the changes could be traced.

This lack of precision just about forces us back into the arms of Almond and Verba (1965) and other behavioralist political scientists of the 1960s

who at least provided definitions—like them or not—for what they called
"political cognition" and the growth of a sense of political efficacy or political competence. Ironically, it may be that these are the terms—rather than
the constitution of new subjects and subjectivities—that come closest to providing a conceptual vocabulary with which social movement analysts might
meaningfully express their observations regarding the transformation of consciousness undergone by the new actors.

A second claim made for social movements is that they win key concessions
for their adherents. Ironically, this is the area of organizational achievement
that receives the least attention because it appears to be the one that most em-
barrasses social movement analysts (Hellman 1992:55–56). In reality, new
movements often do realize many of their concrete goals, winning for their
members the material goods and services they desperately need. But inasmuch
as movements often obtain these concessions only by compromising their independence vis-à-vis the state, the literature on social movements devotes far
less attention to the specifics of organizations' material victories than to their
consciousness-raising or democratizing potential. Yet, although for theorists
the extraction of output from the state may be the least important achievement of a new movement, for the participants themselves this is often, if not
to say usually, the central issue (Hellman 1994b). As Paul Haber points out in
his study of the Committee for Popular Defense (CDP) in Durango, Mexico:

> The ability to deliver goods and extract concessions from the state, combined
> with inspirational ideological positions articulated by a competent and ideally
> charismatic leadership, is the winning combination for most, if not all Mexican
> [urban popular movements]. Many CDP members are first or second genera-
> tion immigrants from rural Durango and most have very low incomes and little
> or no formal education. Within the political culture of the CDP, as is true else-
> where in low-income urban barrios throughout Mexico . . . participation in de-
> cision-making is simply not valued as much as the demonstrated ability to ex-
> tract governmental concessions and services. (1990:234)

The third area of potential achievement for new social movements is the
one that has generated perhaps the greatest interest among analysts. Social
movements are often posited as having an important contribution to make to
the overall process of democratization in Latin America. In general, students
of the transition in South America have emphasized the movements' "democratizing impact on political culture and daily life," and much attention
has been focused on the way in which "grassroots democratic practices [are]
transferred into the realm of political institutions and the state" (Alvarez and
Escobar 1991).

Women's movements, in particular, have been studied in relation to democratization. For example, Jane Jaquette identified as the central question of her
collection "the role of women and of feminism in the transition from authori-

tarian to democratic politics" (1989:1). The place of women in the defeat of authoritarian regimes in Argentina, Brazil, and Chile has, in fact, attracted a great deal of attention to the democratizing aspect of women's struggles. Indeed, a more recent collection of writings on Latin American women that, in fact, covers a much broader range of questions regarding women's political participation, carries a publisher's advertisement on the back jacket that shouts in bold letters: "WHAT ARE THE 'NEW POLITICS' OF LATIN AMERICA? HOW HAVE WOMEN SHAPED THE DEMOCRATIZING PROCESS?" (Radcliffe and Westwood 1993). This marketing approach on the part of Routledge is reiterated in the introductory chapter of many dissertations produced in the same period; the presumed connection between democratization and new social movements often serves to justify concern with the latter.

However, although it is relatively easy to demonstrate the relationship between new movements and the consolidation of democracy in some South American countries, elsewhere in Latin America the connection is not nearly so strong. Moreover, some analysts tend to conflate the internal dynamics of movements with their impact on the political system as a whole. In fact, there is an important distinction to be drawn between a movement's internal practices (which may or may not be more open, less hierarchical, and more participatory than those of traditional political formations) and its capacity to push the whole political system in that direction. As Boschi writes:

> The literature on the new social movements suggests that the attainment of democratic processes and structures flows naturally from pressures toward democratization expressed by the movements in their initial, formative stages. The problem here is twofold. In the first place, there is the issue of assessing whether it is true that the movements' framework really assures more democratic relations internally. Second, and more problematic, is the relation between democratic relations at a non-institutional level (assuming that they in fact prevail) and democratization at the politico-institutional level. (1984:8)

Boschi concludes that although the movements may "allow for some degree of internal democracy at some point of their trajectory, . . . democratization of social relations does not necessarily entail democratization at the institutional level of politics" (1984:8).

A good illustration of this point can be found in the case of Uruguay. Writing on new movements there, Eduardo Canel (1992) finds that the grassroots groups that arose during the eleven years of military dictatorship went into decline shortly after the return to democracy in 1984. Although many observers thought of the movements as "embryos of new, more democratic social practices, with the potential to transform power relations in daily life" and assumed that they would "play a central role in the process of constructing a . . . qualitatively more democratic society," in fact, the restoration of civilian rule in Uruguay was marked by the return of the most traditional forms of party-based political activity. "In this context," writes Canel, "grass-roots activities declined and many of the new organizations disappeared or were assimilated into more traditional ones. The hope of establishing a new way of doing politics did not materialize and the country missed a good opportunity to develop a more open and democratic political system" (1992: 276–277).

In Mexico expectations that the burgeoning social movement sector would find ways to exert pressure for a more open, participatory system (Foweraker and Craig 1992) have come to seem overly optimistic. Although Mexican social movements are numerous, varied, and strong, their democratizing influence, as I have argued elsewhere (Hellman 1994b), has been very modest indeed. A number of different reasons could explain their lack of influence. We might look at the institutional reform process itself: the snail's pace at which it has proceeded and the priority given to economic over political reform in the Salinas administration (1988–1994). We might focus on the official party's control over the means of communication, the undiminished capacity of the regime to play off elements of the Left against one another, or the increased recourse to repression that has marked the Salinas years (Amnesty International 1991; Americas Watch 1990).

However, the characteristic of the Mexican movements that I would identify as most significant in explaining their inability to play a more dynamic role in the push for democracy is their tendency to fall squarely into the logic of clientelism that has always guided the political strategies and tactics not only of the official party organizations but of Mexican opposition movements as well. These movements are, in fact, deeply enmeshed in clientelistic patterns from which they escape only very rarely. Although the emergence of a new movement may challenge the old PRI-linked networks based on *caciques* (rural political bosses), it usually undermines the control of the *caciques* only by replacing the old networks with alternative channels that, generally speaking, are also clientelistic in their mode of operation. In short, the Mexican movements are shaped by the broader political context in which they develop, and that context is one of patronage politics and clientelism.

Under the circumstances, the study of Mexican cases suggests that there is nothing deterministic about the relationship of new movements to the process of democratization. A movement's own practices may be more open and inclusionary—although often they are not (Hellman 1994b:133–135). But even when a movement is more participatory and democratic in its internal structures, it does not necessarily change the system simply by making demands on it. On the contrary, social movement demands may, in fact, reinforce the system of control. This was certainly the case when the Salinas regime (in line with World Bank recommendations) strategically spread around the largesse provided by PRONASOL (National Solidarity Program) of government handouts to the "poorest of the poor." The administration's plan was to meet the demands of independently organized groups in such a fashion as to demobilize the movements and attach (or reattach) the loyalty of movement activists to the official party and the regime.

If Mexico offers a clear example of the conditioning, delimiting effects of the political context, so, too, does Guatemala. In his analysis of Guatemalan social movements, Marco Fonseca (1994) notes that the very emergence of popular organizations in countries like Guatemala is commonly taken as a signal that some kind of "real" democratization is occurring at the grassroots that should stimulate a process of "democratization from above." However, he asserts that, were this the case, "then Guatemala should have already achieved an unparalleled level of democratic development . . . given the fact that popular organizations have been 'emerging' and filling the country's limited political openings and spaces for at least the past thirty years" (Fonseca 1994:3).

Instead, what Fonseca finds is a social movement sector deeply influenced by the specific political context of Guatemalan society, which is characterized chiefly by what he calls "oligarchismo," or patterns of collective activity that are "male-dominated, largely confrontational, violent, and exclusionary." It is this "normative framework of political action" that shapes new social movements in Guatemala, even as it shapes the traditional formations of the Left and Right. Thus, just as Mexican opposition movements reflect the clientalistic nature of the political context in which they arise, in Guatemala Fonseca finds that "revolutionary and popular organizations have reproduced the oligarchic patterns prevalent in the overall sociocultural environment and in public/civic relations" (1994:5).

Because social movements do not arise in a vacuum, they are to some degree products of the political context in which they grow. Under the circumstances it may be disappointing, but it is not surprising that social movements do not manage to democratize the system in every case. Thus, notwithstanding our wishes to the contrary, popular movements do not necessarily bring about an opening of the political system. As Boschi (1984:9) has noted in the case of Brazilian neighborhood movements, the striking thing is not how radical is the influence of new social movements but rather "how little change they bring about in existing institutional formats."

The Future of New Movements

If the new movements do not, in all cases, function to democratize the system as a whole, this is not to say that they have no positive role to perform. The greatest potential of the movements may well lie in the alliances that many analysts and movement activists have previously identified as a threat to movement survival (Hellman 1992:53–54).

The preoccupation with the difference between movements and parties—a preoccupation that has sometimes troubled theorists more than activists—

has come by the mid-1990s to seem an exaggerated concern. Social movements may not be able to transform the political system as a whole, as some analysts had hoped. But in key historical moments they can link up with other formations: other movements and even progressive partisan forces, such as the Workers' Party in Brazil or Cárdenas's Party of the Democratic Revolution (PRD) in Mexico. Moreover, this kind of alliance may be forged in ways that strengthen both the party and the movement.

That social movements can, with relative ease, establish alliances among themselves has been demonstrated by the growth of *coordinadoras,* that is, coordinating committees and other umbrella organizations that allow a wide assortment of movements to join forces around common goals. That they can do this in ways that permit individual movements to retain their distinctive identity has also been demonstrated in practice. Even groups that begin with very antiorganizational values frequently end up establishing links among themselves for their mutual benefit and protection.

In a period like the present, when progressive forces—both social and political—are under attack from the Right, it seems reasonable to predict that alliance strategies may well gain momentum. Distinctions between class-based organizations and social movements have been a focus of this chapter. It is precisely these differences that are increasingly likely to be set aside as social movements of all descriptions form links with independent trade unions and progressive political parties to defend their achievements of the past and to push forward, however haltingly, with a project of economic redistribution, social justice, and perhaps even democratization.

References

Almond, Gabriel A., and Sidney Verba. *The Civic Culture.* Boston: Little, Brown, 1965.

Alvarez, Sonia E., and Arturo Escobar. "New Social Movements in Latin America: Identity, Strategy and Democracy." Panel proposal, Latin American Studies Association Meetings, Washington, DC, 1991.

Americas Watch. *Human Rights in Mexico: A Policy of Impunity.* New York: Americas Watch, 1990.

Amnesty International. *Torture with Impunity.* London: Amnesty International, 1991.

Boschi, Renato. "On Social Movements and Democratization: Theoretical Issues." *Stanford-Berkeley Occasional Papers in Latin American Studies,* no. 9 (Spring 1984):1–17.

Calderón, Fernando, Alejandro Piscitelli, and José Luis Reyna. "Social Movements: Actors, Theories, Expectations," in Arturo Escobar and Sonia E. Alvarez, eds., *New Social Movements in Latin America: Identity, Strategy, and Democracy.* Boulder, CO: Westview Press, 1992, 19–36.

Canel, Eduardo. "Democratization and the Decline of Urban Social Movements in Uruguay: A Political-Institutional Account." In Arturo Escobar and Sonia E. Alvarez, eds., *New Social Movements in Latin America: Identity, Strategy, and Democracy*. Boulder, CO: Westview Press, 1992, 276–290.

Carrillo, Teresa. "Women and Independent Unionism in the Garment Industry," in Joe Foweraker and Ann L. Craig, eds., *Popular Movements and Political Change in Mexico*. Boulder, CO: Lynne Rienner Publishers, 1990, 213–233.

Cleaver, Harry. "The Chiapas Uprising and the Future of Class Struggle in the New World Order." Unpublished English-language draft of an article for *Riff-Raff*, Padora, Italy, February 1994.

Cockburn, Alexander. "Chiapas and the Americas." *Nation*, 28 March 1994, 404.

Craske, Nikki. "Women's Political Participation in Colonias Populares in Guadalajara, Mexico," in Sarah A. Radcliffe and Sallie Westwood, eds., *Viva: Women and Popular Protest in Latin America*. London: Routledge, 1993, 112–135.

Escobar, Arturo, and Sonia E. Alvarez, eds. *New Social Movements in Latin America: Identity, Strategy and Democracy*. Boulder, CO: Westview Press, 1992.

Evers, Tilman. "Identity: The Hidden Side of New Social Movements in Latin America," in David Slater, ed., *New Social Movements and the State in Latin America*. Amsterdam: CEDLA, 1985.

Feijoó, María del Carmen. "The Challenge of Constructing Civilian Peace: Women and Democracy in Argentina," in Jane S. Jaquette, ed., *The Women's Movement in Latin America: Feminism and the Transition to Democracy*. Boston: Unwin Hyman, 1989, 72–94.

Fonseca, Marco. "Guatemala's Popular Movements and the Process of Democratization." Unpublished paper delivered at York University, Toronto, April 1994.

Foweraker, Joe. "Popular Movements and Political Change in Mexico," in Joe Foweraker and Ann L. Craig, eds., *Popular Movements and Political Change in Mexico*. Boulder: Lynne Rienner Publishers, 1990, 3–20.

Frank, André Gunder and Marta Fuentes. "Ten Theses on Social Movements." *World Development* 17, 2 (1989):179–189.

Haber, Paul Lawrence. "Cárdenas, Salinas, y Los Movimientos Populares Urbanos en México: El Caso del Comité de Defensa Popular, General Francisco Villa de Durango," in Sergio Zermeño and Aurelio Cuevas, eds., *Movimientos Sociales en México*. Mexico, Federal District: Universidad Nacional Autonoma de México, 1990, 221–252.

Hecht, Susanna. "Chico Mendes: Chronicle of a Death Foretold." *New Left Review*, no. 173 (January/February 1989):47–55.

Hellman, Judith Adler. "The Study of New Social Movements in Latin America and the Question of Autonomy," in Arturo Escobar and Sonia E. Alvarez, eds., *New Social Movements in Latin America: Identity, Strategy and Democracy*. Boulder, CO: Westview Press, 1992, 52–61.

———. *Mexican Lives*. New York: New Press, 1994a.

———. Mexican Popular Movements, Clientelism, and the Process of Democratization." in *Latin American Perspectives* 21, 2 (Spring 1994b):124–142.

Henry, Etienne. "Urban Social Movements in Latin America—Towards a Critical Understanding," in David Slater, ed., *New Social Movements and the State in Latin America*. Amsterdam: CEDLA, 1985, 127–145.

Jaquette, Jane S., ed. *The Women's Movement in Latin America: Feminism and the Transition to Democracy*. Boston: Unwin Hyman, 1989.

Knight, Alan. "Historical Continuities in Social Movements," in Joe Foweraker and Ann L. Craig, eds., *Popular Movements and Political Change in Mexico*. Boulder, CO: Lynne Rienner Publishers, 1990, 78–102.

Kowarick, Lucio. "The Pathways to Encounter: Reflections on the Social Struggle in São Paulo," in David Slater, ed., *New Social Movements and the State in Latin America*. Amsterdam: CEDLA, 1985, 73–93.

Laclau, Ernesto, and Chantal Mouffe. *Hegemony and Socialist Strategy: Toward a Radical Democratic Politics*. London: Verso Books, 1985.

Levine, Daniel H., and Scott Mainwaring. "Religion and Popular Protest in Latin America: Contrasting Experiences," in Susan Eckstein, ed., *Power and Popular Protest: Latin American Social Movements*. Berkeley: University of California Press, 1989, 203–240.

Maxwell, Kenneth. "The Mystery of Chico Mendes." *New York Review of Books* 38, 6 (March 28, 1991):39–48.

Meyer, Jean. *La Cristiada*, 3 vols. Mexico, Federal District: Siglo Veintiuno Editores, 1973–1974.

Miliband, Ralph. *Marxism and Politics*. Oxford: Oxford University Press, 1977.

Moreira Alves, Maria Helena. "Grassroots Organizations, Trade Unions, and the Church: A Challenge to the Controlled Abertura in Brazil." *Latin American Perspectives* 40 (Winter 1984):73–102.

Nash, June. "Cultural Resistance and Class Consciousness in Bolivian Tin-Mining Communities," in Susan Eckstein, ed., *Power and Popular Protest: Latin American Social Movements*. Berkeley: University of California Press, 1989, 182–202.

Perelli, Carina. "Putting Conservatism to Good Use: Women and Unorthodox Politics in Uruguay, from Breakdown to Transition," in Jane S. Jaquette, ed., *The Women's Movement in Latin America: Feminism and the Transition to Democracy*. Boston: Unwin Hyman, 1989.

Radcliffe, Sarah A., and Sallie Westwood. eds. *Viva: Women and Popular Protest in Latin America*. London: Routledge, 1993.

Scherer-Warren, Ilse. "O carater dos novos movimentos socais," in Ilse Scherer-Warren and Paulo J. Krischke, eds., *Uma Revolucão no Cotidiano? Os Novos Movimentos Socais na América do Sul*. São Paulo: Editora Brasiliense, 1987, 35–53.

Schirmer, Jennifer. "The Seeking of Truth and the Gendering of Consciousness: The Comadres of El Salvador and the Conavigua Widows of Guatemala," in Sarah A. Radcliffe and Sallie Westwood, eds., *Viva: Women and Popular Protest in Latin America*. London: Routledge, 1993, 30–64.

Slater, David, ed. *New Social Movements and the State in Latin America*. Amsterdam: CEDLA, 1985a.

———. "Social Movements and a Recasting of the Political," in David Slater, ed., *New Social Movements and the State in Latin America*. Amsterdam: CEDLA, 1985b, 1–25.

Tamayo, Jaime. "Neoliberalism Encounters Neocardenism," in Joe Foweraker and Ann L. Craig, eds., *Popular Movements and Political Change in Mexico*. Boulder, CO: Lynne Rienner Publishers, 1990, 121–136.

Tarrow, Sidney. *Struggle, Politics, and Reform: Collective Action, Social Movements, and Cycles of Protest*. Western Societies Program Occasional Paper no. 21 (2d ed.), Center for International Studies. Ithaca, NY: Cornell University, 1991.

————. *Power in Movement: Collective Action, Social Movements, and Politics.* New York: Cambridge University Press, 1994.

Tilly, Charles. *From Mobilization to Revolution.* Englewood Cliffs, NJ: Prentice-Hall, 1978.

————. *The Contentious French.* Cambridge: Harvard University Press. 1986.

7

Latin American Women and the Search for Social, Political, and Economic Transformation

FRANCESCA MILLER

One of the most striking phenomenons of the past two decades is the extent to which the central concerns of contemporary life—access to housing, employment, health care, freedom from violence, full citizenship for all people, preservation of the environment—are being effectively articulated by women. Historically, women activists in Latin America, while insisting on the validity and specificity of the female experience, have posited their work as part of the search for social, economic, and political justice for all people. This chapter focuses on the history of women's activism as influenced by and exerting influence on contemporary social movements. Theoretical insights will emerge from my comparison of Latin American women's movements as they developed in specific historical contexts; considerations of class and ethnicity as well as of gender inform the analysis.

In the mid-1990s a focus on women in Latin America reveals the profound changes that have occurred in the region in the past forty years. Far more women now live in urban areas—many in and around megacities such as São Paulo, Buenos Aires, Mexico D.F. (Federal District)—than live in rural regions. Between 1970 and 1990 the number of women employed in the formal economy rose by 83 percent in all regions of Latin America ex cept the Caribbean (Valdés and Gomariz 1993). Access to education for girls has risen steadily since 1950. In Mexico and Brazil the number of chil dren a woman will bear in a lifetime has dropped by half; in Cuba, Venezuela,

Uruguay, Costa Rica, birth rates are comparable to those in southern Europe. Additionally, although most Latin American women may be described as culturally Catholic, their day-to-day lives are imbued with a secular worldview that is reinforced by global communications, internal and international migration, and increased personal autonomy and mobility.

But such a profile masks deep regional variations both within nations and from one country to another. With 150 million people, Brazil is the largest and most populous of Latin American nations. If statistics are taken from Brazil's industrialized central south, female education and employment levels are comparable to those of Colombia, Mexico, Venezuela, and Chile. But if the calculations are derived from the country's north and northeast, they resemble those of Peru and Ecuador, where infant mortality and fertility rates are the highest in South America.

More important, the pattern of greater female involvement in the formal labor force, a pattern driven at least in part by deteriorating standards of living brought about by the crippling inflation and government responses to the international debt pressures of the 1980s, exists simultaneously with the growth in concrete numbers of women whose economic status is precarious in the extreme. In the 1990s an estimated 130 million women and children, living primarily in the urban periphery—*pueblos jóvenes, favelas, barrios pobres*—are attempting to eke out a daily living in the informal economy as petty vendors, laundresses, and part-time domestics.

The present situation raises the following central questions: What do the ongoing changes—many of which are linked to the internationalization of the economy—portend for women and their families? Does the entry of women into the paid labor force in unprecedented numbers indicate not the promise of greater economic and personal independence for women but the "atomization of the labor force" and "deteriorating conditions" for all workers (Fernández-Kelly 1993)? What role are Latin American women playing in trying to shape the future? The issues that women are identifying as central to their present and future circumstances are visible in the focus of the hundreds of women's organizations—local, national, transnational—that are a hallmark of contemporary Latin America. The history of these organizing efforts offers us an understanding of their potential for the future.

A Sense of Place

Every observer of Latin America soon learns that the term "Latin America" serves more to obscure than to illuminate an understanding of the thirty-odd countries and dozen territories that lie between the Rio Grande in the north and Tierra del Fuego in the south. Similarly, it is soon discovered that there is no single type of Latin American woman. Factors of time and place, class, race, ethnicity, age, and marital status, among others, are important considerations whether these women are Mexican, Brazilian, Haitian, or Guyanese and who would not necessarily be able to speak to one another as their respective national tongues are Spanish, Portuguese, French, and English. Moreover, it is not unlikely that a Guatemalan woman's first language might be Maya or Quiché, not Spanish, that a woman of the Andes might speak only Quechua; a woman of the Amazon, a Tupí dialect.

The classical understanding of the peopling of the Americas is built on the deeply sexual metaphor of the "Contact Period," when seafaring European men encountered the indigenous women of Middle, Central, and South America to produce a "new race." The story of Malinche/Malintzin (1504?–1528), a Tabascan woman given as tribute to conquistador Hernán Cortés, who through her knowledge of languages subsequently played a pivotal role in the Spanish overthrow of the Aztec regime in central Mexico, became a founding myth of modern Mexico. But this paradigm ignores the presence of French, Spanish, and Portuguese women who began to arrive as early as 1498 and leaves out women, both free and slave, who came to the Americas from sub-Saharan Africa.

Additionally, since the late nineteenth century the large Latin American nations have received successive waves of immigrants from Europe and Asia. Spanish, Portuguese, Italian, and German immigrants settled in significant numbers in Mexico, Argentina, Uruguay, Chile, and southern Brazil. Brazil has the largest number of citizens of Japanese descent of any nation other than the United States or Japan itself. Koreans, Chinese, and Southeast Asians have emigrated to Brazil and other Latin American nations. In the past forty years, immigrants from India, Pakistan, Syria, Lebanon, Iran, and Iraq have made their way to South America. Though in some cases the first immigrant generation settled in rural areas, the daughters and granddaughters of these European, Asian, and Middle Eastern immigrants live in the cities and should be understood as Latin American women.

Recent research challenges many long-held preconceptions about the roles women played in colonial society (Lavrin 1989; Seed 1988). Distinctions of class, racial heritage, and ethnicity were sharply reinforced by an economy that rested on the institution of forced labor. Prior to the contact period, female roles in indigenous societies varied as widely as did the societies themselves: Women were priestesses, physicians, agricultural laborers, artisans, market vendors, prostitutes, and slaves. The degree to which the customs of the indigenous peoples were disrupted by colonization was dependent on the extent of contact.

Family, church, and state were the central institutions that governed colonial life, especially for Iberian and mestiza women, though the Catholic Church touched all sectors of society through conversion and in the rituals of baptism, confirmation, marriage, and burial. The church determined social mores and reinforced the strictures that propertied families placed on their daughters, for whom marriage or a religious vocation were the respectable choices. The image of the cloistered upper-class Iberian woman, however, must be balanced against examples of the upper-class woman who actively participated in the economy by running large estates and overseeing complex familial business affairs. Similarly, the diverse experiences of poor women should not be subsumed under blanket assumptions that differentiate her life from that of her male counterpart only by her biologic functions.

Women of African descent were present in every region of the Americas. In Brazil, where slavery was not finally abolished until 1888, female slaves were found in larger concentrations in urban areas, working in households or earning money for their owners as street vendors, wet nurses, craftswomen, or prostitutes. To the extent that their particular situation enabled them to do so, they kept alive their religious and cultural practices and deeply influenced the formative national cultures in Brazil, the Caribbean, Colombia, and Venezuela.

One of the best-known women of the colonial era is Sor Juana Inés de la Cruz (1648–1695), who is considered to be one of the greatest lyric poets ever to write in Spanish. Because of her status as a great woman, an exception, Sor Juana cannot be used as an example of women in colonial Latin America. But perhaps the point is that no woman can be, whether she is a domestic slave of Afro-Brazilian heritage in Salvador, Brazil; an Aymará woman of the Bolivian Andes whose male kin are taken by the Spanish to work the silver mines; the mestiza wife of a cattle rancher in northern Mexico; or the illegitimate daughter of a Creole mother, as was Sor Juana, born Juana Ramirez de Azbaje. But it is with a sense of this rich and diverse heritage that the contemporary history of Latin American women must be approached.

Historically the voices of women activists in Latin America have articulated ideas that have driven forward a politics of inclusion. This is traceable in the nineteenth-century push for the education of women, which, in the twentieth century, was articulated as the drive for universal education. It is visible in the history of universal suffrage, despite the ofttimes limited intentions of the early woman suffragists and their male allies.

The following metaphor invoked by a Chilean woman at the IV Encuentro Feminista Latinoamericano y del Caribe (Fourth Feminist Encounter of Latin America and the Caribbean), which convened in Taxco, Mexico, October 19–25, 1987, is apt:

> I think that, from the most radical feminism, deeply transformative ideas have emerged. The early feminists gave the first kick to the soccer ball, the ball is now circulating through the field and is not always controlled by the players themselves and the score is sometimes scored by people who hadn't been participating, but who suddenly succeed in passing a law. On the one hand, the feminist

movement appears to be marginal, but on the other, it is obvious that it has permeated everything. (*Off our backs*, March, 1988:2)

Women and National Formation

The issue of full citizenship for women and access to education for girls was raised in the immediate aftermath of the Wars of Independence (1790–1823). An 1824 petition presented to the government of Zacatecas, Mexico, states: "Women also wish to have the title of citizen . . . to see themselves counted in the census as *una ciudadana*" (Enciclopedia de Mexico, 1970). Women patriots were vital to the success of the independence movements. The histories of these women were used at the time to rouse patriotic fervor. In later years, Latin American women pointed to the patriotism of their precursors in the effort to claim their own right to civil, political, and economic independence.

A central arena for the debate of women's role in the new nations took place around the issue of education. In the struggle between secular and liberal values and religious corporatist politics that marked the nineteenth century, who would educate young women was played out among Catholic female teaching orders, independent dames' schools, and the new public schools, which were established to impart a modicum of learning along with household skills to poor young women.

Women who founded girls' schools were among the first voices calling for women's rights in Latin America. The periodical or political journal first appeared as a central forum for the public debate of women's issues in Latin America in the early nineteenth century. Argentine writer Juana Manuela Gorriti founded *La Alborada del Plata* (1850), which engaged in the intense international debate surrounding women's role in the modern state. Juana Manso, while in exile from Argentina in Brazil, founded *O Jornal de Senhoras*, which dealt primarily with the discussion of female education and politics. Similar journals appeared in Mexico—*La Semana de las Señoritas Mejicanas* (1851–1852); Cuba—*Album Cubano de lo Bueno y lo Bello* (founded in 1860 by Gertrudis Gomez de Avellaneda); Peru and Bolivia—*El Album* (1860s); and elsewhere (Stoner 1989). The linkage of the ideas of independence, the abolition of slavery, and the drive for political and economic modernity with full citizenship for women permeate the writings of these early feminists.

By the latter half of the nineteenth century arguments for women's equality were cast in terms of progressivism and the hope of a better life in the New World. The first issue of *O Sexo Feminino*, edited by Francisca Motta Diniz, was "dedicated to the emancipation of women" and appeared in

Campanha, Minas Gerais, Brazil, on September 7, 1873. September 7 com-memorates Brazil's independence day; the use of national patriotic symbols by Latin American women activists has a long history. *O Sexo Feminino* declared: "It will be seen that America will give the cry of independence for women, showing the Old World what it means to be civilized, that women are as apt for education as young men." *La Mujer*, published in Chile in the 1890s, was committed to the idea that "the woman is the basis for universal progress."

Women and the Process of Modernization

The emergence of women novelists, poets, journalists, and political activists and the development of a shared feminist consciousness in Latin America are directly linked to trends that combined to produce a process of moderniza-tion in certain nations. Women speaking out on behalf of women found their voice—and their audience—in Argentina, Uruguay, Chile, and Brazil, states that received hundreds of thousands of European immigrants, whose urban centers became true cities, and where social and political reform movements were mounted; and in Mexico and Cuba, where major social upheavals took place. Women workers were at the heart of the great Río Blanco textile strike of 1907, and schoolteachers and factory workers played a crucial role in the politics that led to the Mexican Revolution of 1910.

The turn of the century also marked the entry of women into the paid workforce in significant numbers. Women factory workers and piece workers, drawn from the immigrant and rural-to-urban migrant peasant population, were the primary laborers in the textile, food processing, and tobacco indus-tries. They faced great difficulty in organizing to improve their working con-ditions. The hostility of employers and officials, little support from their male cohorts, long working hours, and family demands left scant energy for union work. The call of São Paulo seamstresses Tecla Fabbri, Teresa Cari, and Maria Lopes in the Brazilian anarchist newspaper *Terra Livre* (July 29, 1906) reflects these frustrations: "COMRADES! SHAKE OFF THE APATHY THAT DOMI-NATES YOU. IN THIS CITY WHERE WE ARE SO EXPLOITED, RESOLVE TO MAKE A NEW ATTEMPT TO DEFEND US ALL!"

Women in the white-collar urban workforce were predominantly young single women employed as clerks and in service-related jobs in government and commerce. The Liga de Empleadas Católicas (League of Catholic Women Employees, or LEC), established in the 1920s by the Catholic Church with branches throughout Latin America, was founded to respond to the needs of young working women while keeping them within the Catholic fold. These women were part of the formative urban middle and working classes in Santiago, Mexico City, Havana, Caracas, Río de Janeiro, São Paulo, Montevideo, and Buenos Aires. Argentine writer Alfonsina Storni

(1892–1938) addressed the concerns of this new population in her articles in the newspaper *La Nación*. Working women and their occupations, the relationship of women to national and cultural tradition, the role of the Catholic Church in women's lives were frequent themes not only in her work but also throughout the contemporary press (Kirkpatrick 1990).

Though women were entering new fields in urban areas, in the 1920s the great majority of women were rural. In Andean America, Paraguay, parts of Brazil, southern Mexico, Guatemala, and Venezuela that population was predominantly indigenous. Rural women's work was immensely varied: Women carried out ancient mining-related tasks in Potosí; worked communal agricultural plots, and ran trade networks in the Peruvian sierra; hulled and sorted spices in the Caribbean; worked the sugar, rubber, and banana plantations of Brazil, Haiti, and Cuba; harvested the wheat and grapes of Chile and Argentina; and did domestic labor at the big house on the ranch, *finca,* and hacienda. And everywhere women prepared daily meals, cared for children, cleaned and washed clothes for their own households in addition to whatever other work they might perform.

What is apparent in the examination of women's occupations in the early twentieth century is the emergence of two antithetical patterns that have persisted and intensified over time. One is the new presence of the middle-sector working woman: skilled and unskilled factory workers, teachers, government employees, writers, and sales clerks. Although there are great differences in the social and economic status of these women, their pay and relative job security differentiates them as a group from women whose work lies in the unregulated, informal sectors of the economy, a sector that includes female domestics, market women, vendors, laundresses, prostitutes, and nearly all the work performed by women in rural areas.

It was female schoolteachers who formed the nucleus of the first women's groups to articulate what may be defined as a feminist critique of society; that is, to protest the pervasive inequality of the sexes in legal status, rights over children, marriage, and access to education and political and economic power. The teachers represented a new group in Latin American society—the educated middle sector—which included skilled workers, clerks, and government employees as well as educators. They were in touch with one another through their institutions of learning and through professional associations—forums in which they could share their common experiences. The critical change was that their activities were collective, not individual.

In Mexico in 1870, poet and educator Rita Cetina Gutierrez, Cristina Farfan de Garcia Montero, and several primary-school teachers formed La Siemprevivia, a female society dedicated to overcoming women's unequal status in society and to combating social problems by improving hygiene and educating mothers in nutrition and child care. In their decision to found a publication to espouse their ideas and to open schools to train a new generation, the members of La Siemprevivia employed tactics used by the earlier advocates of women's rights.

In South America a collective female critique of discriminatory practices based on gender was visible at a series of scientific congresses held between 1898 and 1909. Men and women delegates presented papers on health care, hygiene, mothers' welfare, and scientific research. In conference discussions, the divisive issue proved to be female education: Should women have equal access, or be educated only in "suitable" professions, such as primary teaching? The women delegates were indignant that the debate should be cast in these terms and broadened the discussion into a wide-ranging attack on the pervasive inequality of the sexes within their societies (Miller 1991).

In the next decades, women called numerous conferences to discuss these issues. On May 10, 1910, the date of the centennial celebration of Argentine independence, the first Congreso Femenino Internacional (International Congress of Women) convened in Buenos Aires with more than two hundred women from Argentina, Uruguay, Peru, Paraguay, and Chile in attendance. The congress was organized by the Consejo Nacional de Mujeres (National Council of Women) and presided over by Cecilia Grierson. Sponsoring groups included the Asociación Nacional del Profesorado (National Association of Professors), the Asociación Nacional Argentina Contra la Trata de Blancas, Centro Socialista Femenino (Socialist Women's Center), Escuela Normal de Maestras de Tucumán (Teacher's Normal School of Tucumán), Grupo Femenino Unión y Labor (Women's Union and Labor Group), Liga Nacional de Mujeres Librepensadores (National League of Free-Thinking Women), and many more.

The wide differences in the political orientation of the women at the Congreso Femenino reflected the great political diversity between Buenos Aires, Montevideo, São Paulo, Santiago, and Lima in that period. Many of the reformist women belonged to the Socialist Party; others rejected the Socialist platform as too concerned with class and labor and aligned themselves with the anarchists, whose platform called for a complete reform of the bourgeois household. The loyalties of others lay with the Argentine Radical Party, a more conventional form of political opposition. Topics addressed ranged from international law, particularly as it related to the rights of married women to retain their citizenship, to health care, the problems of the married working woman, and equal pay for equal work. A resolution commending the government of Uruguay for the enactment of a bill of divorce in 1907, the first in Latin America, was also passed.

Universal suffrage was part of the Socialist Party platform and was debated at women's congresses in Latin America during the first half of the twentieth century. In 1916 two feminist congresses were convened in Mexico to discuss the role of women in postrevolutionary Mexico and to attempt to influence the Mexican Constitutional Convention then meeting in Queretaro. On its promulgation in 1917, the Mexican Constitution was hailed as the most advanced social and political document of its day. Political rights, including the right to vote, were granted "to all Mexican citizens." Women, however, were excluded from the category of citizen (Soto 1979).

The history of feminism in Peru offers an example of the women's movement in a country where a strong middle class did not develop in the early twentieth century and secularization of schools did not occur. Maria Jesús Alvarado Rivera—who studied at the private school for girls formed by feminist thinker and author Elvira García y García—founded Evolución Femenina in 1914 to discuss "the woman question." The core group of members had all attended the Congreso Feminino Internacional in 1910. The conservatism and class bias of the Peruvian political milieu is apparent in the women's twelve-year campaign not for access to government positions but for the right of women to be appointed as directors of the powerful private charitable organization, Sociedades de Beneficencia Pública (Societies for Public Beneficence).

In the 1920s and 1930s a number of national and international women's conferences met to discuss civil, legal, and educational reform, suffrage and the rights of working women. In 1922 with the example of U.S. women's successful drive for suffrage (1920) and in the wake of the war to "make the world safe for democracy," two thousand women from throughout the hemisphere convened in Baltimore and formed the Pan-American Association for the Advancement of Women. Veterans of the scientific congresses, such as Lamanda Labarca of Chile and Flora de Oliveira Lima of Brazil, were among the Latin American delegates, as were a rising generation of feminist leaders that included Elena Torres, who was at that time designing the radical rural literacy program in postrevolutionary Mexico; Sara Casal de Quiros of Costa Rica; and Bertha Lutz, founder of the Liga para Emancipação Intelectual Feminina (League for the Intellectual Emancipation of Women) in Río de Janiero (1920). Lutz's vision of feminism was that "in Brazil, the true leaders of feminism are the young women who work in industry, in commerce, in teaching" (Hahner 1991).

In the 1920s Cuban women were heavily involved in the effort to establish democracy and social equality in their newly independent nation. In 1923 the Club Femenino de Cuba (Women's Club of Cuba, which was founded in 1917) formed the Federación Nacional de Asociaciones Femeninas (National Federation of Women's Associations), an umbrella group of thirty-one women's organizations, which planned the First National Women's Congress in Havana, April 1–7, 1923. Government officials were invited to the event in an effort to influence national reform policy. A second women's congress met in Havana in 1925 to call for (1) social equality between men and women; (2) child protection; (3) equal pay for equal work; (4) equality for illegitimate children; (5) elimination of prostitution; and (6) prohibition of the unequal treatment of women.

In Mexico, in July 1925, Sofia Villa de Buentello organized the Congreso de Mujeres de la Raza (Congress of Women of the Race), where the class and ideological splits that characterized the women's movement in the hemisphere in the following decades first appeared. Irreconcilable differences emerged between the socialists, who insisted on the economic basis of women's problems, and the conservatives and moderates, who believed female inequality to be rooted in social and moral conditions.

In Argentina, feminists Alicia Moreau de Justo and Elvira Rawson joined with other reformist groups, including the conservative Catholic women's trades' union, to support passage of protective legislation for women industrial workers in 1924. Encouraged by this success, the National Feminist Union and the Women's Rights Association formed a coalition to push a comprehensive reform of the civil code through the Argentine congress in 1926; the reform granted married women equal civil rights with adult men, mothers parental rights over their children, and married women the right to enter professions, make contracts, and dispose of their earnings without spousal permission. In order to maintain the coalition, the Argentine National Women's Council agreed not to connect the reform to the divisive issue of women's suffrage.

In 1928 Cuban women's associations hosted women from all over the hemisphere who came to Havana as unofficial delegates to the Sixth International Conference of American States. By the end of the conference the women had presented an equal rights treaty for the consideration of the governments of the hemisphere and successfully lobbied for the creation of an officially designated body, the Comisión Interamericana de Mujeres (Interamerican Women's Commission, or CIM), which was charged with the investigation of the legal status of women in the twenty-one member states. The use of the international forum for the discussion of women's issues proved particularly efficacious for those Latin American women who found it difficult to create sympathetic political space in their home countries. Bringing international attention to an issue was a political strategy that Latin American feminists helped to pioneer, and it was one that would serve them well over time (Miller 1991).

The Change in Legal and Civil Status of Women

Prior to the early twentieth century, the legal and civil status of Latin American women was governed by a complex body of legislation rooted in Iberian and ecclesiastic law; in practice, the legal status of most women was determined by their relationship to the male head of household. Indigenous women living within their traditional communities (Maya, Guajira, Aymará, Guaraní) were governed according to the customs of that community. Although elaborate sets of laws governing slave women had evolved by the nineteenth century, individual slave women had little recourse to these laws. In all cases, full citizenship was limited to men of property.

The history of female suffrage illustrates the politics involved in seeking redress through legal change. Effective universal suffrage, male or female, did not exist in any Latin American nation until after World War II. Property, type of employment, and residence requirements restricted the vote to certain sectors of the population. Moreover, irregular transitions in power and the suspension of civil liberties, including elections, characterized the political scene in many Latin American nations during the period between 1929, when Ecuador became the first Latin American country to make female suffrage the law, and 1961, when women finally received the right to vote in Paraguay, the last country in Latin America to do so. Three periods of enactment may be distinguished:

1. **Pre–World War II:** Ecuador, 1929, Brazil and Uruguay, 1932, and Cuba, 1934
2. **World War II:** El Salvador, 1939, Dominican Republic, 1942, Panama and Guatemala, 1945
3. **Post–World War II:** Venezuela and Argentina, 1947, Chile and Costa Rica, 1949, Haiti, 1950, Bolivia, 1952, Mexico, 1953, Honduras, Nicaragua, and Peru, 1955, Colombia, 1957, and Paraguay, 1961

The enactment of female suffrage should not be viewed, however, as a signpost that the women's program had triumphed in a country. An examination of the first group of states to enact suffrage for women reveals a variety of motives prompted the governments of Brazil, Uruguay, and Cuba to bring women into the national polity. The enactment of female suffrage in these countries was the result of years of hard work and carefully planned campaigns by groups of women and their male allies, who were prepared to act when a political opening occurred. When the Brazilian Revolution of 1930 brought a reformist government to power, the Federação Brasileira pelo Progresso Feminino (Brazilian Federation for Women's Progress), led by Bertha Lutz and Carolota Pereira de Queiroz, presented the leaders with a platform of thirteen principles, which included female suffrage and equality before the law. In Cuba, numerous women's organizations, including the Alianza Naciónal Feminista, the Partido Naciónal Sufragista, and the Partido Democrática, were in the forefront of groups fighting for political reform and poised to demand the extension of the franchise to women when the new provisional constitution was drafted in 1934.

By way of contrast, in Ecuador, the political coalition that lobbied for the female vote was deeply conservative; it viewed women as loyal to the Catholic Church and politically malleable and believed the female vote would buttress the Conservative's political base vis-à-vis a challenge from the Socialist Party. Ironically, many members of the political Left concurred with the Conservative Party's assessment of women's political acumen.

In Argentina, Eva Maria Duarte de Perón is often credited with the passage of female suffrage, but by 1947 Argentine women had waged a half-century-long campaign for the vote, suffrage laws had been passed in many other Western Hemisphere nations, and commitment to equal political rights was part of the U.N. Charter, to which Argentina was a signatory. What Eva Perón did was deliver the new female vote for the Peronist Party.

Despite the passage of female suffrage laws in every Latin American country by 1961, the right of women to vote continued to be limited by language and literacy requirements. Rural women were especially affected by these requirements. In some countries, such as Guatemala, male suffrage was universal but female suffrage was restricted to women who could read and speak Spanish. In Peru, Quechua-speaking Peruvians did not receive the franchise until 1980, a restriction that affected women who stayed in the sierra and maintained the home community while the men migrated out of the area to work or fulfill military service.

Although female literacy remained comparatively low in most Latin American countries until the 1960s, by the late 1920s the number of women attending postelementary schools was nearly equal to that of male students in Cuba, Argentina, Uruguay, and Chile. New associations of women seeking broad-based reform, including female suffrage, appeared in the 1930s. One was the Movimiento Pro-Emancipación de la Mujer Chilena (MEMCH, 1935–1955), established by Chilean university women (Antezana-Pernet 1994). Journals such as Nelly Merino Carvallo's *Mujeres de America* (1930–1935, Buenos Aires) appealed to an international audience and carried articles written by Bolivian, Paraguayan, Peruvian, and Uruguayan women as well as Argentines; themes of peace and transnational sisterhood were among those discussed.

Women leaders also emerged within the political Left, although their politics as spokeswomen on behalf of their own sex often put them in dire conflict with their male comrades, as is illustrated by the career of Patricia Galvão, known as Pagú, who joined the Partido Comunista Brasileira (PCB) in 1930. Pagú, like most radical women, felt scorn for the bourgeois feminists, but she had a feminist vision of her own. In her book, *Parque Industrial* (1933), she described the sexual discrimination and duress experienced by female industrial workers. Pagú had the temerity to link sexism with racism in the Brazilian workforce and thereby so outraged the male leadership of the PCB that they ordered her book destroyed.

In Mexico women loyal to the Revolutionary Party were deeply disappointed when reformist president Lázaro Cárdenas (1934–1940) failed to fulfill his promise to reform the constitution to grant equal rights. At the Eighth International Conference of American States (Lima 1938), it was the Mexican delegation to the CIM, led by Amalia Caballero Castillo de Ledón, that successfully lobbied for the passage of the Declaration in Favor of Women's Rights. The resolution established the precedent for the incorporation of the phrase "the equal rights of men and women" into the charter draft of the United Nations in Chapultepec, Mexico, in March 1945.

The democratic opening that followed World War II in many Latin American nations was brief. The Río Pact, signed in 1947 at the Inter-American Conference for the Maintenance of Continental Peace and Security in Petrópolis, Brazil, marked the beginning of the cold war in the Western Hemisphere and served as the blueprint for North Atlantic Treaty Organization (NATO). Less well known is the history of the Primero Congreso Interamericano de Mujeres (First International Congress of Women), which was convened that same year by women from every nation in the Western Hemisphere to protest the arming of the Americas and to plead that the Río Conference turn its attention and resources not to a military buildup but to social and economic problems. The women's agenda did not prevail. The congress's resolutions on the peaceful use of atomic power, on the dedication of financial resources to economic and social development, not a military buildup, and the denunciation of dictatorships in Honduras, the Dominican Republic, and Haiti were not included in the Río Pact.

The concerns voiced at this women's conference did persist, however. They were at the heart some years later of the Alliance for Progress and burned bright in the declarations for social justice made by liberation theologians, reformers, and revolutionaries in the 1960s and in the rising concern for human rights in the 1970s.

The Contemporary Historical Context

January 1959 marked the triumph of the Cuban Revolution. Whether women supported revolution, favored reform, or were ardent counterrevolutionaries, politics became permanently altered after this date. Throughout the region, among those committed to change through revolution, women were most active in the urban movements. Young women made up almost half of the "soldiers" of the urban revolutionary Tupumaro movement in Montevideo, Uruguay. Among rural guerrilla groups, women were more apt to be seen as *compañeras,* companions of the male revolutionaries. "Tania" (Haydée Tamara Bunke Bider, 1937–1967) was an exception; she played a key role in Ché Guevara's effort to establish a revolutionary front in Bolivia and became a martyr to a generation of young women after her death under fire.

Liberation theology, which emerged from the Latin American Catholic Church in the wake of Vatican II (1962) and the Medellín Conference (1968), did not address the specific needs of women. However, women of the church—laywomen, nuns, congregants, and participants in the base communities—were deeply involved in the church's commitment to the poorest of the poor. Women were also active in defending traditional ways of life that they believed were threatened. In Brazil in 1964 and Chile in 1972, upper- and middle-class women organized street demonstrations to protest the erosion of homemakers' buying power, the specter of communism, the supposed threat to the family, and to call on the military to "restore order."

Taking their cue from the Cuban Revolution, women who joined the revolutionary Left in the 1960s adopted a class analysis that repudiated feminism as bourgeois and divisive to the cause. But it was from this generation of women activists—the most highly educated generation of women in Latin American history—that the feminists of the 1970s emerged, giving up not a whit of their commitment to social change but adding to it a new, gendered brand of social criticism. By 1985 this generation of Latin American feminists had developed a stinging critique of the traditional Left within their own communities, challenged the "First World" view of feminists from Europe and the United States, and contributed organizational models, political strategies, and a new understanding of grassroots social movements and global feminism.

In 1975 the Conferencia Mundial del Año Internacional de la Mujer (World Conference of the International Year of the Woman) convened in Mexico City to draw up the "world plan of action" for the U.N. Decade for Women (1976–1985). It was at sessions of the Tribune for nongovernmental organizations, held parallel to the conference, where nongovernmental organizations and individuals could speak and where the Latin American women were especially influential. The majority of the six thousand women who attended the tribune were from North, Central, and South America; two thousand were from Mexico alone. The lines of debate that dominated the first half of the U.N. Decade emerged in the confrontation between Betty Friedan and Domitila Barrios de Chungara, who came to Mexico to represent the Housewives' Committee of Siglo XX, an organization of Bolivian tin miners' wives.

By 1977 a feminist political critique was being included in the women's movements emerging throughout Latin America. During the next decade more than two hundred newsletters, feminist journals, and women's movement periodicals appeared, indicating the presence of women's groups in every region of the continent. One of the earliest and most notable was *fem*, which has been published since 1976 by a collective editorship, Nueva Cultura Feminista, in Mexico City. The subjects addressed in this periodical provide a microcosm of the concerns of Mexican feminists over the years: abortion, work, sexuality, feminism, language, family, education, mothers and children, women writers, the history of women in Mexico, women in the struggle for social justice, and so on. *MUJER/fempress,* published monthly in Santiago, Chile, since 1981, carries articles by correspondents from every country in the hemisphere.

In 1984 the Grupo de Estudios sobre la Condición de la Mujer en Uruguay (Study Group on the Condition of Women in Uruguay) began the publication of *La Cacerola* (The Casserole), explaining: "The name has many meanings, but one above all: in these months of perilous transition to democracy, the casserole has been converted into a symbol of liberation." In Peru, the Centro de Flora Tristán publishes *VIVA*; the Movimiento Manuela Ramos ("Manuela Ramos" signifies "everywoman") issues pamphlets on health and community resources; and *Mujer y Sociedad* addresses the politics of violence in the nation and the home. Brazilian women have been leaders in the innovative use of film and have succeeded in incorporating the concerns of the women's movement into popular *telenovelas,* long-running stories of Brazilian life, such as "Malu Mulher."

In the 1990s new journals have continued to appear. For example, there is *Feminária* in Buenos Aires, which states on its masthead, "FEMINÁRIA IS FEMINIST BUT IS NOT LIMITED TO ONE CONCEPT OF FEMINISM." *Enfoques de Mujer* is published in Paraguay by the Grupo de Estudios de la Mujer Paraguaya. Like their counterparts in Brazil, Argentina, Uruguay, and Chile, the Paraguayan women who founded the journal were participants in the struggle to end the military dictatorship and bring democracy to their country.

Many of the women's groups have also established documentation centers, realizing how little information was available on women. And, without adequate data, a critical analysis of women's situation would not be possible. In Chile ISIS International continues to gather information and publications on women from throughout the hemisphere; its publication *Documentas* offers monthly updates of their computerized listings. ISIS also coordinates, via computer, the Women's Health Network of Latin America and the Caribbean and the Program for Information and Politics on Violence Against Women.

In 1992 the Facultad Latinoamericana de Ciencias Sociales (The Latin American Faculty of Social Sciences, or FLACSO) in Santiago, Chile, began publication of a new country-by-country series, entitled *Mujeres Latinoamericanas en Cifras* (Latin American Women in Numbers). The editors state in the preface:

> Mujeres Latinoamericanas en Cifras is the first systematic, universal effort to document in numbers the situation of women in a continent of multiple hues and geographies, that also takes into account the great political, social, ethnic, cultural and economic disparities that exist in the hemisphere. The subordination of women, broadly debated throughout the whole world, is today an

inarguable reality. . . . Mujeres Latinoamericanas en Cifras is intended to be an
instrument for the transformation of this situation.

Statistics, gathered from the sources each country-team deemed most reliable,
are presented in sophisticated graphics that offer socioeconomic and demographic profiles for each of the nineteen countries covered in the series, including statistics on women in the workforce, in education, and in the political process; medical and actuarial statistics; legislation affecting women; and at
the end of each volume a listing of *organismos y acción de promoción de la
mujer* (organizations and action concerned with the promotion of women).

The Chilean editors write that the latter section proved the most difficult
to find information on "due to the absence of official sources and the nonex-
istence of central data repositories" (Chile 1993:127). Pointing to informational lacunae is part of the political intent of these documentation centers.
In contexts where people's very lives have been "disappeared" from the official story, the creation of a new historical record in which women's lives are
visible is extremely important.

The strategies developed by Latin American women activists over the past
century have been widely adopted in other areas of the world. The Organizaciones de Trabajadores del Hogar de America Latina y el Caribe (Organizations of Latin American and Caribbean Home Workers), founded in 1988
by women household workers, has been a model for similar organizations in
Africa and Southeast Asia. Violence against women, in all its forms, is a central concern of the contemporary women's movement in Latin America. The
celebration of November 25 as an International Day Against Violence
Against Women, was initiated in 1987 by Latin American feminists at the IV
Encuentro Feminista in Mexico to commemorate the tortured deaths of six
Dominican peasant women for resisting sexual violation at the hands of military troops. In 1992 the United Nations declared November 25 a global day
of commemoration with regard to violence against women.

The Encuentro resolution was intended to protest violence against women
perpetrated by the state as well as in the home. Since the proclamation of this
day, thousands of women have gathered in public squares across Latin America to show their solidarity on the issue. This event is a quintessential expression of Latin American feminism since it has involved the use—in this case,
the creation—of an official, international event to make a statement in the
local arena and thereby gather a bit of political *sombra,* or coverage. November 25 is a protest against the violence women experience on a daily basis at
the hands of the men with whom they share their lives, and it is a protest
against official tolerance of rape and domestic battery.

In instituting the International Day Against Violence Against Women,
Latin American feminists did not attempt to separate public from private or
national politics from domestic concerns. Their activism obviates neat dis-

tinctions between what is "feminist" (for example, a gendered understanding of women's position within the family) and the gendered expression of a larger political issue (e.g., violent, state-sponsored political repression). The blending of the political activism of women on the Left with the feminists' gendered analysis has produced a profoundly ethical expression of principle that abhors both state-sponsored violence against the general populace and the day-to-day violence women withstand because they are women.

The proliferation of women's organizations and activism in the 1990s reflects the urgency of women's concerns. The opening editorial of the summer 1993 edition of *Mujeres en Acción* (published in Santiago, Chile) states: "To participate as actors in changing the world . . . is a human right that nobody can take away from us." In the southern Mexican town of San Cristóbal de las Casas, Chiapas, the center of recent armed protests against the government, the Grupo Mujer (GM) was formed in 1989 by female migrants to address their problems in securing work and caring for their families. GM's membership included women who had been resettled from northern Mexico as well as Mayan women from Guatemala who had fled the counterinsurgency campaigns in their country.

Two recent examples from Nicaragua illustrate the strategies of these new groups. On December 4, 1992, Radio Mujer, created by the Fundación de Mujeres Comunicadoras (Foundation of Women Communicators), began broadcasting in Managua. When asked if Radio Mujer had "a political line," spokeswoman Luz Monterrey answered: "We are a multi-party emissary because gender does not have a political party. It is certain that many of us are Sandinistas. I am a Sandinista and will be until I die. I strongly oppose the government of Violeta Barrios de Chamorro. But when the station was inaugurated in December, we invited the president, and she came. She gave her strong support to the project." Monterrey also stated that Radio Mujer was not necessarily feminist but that their purpose was to bring information directly to women: "The great majority of women do not know the law and therefore cannot defend themselves. We have programs about women's health, and sex education for young people. 'Eco-mujer' addresses the ecology. In the program 'Noti-mujer' we analyze the news from a woman's perspective" (Monterrey 1993:4).

The second illustration is drawn from El Encuentro de Mujeres Nicaraguenses "Diversas pero Unidos" (The Encounter of Nicaraguan Women "Diverse but United"), which met in Managua in January 1992. This conference of representatives from diverse backgrounds was a product of the aspirations expressed by many Nicaraguan women in the two-year period since the defeat of the Sandinista Front for National Liberation (FSLN) in the elections of 1990. The idea arose as part of the reactivation of the movement, which since 1977 has been conducted under the aegis of the Asociación de Mujeres Nicaraguenses "Luisa Amanda Espinoza" (The "Luisa

Amanda Espinoza" Association of Nicaraguan Women, or AMNLAE). The AMNLAE leadership declined to participate in the conference, entitled the "Festival de las 52%" (Festival of the 52 Percent; i.e., in reference to the percentage of women in the population). But the organizers went forward with their plans, which they described "as a learning experience for us all." The minutes indicate that eight hundred women attended, among them "women from the interior zone of Mulukukú and from the autonomous Atlantic regions, from whom we learned of the extremely difficult economic situation that population faces" (Conference of Nicaraguan Women 1993:3).

In the Caribbean, women writers and feminist activists write and broadcast in their "nation language" in a threefold strategy: First, to reach the majority of women in the country; second, to disavow the superiority of the colonial language—French, Spanish, or English; and, third, to thumb their noses at those who do not/would not understand the nation language of the people. In Haiti, ENFOFANM was founded in 1987 as "the only institution for documentation on Haiti's women." In 1991 it began publication of a women's journal in Creole.

In February 1993 the Programa Interdisciplinario de Estudios de Genero (Interdisciplinary Program of Gender Studies, or PRIEG), the women's studies program instituted at the University of Costa Rica in 1987, hosted the V Congreso Interdisciplinario y Internacional de Mujeres (Fifth Interdisciplinary and International Congress of Women). Although the two thousand participants represented women from throughout the world, the organization and content of the program were telling indicators of the breadth and depth of Latin American feminist thought in the 1990s. The program addressed women and the environment, heterosexual Acquired Immunodeficiency Syndrome (AIDS), sexual preferences, indigenous women and peoples, feminism and democratic practice, and other concerns in Central America and elsewhere in Latin America. The weeklong event culminated in a march from the university campus to the Plaza de la Democrácia (dedicated in 1989 by former president Oscar Arias Sánchez, winner of the 1987 Nobel Peace Prize) to celebrate women's rights/human rights.

In the 1990s Latin American women are more highly educated, more urban, more engaged in activities outside the household—economic, political, and social—than has been previously true. But throughout the region deep, persistent political and economic instabilities threaten efforts to revise social and cultural attitudes. The ostensible gains—political citizenship for women, a focus on the double burden of poor women, greater access to schooling for girls, labor regulations that take women's work into account—are under constant threat of erosion. Ironically, years of pointing out the importance of women in the economic life of developing countries appear to have convinced governments that women will devise a means to help sustain themselves and their children without aid from government agencies. UNICEF analysts describe the process as the "invisible adjustment," in which the crisis of social disinvestment is financed by the superhuman efforts of poor women. A gendered understanding may have emerged, but the use to which that understanding is being put demonstrates that caring for poor, usually ethnically different women and their children is still regarded as an expendable luxury by governments.

The slogan "We want democracy in the nation . . . and the home" was coined by the Chilean women's movement in the 1980s. In the 1990s true democracy in Chile remains a radical vision but perhaps not as radical as that of democracy in the home. The struggle to be included in a full definition of what it means to be human ultimately demands that all people, male and female, of all backgrounds, must be included in the polity.

In Latin America, the women's movement of the early twentieth century arose as part of a critique of politics as usual. This is still true. Women were active leaders in the redemocratization efforts in Chile, Brazil, Uruguay, Argentina, and Paraguay. Women are vital to democracy if democracy is to be viable, and they are central to overcoming seemingly implacable social and economic problems. In this effort, the importance of collective memory, of bearing witness, of knowing the history of women cannot be underestimated. The concepts of *abertura* (which means "opening" in Portuguese and came into use to describe the military's gradual retreat from the executive branch of the government in Brazil between 1974 and 1984) and *parenthése* (a Haitian term connoting a brief break, but little change, in politics as usual) are useful in the attempt to discern themes and trends in the history of women's political engagement in Latin America. Throughout the national period, from independence to the present, debates over full citizenship for women have been a hallmark of the political *abertura*. Some examples are the demand for citizenship for female as well as male patriots in the wake of the Cuban independence movement in 1917; the insistence at the Constitutional Convention in Querétaro, Mexico that universal suffrage must extend to women; the articulation of a gendered understanding of revolution in the late 1970s; and feminist participation in the politics of redemocratization in the 1980s. The presence or absence of a gendered consideration of the political situation may be seen as an accurate indication of whether a true *abertura* has occurred, or whether the political change is in reality a *parenthése*— just another period of disorder marking the fall of one leader or party and the rise of another. Such an understanding emerges only from a gendered analysis of events.

In the 1990s the question of de facto citizenship for women is being posited in new ways by women activists in Latin America and the Caribbean. In 1987 Brazilian feminists successfully pressed for the enactment of a law that would condemn so-called killings of honor. To win convictions against men who killed their wives or partners because of suspicion of adultery, these women believed a specific law was needed to end the cultural tolerance for this crime.

Of equal concern to women activists is the ways in which women may be excluded from 'the imagined national community' (Pratt 1990). The disaffection of women from the national political process can be politically costly to those in power. It is speculated that in Nicaragua the Sandinistas lost the allegiance of many women as the civil war cooled down and women were in effect asked to return to the home or at least to raising a family and to part-time and, relative to their male counterparts, low-paid work. The loss of that constituency proved crucial in the 1990 elections.

The resistance of the Latin American political Left to feminist analysis is well documented (Miller 1991; Vargas 1983). The most passionate criticism has arisen from women who supported the revolutionary movements. Margaret Randall's testimonial essays on Cuba and Nicaragua, published in 1994, are aptly titled *Gathering Rage: The Failure of Twentieth-Century Revolutions to Develop a Feminist Agenda*. The Cuban Women's Federation (Federación de Mujeres Cubanas, or FMC), while rejecting the term *feminism*, openly acknowledges the gap between de jure equality and daily life: "Family dynamics, that is, the division of labor and responsibilities within the family, continue to be marked by traditional constructs that translate into a difference of opportunities that is disadvantageous for the woman" (1993).

In *The Morning After: Sexual Politics at the End of the Cold War*, Cynthia Enloe writes: "Now that the war is over, Esmeralda has had her IUD removed." Enloe explains that a Salvadoran woman, Esmeralda, who fought as a guerrilla in the Farabundo Martí National Liberation Front (Frente Farabundo Martí de Liberación Nacional, or FMLN), had understood that it would have been "politically irresponsible" to have allowed herself to become pregnant during the civil war: "But now she was being urged by men in the political leadership to imagine her postwar life as one devoted to being a good mother" (1993:1). Enloe goes on to explain that although some women may have acceded to such pressures, many are challenging them. For these young women, the alleged status ante bellum is one that can be known only through the stories of others, not through their own reality.

Conclusion

In the 1990s the Latin American women's movement is distinguished by several characteristics. The emphasis on individual fulfillment that characterized the mainstream women's movement in the United States in the 1970s and early 1980s remains muted in the Latin American context. In Latin America a politics of *concientización* has developed in which women have sought to awaken one another's awareness and understanding of their specific historical situation while providing the analytic tools and organizational modes to participate in the transformation of social conditions.

Women's attempts to raise public consciousness have merged with the efforts of socialists, liberal reformers, liberation theologians, and/or revolutionaries such as the Tupumaros to publicize the plight of the poor. The fusion of a radical critique of economic, political, and social injustice with a gendered analysis has resulted in a syncretic understanding that has transformed both feminism and the politics of social change in Latin America. It has also deeply influenced the global women's movement.

References

Alvarez, Sonia E. *Engendering Democracy in Brazil: Women's Movements in Transitional Politics.* Princeton, NJ: Princeton University Press, 1990.

Antezana-Pernet, Corinne. "Peace in the World and Democracy at Home: The Chilean Women's Movement in the 1940s," in David Rock, ed., *Latin America in the 1940s: War and Postwar Transitions.* Berkeley, University of California Press, 1994.

Bergmann, Emilie. "Sor Juana Inés de la Cruz: Dreaming in a Double Voice," in Seminar on Feminism and Culture in Latin America, *Women, Culture, and Politics in Latin America.* Berkeley: University of California Press, 1990.

Chaney, Elsa, and Mary Garcia Castro. *Muchachas No More: Household Workers in Latin America and the Caribbean.* Philadelphia: Temple University Press, 1989.

Conference of Nicaraguan Women. "Diverse but United: Minutes." *La Boletina* (January 1993):3.

Enloe, Cynthia. *The Morning After: Sexual Politics at the End of the Cold War.* Berkeley: University of California Press, 1993.

Feijóo, Maria del Carmen. "Las Feministas," in *La Vida de Nuestro Pueblo: Una Historia de Hombres, Cosas Trabajos, y Lugares,* no. 9. Buenos Aires: Centro Editor de America Latina, 1982.

Fernández-Kelly, Maria Patricia. "Political Economy and Gender in Latin America: The Emerging Dilemmas." Paper presented at the Seminar on Women in Latin America, Woodrow Wilson Center, Smithsonian Institution, Washington, DC, October 29, 1993.

Greenberg, Janet. "Toward a History of Women's Periodicals in Latin America: A Working Bibliography," in Seminar on Feminism and Culture in Latin America, *Women, Culture, and Politics in Latin America.* Berkeley: University of California Press, 1990.

Hahner, June. *Emancipating the Female Sex: The Struggle for Women's Rights in Brazil, 1850–1940.* Durham, NC: Duke University Press, 1991.

Jaquette, Jane, ed. *The Women's Movement in Latin America.* Boston: Unwin Hyman, 1989.

Kirkpatrick, Gwen, "The Journalism of Alfonsina Storni: A New Approach to Women's History in Argentina," in *Women, Culture, and Politics in Latin America.* Berkeley: University of California Press, 1990.

Lavrin, Asunción. ed. *Latin American Women: Historical Perspectives.* Westport, CT: Greenwood Press, 1978.

———. *Sexuality and Marriage in Colonial Latin America.* Lincoln: University of Nebraska Press, 1989.

Leitinger, Isle, ed. *The Costa Rican Women's Reader.* Pittsburgh: University of Pittsburgh Press, 1994.

Macías, Anna. *Against All Odds: The Feminist Movement in Mexico to 1940.* Westport, CT: Greenwood Press, 1982.

Masiello, Francine. "Women, State, and Family in Latin American Literature of the 1920s," in Seminar on Feminism and Culture in Latin America, *Women, Culture, and Politics in Latin America.* Berkeley: University of California Press, 1990.

Miller, Francesca. "Latin American Feminism and the Transnational Arena," in Seminar on Feminism and Culture in Latin America, *Women, Culture, and Politics in Latin America.* Berkeley: University of California Press, 1990.

———. *Latin American Women and the Search for Social Justice.* Hanover, NH: University Press of New England, 1991.

Monterrey, Luz. "Interview." *La Boletina* (January 1993).

Morello-Frosch, Marta. "Alfonsina Storni: The Tradition of the Feminine Subject," in Seminar on Feminism and Culture in Latin America, *Women, Culture, and Politics in Latin America.* Berkeley: University of California Press, 1990.

Pratt, Mary. "Women, Literature, and National Brotherhood," in Seminar on Feminism and Culture in Latin America, *Women, Culture, and Politics in Latin America.* Berkeley: University of California Press, 1990.

Programa Interdisciplinario de Estudios de Mujer (PIEM). *Presencia y transparencia: La mujer en la historia de Mexico.* Mexico City: Colegio de Mexico, 1987.

Randall, Margaret. *Gathering Rage: The Failure of Twentieth-Century Revolutions to Develop a Feminist Agenda.* New York: Monthly Review Press, 1994.

Seminar on Feminism and Culture in Latin America. *Women, Culture, and Politics in Latin America.* Berkeley: University of California Press, 1990.

Soto, Shirlene. *The Mexican Woman: A Study of Her Participation in the Revolution, 1910–1940.* Palo Alto, CA: R&R Research Assocs. 1979.

Stoner, K. Lynn. *From the House to the Streets: The Cuban Women's Movement for Legal Reform, 1898–1940.* Durham, NC: Duke University Press, 1989.

Valdés, Teresa, and Enrique Gomariz, eds. *Mujeres Latinoamericanas en Cifras: Chile,* 2d ed. Santiago, Chile: Facultad Latinoamericana de Ciencias Sociales (FLACSO-Chile), 1993.

Vargas, Virginia. In Jeanine Anderson de Velasco, ed., *Congreso de investigación acerca de la mujer en la region andina,* Lima, Peru: Asociación Perú-Mujer, 1983.

8

Latin America's Indigenous Peoples: Changing Identities and Forms of Resistance

MICHAEL KEARNEY AND STEFANO VARESE

Any attempt to make meaningful and valid generalizations about the contemporary indigenous peoples of the Americas is a daunting task given their vast geographical extension and wide variation in social forms and living conditions. There are tens of millions of indigenous peoples, or *indígenas*, in Latin America. Their distribution today generally follows that of pre-Columbian population patterns. Thus, they range from a majority of the population in Bolivia, Peru, and Guatemala to large minorities in Mexico, Colombia, Venezuela, Ecuador, Paraguay, and Chile. A small minority in the vastness of Brazil, *indígenas* nevertheless have acquired unanticipated importance in the politics of their country.

Contemporary indigenous identities are best understood through historical examination. Several major epochs have shaped the economic and political conditions affecting indigenous communities. Furthermore, these conditions continue to change, just as anthropological understandings about indigenous identity have evolved. Therefore, in reviewing the status of the contemporary *indígenas* in Latin America, we must also comment on the development of the concepts that have been used to interpret these identities.

There are various ways to approach the history and identity of indigenous peoples. Anthropological thinking was dominated until recently by the assimilation model. In this view, the *indígenas* possess traditional social forms and cultures that will eventually give way to modern society, a process that is thought to occur through the acceptance of modern technology and cultural

forms whereby *indígenas* are supposed to be acculturated into modern society. This perspective sees contemporary indigenous identities largely as sur-
vivals from earlier periods, especially pre-Columbian times. One implication
of this acculturation perspective is that indigenous communities are destined
to disappear as successive generations lose their traditional traits and assimi-
late into modern society. To be sure, there has been much acculturation and
assimilation of *indígenas* who have retained few traits stemming from their
original cultures. Hundreds of local indigenous communities and their languages have completely disappeared over the past five hundred years. But at
the same time, many *indígenas* have displayed a remarkable staying power,
and in recent years their presence has become ever more notable.

The durability of the *indígenas* called for a different theoretical perspective. The working notion of this theory is that social identity is formed
largely in opposition to others in a dialectic of what are called "othering" and
"self-attribution." The rest of this chapter explores this twofold phenomenon of leveling and differentiation and assumes that it is inherent not only in
local but also in global economic and cultural relations.

From Pre-Columbian to Colonial Societies

At the end of the fifteenth century, when the first appreciable numbers of
Europeans came into their midst, the native peoples of what is now Latin
America were arrayed in numerous and diverse types of societies ranging
from nomadic foraging bands to complex state civilizations comparable to
those of Asia and Europe. In the two centuries after the arrival of Columbus,
the destinies of *indígenas* of the region were overwhelmingly shaped by the
devastating impact of this encounter; numerous communities disappeared
completely while others suffered population declines of 80 to 100 percent
(for an overview of the human tragedy associated with the Conquest, see
Galeano 1973). During the ensuing three hundred years the identity of *indígenas* was shaped by their subordinate position as colonized subjects and,
later, as subordinated ethnic groups within the postcolonial nation-states
dominated by non-*indígenas*.

The Conquest irrevocably incorporated the indigenous peoples into global
relationships with European states in what was becoming a world capitalist
system (Wolf 1982). As the logic of that new world order was understood by
the political leaders of the time, European nations, to prosper and to be
strong vis-à-vis other nations, needed colonies as sources of wealth. According to the theory of mercantilism that gained favor in sixteenth-century Europe and influenced economic thought through the eighteenth, the ideal
colonies possessed both natural resources and the native populations needed
to extract them. The resources produced by cheap labor in the colonies could

supply industries in the home countries, which in turn would produce merchandise for sale back to the colonies and on the world market in general.

The identity of the *indígenas* during the Conquest and colonial periods was shaped mainly by Spanish, Portuguese, French, and English policies designed, first, to maintain distinctions between the European nations and their colonies in what was called the New World and, second, to maintain, within the colonies, the distinctions between Europeans and the non-Europeans found there. Spanish occupation of the Americas and Spanish colonial policies regarding the *indígenas* contrasted sharply with those of the English in their colonial project in North America, which was effected largely through the migration of prosperous dissident religious communities consisting of entire families. Imbued with notions of religious and economic freedom, they sought worldly and spiritual salvation through industry and commerce in which the indigenous peoples were seen as having no significant role. Indeed, the English colonists of North America saw the *indígenas* more as obstacles to their projects than as resources.

At the time of its conquest of the Americas, Spain had emerged from several hundred years of military struggle against the (non-European) Moors on the Iberian Peninsula. Indeed, the final episode in that long war, the fall of Grenada in 1492, coincided with Columbus's first voyage to the islands of the Caribbean. To a great extent the subsequent conquest of what became Spanish America was a continuation of Spain's reconquest of the peninsula and was carried out largely as a military and religious crusade. Whereas English settlement in North America sought to clone the communities of England, Spanish America was occupied by battle-hardened military men, for the most part unaccompanied by women and children. Furthermore, whereas the English settlers went to North America to stay, the first waves of Spanish into the Western Hemisphere went to acquire wealth with which to improve their status upon their return to Europe. Unlike the English in North America, who generally viewed the natives as obstacles to their enterprises, the Spanish regarded indigenous labor as essential to extract wealth from the gold and silver mines and from plantations that produced commodities such as sugar, silk, indigo, and cochineal for the world market.

In Spanish America, the indigenous peoples were an essential economic resource that needed to be protected so that it might be perpetually exploited. To this end many existing indigenous communities were legally recognized and given resources so that they might endure as sources of labor and other forms of wealth for the Spanish crown, the Spanish colonists, the church, and various Catholic religious orders. The catastrophic post-Conquest population declines noted above made labor scarce, however, and necessitated stronger policies for the husbandry of these communities. The subsequent social identities and destinies of the *indígenas* and their communities in

Spanish America thus developed under markedly different conditions from the English colonies.

Whereas in North America the indigenous peoples were not greatly valued as an economic resource and were mostly exterminated outright or forced onto reservations, in Spanish Latin America the larger populations of *indígenas* were concentrated in communities that were in effect internal colonies. By way of contrast, the Portuguese colonists in Brazil regarded the *indígenas* much as the English (and subsequently the Americans) had the *indígenas* in North America. Although many *indígenas* were incorporated into rubber tapping and mining, African slaves assumed a much more important role in the overall economy of Brazil than they did in most of Spanish America.

From Independence to the Mid-Twentieth Century

By the early nineteenth century criollos throughout Spanish America had come to think of themselves as more American than Spanish; that is, as residents of the regions in which they were born and with which they identified. When these sentiments culminated in successful independence movements, the independent criollos were faced with the challenge of building nation-states out of the former colonies. Central to the concept of a modern nation-state was the idea of a common national cultural identity. The postcolonial nation-states, striving as they were to create more or less culturally homogeneous citizenries, swept away colonial laws that defined peoples as members of racial castes such as "Indian," "white," "black," and combinations thereof. Although racism did not disappear, it now became imbricated more in a social structure based on class. The main distinctions in this class structure grew out of how one earned a living, and the major divide was between those who did manual labor and those who did not. Of course, the *indígenas* fell almost exclusively into the former category. Thus, although the formal structure of the caste system was dismantled, the position of the *indígenas* on the bottom rung of the social hierarchy was perpetuated.

The architects of the Latin American nation-states assumed that the *indígenas* would disappear from history along with the system of castes. And toward this end some of them enacted reform programs in the mid-eighteenth century aimed at eliminating the colonial laws that protected the indigenous communities. In Mexico, for example, the liberal procapitalist elements that enacted the 1857 constitution dissolved the corporate legal basis of the indigenous communities that had prevailed during the colonial period. The assumption was that exposure of the communal resources (primarily communal lands) of the *indígenas* to market forces would break down the backwardness of these communities. Thus, they ceased to be regarded as primarily economic resources and were now seen as barriers to the development of the types of modern agriculture and manufacturing taking place to the north in the United States. Indeed, the liberals saw development in the United States as due in large part to the absence of large indigenous peasant communities such as those in Latin America. In contrast to the colonial period, therefore, in which the *indígenas* were seen as sources of wealth, the indigenous communities were now regarded as pockets of backwardness that were inhibiting progress.

This situation prevailed for the most part until after World War II, when the United States took a renewed interest in Latin America in the context of the cold war. Concerned to maintain its hegemony in the Western Hemisphere in the face of a presumed communist threat, the United States and various international agencies such as the World Bank sought to promote economic development in Latin America. Indeed, the policies and projects of this period were variations on nineteenth-century developmental goals, except they were now promoted in the cold war context, with the U.S. government and international agencies assuming considerable responsibility for the economic and political development of "backward" communities. In this period the Indians were largely identified as peasants. That is to say, they were seen according to economic and developmental criteria rather than for their identity as indigenous peoples. The assumption was that "underdeveloped" communities would be transformed into modern developed ones.

During this period the population growth rate in many countries of the hemisphere exceeded the rates of socioeconomic development measured in terms of job creation and improved standards of living. The population growth also affected indigenous communities, and earlier prognostications about their demise were shown to be inaccurate. Indeed, the simultaneous growth in poverty and numbers of the indigenous peoples suggested that modern history was taking a turn other than that predicted by the architects of the modern Latin American states and the theorists of development.

The Persistence of the *Indígenas*

After the disastrous biological holocaust caused by the epidemics of the "Columbian exchange" (Crosby 1972), which produced probably the greatest population decline in human history (Denevan 1976; Borah and Cook 1963; Dobyns 1966), the indigenous peoples of colonial Spanish and Portuguese America began a slow demographic recuperation that by the early 1990s had brought their population to the vicinity of 40 million (Mayer and Masferrer 1979; World Bank 1991). This number, however, is far below the estimates of the hemisphere's original indigenous population.

There is an intriguing paradox in regard to this obstinate biological and cultural perseverance of the Native American people: How could they outlast the European military invasion, the resulting biological disaster, the systematic "ecological imperialism" (Crosby 1986), the meticulous destruction of their institutions, and still undergo a cultural, social, and political recuperation that has allowed for their continuous and increasing presence in the social and biological history of the continent? The answer to this question has to be sought in the complex forms of resistance and adaptation of the various indigenous peoples over the past five centuries.

Four fundamental forms of ethnic resilience and opposition recur in this long history. The first is what we may call the "moral management" of the cosmos, a type of environmental ethic and practice found in the majority of indigenous societies (Varese 1995). The second is an economic rationality and a social philosophy that contrasts with the individualism and market-based economies of modern societies. This "moral economy," as Scott (1976, 1985) refers to it, occurs among some peasant societies and operates with a logic informed by the ecological cosmology noted above. It seeks to preserve the common resources of the community and minimize internal economic differentiation. Basic economic resources are held in common, and access to them is determined by good citizenship, defined by one's willingness to serve the community in ways that often involve considerable self-sacrifice. Such an economy is centered more on use-value than exchange-value, and economic transactions are mediated primarily by reciprocity rather than by market or profit considerations.

Related to the specifically indigenous nature of these two factors is a third: the tendency of *indígenas* to conceal their ethnobiological knowledge while maintaining an active exploration, investigation, experimentation, and conservation of biodiversity. Finally, indigenous peoples have been extremely adaptable in restructuring their political action to respond to a constantly changing world.

Latin America's indigenous communities were able to establish a new, decolonized institutional, political, and cultural relationship not only among themselves but also with the nonindigenous peoples of the Americas in a number of ways. A reconfiguration of this nature implies a demise of nineteenth-century nationalistic ideology and practices and the negotiation of autonomy and sovereignty with national and international entities (the nation-states, intergovernmental organisms, the transnational corporations, etc.).

Since the European invasion of the Americas, indigenous societies have attempted to conceal their biotic and biotechnological knowledge, well aware that such knowledge was among the most contested cultural domains of the colonial mercantile and evangelical enterprise. For most of the indigenous peoples, agricultural and food production, as well as environmental management, were suffused with religious significance. As such, these social practices were extremely vulnerable to repression by the colonial authorities.

It is well documented that the Spaniards' early ambiguous attitudes toward the Native American biotic heritage induced a series of repressive measures against the cultivation and use of certain plants and resources. The most notorious example is the Mesoamerican *alegría* (amaranth—called *tzoalli* and *huautli* by the Mexicans), whose cultivation, trade, and consumption were banned throughout New Spain during the early colonial period with the argument that it was a pagan sacrificial plant. However, use of medicinal and psychotropic plants and substances, use of stimulants like coca and of animal and insect foods, techniques of preparation of food and fermented beverages, and techniques of food production (e.g., various types of swidden cultivation) have been contentious areas of cultural and political control throughout the colonial period and up to the present.

In Mexico, Bishop Zumarraga, "wished to outlaw pulque [fermented maguey juice] in 1529 because it smacked of idolatry," and for the missionary "drinking, with its ritual vestiges, was a major obstacle to evangelical expansion" (Super 1988:75). But similar aspirations are still at the core of various types of evangelical fundamentalism practiced, for example, by the Summer Institute of Linguistics or a number of Protestant missionaries working with the *indígenas* (Stoll 1985). In sum, European colonialism brought to the Americas definite ideas about food and food production that are still very much part of the hegemonic culture and the ideology that informs most development planning and policy affecting the indigenous regions.

The indigenous peoples did not simply react to colonial impositions. Their responses reflected a variety of strategic accommodations and initiatives. For example, immediately following the Spanish invasion of Mexico, the Maya people of Yucatan repeatedly resisted the invaders—actions that often turned into armed insurrections. These rebellions were motivated by a call to reconstitute the precolonial order and to restore the world's sacredness: to purify a nature contaminated by foreign oppressors. In 1546 the *chilam* (prophet-diviner) Anbal brought together a coalition of the Maya people. On the calendar date of Death and End (November 9), they initiated a war of liberation that sought to kill the invaders, end colonial domination, and purify the earth. The rebels killed Spaniards and their Maya slaves in sacrificial rites and meted out the same fate to all the plants and domesticated animals brought by the Europeans (Barabas 1987; Bartolomé 1984).

In 1786 the Totonacs of Papantla, in southeastern Mexico, rose in rebellion against the Spanish authorities in defense of their threatened trees. A Spanish source observed that "the trees give shade to people and help them to persevere, are useful to tie animals, protect houses from fires, and the branches and leaves are used as fodder for animals" (cited in Taylor 1979: 137).

Earlier, in 1742, in the Amazon jungle of Peru, a Quechua messiah, Juan Santos Atahualpa Apu Capac Huayna, fomented a rebellion that mobilized thousands of Ashaninka, Quechua, and a dozen other ethnic groups and kept the Spaniards and Creoles out of the region for a century. Some of the insurgents' revolutionary demands and proposals were informed by an ecologically based morality: the right to live in dispersed villages and households to allow a rational use of the tropical rain forest; the eradication of European pigs considered harmful to farming and human health; the right to freely cultivate and use coca, known as the "the herb of God"; and the right to produce and ceremonially drink *masato,* a fermented manioc beverage of substantial nutritional value (Brown forthcoming; Varese 1973; Zarzar 1989).

Two centuries later, in 1973, among the Chinantecs of Oaxaca, Mexico, an intense messianic movement flared up in opposition to a proposed dam that would flood their territory and force them into exile to distant lands (Barabas and Bartolomé 1973; Barabas 1987). To defend the ecological integrity of their territory, which they considered sacred, the Chinantecs resorted to a diversified strategy that ranged from legal and bureaucratic negotiations with the government and alliance-building with poor mestizo peasants to the mobilization of shamans, the "caretakers of the lines" (the ethnic borders) whose 'lightning' or *nahuals* would kill the president of Mexico, Luis Echeverría Alvarez. The Chinantec messianic movement gained cultural and social legitimacy with the sacred appearance of the Virgin of Guadalupe and the "Engineer Great God," who ordered the performance of a series of rituals to strengthen the physical and spiritual integrity of certain ecocultural features such as rivers, mountains, trees, springs, caves, and trails.

On January 1, 1994, Tzeltal, Tzotzil, Chol, Tojolabal, and Zoque Maya *indígenas* organized into the Zapatista National Liberation Army (*Ejército Zapatista de Liberación Nacional,* or EZLN) and declared war on the government, quickly establishing the military occupation of four major municipalities in Chiapas, Mexico. An *indígena* army of eight hundred combatants occupied the city of San Cristobal de las Casas, seized the municipal palace, and proclamed their opposition to the "undeclared genocidal war against our people by the dictators," and described their "struggle for work, land, shelter, food, health, education, independence, freedom, democracy, justice, and peace" (EZLN 1994).

Of the six points stated in the EZLN's Declaration of War, the first five spelled out their rules of engagement; the sixth stated that the EZLN would "suspend the looting of our natural resources" in the areas the rebels controlled. This armed movement of an estimated two thousand persons was essentially composed of the Mayan ethnic groups noted above. A fundamental objective of the insurrection was the defense of their lands and natural resources. In other public declarations and communiqués, the EZLN also stressed its opposition to the North American Free Trade Agreement (NAFTA), which it considered a "death certificate" for the indigenous peasants, and to the modification of Article 27 of the Mexican Constitution, which permits the privatization of indigenous and peasant collective and communal lands. "This article 27 of the Constitution, they changed it without asking us, without requesting our input. Now it is time for them to listen to us, because to take our land is to take our life" (IATP 1994). These are but a few examples taken from innumerable historical and contemporary cases illustrating the moral economy that has guided indigenous resistance to economic exploitation and political oppression.

Nevertheless, since at least the mid-seventeenth century, local indigenous communities have participated in an economic system in which part of the production satisfies subsistence needs while the rest, the surplus, enters circuits of commercial exchange (Varese 1991a). Contemporary indigenous communities are thus not uncontaminated citadels of precapitalist economy. They are ruled first by the basic principles of moral economy founded on the logic of reciprocity and on the "right to subsistence," and, second, by the necessity of exchange with the surrounding capitalist market. Both principles permeate the social life of prepeasant, peasant, and even some postpeasant *indígenas* who, self-exiled from their communities because of poverty, partially reconstitute this moral economy as urban subproletarian or transnational migrant workers in the agricultural fields of California (Kearney and Nagengast 1989; Zabin et al. 1993).

Analysis of Indian social movements reveals a history of parallel forms of existence between the indigenous communities and the dominant national communities. These indigenous communities and the dominant national communities reproduce themselves with contradictory cultural principles that are negotiated over and over again, at times violently, when an indigenous community is cornered by the oppressor, cannot avoid direct confrontation, and is thus forced to choose the desperate option of open opposition. In this sense, the violent rebellions of indigenous people embody and condense in heroic moments their daily, nonviolent forms of resistance to the dominant culture. Among such forms of resistance is their indifference to the logic of economic accumulation and their commitment, on the contrary, to the dictates of reciprocity, ceremonial squander, and other forms of social generosity that serve to impoverish them economically while equalizing and empowering them politically.

New Conditions and New Identities

For the sake of discussion, the contemporary period can be seen as beginning in the late 1970s and early 1980s and extending into the twenty-first century. Several notable events have punctuated this period, including the five-hundredth anniversary (1992) of the first encounter of *indígenas* with Europeans. After five centuries of colonization and oppression and the best efforts of modern nation-states and their international agencies to develop the *indígenas* out of existence, it was clear that they were still very much present and in a number of cases growing in numbers and in political significance. Rather than being passive subjects of history made by Europeans and other non-*indígenas,* they have assumed new social forms, new relationships with the nation-states that seek to contain them, and indeed in many cases are assuming new identities that no one had previously imagined. The contemporary situation thus requires a shift in how *indígenas* are conceptualized and, perhaps more important, how they conceptualize themselves.

With respect to the unanticipated turns in the demography and identity of indigenous communities noted above, several major contemporary themes can be identified in this regard. The failure of modern history to bring about the cultural demise of the *indígenas* and to contain their demographic expansion and political power is associated with the stagnation of overall economic development that has failed to stay ahead of growing poverty and population in many areas of Latin America. Indeed, some observers have noted that the global economy has entered a postdevelopment phase of history (e.g., Escobar 1992).

In contrast to the economic and social development of the First World countries, which was based on relatively immobile extractive and heavy industries, postdevelopment economies are based on flexible, light manufacturing, and service industries organized on a global scale to take advantage of the most competitive sources of supplies, labor, and markets. These kinds of industries do not provide their employees with working conditions that have traditionally helped to support a stable working class. Workers receive low wages, no benefits, and no job security. Related to this expansion of "flexible capital" is the growth throughout Latin America of small-scale informal economic activities such as independent home manufacturing and street vending.

In the 1980s many Latin American nations introduced neoliberal policies of development that dismantled the import substitution policies designed to protect domestic industries from the penetration of foreign commodities. With the removal of tariffs and other forms of protection affected by the General Agreement on Tariffs and Trade (GATT) and the formation of free trade agreements such as NAFTA, the balance-of-payment problems for many Latin American countries have been alleviated, but typically at a tremendous cost to the middle and lower classes, which have suffered a general lowering of their income and standards of living. The inhabitants of urban shantytowns and peasant communities have been especially hard hit by these trends (see the chapters by Kay and Halebsky in this volume).

The proliferation of flexible capital, the spread of the informal economy, and the rapid growth of the population mock the orthodox modernist visions of development and its supposed power to level social and cultural differences. More and more indigenous peoples are being drawn into postdevelopment conditions of production and reproduction. It is in such contexts that indigenous identities are not only destroyed but also recreated. That is to say, these contexts both destroy and preserve traditional social and cultural forms; even more notable, postdevelopment conditions also stimulate and support the emergence of forms of indigenous identity that are strictly speaking neither modern nor traditional. Indeed, one of the most notable characteristics of the contemporary era is the collapse of the distinction between modern and traditional. An understanding of this rather novel cultural, economic, and political context is essential for comprehending the formation of contemporary indigenous identities. A major feature of this new context is that it is increasingly transnational.

Transnationalization

Modernist theories of indigenous societies assumed that the identities of indigenous peoples were being modified within the context of the nation-states in which these societies were encapsulated. But the dynamics of identity formation in the contemporary era are increasingly being influenced by transnational forces and events. Furthermore, specific groups of *indígenas* have begun to operate outside the nations that have historically confined them. In other words, identity formation is no longer restricted mainly to national contexts.

In many Latin American countries indigenous groups span national borders. This transnational, transborder, transstate character of Native American ethnic groups is rooted in colonial territorial partitions and their postcolonial confirmation: Aymara live in Peru, Bolivia, Chile, and Argentina; Quechuas in Bolivia, Ecuador, and Peru; Shuar-Aguajun in Ecuador and Peru; Embera in Panama and Colombia; Yanomamo in Brazil and Venezuela; Miskito and Garifunas in Belize, Honduras, and Nicaragua; Mayas in Mexico, Guatemala, and Belize; Mapuches in Chile and Argentina; Yaqui, Kikapoo, and O'hotam (known also as Papago), and so forth in Mexico and the United States. The transnationalism of numerous indigenous peoples is also accentuated by their migration across national boundaries. Thus, the conventional anthropological image of indigenous people living in relatively isolated and stable rural agricultural communities is challenged by a new and more complex reality in which *indígenas* from Mexico, Central, and South America migrate to the United States, for example, as rural and urban workers and as political and economic refugees. Mixtecs, Zapotecs, Chinantecs, Triques, Purepechas, Kanjobales, Quiche, Keqchi, Mam, Ixil, Garifuna, Miskito, and even Peruvian Quechua and Ecuadorian Quichua have become a substantial component of the so-called Latino community of the United States (Altamirano 1991; Zabin et al. 1993; Varese 1991b).

Since the early 1970s massive demographic movements of indigenous peoples in Latin America have taken the shape of migrations to other rural areas and to urban centers with better economic opportunity, both within the same country or in other countries. In fact, the rural-to-urban migration of *indígenas* has created what Albo (1991) calls "cities of Indians," such as Cochibamba in Bolivia. Throughout Latin America, indigenous peoples unable to make ends meet in the countryside have been forced to move into urban areas. They typically retain close ties with their family and community in the countryside. Indeed, in many cases households and entire communities are able to endure from year to year because of complex strategies that effectively blur the distinctions between rural and urban identities and spaces. The large number of *indígenas* in many Latin American cities is comparable to the situation in the United States, where more Native Americans now live in urban areas than on reservations.

Just as pollution and ozone depletion in the atmosphere do not obey national boundaries, so is concern with the ecological well-being of the planet and the rights of indigenous peoples in general an imminently global issue. In recent years, concern for the health of the planet has become linked to the well-being of indigenous peoples in Latin America and elsewhere. Indeed, as concern with the degradation of ecosystems rises, people in and outside of Latin America have increasingly come to appreciate how the *indígenas* have most often lived for centuries in ecological balance with their environments and how this might offer alternative models to the environmentally destructive forms of modern development. Consequently, indigenous communities, whose organizations may be numerically quite small or otherwise relatively powerless within their own national contexts, have come to find that they have powerful allies elsewhere in the world.

International concerns about protecting the global ecosystem have drawn indigenous peoples into the international area. In a similar manner, the growing international concern with the protection of human rights has also brought indigenous peoples to the attention of potential allies outside Latin America. Sometimes both types of concerns are intermixed as, for example, when mining, oil, and timber companies, cattle ranchers, or nonindigenous colonists invade indigenous life spaces and begin to destroy them. Until recently, awareness of and concern with such conflicts did not extend significantly beyond local regions or national boundaries. Now, however, the presence of international nongovernmental organizations (NGOs) that are concerned with environmental issues and human rights use sophisticated networking and communication facilities to publicize the plight of indigenous communities whose environment and rights are being violated. One of numerous examples in which the human rights of *indígenas* and ecological issues were interwoven was the international mobilization to protest the assassination of Chico Mendez, leader of the Amazonian rubber tappers' union (see the chapter by Dore in this volume).

In responding to the invasion of their life spaces and the depredation of their natural resources, indigenous peoples have resorted to legal strategies that often involve seeking territorial rights, semiautonomy within the nation-state, cultural autonomy and/or recognition of their indigenous language, as well as judicial reforms that recognize indigenous legal forms (e.g., see Stavenhagen 1988). By advancing and occasionally winning such causes, existing *indígena* identities are not only reinforced, they acquire new dimensions and content.

The old units of anthropological analysis and policymaking—the rural agrarian community, the indigenous region, multiethnic areas, and even the nation-state—are alone inadequate for comprehending the emergent trans-state networks of indigenous and nonindigenous peoples concerned with the environment and human rights. Latin American indigenous peoples who were formerly marginalized are now actively engaged in establishing a transnational civil society in an effort to bypass state mediation and to situate themselves in a global civil society while maintaining strong ethnic, cultural, and local loyalties (Brecher et al. 1993; Brysk 1992; Kearney 1991).

The existence of transnational indigenous peoples' movements that articulate local struggles for communal sovereignty with an agenda of universal political, cultural, and environmental indigenous rights demands a corresponding analytical paradigm and political praxis. Today, transnational multiethnic indigenous organizations understand clearly that the economic and political power that threatens local indigenous sovereignty is unevenly distributed between transnational corporations, intergovernmental institutions, and national governments. They understand that the proposed new world order is a form of neoimperial globalization that is changing the rules of the game and debilitating nation-state sovereignties in order to open more space for the transnational corporations that are the primary organizers of the world political economy at the end of this century.

Most important for the indigenous leadership is the understanding that in the past five centuries the entrenchment and consolidation of the colonial and republican states have been based on the maximization of labor exploitation carefully organized along the lines of ethnic divisions and ethnoterritorial delineation. The incorporation of indigenous ethnicity into the global division of labor shaped intraethnic class differentiation as well as interethnic economic inequality and differential access to political power. The result of the differential treatment of ethnic groups and regions by states and by capital has produced a complex class structure that cuts across and permeates the multiethnic configuration of the Latin American societies. In this regard, it is interesting to note that indigenous intellectuals in Mexico have coined the term "ethnocracy" to define the contemporary Latin American states, ruled and controlled by cliques of nonindigenous people (CONEI 1994). An intricate panorama of indigenous political organizations and platforms with different levels of class and ethnic consciousness has emerged within this complex ethnoclass structure.

One common characteristic, however, appears throughout the hemispheric indigenous movement and its national and transnational organizations: The organized indigenous peoples display a lukewarm national loyalty, a nonconformity, and opposition to the nation-state's political project, which has, after all, been the class and cultural expression of mestizo and creole elites and which for centuries has assaulted indigenous sovereignties with racist and ethnocentric arguments. This indigenous tendency toward denationalization is a fertile ideological and cultural terrain for developing collective identities based on alternative forms of ethnopolitical identification.

Indigenous organizations are thus increasingly taking their fight for the ethnic sovereignty of their constituencies into transnational spaces, where the balance of power between nation and ethnos is realigned, often to the benefit of the latter. One form of such realignment stems from the confrontation between indigenous peoples and transnational corporations seeking to appropriate resources in indigenous areas, usually counting on the complicity or indifference of the nation-state to facilitate their operations. The struggle of Ecuador's Amazonian Indian communities against twenty-two transnational oil companies is a good example of this trend (SAIIC 1991). The foreign companies operate in indigenous territories under army protection provided by the Ecuadorian government, in a style reminiscent of colonial military occupations. In this conflict, indigenous communities defending their ethnic heritage (territory, environment, and natural resources) directly confront multinational development agencies and transnational corporations.

As soon as the revolutionary Sandinista government of Nicaragua was replaced in 1990, the Sumo, a small ethnic group on the Atlantic Coast, were besieged by the transnational Taiwanese company Equipe Enterprise, which had obtained a concession of 350,000 hectares of tropical rain forest on indigenous territory from the newly elected conservative government. The Sumo responded by looking for support from international NGOs, thus avoiding engagement with the government (SAIIC 1991). The Huaorani of Ecuador were able to mobilize national and international environmental groups against the planned oil exploitation of their territory by DuPont-Conoco Oil Company. The Huaorani campaign, which gained the support of South and Mesoamerican Indian Information Center (SAIIC) of Oakland, California, and the Sierra Club Legal Defense Fund, succeeded, and the oil company halted its operation in the Huaorani's territory (SAIIC 1991). Peruvian Amazonian indigenous organizations obtained a similar victory when in September 1991 the Houston-based Texas Crude Oil Company canceled its contract with the Peruvian government for the exploration of the Pacaya Samiria Indian region (SAIIC 1991).

The strategy of internationalizing the defense of collective indigenous rights appears to be more successful than the exclusive exercise of conventional mobilizations at the national level. By globalizing the conflict, the in-

digenous organizations open various fronts in the international arena and
thus gain the support not only of international environmental and human
rights movements but also the legal, financial, and technical assistance of international NGOs and intergovernmental organizations such as the International Labor Organization (ILO). Finally, since the early 1980s, the indigenous peoples of the Americas have carried their struggles to the United
Nations, demanding that it become more democratic and adopt less nationalist positions and a more stateless orientation. Similar international pressure
has also moved the World Bank and the Inter-American Development Bank
(IDB) to reformulate their policies for indigenous regions. Also, new opportunities are emerging within international law for the defense of indigenous
peoples (Anaya 1994); similar developments are evident at the United Nations with that world body's Draft Declaration on the Rights of Indigenous
People. The ILO's Convention on Indigenous and Tribal Peoples is also an
auspicious document (Coulter 1994; Barsh 1994; see also Stavenhagen
1988).

Changing Forms of Political and Symbolic Representation

As new *indígena* political issues connected with environmentalism and human
rights have emerged, so have new organizations taken shape to express these
issues. Generally speaking, they have taken the form of new social movements,
or NSMs, that have become powerful voices for grassroots concerns (as discussed in the chapter by Hellman in this book). Forsaking conventional organizational forms such as parties and unions, these NSMs tend to be looser
networks of individuals and groups, often formed around a single issue. A particular organization may have a name and officers, but its structure and membership tend to be fluid and prone to fragmentation and lack of cohesion.
Nevertheless, the recent general history of new indigenous movements in
Latin America reveals a growing coalescence of small movements into larger
alliances and confederations. Thus, local groups may form a regional alliance
that then allies itself with other regional groups to form an overarching national or supranational organization that coordinates its member organizations. This tendency for expansion has now reached the continental level via,
for example, the efforts of the International Treaty Council and SAIIC to
"link natives of North and South America" (Brysk forthcoming). This organizational transcendence of the boundaries between North American and Latin
American groups is a logical progression of the political and cultural self-as-
sertion of the *indígenas* of the Western Hemisphere. Whereas at the time of
their first contact with Europeans the peoples of the Americas were largely
isolated from one another by distance and their differences, now, on the eve of
the twenty-first century, they are creating transnational organizations that
reach from within the Arctic Circle to Tierra del Fuego.

Brysk has observed that "the Indian rights movement internationalized so quickly" because *indígenas* were forced into the international arena as a result of their powerlessness at home and "contrary to the implicit assumptions of a levels of analysis model, international activity required fewer resources than domestic mobilization and was more amenable to information politics" (Brysk 1995). In other words, Brysk argues that they were able to turn their "weakness into strength." Indigenous organizations have also greatly benefited from the international prominence granted them by the global media of communication, allowing them to proceed "from oral history to sound bites in one generation" (Brysk forthcoming). The direct utilization of electronic means of communication, such as facsimile machines, video cassettes, and electronic networks, has also made the indigenous movements an effective political force.

In the late twentieth century, individual indigenous personalities have begun to vie with other notable persons in public. Formerly, only mythic figures appeared in public spaces; that is, individuals who were glorified after their deaths, such as Tupac Amaru or Moctezuma. But now living persons are becoming world figures in real time rather than in some mythic past. Parallel to the remarkable appearance of major indigenous political figures in the international media is the recent emergence on the international scene of a new type of literature that portrays the lives of *indígenas*. Perhaps the most notable example is that of Rigoberta Menchú (1983), a Mayan woman of Guatemala who received the 1992 Nobel Prize in Literature for her autobiography. Menchú's book is a prime example of testimonial literature, a form advanced in large measure by *indígenas* who are increasingly speaking up for themselves rather than being the passive subjects described by nonindigenous writers. Such testimonial literature is especially notable in that it has been written to a great extent by women (Gugelberger and Kearney 1991).

Debate over the indigenous movement has centered on two main issues: (1) Are these new organizations legitimate, and (2) is their autonomous presence on the political scene a divisive force? For the past twenty years, social scientists, as well as mestizo and criollo political activists, politicians, and policymakers, have debated these questions. Only occasionally have invitations to participate in these discussions been extended to indigenous leaders and intellectuals. Charges of illegitimacy and suggestions that they should become subordinate to nonindigenous political parties have been the main focus of debate and struggle. Although risky to generalize, it can nevertheless be argued that the indigenous organizations of Latin America, with the exception of those of Mexico, have generally perceived political parties as an extension of the neocolonial state (see Smith 1985).

With the support of marginal sectors of the Catholic Church and a handful of progressive social scientists, a new generation of indigenous grassroots organizations have emerged within the neoliberal state, multiplying, expanding, and consolidating their support (for an extended discussion of these developments see Albo 1990; Juncosa 1992). In view of the critical situation of the Left, the demise of the Socialist Bloc, the profound cultural crisis of both liberal and Marxist utopias, and the messianic escapism of the Shining Path guerrillas of Peru, it is reasonable to argue that the indigenous movements of the 1990s in Latin America provide a strong and coherent—although multi-faceted and plural—voice of opposition as well as cultural and political innovation.

This perspective on the indigenous movements in contemporary Latin America contrasts in nearly all respects with the reductionism of mainstream social scientists who see indigenous movements only in terms of how they are subordinate to the dominant society's social agenda, confining the analytical discussion to narrow political dimensions and shallow historical perspectives. Their fragmented ethnography—informed by a Eurocentric epistemology of eventfulness—has obscured the cultural history of the *indígenas*. For them, the political resistance of indigenous people appears to have no historical depth, taking on significance only when they behave like Europeans or use an idiom considered to be politically valid. This conception of the *indígenas* is suffused with the ideology of expanding capitalism and colonialism; it assumes that intellectual and ethical innovations have been transmitted to a passive, uncivilized native periphery from a vibrant European center.

The chronicle of post-Conquest history reveals, however, that the indigenous peoples of the Americas have confronted profound and radical issues throughout their five centuries of resistance. Proposals for a radical change of the global economic and political system, criticism of the social order imposed on the Americas by the Europeans, and denunciations of the disruption of nature caused by colonialism, have motivated numerous indigenous uprisings, provided the basis for persistent, daily resistance, and served as an integral part of the critique of the dominant culture developed by the indigenous intelligentsia. For five centuries, the indigenous peoples of the Americas have striven to maintain a critical distance from the worldview and values of the colonizers in an effort to preserve the minimum conditions for their moral autonomy, cultural independence, and political sovereignty.

The rapid growth of transnational indigenous political movements indicates that the indigenous peoples have been able to turn their domestic weakness and marginality into a basis for international recognition and support. Under the contemporary conditions of "globalization from the top," the *indígenas* have been able to respond with a "globalization from below" (Falk 1993) by shifting the target of their activism to the international political and economic actors.

An expanded conception of ethnicity, one that incorporates a political project encompassing the whole multicommunal territory and biocultural resources of a state or region, requires dramatic changes in the political culture, social practices, and organizational forms of the indigenous peoples affected by this conception. Larger, more complex ethnopolitical organizations, which require extensive innovations in management and new indigenous democratic mechanisms, must be imagined and implemented. The following examples, drawn from Amazonia and Mesoamerica, illustrate these new indigenous political and cultural forms.

Building Indian Sovereignty in the Amazon

The creation of the Federation of Shuar Centers in 1964 is a benchmark in the development of new forms of resistance by indigenous peoples in Latin America. This surprising form of political organization had by 1987 incorporated 240 centers and more than 40,000 Shuar people into a unique social program of economic and cultural self-determination. Four years after the Shuar Federation was formed, the Amuesha people (Yanesha) of the Peruvian Upper Amazon convened the first Amuesha Congress, which was later transformed into a permanent political body called the Amuesha Federation.

Between 1970 and 1974, in an intense series of mobilizations, Colombian *indígenas* organized the Indian Regional Council of Cauca and several other organizations. During the 1970s in Peru, the indigenous people of the Amazon region formed many local organizations and regional federations—for instance, the Ashaninka Congress of the Central Jungle, the Shipibo Congress and Defense Front, and the Aguaruna Huambisa Council. In the highlands of Bolivia the organized expressions of a strong Aymara and Quechua nationalism were initially shaped by the Katarist movement. To the south in Chile, under the safeguard of Salvador Allende's socialist government, the Mapuches participated in the elaboration and implementation of a *Ley de Indígenas* (Law of the Indígenas). This short-lived taste of multiethnicity ended in 1973 with General Augusto Pinochet's military dictatorship and the death, imprisonment, and exile of the Mapuche leadership.

In March 1984 representatives of five indigenous organizations from the Amazonian countries of Brazil, Bolivia, Colombia, Ecuador, and Peru met in Lima and founded the international organization called the Coordinating Body of Indigenous Peoples' Organizations of the Amazon Basin (*Coordinadora de las Organizaciones Indígenas de la Cuenca Amazónica,* or COICA). COICA's main political objective was to became a coordinating body that would present a common policy position for all the organized *indígenas* of the Greater Amazon Basin before the region's governments and the international community. COICA's origins can be traced to the three regional, community-based organizations of the early 1960s noted above: the Shuar Federation in Ecuador, the Congress of Amuesha Communities in Peru, and the Regional Indigenous Council of the Cauca in Colombia (Smith 1993). These local organizations, initially unknown to one another, established a model of social mobilization that gave voice to each local community's problems of territorial loss, human rights abuses, and cultural oppression. Throughout the 1970s, numerous other organizations emerged among the Amazonian peoples and began to establish contacts facilitated by the solidarity of various nonindigenous groups, such as sympathetic Catholic missionaries, proindigenous NGOs, and environmentalists.

COICA has primarily been concerned with territorial and environmental rights; human, cultural, and linguistic rights; and rights to economic and political self-determination (Smith 1993; Varese 1991a). Today COICA comprises more than one hundred interethnic confederations of Amazonian groups from Bolivia, Brazil, Colombia, Ecuador, Guyana, French Guyana, Peru, Suriname, and Venezuela, which represent approximately 1.5 million indigenous people (Chirif et al. 1991; Smith 1993).

COICA's active involvement in the U.N. Working Group on Indigenous Peoples' Rights, in the discussions concerning the ILO's Covenant 169 on Indigenous and Tribal People approved in 1989, and in various committees of the Amazon Treaty Cooperation sponsored by the Inter-American Indigenous Institute, brought the members of the organization in contact with an increasing number of international bureaucrats, advocates, indigenous support groups, the leaders of other ethnic minorities, parties, labor organizations, the European Green movement, and funding agencies. In 1986 COICA won an ecological prize, the Right Livelihood award, which gave the organization front-page international coverage and major exposure to official circles. During 1989 COICA was recognized by the World Bank and had established official contact with the European Community (now the European Union). In 1991 COICA gained official advisory status with the Indigenous Commission of the Amazon Cooperation Treaty. Moreover, between 1990 and 1991, it was one of the founding members of the Alliance for Protecting the Forest and Climate, formed with representatives from more than one hundred cities in five European countries (Smith 1993).

This relatively rapid success brought strains to COICA, revealing its structural limitations in representing its constituencies and its lack of means and methods for efficient communications between its community-based units, the regional and national federations, and its central administrative body. And, finally, the central administration had become somewhat autocratic (Smith 1993). By 1992 a general congress of COICA unanimously decided to create a less hierarchical structure and to facilitate communications and accountability by decentralizing decision-making. COICA headquarters were also moved from Lima to Quito.

Mesoamerican Indigenous Peoples in the United States

The activities of migrants from Guatemala and southern Mexico to the United States have been one of the most notable developments in the recent history of new Latin American indigenous movements. Since the outbreak of war in Guatemala during the late 1970s between several indigenous-based guerrilla groups and the government, some tens of thousands of *indígenas* have been killed, and many thousands more have fled the country to seek sanctuary either in Mexico or in the United States. Those who sought refuge in the United States in the past fifteen or so years have settled mainly in Los Angeles. Within the Guatemalan indigenous community in Los Angeles, many different ethnic groups are represented, each of which is from a distinct community that speaks its own Mayan language. Whereas these refugees were isolated by distance and culture in Guatemala, they have been thrown together in the city's sprawling Latino neighborhoods, where they found common cultural and political bonds. On the basis of this shared heritage, the need to defend themselves as aliens in a strange and often hostile land has motivated them to form several interethnic associations. The largest of these, known as "Ixim," takes its name from the Mayan word for maize, which in cognate forms is found in the languages of all the Guatemalan indigenous peoples in Los Angeles.

Comparable to the presence of indigenous Guatemalan refugees in Los Angeles is the presence in California of tens of thousands of *indígenas* from the state of Oaxaca in southern Mexico. At any given time there are some 25,000 to 40,000 Mixtec migrant farm workers in California (Runsten and Kearney 1994). Whereas the Guatemalan *indígenas* are refugees from a horrendous war waged against them, the Mixtecs are mainly economic refugees from a region in which the environment has been steadily deteriorating, undermining the subsistence farming that is their primary livelihood. In the 1980s, Mixtec migrants from various towns formed self-help associations based on their communities of origin, and by the early 1990s these local groups had come together to form a common Mixtec front.

Since the 1960s, uncounted thousands of Zapotecs from Oaxaca have migrated to California to work temporarily or to settle, primarily in the Los Angeles area. As in the Mixtec case, the Zapotecs have formed migrant associations based on their communities of origin, some twenty of which came together in the late 1980s to create a coordinating body, the Oaxacan Regional Organization (ORO).

The objectives of the Zapotec and the Mixtec federations are binational in scope in that they seek to protect and promote the well-being of their members in the United States and also to defend and otherwise support their communities of origin in Oaxaca through financial and symbolic support and by intervening in government policies directed at the indigenous communities. A major milestone in Oaxacan political evolution in California was the coming together in 1991 of most of the Mixtec and Zapotec groups to form the Mixtec-Zapotec Binational Front, which has since acquired considerable legitimacy with the Mexican government and international agencies. In 1994 other indigenous groups in Oaxaca asked to join the front. These groups represent Mixe, Triques, and Chatinos, thus occasioning another name change, this time to the all-inclusive Frente Indígena Oaxaqueña Binacional (FIOB), which can without terminological inconsistency now accept groups representing any of the sixteen indigenous peoples of Oaxaca.

The history of the formation of the Guatemalan and Oaxacan indigenous groups in California is perhaps the most notable example of the transnationalization of Latin American indigenous politics in that the primary locus of these international groups has been outside not only their home territories but also Latin America. In their organizational forms, as in their personal lives, the members of these groups transcend the boundaries between the United States, Guatemala, and Mexico, and also between the so-called industrial and developing worlds, a distinction that has become largely obsolete as Mesoamerican indigenous peoples increasingly live transnational lives.

Lessons from Experience and Future Perspectives

An assessment of the Latin American indigenous movement in the 1990s reveals two crucial concerns of the indigenous people. The first is the right of self-government and autonomy. These rights are becoming an increasingly prominent part of the democratization process in various Latin American countries. The demands of the Mayan rebels of Chiapas presented to the Mexican government in 1994 are a good example. As mentioned above, the indigenous insurgents demanded communal and regional autonomy, free elections, self-rule, and guarantees of nonintervention on the part of the government in their internal affairs. The second concern is their right to territorial and resource sovereignty. Their demands for ethnic self-determination and autonomy include full control over the lands, water, and resources that fall within their newly defined ethnic boundaries.

The recuperation of ethnic territories and political autonomy is based on three principles, the first of which is the historical depth of the claim. The current territorial fragmentation and reduction in Latin America is the result of centuries of colonial and postcolonial expropriation; therefore, restitution of land and/or reparations are major issues.

The second principle is based on the ethnobiological integrity of territories traditionally occupied by specific indigenous groups. In other words, bioregions and ethnoregions were largely coincident before the territorial disturbances of the Europeans. There is no such thing in the contemporary period as natural, untouched landscape: Rational intervention by *indígenas* over the millennia has shaped and molded the environment and its biotic resources (see Chirif et al. 1991).

The third principle is the repudiation of any solution to territorial and environmental claims that would involve the commoditization of nature. As one indigenous leader is reported to have stated in objection to the celebrated debt-for-nature swaps promoted by some Northern environmentalists: "It is our nature—and it's not our debt" (Brysk 1992).

Recognition of and respect for these three principles must constitute the ethical framework for any political and economic negotiations between the indigenous peoples and national and international entities regarding political, territorial, and resource sovereignty. Some of the specific practical aspects of ethno-sovereignty rights that will have to be jointly addressed by *indígenas* and nonindigenous peoples are briefly mentioned below.

First of all, there is the important question of the social and spatial definition of indigenous peoples and groups. According to the indigenistic legislation of various national governments, the indigenous ethnic groups are legally defined by their respective constituent communities (e.g., the *resguardo* in Colombia, the *comunidad nativa* and *comunidad campesina* in Peru, the *comunidad indígena* and *ejido* in Mexico, etc.). The whole ethnic group, even if legally recognized in some capacity by the state, does not constitute a juridical subject. Nevertheless, the indigenous organizations of Ecuador have succeeded in obtaining the state's recognition of the term "nationalities" for the various indigenous ethnic communities, but this is a definitive exception in Latin America.

In view of the disagreement and confusion throughout the continent about ethnosocial definitions and boundaries, indigenous intellectuals and leaders are addressing two levels of sovereignty that are rather complementary: One is "communal sovereignty," which is usually legally recognized by the state. At this level there are local indigenous institutions and authorities and clear social-ethnic boundaries; the rather murky and more complicated biotic boundaries therefore pose a more complex problem of genetic and resource sovereignty.

In contrast, the concept of "ethnic sovereignty" is legally rare or nonexistent from the state's point of view. However, some groups are beginning to define this type of sovereignty (Varese 1988). Total ethnic sovereignty is represented in the numerous indigenous ethnic organizations that have a legal and fully institutional existence. In this case, negotiated restitutions and formal interinstitutional agreements are required at various organizational levels, including the local community, the ethnic organization, local and central government agencies, and external investors and/or scientific parties. In instances of this type, the issue of biotic, cultural, and resource boundaries is easiest to resolve since there may be an approximate coincidence between ethnopolitical and ethnobiotic boundaries. By "ethnopolitical boundaries," the indigenous people mean the historically traceable ethnic frontiers, even if they are not actually under ethnic control and are not being reclaimed by the organization as a political objective.

Finally, there is the challenge of further developing organizational and legal forms that recognize and meet the needs of the ever-growing numbers of de-territorialized indigenous peoples who reside in cities and in nations far removed from their traditional homelands and modes of existence. These issues of boundaries and identities, of sovereignty and self-determination, promise to be increasingly salient issues to the indigenous peoples of Latin America in the twenty-first century.

References

Albo, Xavier. "De MNRistas a kataristas a Katari" in Steve Stern, ed., *Resistencia rebelión y conciencia campesina en los Andes*. Lima: Instituto de Estudios Peruanos, 1990.

———. "El retorno del Indio." *Revista Andina* 9, 2 (December 1991).

Altamirano, Teófilo. "Pastores Quechuas en el Oeste Norteamericano." *América Indígena*, no. 2–3 (1991).

Anaya, S. James. "International Law and Indigenous Peoples." *Cultural Survival Quarterly*, no. 1 (1994):42–44.

Barabas, Alicia M. *Utopias Indias: Movimientos Socio-religiosos en México*. Mexico City: Grijalbo, 1987.

Barabas, Alicia M., and Miguel A. Bartolomé. *Hydraulic Development and Ethnocide: The Mazatec and Chinantec People of Oaxaca, Mexico*, IWGIA Document No. 15. Copenhagen: IWGIA, 1973.

Barsh, Russell L. "Making the Most of ILO Convention 169." *Cultural Survival Quarterly*, no. 1 (1994):45–47.

Bartolomé, Miguel A. "La dinámica social de los mayas de Yucatán." Ph.D. diss., Facultad de Ciencias Políticas y Sociales de la UNAM, 1984.

Borah, Woodrow, and S. F. Cook. *The Aboriginal Population of Central Mexico on the Eve of the Spanish Conquest*. Berkeley: University of California Press, 1963.

Brecher, Jeremy, John Brown, Robert Childs, and James Cutler. *Global Visions: Beyond the New World Order*. Boston: South End Press, 1993.

Brown, Michael F. "Facing the State, Facing the World: Amazonia's Native Leaders and the New Politics of Identity," in Philippe Descola and Anne-Christine Taylor, eds., *L'Homme: Anthopologie et histoire des sociétés amazoniennes*. Forthcoming.

Brysk, Alison. "Acting Globally: International Relations and the Indian Rights in Latin America." Paper presented at the Seventeenth International Congress of the Latin American Studies Association, Los Angeles, September 24–27, 1992.

———. "Turning Weakness into Strength: The Internationalization of Indian Rights." *Latin American Perspectives* (1995).

Chirif Tirado, Alberto, Pedro Garcia Hierro, and Robert C. Smith. *El Indígena y su territorio son uno solo: Estrategia para la defensa de los pueblos y territorios indígenas en la cuenca amazónica*. Lima, Peru: Oxfam America, 1991.

CONEI *(Convención Nacional Electoral Indígena)*. "Declaración de los pueblos indios de México en torno a la respuesta del gobierno al EZLN." Mexico City, March 4–5, 1994.

Coulter, Robert T. "Commentary on the U.N. Draft Declaration on the Rights of Indigenous Peoples." *Cultural Survival Quarterly*, no. 1 (1994):37–41.

Crosby, Alfred W. *The Columbian Exchange: Biological and Cultural Consequences of 1492*. Westport, CT: Greenwood, 1972.

———. *Ecological Imperialism: The Biological Expansion of Europe, 900–1900*. Cambridge: Cambridge University Press, 1986.

Denevan, William M., ed. *The Native Population of the Americas in 1492.* Madison: University of Wisconsin Press, 1976.

Dobyns, Henry F. "Estimating Aboriginal American Populations: An Appraisal of Techniques with a New Hemispheric Estimate." *Current Anthropology,* no. 7 (1966):395–416.

Escobar, Arturo. "Imagining a Post-Development Era? Critical Thought, Development and Social Movements." *Social Text* 31–32 (1992):20–56.

EZLN. *Comunicados del Ejército Zapatista de Liberación Nacional,* January 1, 6, 11, 12, and 13, 1994.

Falk, Richard. "The Making of Global Citizenship," in Jeremy Brecher, John Brown, Robert Childs, and James Cutler, eds., *Global Visions: Beyond the New World Order.* Boston: South End Press, 1993.

Galeano, Eduardo. *The Open Veins of Latin America.* New York: Monthly Review Press, 1973.

Gugelberger, Georg, and Michael Kearney. "Voices for the Voiceless: Testimonial Literature in Latin America." *Latin American Perspectives* 18, 3 (1991):3–14.

IATP (Institute for Agriculture and Trade Policy). "Chiapas Digest." 1994. Via E-mail.

Juncosa, José, ed. *Documentos indios: declaraciones y pronunciamientos,* in Colección 500 Años, no. 32, 1991; no. 57, 1992. Quito: Ediciones Abya Yala, 1991–1992.

Kearney, Michael. "Borders and Boundaries of the State and Self at the End of Empire." *Journal of Historical Sociology* 4, 1 (1991):52–74.

Kearney, Michael, and Carole Nagengast. "Anthropological Perspective on Transnational Communities in Rural California." Working Paper No. 3 of the Working Group on Farm Labor and Rural Poverty. Davis: California Institute for Rural Studies, 1989.

Mayer, Enrique, and E. Masferrer. "La población indígena de América en 1978." *América Indígena,* 39, 2 (1979).

Menchú, Rigoberta. *Rigoberta Menchú: An Indian Woman in Guatemala.* London: Verso, 1984.

Runsten, David, and Michael Kearney. *A Survey of Oaxacan Village Networks in California Agriculture.* Davis: California Institute for Rural Studies, 1994.

SAIIC (South and Mesoamerican Indian Information Center). *SAIIC Newsletter* 6, 1–2 (Spring–Summer 1991).

Scott, James. *The Moral Economy of the Peasant: Rebellion and Subsistence in Southeast Asia.* New Haven: Yale University Press, 1976.

———. *Weapons of the Weak: Everyday Forms of Peasant Resistance.* New Haven: Yale University Press, 1985.

Smith, Richard C. "A Search for Unity Within Diversity: Peasant Unions, Ethnic Federations, and Indianist Movements in the Andean Republics," in Theodore Macdonald Jr., ed., *Native Peoples and Economic Development: Six Case Studies from Latin America.* Occasional Paper No. 16. Cambridge, MA: Cultural Survival, 1985.

———. "COICA and the Amazon Basin: The Internationalization of Indigenous Peoples' Demands." Paper presented at the Thirteenth International Congress of Anthropological and Ethnological Sciences, Mexico City, July 29–August 5, 1993.

Stavenhagen, Rodolfo. *Derecho indígena y derechos humanos en América Latina.* Mexico City: El Colegio de México and Instituto Interamericano de Derechos Humanos, 1988.

Stoll, David. *Pescadores de hombres o fundadores de Imperio?* Lima: DESCO, 1985.

Super, John C. *Food, Conquest, and Colonization in Sixteenth-century Spanish America.* Albuquerque: University of New Mexico Press, 1988.

Taylor, William B. *Drinking, Homicide, and Rebellion in Colonial Mexican Villages.* Stanford, CA: Stanford University Press, 1979.

Varese, Stefano. *La sal de los cerros: Una aproximación al mundo campa.* Lima: Ediciones Retablo de Papel, 1973.

———. "Multi-ethnicity and Hegemonic Construction: Indian Plans and the Future," in Remo Guidieri, Francisco Pellizzi, and Stanley J. Tambiah, eds., *Ethnicities and Nations.* Austin: University of Texas Press, 1988.

———. "The Ethnopolitics of Indian Resistance in Latin America." Working Paper. Cambridge: M.I.T. Center for International Studies, 1991a.

———. "Think Locally, Act Globally." *NACLA Report on the Americas, 25, 3 (1991b):13–17.*

———. "The Ethnopolitics of Indian Resistance in Latin America." Latin American Perspectives (1995).

Wolf, Eric R. *Europe and the People Without History.* Berkeley: University of California Press, 1982.

World Bank. *Informe sobre el desarrollo mundial.* Washington, DC: World Bank, 1991.

Zabin, Carol, Michael Kearney, Anna Garcia, David Runsten, and Carole Nagengast. *Mixtec Migrants in California Agriculture: A New Cycle of Poverty.* Davis: California Institute for Rural Studies, 1993.

Zarzar, Alonso. *Apo Capac Huayna, Jesús Sacramentado: Mito, utopia y milenarismo en el pensamiento de Juan Santos Atahualpa.* Lima: Ediciones CAAP, 1989.

9

Whither the Catholic Church in the 1990s?

JOHN M. KIRK

If this chapter had been written in the late 1970s or early 1980s, the future of organized religion would have been far more difficult to predict than it is now largely because the number of variables was so much greater then. Confusing (and at times contradictory) signals emanated from the church hierarchy in Latin America and the Vatican, while the active participation of Christians in the Nicaraguan Revolution against the Somoza regime revealed a vastly different potential role for the church. Finally, the religious competition posed by fundamentalist Protestantism was quickly becoming intense, and it was unclear how much of a challenge Protestantism would present to the established Roman Catholic Church.

Much has changed since then. This chapter reflects on the major changes and assesses the probable role of the Catholic Church as the new millennium approaches. It also examines the role of the hierarchical church and the path taken by the grassroots church in an attempt to trace the evolution of these two significant facets of religious life in Latin America. Finally, it concludes with some observations concerning the major challenges facing the church and some probable future developments.

Historical Overview

The Catholic Church has always played a major role in Latin American politics. Indeed, since the time of the Conquest in the 1520s (when one of its fundamental goals was to impose Christianity on the indigenous population, by force of arms if necessary) the church has enjoyed tremendous political and social power in Latin America. This general situation continues to this day.

It is extremely important to understand the traditional militant role of Catholicism in the Americas. The Conquest was in many ways waged with the cross and the sword, in every sense a struggle against "the infidel"—one in which the indigenous population would accept Catholicism whether they wanted to or not. This belligerent, unquestioning approach to religious conversion, together with the absolute conviction that Catholicism constituted the only path to eternal salvation, clearly left its mark on the cultural psyche of the Americas. The ensuing blend of political power, economic well-being (which lasted largely until the liberal reforms of the nineteenth century), and religious triumphalism was a heady combination indeed.

It is worth reflecting on the significant moral and political authority enjoyed by the church since the 1520s. In part it stems from the deeply rooted psychological justification that the Spanish conquistadores were carrying out a divine religious mission in converting the natives. The resulting political influence was therefore also presented as God's will. Given that the church schools (the only ones in existence for more than three centuries, and still the most prestigious) catered to the colonial elite and that the church itself was one of the wealthiest landlords, it was inevitable that its authorities would identify their interests with those of the landholding minority and form an alliance with them. This alliance, with some notable exceptions, has lasted until the present.

Often overlooked by political historians, however, is that despite this inherently conservative, mainstream Catholicism for more than four-and-a-half centuries, the church has always harbored a radical minority. Supporters of liberation theology in the 1960s and 1970s often forgot this rich radical legacy, dating back to the early days of colonialism, when church representatives rejected the goals of Madrid and the Vatican. Bishop Antonio Valdivieso, for example, was assassinated in Nicaragua in 1550 by the family of Rodrigo Contreras, former governor and wealthy landlord, after the bishop complained about the way he treated his Indian workers.

Like Valdivieso, many church representatives—Bartolomé de las Casas (known as the "Protector of the Indians") and priests such as Hidalgo and Morelos in Mexico (who led the first social revolution in Latin America, seeking in 1810 to implement a program of far-reaching social reform)—sought to distance themselves from the overwhelming majority of their colleagues who supported the right of the crown and the Vatican to maintain the status quo. In essence, they were practicing what in the late 1960s would be defined as the "preferential option for the poor." Like Oscar Romero in El Salvador, many of them paid for their opposition to the rich and powerful with their lives.

The Vatican's Reformist Stance

The Latin American church exercises limited autonomy in that the Vatican, an inherently conservative institution, tells it what to do. On two occasions

in the past century, however, the Vatican sought to modernize church magisterium in the face of dramatically evolving world circumstances. The first of
these can be seen in the 1891 encyclical, "Rerum Novarum," issued by Pope
Leo XIII. Although in the modern context it appears as an extremely conservative document, at the time (largely because of its criticism of the exploitation of workers) it was viewed as being remarkably radical.

The document clearly acknowledged the excesses of organized capitalism—as well as the dangers of Marxism, which, it warned, could well result
from this form of exploitation. Although a conservative document (for instance, it emphasizes the blessed nature of the poor in God's eyes, rejects socialism—much less any form of class struggle—and appeals to the conscience
of the rich to provide sufficient benefits to the poor so that class tensions will
not result), it nevertheless represents a major effort by the Vatican to seek a
more just balance between capital and labor.

Far more significant, however, was the desire for an *aggiornamento* (updating) of the church that Pope John XXIII sought in the momentous Vatican II, a major conference for the world's Catholic bishops held at the Vatican between 1962 and 1965. Edward Cleary correctly called it "the most
important event in the Latin American Church in almost five hundred years
of experience" (1985:18); Vatican II brought together more than six hundred bishops and three hundred specialists to seek to make the church more
pertinent to a quickly changing world.

That goal meant very different things for the Latin American church. The
wrenching poverty of the Americas, the culture of violence, and a flagrantly
unjust socioeconomic structure—entrenched for more than five centuries
and, it was increasingly noted, firmly supported by the church—were now
analyzed in a totally different way. For the first time, too, a homegrown theology rapidly took root and flourished as church thinkers sought to break
away from a dependency on European analytical models, breathing a spirit of
self-confidence and independence into the Latin American church; a variety
of specifically Latin American modifications of church practices soon took
hold.

In sum, the call for updating church magisterium as represented by John
XXIII's desire for change was heeded with great enthusiasm by the Latin
American bishops. As a result, both at Medellín (1968) and to a lesser extent
at Puebla (1979), the Latin American Bishops Council (CELAM) sought to
channel the broad sweep of Vatican II into a Latin American context.

The Medellín meeting was exceptional in many ways. Not only was the
pope present (the first visit to Latin America by a pontiff), but also the conclusions of the CELAM meeting were like nothing ever seen before, or indeed since. A thorough self-criticism of the church's role in a society that was
flagrantly unjust (in which the church legitimized socioeconomic injustices)
was, of course, important. More significant, however, was the decision on

the part of the church leaders to accept that they now had a biblical imperative to side with the poor and exploited—even though this would inevitably lead to a loss of their own power and privilege. Radical change was required, and in order to atone for its corporate sins of more than five centuries, it now fell to the church to practice its faith in an innovative fashion, showing solidarity with the marginalized sectors of Latin American society.

The concept of neutrality was now officially rejected since the church had to choose sides—and it had to do so, if it were true to its Christian roots, with the poor and oppressed. This preferential option for the poor, as it came to be known, was extremely important because it placed the church not only in uncharted waters but also on a direct collision course with the rich and the powerful of Latin America, who had over the centuries been its greatest allies in maintaining the same patently unjust status quo that they were now seeking to change.

A battery of innovative approaches was developed in order to provide this pragmatic *aggiornamento* of the Latin American church. The model that began to emerge (following the central thrust of Vatican II reforms, but with a distinctly Latin American flavor that sought a fast-track application of these changes) encouraged the development of lay participation in church activity. In part this was due to a very clear need for greater lay involvement: The majority of the world's Catholics will live in Latin America by the year 2000, yet it possesses one of the worst priest-to-parishioner ratios. The ratio of priests to Catholics in Latin America (where most inhabitants are Catholics) is approximately one-fifth that found in a minority Catholic country like the United States (1.9 per 10,000 and 9.8 per 100 respectively).

The Latin American church thus encouraged the formation of a more horizontal approach to religious formation, with more lay Catholics becoming involved both at the grassroots level (largely through the ecclesiastical base communities) and in assuming leadership roles in many functions. Although not always well regarded by the Vatican under the leadership of John Paul II, most changes had taken root in the decade before his election as pontiff and are now fairly well established. Many traditionally held approaches and beliefs were transformed: The "delegates of the word" now substituted as priests; congregants now increasingly saw their religious lives as more than providing spiritual solace. The church also became a means of directing their frustration, following biblical reflection, toward the search for a solution to their daily difficulties; it no longer told them it was God's will that they suffer with resignation.

It is important to point out that this was not an easy transformation, largely because the countries of Latin America are very different, and the Catholic influence varies among them. Some countries (such as Argentina and Cuba) possessed an extremely conservative church, and change came slowly; conversely, others (such as Brazil and Chile) embraced the need for a radical transformation. Moreover, many Catholics, schooled in traditional ways, were simply unable to comprehend the rapid pace of change, while others preferred to cling to a simpler belief system. Divisions among the clergy themselves mirrored these conflicts. The election in 1978 of Pope John Paul II, very much a solid conservative (in both political and ecclesial terms), strengthened the hand of those opposed to change (particularly after Msgr. Alfonso López Trujillo of Colombia took over as secretary general of CELAM). Throughout the 1970s tension and religious polarization increased between the two camps.

The role of Pope John Paul II should not be underestimated in seeking to understand this dynamic. He has clearly been the prime mover in seeking to undo much of the reformist zeal so visible in Medellín and Puebla. In particular, his enthusiastic crusade against liberation theology, his condemnation of any relationship between church representatives and Marxists, and his insistence on a rigid chain of ecclesial authority all were antithetical to the central thrust of the CELAM meetings and indeed Vatican II itself. A proper understanding of how all three fused can be seen in his single-minded opposition to the Sandinista government in Nicaragua (Kirk 1992:100–209).

The Impact of Liberation Theology

Notwithstanding the pontiff's unswerving opposition to much of the reform program (significantly instituted before his term began), it is clear that the decade between Medellín and his election had been extremely important. The broad sweep of reform introduced by the 1968 CELAM meeting at Medellín produced major changes in the Latin American church. Writing in 1992, Hannah Stewart-Gambino referred to these major innovations:

> After over two decades of dramatic theological and pastoral change, liberation theology, a theology born of the Latin American experience and grounded in the perspective of the poor, not only has survived attacks from opponents in and out of the Church but also has influenced theological discourse among First World, minority, and feminist theologians. In many Latin American dioceses, the institutional Church has flourished as a result of bishops' adoption of a preferential option for the poor. At the national level, the Church in its role as "voice of the voiceless" has led hierarchies throughout the region to champion human rights and the struggles against oppressive regimes. Thus, on one hand, the terms of theological debate as well as the institutional pattern of the Latin American Church appear to have been permanently, if not uniformly, altered. (Cleary and Stewart-Gambino 1992:1)

In 1968 Gustavo Gutiérrez, a Peruvian priest, published his landmark study *Teología de la liberación*. As the introduction states, it is "an attempt at reflection, based on the Gospel and the experiences of men and women committed to the process of liberation in the oppressed and exploited land of

Latin America" (Gutiérrez 1973:ix). In a closely argued text, Gutiérrez stresses the need for theological analysis and a resulting social praxis. It was time, he writes, to develop a religious philosophy that channels biblical reflections toward the goal of establishing the Kingdom of God on earth. He emphasizes, however, the need for a practical application of these theological reflections since "all the political theologies, the theologies of hope, of revolution, and of liberation, are not worth one act of genuine solidarity with exploited social classes" (Gutiérrez 1973:308).

Gutiérrez's book has become the classic study of liberation theology, as relevant now as it was a quarter-century ago. At that time it constituted a clearly founded theological rationale for the positions developed at Medellín, outlining both the biblical justification and the social imperative for a new approach to be followed by the church. For the church in Latin America, it clearly represented a challenge to undertake its mission in a vastly different manner, in short to radicalize its faith. Gutiérrez starts the book's conclusion in characteristically direct fashion: "The theology of liberation attempts to reflect on the experience and meaning of the faith based on the commitment to abolish injustice and to build a new society; this theology must be verified by the practice of that commitment, by active, effective participation in the struggle which the exploited social classes have undertaken against their oppressors." At the same time, however, Gutiérrez warns that this commitment to abolish social injustice must be uncompromising for authentic Christians: "If theological reflection does not vitalize the action of the Christian community in the world by making its commitment to charity fuller and more radical, if—more concretely—in Latin America it does not lead the Church to be on the side of the oppressed classes and dominated peoples, clearly and without qualifications, then this theological reflection will have been of little value" (Gutiérrez 1973:307).

The impact of the work of Gutiérrez on other church theologians in Latin America has been profound. Since his work was published in 1968, theologians such as Leonardo Boff (Brazil), Jon Sobrino (El Salvador), Juan Luis Segundo (Uruguay), José Míguez Bonino (Argentina), Ronaldo Muñoz (Chile), and many others have also published their work—which still retains much influence on church teachings in the 1990s. All have sought to direct the basic spirituality toward the liberation of oppressed peoples—and as proof of the universality of their message, it has also been adopted by their counterparts in Africa and Asia.

Yet the vibrancy of the message so clearly enunciated in 1968, while losing none of its universal appeal, has been muted by an increasingly doctrinaire and authoritarian approach of the Vatican. Perhaps the best synthesis of Rome's position can be seen in the report "Instructions on Certain Aspects of the Theology of Liberation" by Cardinal Joseph Ratzinger, prefect of the Vatican Congregation for the Doctrine of the Faith in August 1984. It begins by noting that the gospel is indeed a message of liberation from sin and that the church indeed supports all those theologians who espouse Medellín's "preferential option for the poor," although it soon passes to a warning against potential deviations from this option.

Cardinal Ratzinger condemns liberation theology for its "classist viewpoint, which it has adopted a priori and which has come to function in it as a determining principle." There is a resultant difficulty in establishing a debate or in pursuing any objectivity, claims Ratzinger, because liberation theologians have as a point of departure the viewpoint of the oppressed class and are not willing to listen to that of the oppressor. As in the case of "Rerum Novarum" nearly a century earlier, the cardinal rejects the concept of radical reform ("class struggle as a road toward a classless society is a myth that slows reform and aggravates poverty and injustice") and returns to the need for individual conversion: "The acute need for radical reforms of the structures which conceal poverty and which are themselves forms of violence should not let us lose sight of the fact that the source of injustice is in the hearts of men. Therefore it is only by making an appeal to the moral potential of the person and to the constant need for interior conversion that social change will be brought about which will be truly in the service of man" ("Instructions . . ." 1984:20).

The congregation's repudiation in 1985 of what it termed the "Marxist content" of a work by Brazilian liberation theologian Leonardo Boff is instructive in this regard. Boff was summoned to the Vatican in 1984 to answer charges against his book *Church, Charism and Power: Liberation Theology and the Institutional Church.* The Franciscan's book criticizes the Vatican of elitism and of failing to take a firm stand on many pressing social problems. He also condemns the lack of collegiality and consultation in the church, which he says marginalizes the majority of Catholic laity as well as women religious. The centuries-old model of ensuring doctrine and discipline is also seen as being severely outdated. Church authority is of course essential, in Boff's view, but the administration of this authority is found sorely lacking.

In place of this conservative authoritarian approach, Boff suggests the ecclesiology of Vatican II and the local application found in base ecclesial communities of Latin America. This "church of the poor," he suggests, embodies the message of Christ—a far cry, he insinuates, from the authoritarian, dry model defended by the Vatican. Yet in seeking this internal conversion of the church, Boff clearly offended the Vatican leadership. Boff was silenced in 1985, forbidden to speak about or publish his views for a year. He was also stripped of the editorship of the *Brazilian Ecclesiastical Review* and had to submit all that he wrote to a team of censors.

After his suspension was lifted, and in strict defiance of canon law, Boff's work in a multivolume compendium of theology was singled out for special scrutiny, despite having the imprimatur of his bishop and support of the superior of his religious order. In 1991 he was also forced by the Vatican to resign from a Catholic publishing company. Finally in summer 1992 Boff, the author of about fifty books on liberation theology, decided to leave both the Franciscan order and the Catholic priesthood and since then has worked as a lay person on a variety of theological projects.

Given that, on the one hand, there has been a dramatically new theological direction indicated without compromise by Gutiérrez and a new generation of Catholic thinkers, while on the other the Vatican has steadily sought to corral what it clearly sees as black theological sheep, what can one expect for the rest of the 1990s—and indeed into the next century?

It seems clear that the Vatican, under John Paul II, will continue its unrelenting pressure against proponents of liberation theology as defined by Gutiérrez. The pontiff, greatly influenced by his own formative experiences under communism in Poland, is clearly fearful of a radical sociopolitical praxis forming in Latin America. He is both aware of the tremendous appeal of liberation theology in the Americas and ill prepared to put aside his European prejudices in order to appreciate the conditions that spawned it. As Boff put it so well, "In Europe the Church is engaged in a dialogue with the nonbeliever. In Latin America, it is with the poor and oppressed" ("Brazil . . ." 1980:9).

The center of church gravity threatened to slip from Europe to Latin America in the 1980s as liberation theology became enormously popular throughout the developing world. The Vatican, buoyed by John Paul II's own profound reservations about the sociopolitical praxis inherent in this theological expression, therefore responded with great alacrity. European control of the church should not be underestimated, for it clearly sets the standards around the world for acceptable ecclesial discourse. Writing in 1984, Alberto Iniesta, Madrid's auxiliary bishop, criticized the ensuing filter placed on theology:

> Ever since the Renaissance and on through the Enlightenment, theology has always responded with a time lag to the demands, needs and questions of a European bourgeois society that was liberal, enlightened and capitalist. . . . Today, then, theology, ecclesiology, ethics, spirituality and pastoral practice come to us heavily weighted by the bourgeoisie. While at one time they did perform the service of mediating faith, today they constitute more of a burden, a stumbling block, a prison even: a kidnapping of the Gospel of Christ and the Church. (Iniesta 1984:6)

Throughout the 1980s and into the 1990s the Vatican has maintained its opposition to Latin American liberation theology, while claiming that it is fully in favor of authentic liberation (which revolves around individual conversion). Indeed in July 1985, following a grueling Latin American tour, the pope repeated the two basic themes in his approach to the controversy: First, he noted the need to "purify" liberation theology "from the dangers of doctrinal detours"(Arias 1985:7). Second, he added that he too is a "liberation" theologian. Once again, however, the pope holds a vastly different (and in many ways totally opposing) interpretation of the term.

Should there remain any doubt concerning the Vatican's visceral opposition to anything smacking of liberation theology, one has only to reflect on its opposition to Bishop Samuel Ruiz of San Cristóbal de Las Casas in Chiapas, Mexico, the site of a major uprising by impoverished Mayan peasants in January 1994. The bishop sent a letter to the pope on August 6, 1993, complaining of the impact of the Salinas government's neoliberal policies on the poor of Chiapas. Just under three months later the papal nuncio asked the bishop to resign, following the receipt of instructions from the Vatican. Nuncio Girolamo Prigione later informed the press that Ruiz's removal was brought on by the bishop's "doctrinal, pastoral and administrative" mistakes for some twenty years.

The fundamental position of the Vatican is that liberation theology as outlined by Gutiérrez, Boff, and others is too partialized a view of church teaching. Not only does it emphasize a praxis that encourages a class struggle (something that traditional Catholic social teaching rejects), but it also favors the poor—thereby reducing the universality of the church's mission. Opponents argue that the gospel excludes nobody, but that—as Jesus showed by coming to live with a carpenter's family—the church has to show its preferential option for the poor (a position established clearly at Medellín). For over a decade pressure has been exerted on practitioners of liberation theology to accept Vatican orthodoxy on the subject—a policy that has been largely successful. For the foreseeable future, under John Paul II, this tendency will continue. A useful symbol of this push for conformity can be seen in Gutiérrez's current work on the great sixteenth-century priest, Bartolomé de las Casas (clearly a topic less likely to provoke Cardinal Ratzinger), while Boff is now a lay theologian.

The Contribution of the Ecclesial Base Communities

Although substantial attention has been paid to the controversies surrounding the evolution of liberation theology in Latin America, a far more significant development in the long-term development of the Catholic Church has been its steady laicization. In Honduras, for instance, in 1957 there were some 350 Protestant missionaries—more than twice the number of Catholic priests. Yet in the wake of Medellín and Puebla, the shortage of priests was resolved by the development of a successful program to train lay church workers and the strengthening of the ecclesial base communities (CEBs). In fact, by 1971 there were more than 5,000 "delegates of the word" who led church services and developed CEBs (Brett and Brett 1988:117).

Base communities in Latin America are in general driven by a new, original model of consciousness based on an invigorated awareness of faith and the need to harness it toward improving self or community. Members are united by a desire to develop a better understanding of their socioeconomic reality, of their experience as a group, in the light of the gospel. Writing in 1980, Gottfried Deelen put this in the appropriate context: "A person is not a member of a [CEB] for professional reasons, for educational or political reasons: the main motivation for membership stems from religion. . . . Above all, however, there is the hope of being able, in the company of others, to build a better future" (1980:4). In many cases, too, there is a commitment to resolve their difficulties, as a community, based on the religious reflections of the group. It is this new understanding of religion, involving religious inspiration and concrete praxis, which is such a prominent feature of the post–Vatican II Latin American church.

That said, it is important to bear in mind that there are many different kinds of base communities. Deleen cites three fundamental categories of CEBs: (1) those concerned specifically with "the formation of religious groups and the strengthening of ecclesial and sacramental life"; (2) communities that in addition dedicate themselves to social tasks, mutual aid within the neighborhood, and to acts of charity; and (3) those that "go a step further along the road to political awareness and begin to demand social reforms" (1980:5). It is generally estimated that there are some two hundred thousand CEBs in Latin America, of which approximately one-half are to be found in Brazil. They usually average between fifteen and twenty families—not too large, so that all can participate actively.

Participation is both the rationale for their existence and the key to their success, essential because many of the community are often faced by the same reality and know that their most successful course is through united, collective action. The result is a very concrete form of spirituality: "Scripture is understood in the light of the problems the community is struggling with at the time: unemployment, drug and alcohol abuse among youth, landlessness in the countryside, lack of sanitation, transport, schools and other services the government should be supplying and so on" (Sheppard 1986:8).

Yet CEBs are not the same everywhere. In addition to their prevalence throughout parishes of varying socioeconomic backgrounds, in both rural and urban settings, CEBs also have different views of their functions and roles. For example, a CEB in the east of Managua that struggled against the Somoza dictatorship in 1978 is now probably more concerned with running the parish cooperative or soup kitchen; similarly, CEBs in Pinochet's Chile now have vastly different preoccupations under Frei. Moreover, many conservative parishes have also developed their own CEBs, although they are often more concerned with liturgical questions, or praying, than with direct social praxis.

Carol Ann Drogus indicates three basic categories of CEBs: people-concerned, self-concerned, and integrated religionists. The first is perhaps most typical: It is more politically aware, more committed to improving the lot of its members, and more involved in the community. The second broad grouping represents CEBs that, although concerned with community social problems, are "absorbed with their personal relationship with God, with individual salvation. . . . This group views religion as a source of comfort in a harsh world, in contrast to the people-concerned religionists' perception of religion as challenge" (Drogus 1992:71). The final group, and probably the largest sector, is that which belongs in the middle of these two extremes and is concerned both with personal salvation and with the need for acts of compassion and charity (but not necessarily social justice).

Because the Brazilian church is both the largest and the most progressive in Latin America, it is instructive to look at its evolution. Formed at a time of military repression, CEBs have developed in the mold of the "voice of the voiceless." Headed since the 1960s by progressives, the church in Brazil consistently advocated significant political change, offering its protection to those who opposed the military government while supporting the reconstruction of civil society. Yet times have changed since the heady days of the birth of the CEBs. The military have returned to the barracks, the Vatican has steered the church in an increasingly conservative direction, and the initial raison d'être of the CEBs has been greatly reduced.

As a result, as Bruneau and Hewitt have shown, the profile of the CEBs (in ecclesial and political terms) has decreased greatly in Brazil since the late 1980s. Official church documents rarely make reference to CEBs, and their mission is increasingly changing its focus away from traditional sociopolitical objectives:

> Much was expected of the CEBs, and indeed their importance in the late 1970s and early 1980s in providing alternate forms of organization and mobilization cannot be denied. Nevertheless, thay have not matched expectations, despite inflated figures on their numbers. An independent lay leadership has not emerged from the CEBs, and they still rely very much on clergy and bishops. They have not been unified on sociopolitical matters, and their general impact is weak. (Bruneau and Hewitt 1992:58)

It is clear that the tradition of the CEBs will continue in Latin America throughout the 1990s and well into the next century—although it is also clear that their goals will continue to move away from the political positions espoused as recently as a decade ago. There are several reasons for this continued growth. Chief among them is that despite a dislike for many of the more politically progressive stances taken by the CEBs, the church leadership recognizes that they are indeed a positive force in improving basic social conditions for the community.

It is also true that what was presented as the typical base community, active in social justice campaigns and militant action against political repression, has slowly been ceding ground to the second and, more noticeably, the third categories noted by Drogus above. In general, then, in the 1990s the CEBs are not seen as a source of competition with the church hierarchy—as may have been the case a decade ago. It can also be argued that the CEBs have reduced the possibility of Catholic members being converted to Protestantism (often perceived as offering greater practical benefits). Moreover, the spiritual activities of the CEBs often fill the vacuum created by insufficient clergy. They are thus perceived as helping to keep the faith alive—another important fact in the face of the growing tide of Pentecostalism in the past decade.

Yet even though there has been a general depoliticization of the CEBs in the 1990s, it is important to note that there has been a significant development in the strengthening of self-confidence among the Catholic laity. From the perspective of the grassroots, the development of the CEBs has had, and continues to have, a major influence on the manner in which the church is viewed. Prior to the CEBs, religious life revolved in large part around initiatives undertaken by the parish priest. He was traditionally seen by Catholics as the keeper of the faith, the man to whom all turned for religious leadership and inspiration. In turn, the bishop was perceived as an all-powerful figure, whose opinions were to be accepted unthinkingly. Church magisterium was always laid out by the bishops and passed along by the parish priest, with criticism, much less dissent, unthinkable.

That has, to a large degree, changed. Although respect for the hierarchy and other ecclesial superiors remains the glue that holds together a large part of the faithful, the decentralization resulting from the empowerment of the laity, especially in the CEBs, has given a far greater sense of self-confidence than is widely thought. Although that confidence diminishes as the CEB members direct their energies toward eking out a living (therefore devoting less time and energy to parish work), nevertheless the foundation on which it has been built remains fairly well grounded.

Challenges to the Church in Latin America

As the new millennium looms on the horizon, it is instructive to reflect on the evolution of the church during the past century, one that has seen significant ferment and much discord. It appears that the future is more uncertain for the Latin American church than ever before, with several key variables ultimately responsible for its fate. Although other factors will exercise some influence on this evolution, the main ones are the role of Protestantism (particularly the fast-growing fundamentalist form) and the future direction of the church hierarchy—both at the Vatican and in the Latin American leadership.

The challenge posed by the growth of Pentecostalism is perhaps the most serious faced by the church. Estimates concerning the number of Protestants, and the type of religious adherents within this broad religious grouping, vary wildly. Yet it is absolutely clear that a trend is clearly in place, and that the rate of growth—particularly among fundamentalist Pentecostal churches—has increased significantly in the past two decades. In Brazil, the largest Catholic country, Protestant growth has been steady, if unspectacular: up from 2 percent in 1950 to an estimated 10 percent in 1991. (That said, the growth in recent years has been staggering: 77 percent between 1960 and 1970, and 155 percent the following decade.)

In his seminal work, *Is Latin America Turning Protestant?* (he shows clearly that it is), David Stoll provides an astonishing survey of Protestant church growth rate figures: Since 1960 evangelicals have doubled their proportion of the population in Chile, Paraguay, Venezuela, Panama, and Haiti; tripled their proportion in Argentina, Nicaragua, and the Dominican Republic; quadrupled in Brazil and Puerto Rico; quintupled in El Salvador, Costa Rica, Peru, and Bolivia; sextupled in Ecuador, Colombia, and Honduras; while in Guatemala it has increased by a factor of seven (Stoll 1990:8–9). What this means is that Protestants now represent a third of the population of Guatemala, 28 percent in El Salvador, and 20 percent in Chile and Panama. Their numbers have grown from 4.23 million in 1957 to 15 million in 1970, 28 million a decade later, and an estimated 48 million in 1989 ("Robbing Peter" 1989:2).

In addition, given the preponderance of nominal Catholics (who rarely attend religious ceremonies) on the one hand, and the rapid growth of Pentecostals (who regularly do) on the other, it is clear that Catholicism is being eclipsed in several Latin American countries. Cleary puts this in context: "For every practicing Catholic in Brazil, Chile and Guatemala there is, most likely, an equal or greater number attending Protestant or native religious services" (Cleary and Stewart-Gambino 1992:214). The numbers of evangelicals and, more important, their rate of growth are extraordinary indeed. It is estimated, therefore, that several Latin American countries—and in particular Guatemala—may well have Protestant majorities by the end of this decade.

Literally tens of thousands of Pentecostal churches have sprung up in the past decade in Latin America. Professing a fundamentalist interpretation of the Bible, they now comprise between two-thirds to three-quarters of the continent's approximately 50 million Protestants. Significantly, the number of their adherents continues to grow.

Edward Cleary shows that in Guatemala—commonly cited as the country closest to having a Protestant majority—there has been a religious revival, with both Pentecostalists and reformist Catholics increasing their followers. The number of Catholic seminarians increased 637 percent between 1972 and 1987, while the same period saw a 32 percent increase in the number of sisters (Cleary and Stewart-Gambino 1992:186). His closely argued thesis is that it is too soon to claim that the evangelical tide has swept completely over

Guatemala. He notes that despite the presidencies of two Pentecostalists in recent years (Ríos Montt and Jorge Serrano) and significant growth in the number of Protestant fundamentalists, the Catholic Church is also "enjoying an awakening to a degree unknown in contemporary history" (Cleary and Stewart-Gambino 1992:215).

Although that may be true for certain areas of Guatemala (where some re vitalized clergy are pursuing initiatives to win over converts), it is hardly the paradigm for Latin America as a whole. There one encounters waves of people (both former Catholics and others) converting to Pentecostalism. There are a whole host of reasons for their conversion, and although some of them are less pertinent now than in the 1980s (such as a rejection of the politicized church and a well-founded fear of repression from the scourge of military regimes that plagued the region in the 1980s), most remain pertinent to my analysis in this chapter.

The inadequate number of priests needed to minister to the region's Catholics and the length of time required to train them (compared with the vast number of their fundamentalist counterparts and the relatively short period of religious formation) are of course key points in explaining the conversion of many Latin Americans to Pentecostalism. The traditional lack of native clergy and dependence on foreign priests, who often import unworkable ideas and approaches, are related arguments.

Perhaps more important, however, has been the comparative inability of the Catholic Church to reach out in practical ways to the victims of the continent's structural adjustment programs. The major cities contain many *campesinos* seeking a better life. Their truly daunting difficulties and stresses have created a population into which the Pentecostalists have made their greatest inroads. Their aggressive campaigns to seek out and help marginalized sectors of society have reaped significant rewards, and their large numbers of ministers have made this task relatively straightforward.

A related note is perhaps pertinent here. A decade ago the Pentecostalists were able to provide food and clothing to these marginalized sectors largely because of their affiliation with North American churches. Although it is not clear to what extent funding is provided by U.S. churches today, it is clear that significant financial aid is still funneled to Latin America by parent churches. During the worst of the civil war in El Salvador and the U.S.-supported contra rebellion in Nicaragua, this aid was undoubtedly helpful to evangelical Christians, who are politically conservative, reject communism, and are opposed to liberation theology.

A final factor (and perhaps the most important) needs to be assessed in explaining this growth of religious fundamentalism. Many Latin Americans have shunned the mixture of the sacred with the secular found in Catholicism, preferring the spiritual mysticism and personal relationship with Christ as savior found in evangelical Protestantism. This has led to members seeking to pursue their personal salvation, rejecting political activity, and concentrating on individual morality. The emphasis given to the emotional appeal of Pentecostalism and the tightly organized mission campaigns that skillfully use modern media have also been instrumental in aiding the religion's spread. The dependence on inspiration of the Holy Spirit and free rein given to emotional testimonies, speaking in tongues, and exorcism of the possessed have also helped its development.

The essential point about this variety of factors is that virtually all are as pertinent now as they were over a decade ago. Notwithstanding, therefore, Cleary's example of Catholic revitalization in Guatemala, it is clear that the greatest challenge facing the Catholic Church as a new millennium approaches is the continuing evangelical tide. Admittedly, the tide has slowed somewhat in recent years. It still, however, will continue to win converts at an alarming rate. It is unclear how the Catholic Church, divided in its approach to missionary work, limited by the number of clergy, and uncertain about the Vatican's understanding of the fundamental dynamics at play in Latin America, will rise to the challenge.

The direction taken by the Vatican will largely revolve around the personal agenda of the pontiff. John Paul II is an extremely conservative leader. His relentless pursuit of liberation theology is instructive in this regard. Both through his own many observations on what he perceives as the misguided nature of much of liberation theology, and through the actions of the watch-guard of orthodoxy, the Congregation for the Doctrine of the Faith (headed by the conservative Cardinal Ratzinger), John Paul II has gone out of his way to overturn the influence of liberation theology.

In particular, his criticism of the work of Gutiérrez, the summoning to the Vatican of Leonardo Boff to defend his position, the thirty-five-page critique of liberation theology issued by Ratzinger, and the eventual silencing of Boff were all important in showing the steadfast opposition of the Vatican. Boff, one of the best-known proponents of liberation theology, was in part singled out because he is from Brazil, where the grassroots church is particularly strong. The targeting of the Brazilian church is not coincidental. It is the largest in Latin America and, since the late 1960s, it has been the most progressive wing of the church in political terms.

It is also important to bear in mind that, although the Catholic Church is not a monolith, it is directed from the Vatican—which makes decisions about the nomination of bishops and their replacement when they reach retirement age. Accordingly, a steady stream of conservative nominees has replaced more liberal colleagues. Two examples will perhaps help to illustrate the importance of the power of nomination and its impact on the church in particular countries. In the case of replacements to the Brazilian hierarchy in recent years, for example, almost all new appointments are conservatives. (This is seen most clearly in Recife, where Dom Helder Camara was replaced by Dom José Sobrinho.) The promotion of two conservative archbishops to the rank of cardinal in 1988, and the division of the São Paulo archdiocese into five in 1989—in an attempt to undermine the influence of progressive Cardinal Arns—are also evidence of the power of the Vatican. Violeta Manoukian, referring to the differences of opinion between Brazilian church leaders and the Vatican in recent years, has described the dynamic well: "In the concert of human events, these are two musicians at times playing separate tunes simultaneously" (Manoukian 1992:242). The problem in recent years, however, is that the Vatican has continually replaced the first violins and leading musicians from other sections and, if it could, would replace the conductor, too.

A decade ago, undoubtedly the greatest challenge to the Vatican's authoritarian, conservative approach to ecclesiology came from Sandinista Nicaragua, where the blend of nationalism (Sandinismo), Marxism, and Christianity was a potent combination indeed. For the Vatican it was a volatile mixture, particularly in light of the four priests holding key cabinet roles in the Sandinista government. Accordingly, Rome set out to deliberately undermine the role of the progressive church while strengthening the conservative leadership of Archbishop Obando y Bravo. (Obando was himself elevated to the cardinalate in 1985, despite the fact that there were arguably far better qualified candidates in Central America.) The Vatican also sought to oblige priests and religious to accept the traditional stance by expelling those who supported the progressive church. As a result, London's Catholic Institute for International Relations estimated that by 1987 at least forty pro-Sandinista religious had been forced to leave Nicaragua because of pressure from Cardinal Obando y Bravo (CIIR 1987: 94).

Once again orthodoxy triumphed following this ecclesial muscle flexing—a pattern that John Paul II has repeated throughout his papacy. Under the leadership of John Paul II, then, one can expect the maintenance of this traditional line, which will inevitably place a conservative stamp on the church position.

The Future for the Latin American Church

In a well-argued synthesis of the three dominant models of the church debated in recent decades, Margaret E. Crahan outlines the characteristics of each. These can be termed the Christendom, neo-Christendom, and people's church models. The first of these, "rooted in the Catholic Church's constitution and historical evolution, conceives of the Church as strongly hierarchical and molded by undeviating religious principles" (Crahan 1992:157). The second "views society as broadly infused with Christian beliefs and values," with the church's role as the "sacramental mediator between the individual and God." The final model sees the church "allied with the poor majority in a struggle for liberation that will transform society" (Crahan 1992:158).

If we accept this useful framework for discussing the church's future, then the variables noted in the previous section of this chapter will exercise a major influence on which model will come to dominate. To take but one example, a liberal theologian like John XXIII could reverse the conservatism of the past fifteen years and encourage the strengthening of the *aggiornamento* process initiated in 1962, while, conversely, another pontiff with the ideology of John Paul II would inevitably solidify the conservative bent that has been steadfastly pursued in recent years. Similarly, the election of a pope from the developing world (particularly a Latin American one) would probably leave a different imprint altogether. (Given the preponderance of Italian pontiffs, this latter option is hardly likely. Although since slightly more than one-half the world's Catholic population within the next decade will live in Latin America, a case can surely be made for such an appointment.)

It is also important to recognize that the church's discovery of liberation theology, its solid alliance with popular organizations, and its encouragement of base communities all transpired in a climate of political repression and harassment by the armed forces. In other words, the Latin American church in the 1970s and the 1980s discovered its mission in a society in the throes of military dictatorship. Yet with the reappearance of incipient democracy, or at least a lack of prestige for the military and some strategic peace accords in the region, much of its raison d'être has disappeared. It becomes more difficult to understand, for instance, the pertinence of the Vicaría de la Solidaridad and its original mission during the days of the Pinochet dictatorship in today's Chile, much less the presence of guerrilla priests like Gaspar García Laviana in Nicaragua and Camilo Torres in Colombia. New times pose fresh challenges for the church, undercutting some of the bases for its outspoken role in the face of military repression.

If we stand back from the (occasionally sensational) localized debate between reactionaries and radicals that has dominated the discussion on the church's direction in the last half of the twentieth century, it is clear that the overall picture is of an extremely conservative institution that is inherently reluctant to change. Its fundamental goals are to maintain its internal unity in the face of a massive onslaught of commercialism and secular concerns and the steady evolution of Protestant fundamentalism. It must also provide a message for all Catholics around the entire world. Given the vast differences encompassed in this ultimate challenge, it is obvious that logically the church will err on the side of conservatism in order to protect its corporate, catholic (in both upper and lower case) identity—an approach that has been remarkably successful for most of its two thousand years of existence.

Latin American critics of this tradition will point to the signals given by Medellín and Puebla, the need for a prophetic stance, the innovations since Vatican II, and the legacy of the martyrs—from Valdivieso to Romero. They will argue that with the majority of the world's Catholics now living in Latin America, *their* needs—and not those designated by European theologians— must set the agenda for the church. They will also argue that the church is not, and cannot be, a monolithic bloc, and that the richness of the Catholic faith is its ability to offer a message to people from a variety of backgrounds, races, and stages of development. They will also take offense at the official position that liberation theology and a people's church approach to social inequity are divisive:

> The popular Church does not create division; rather it creates a new vision of Church. And this division is fundamentally characterized by a working relationship between faith in the Gospel and action in society. It is a different model of Church and creates tension with the other model of Church, which is more sacramental, more devotional, more linked to the dominant social classes. (Boff 1983:7)

Yet, however appealing their assessment may appear to be, they will ultimately lose the debate because they have neither power nor history on their side. The demands on the universal Catholic Church are so great, the conservative agenda so deeply rooted, and the ecclesial track record so firmly established, that their position in the overall scheme of things (and their relevance) will be overlooked. That is not to say, however, that their arguments will be dismissed so easily or indeed that they will not exercise any influence. (Indeed, the church reforms unleashed by Vatican II will prove difficult to tame, in no small measure because the unjust socioeconomic conditions in Latin America persist.)

What it does mean, though, is that their input will be severely limited. For, despite the horrendous inequities continuing to plague the developing world in general, the appeal to heed the conversion of Oscar Romero and the call for Christians to "radicalize their faith" will fall on deaf ears. Many Catholics in Latin America will undoubtedly sympathize with the goals of liberation theology and the need to strengthen a lay-driven, practical Christian community in which congregants set the parameters for development. But these sympathies will inevitably lose out to the status quo.

The rest of the 1990s, and continuing into the twentieth-first century, will thus see conservative orthodoxy continue to steer the church back toward its traditional role—with a brave minority struggling against this doctrinaire tide (as always). Meanwhile the Pentecostal challenge will continue to grow rapidly, and several countries may well have a conservative Protestant majority within the decade. This is hardly the reality one would have expected even a decade ago; it is, however, a reflection of the harsh realities facing both Latin America and the church.

References

Arias, Juan. "El Papa Se Declara 'Teólogo de la Liberación.'" *El País* (International Edition), February 11, 1985:7.

"Brazil at Centre of Church Controversies." *Latin American Weekly Report.* WR-80-06, February 8, 1980:9.

"Brazilian Theologian Responds to Criticisms." *Catholic New Times,* November 27, 1983: 7.

Brett, Edward T., and Donna W. Brett. "Facing the Challenge: The Catholic Church and Social Change in Honduras," in Ralph Lee Woodward, ed., *Central America: Historical Perspectives on the Contemporary Crisis.* New York: Greenwood Press, 1988, 107–129.

Bruneau, Thomas C., and W. E. Hewitt. "Catholicism and Political Action in Brazil: Limitations and Prospects," in Edward Cleary and Hannah Stewart-Gambino, eds., *Conflict and Competition:* 45–62.

CIIR (Catholic Institute for International Relations). *Right to Survive: Human Rights in Nicaragua.* London: CIIR, 1987.

Cleary, Edward L. *Crisis and Change: The Church in Latin America Today.* Maryknoll, NY: Orbis, 1985.

Cleary, Edward L., and Hannah Stewart-Gambino. *Conflict and Competition: The Latin American Church in a Changing Environment.* Boulder, CO: Lynne Rienner, 1992.

Crahan, Margaret E. "Religion: Reconstituting Church and Pursuing Change," in Alfred Stepan, ed., *Americas: New Interpretive Essays.* New York: Oxford University Press, 1992, 152–171.

Deelen, Gottfried. "The Church on Its Way to the People: Basic Christian Communities in Brazil." *Pro Mundi Vita Bulletin* (April 1980): 2–18.

Drogus, Carol Ann, "Popular Movements and the Limits of Political Mobilization at the Grassroots in Brazil," in Edward Cleary and Hannah Stewart-Gambino, eds., *Conflict and Competition,* 63–86.

"Government Gets Vatican to Drop a Bishop." *Mexico and NAFTA Report* (Latin American Regional Reports), November 18, 1993, 8.

Gutiérrez, Gustavo. *A Theology of Liberation.* Maryknoll, NY: Orbis, 1973.

Iniesta, Alberto. "Today Latin America Is Evangelizing Europe." *Latinamerica Press* 16, 18 (May 17, 1984):6.

"Instructions on Certain Aspects of the 'Theology of Liberation.'" *Origins* (NC Documentary Service), 14, 13 (September 13, 1984):195.

Kirk, John M. *Politics and the Catholic Church in Nicaragua.* Gainesville: University Presses of Florida, 1992.

Manoukian, Violeta. "Liberation in Action: Brazil's Christian Base Communities and Their Relevance to Development," in Jorge García Antezana, ed., *Liberation Theology and Sociopolitical Transformation.* Vancouver: Institute for the Humanities, 1992, 237–251.

"Robbing Peter to Pay Paul: The Evangelical Tide." *Latinamerica Press,* 21, 24 (June 29, 1989):2.

Sheppard, Jim. "Basic Ecclesial Communities: What Are They?" *Catholic New Times,* June 1, 1986:8.

Stoll, David. *Is Latin America Turning Protestant? The Politics of Evangelical Groups.* Berkeley: University of California Press, 1990.

Torres, Sergio, and John Eagleson, eds. *The Challenge of Basic Christian Communities.* Maryknoll, NY: Orbis, 1981.

10

Latin America and the Social Ecology of Capitalism

ELIZABETH W. DORE

Environmentalism has emerged as one of the main forms of oppositional politics in Latin America at the end of the millennium. Ecological struggles in the region have tended to concentrate on ameliorating particular examples of environmental degradation rather than on addressing the wider issue of the social causes of ecological change. As part of a generalized repudiation of socialism and acceptance of capitalism, environmentalists have rarely focused on the class politics of natural resource use. This chapter takes a different approach. First, it discusses the possibilities for the rational use of natural resources within the framework of the dominant economic system and argues that capitalism tends to be incompatible with environmental sustainability. Second, it examines the environmental debates in Latin America and concludes that the radical ecologists' critique of industrialization may be too sweeping. Analysis of the social context of technical innovation may indicate that modern industry, if it were separated from the context of capitalist production, could be compatible with sustainability. Third, with reference to three major environmental crises and the social struggles they gave rise to in Latin America, this chapter demonstrates that conflicts over the environment can best be understood as class struggles over the use of natural resources.

Capitalism, Socialism, and Ecology

The capitalist system of production and consumption that dominates the world is fundamentally incompatible with ecological sustainability. Under capitalism, the appropriation and transformation of the natural world is driven by profit-making. The objective of production is not to satisfy people's needs and desires but to make profits. This lends a particular character to the exploitation of natural resources.

Working people have little say about what to produce, how to organize production, and how to distribute the products of their labor. Competition among capitalists for profits is the system's driving force: it sets the character of production and consumption. In their quest to reduce unit costs, competition compels firms to endeavor to diminish the amount of labor used to make each commodity. At the same time, they continually strive to increase the volume of commodities produced and consumed in order to maximize profits (Weeks 1981:1–94). Consequently, production techniques are selected with reference to profitability, not sustainability. Inherent in the system is a drive to expand output, regardless of needs. As such, capitalism continually engenders the expansion of consumption, and of waste, because growth is the key to greater profits. This dynamic makes capitalism incompatible with the sustainable use of natural resources. Relentless expansion of production and consumption threatens the environment. Yet restrictions on the drive to increase output threaten profitability and are resisted by the dominant classes, as are production techniques that raise the costs of production even when they diminish environmental destruction.

This does not imply that a juggernaut has been set in motion—that capitalism will destroy the environment or be destroyed. Environmental damage can be contained and managed in numerous ways. The state's relative autonomy from the immediate economic interests of dominant classes gives it substantial latitude in introducing environmental reform (Kaimowitz 1993). For instance, to contain deforestation and erosion in Latin America, governments regulated logging through measures that have been vigorously opposed by a sector of industrialists. Industries have also introduced "environment saving" methods of production when they reduced costs or when pressured by green movements.

Nevertheless, the extent to which governments have resisted environmental reform is alarming. To cite just two prominent examples, despite scientists' warnings of the impact of increased carbon dioxide emissions on global warming, the U.S. government refused to sign a convention to limit those emissions at the Earth Summit in 1992. This refusal was particularly flagrant, given that the United States, with only 5 percent of the world's population, accounted for 25 percent of the earth's greenhouse-gas emissions. In Mexico, for decades the government did little to curtail carbon monoxide emissions in the federal capital even though morbidity and mortality rates amply demonstrated that the population suffered as a result of the extensive pollution. Nonetheless, in spite of such instances of government resistance, increased mobilizations against environmental damage and evidence of dramatic destruction of natural resources forced environmental reform to a more prominent position on the global political agenda. Nevertheless, a radical restructuring of relations between society and nature remains difficult within the confines of capitalism.

Eliminating capitalism could have revolutionary implications for natural resource use. Without the imperatives of profit-making there would be no inherent drive to produce beyond the satisfaction of needs and desires. Compulsion to produce each commodity with minimum labor might be balanced against other objectives, such as ecological sustainability, gender equality, product quality, and so forth. Organization of production and patterns of consumption could evolve out of political debate. Yet, as demonstrated by the ecological disasters in the former Eastern Bloc countries, central planning proved to be as environmentally devastating as capitalism. A radical transformation of the relationship between society and the environment requires a conscious critique of both the current norms in natural resource use as well as the dominant relations of property. The environmental movement facilitated the former by creating a mass consciousness of the consequences of environmental destruction. When that new awareness is joined to an ecological critique of capitalism, it could provide the framework for a powerful movement for social and environmental change.

Environmental Debates in Latin America

The environmental question occupies a prominent position in Latin American debates over economics and politics, possibly reflecting the importance of the environmental lobby in the United States and Europe more than an indigenous preoccupation with the environmental conditions. As with such debates worldwide, there is no unified Latin American discourse but, rather, a wide spectrum of perspectives on the causes, implications of, and solutions to regional and local environmental problems. The discourse nevertheless has two broad strands. One focuses on how to achieve sustainable development; a second centers on the ecological consequences of imperialism. In practice, the approaches overlap to form a rich, if sometimes eclectic, discourse.

Sustainable Development

"Sustainable development" is a catchall term used by policymakers and activists to frame environmental issues. Its commonly accepted definition is "development that meets the needs of the present without compromising the ability of future generations to meet their own needs" (WCED 1987:5). Malleable and moral, sustainable development became the basic doctrine of environmentalism. As such, it has tended to obscure ideological differences as to the causes of and solutions for environmental destruction. Unifying the eclecticism of sustainable development is the implicit belief that there exists a trade-off between development and environmental sustainability, in which more of one necessitates less of the other. With this assumption advocates of sustainable development have concentrated on how to manage the economic system to make it less polluting, less wasteful of resources, and less destructive of ecosystems. Their solutions reflect different approaches, from liberalizing markets to expanding the power of the state. None of these solutions have explicitly challenged capitalist accumulation. Sustainable development spawned an array of proposals to reform the status quo, but few that promised to achieve both equitable development and sustainability.

Notwithstanding its reformist character, sustainable development represents a significant advance in environmental politics in Latin America. In the past the environmental movement focused on how to protect all species except *Homo sapiens*. It concentrated on conservation of rain forests, watersheds, and animals. People living in endangered areas were usually ignored or, worse, considered threats to a region's ecosystem. With sustainable development, the environment has become a human issue by linking the analysis of ecosystems with the conditions of human survival. Nevertheless, within this framework environmentalists and politicians have rarely explored the connections between property relations, political power, and environmental destruction.

Sustainable development is ostensibly about the link between ecosystems and people's lives. As a development policy and a social movement in the United States and Europe, its primary focus was tropical rain forests, especially Amazonia. Although relatively few people live in or are directly affected by rain forests, they have captured world attention for their beauty, mystery, and putative role in global climatological change. Meanwhile, the urban and rural ecosystems populated by the vast majority of Latin Americans have attracted minimal international interest.

In the 1980s the multilateral lending agencies adopted the concept of sustainable development. Institutionalization has threatened to make it the most recent in a long parade of ephemeral development fads: growth with equity, integrated rural development, basic needs, appropriate technology, and women in development. Each began as a critique of the orthodoxy of the development establishment; each in turn was appropriated by those same agencies as a way of defusing opposition; and each left the traditional agenda of the major development agencies virtually unchanged. Sustainable development has threatened to follow the same life cycle (Hawkins and Buttel n.d.:4–5). In its 1992 *World Development Report,* the World Bank announced that "working for a better environment" was a major policy goal. In the late 1980s sustainability rose to a prominent place within the development establishment. Speeches and working papers heralded the new policy. New program departments and professional specializations created vested interests in sustaining the fad. The World Bank appeared to have assumed the mantle of environmentalism, but it was form over essence. Environmentalism made little impact on the Bank's core activities: adjustment lending and project aid. Notwithstanding high-profile pronouncements as to the importance of sustainability, concrete measures to improve the environmental impact of the Bank's activities were minimal.

But the Bank's pronouncements proved less important than the environmental impact of the economic policies adopted by the multilateral lending agencies (see Weeks's chapter in this volume). The agencies' development agenda in Latin America in the 1980s and first half of the 1990s were disastrous for both development and the environment. To make sure Latin American states serviced the debts that they accumulated in the previous decade, the International Monetary Fund (IMF) and the World Bank imposed neoliberal adjustment policies on them. These policy packages were an extreme form of monetarist and laissez-faire economics, designed to ensure that the Latin American countries earned as much foreign exchange as possible in order to pay the interest on their loans (Dore 1992:79–85). To do this, they were required to increase their trade balances, one part of which involved promoting exports.

To comply with bankers' demands, governments sought private investment to expand export production. They competed over which could provide more attractive conditions for foreign and domestic capital to enhance competitiveness in the world market. This required, among other things, ensuring low wages, a submissive labor force, and few environmental restrictions. The policy was successful on its own terms. Exports of natural resources rose spectacularly. In the 1980s the value of Latin American fishery exports was almost four times greater than it had been in the previous decade. The value of forestry exports rose as well, though not as rapidly (FAO 1989:327). Production of iron and copper in the 1980s was well above levels of the decade before (MOPU 1990:188–190). In addition, exports of agricultural products grew significantly over the same period (FAO 1989:327). A few countries in the region succeeded in attracting low-wage, high-pollution industries, especially Mexico. The pressure to export, and generally to comply with IMF and World Bank economic conditionality, compelled most of the Latin American governments to implement development strategies that were antithetical to environmental sustainablity.

The irrational use of natural resources that accompanied the drive to export was compounded by the economic orthodoxy promoted by the development establishment. Free market economics became an article of faith within the multilateral lending agencies in the 1980s as well as in the economics profession at large. Notwithstanding lip service to the environment, this model of capitalist development accentuated ecological destruction. Free marketeers argued that private sector cost-benefit calculations would result in improvements in the environment; that is, that the costs to capital of environmental degradation and natural resource depletion would compel firms to reduce pollution and conserve ecosystems. In this theory, market liberalization, free enterprise, and reduction in the role of the state were the keys to improving environmental quality (World Bank 1992:10).

Notwithstanding these articles of faith, the environmental impact of liberalization was not positive in Latin America. Weak regulations encouraged entrepreneurs to adopt production methods that ensured large profits in the short term without regard for natural resource preservation. Industries were attracted to Latin America because they could pollute, dispose of toxic wastes, and extract resources with little state interference. Where governments introduced environmental regulations, responding at times to pressure from the lending agencies themselves, their monitoring capacity was negligible. With pared-down budgets and staffs, state agencies charged with implementing environmental regulations were unable to enforce their mandate. Environmentalism became yet another avenue for market liberalization and reduction in the ambit of the state.

Few professionals challenged the terms of debates set by the development establishment. To retain credibility, and prevent exclusion from the corridors of power, environmentalists framed issues of sustainability in terms acceptable to the agencies. Instead of the environmental movement transforming the priorities of the multilateral agencies, the reverse occurred. The agenda of the World Bank and the IMF—export promotion, free markets, a small state—became the central issues in the environmental debate. Assuming the mantle of environmentalism, development agencies tamed their opposition.

By the 1990s it was clear to the progressive wing of the environmental movement that the international development establishment had wrapped itself in the rhetoric of environmentalism to legitimate a structural adjustment agenda that was contrary to sustainability and human development. In addition to directly fomenting irrational resource use, structural adjustment intensified poverty throughout Latin America. In 1980, 35 percent of the population of the region lived below the poverty line. Five years later the figure was 40 percent (MOPU 1990:157). The rise in poverty intensified pressure on the environment in numerous ways. In the countryside farmers resorted to cultivating plots that had been considered too eroded for agriculture, thereby intensifying soil depletion. In urban areas, reductions in subsidies and incomes put the price of fuel beyond many people's means. As a result, urban dwellers cut firewood in zones surrounding the cities, denuding those regions of trees.

Ecological Marxism

Progressive Latin Americans embraced dependency theory in the 1960s and 1970s to explain underdevelopment. They argued that the Latin American countries were underdeveloped because the advanced industrial countries had appropriated their economic surplus. In addition to causing underdevelopment in their region, this transfer accounted for the rapid economic growth of the imperialist countries. One of the dominant forms of anticapitalist environmentalism in Latin America derived from dependency theory. In that theory, surplus extraction takes the form of ecological pillage. By exploiting ecosystems in peripheral countries, imperial capital earned a higher rate of profit than it could at home. This contributed to underdevelopment in Latin America because it devastated the region's natural resource base and reduced the long-term potential for capital accumulation (Leff 1989:49–78; 1986).

A variant of the above was that foreign methods of production that were incompatible with the tropical climate and soils of much of Latin America degraded the fragile ecosystems of the region. It was argued, for example, that cattle grazing and monocrop agriculture were sustainable in the ecosystems of Europe and the United States, but not in Latin America. Imposed after the Conquest, these methods of production caused a long-term, irreversible loss of the region's natural productive potential. In this view, underdevelopment was a consequence of foreign technological dependence.

Related to the above was a more explicitly antimodern strand of ecological Marxism. It stressed the positive ecological aspects of indigenous culture. Within this perspective Indian production systems were inherently respectful of the environment, and European practices were intrinsically exploitative. Ecologists who adopted this framework suggested that economically rational strategies of development might be found in the technical wisdom of different social groups, in particular of indigenous peoples. They also viewed small-scale production as more economically sustainable than large-scale production (Toledo 1992; Varese cited in Mires 1990:65; Leff 1986).

The antimodern current ran deeply through the Latin American tradition of ecological Marxism, whose adherents were highly critical of industrialization in the abstract. They argued that modern technologies were incompatible with sustainability and favored a return to scientific-technical knowledge rooted in local conditions. Yet given that technological innovation has been linked with the requirements of capitalist profitability, there is reason to believe that de-linking industrialization from the capitalist drive for profits might alter the ecological impact of technical innovation. In theory, one goal of technical innovation could be sustainability, instead of the expansion of output and reduction in costs (Leff 1986:9–21).

A world without modern technology would be unsustainable. Given present population growth trends, in the year 2025 the world population will be about twice that of 1990. To feed that population, food production will need at least to double. Without the modernization of agricultural production, much of the world's population would face starvation. The challenge was not to do away with industrialization but to de-link it from profit-making so that technological change can serve the needs of development and sustainability.

Judgments about the environmental consequences of methods of production, without reference to their particular ecosystems and class relations, suffered from the same flaw as assessments of the merits of technology in the abstract. Small-scale production may or may not be ecologically preferable to production on a large scale. The central issue is not size of the production unit but who controls it. When the accumulation of capital is the objective of production, ecological considerations may be disregarded whatever the scale. Insofar as Indian and peasant communities practice more rational forms of natural resource use it is because they are not driven by the capitalist imperative to expand output beyond needs. This leads to the conclusion that where production is consciously and collectively designed to enhance social needs, there is more possibility that choice of technique, including scale, might reflect environmental considerations, among others.

Environmentalism and Struggles for Social Justice

Resource use and social justice are inseparable in Latin America. Most environmental issues have involved conflicts among social groups over the rights of property, although the class nature of these conflicts was frequently obscured. I examine major environmental crises in three areas of Latin America: Amazonia, Central America, and Mexico City. In each I analyze the social forces that have given rise to severe ecological deterioration and the class conflicts that have developed over how to respond to the situation.

Amazonia

Possibly nowhere else in Latin America have conflicts over natural resources been more directly tied to property relations than in Amazonia. At the same time, these struggles have been obfuscated by myth. The myth of Amazonia is encoded in popular environmentalism in the United States and Europe. It is a tale of rapid and irreversible deforestation and species extinction, a process that has contributed to global warming. Although not without truth, this account hides social processes that would determine the fate of the forest and of the 15 million people who live there.

The Brazilian Amazon has represented the vortex of contradictory agendas of many competing social groups: local, national, and international (Schmink and Wood 1992:18). Each has a different, often conflicting, vision of how the natural resources of the region should best be used. Farmers, ranchers, miners, land speculators, indigenous groups, rubber tappers, and politicians—a volatile mix—have competed to determine the future of the region. Over the past twenty years or so the terms of that struggle have changed dramatically. In 1970 the debate was about how to modernize the region: how to turn the "empty" forest into a productive resource. By 1990 the discourse was colored green; all the actors made their demands and outlined interests in an environmental framework. Environmental sustainability and social justice became key words in the discourse on the future of Amazonia. Yet deforestation and social violence against subordinate groups that have loudly pressed their claims have continued almost as before.

In the twentieth century the expansion of pastureland was the leading cause of deforestation in Latin America. By 1990 an estimated 8 to 10 percent of the rain forest of Amazonia had been cleared, mostly for cattle grazing. Despite this, beef production as such proved to be unprofitable on the poor soils found in the region. It remained the dominant economic activity, however, serving as a vehicle for real estate speculation and financial manipulation that have been at the root of deforestation in Amazonia.

In the early 1970s the military regime in Brazil embarked on an ambitious project to open the Amazon. The rain forest, like tropical forests elsewhere, was seen as a vast, empty space that called out for development. Development meant building roads, bringing in settlers, promoting economic activities, and taking out products. All groups with a voice in the public debate favored clearing the forest. The principal issues were how to do it and which groups would benefit. The government of Brazil financed construction of the Transamazon Highway, with generous support from multilateral lending agencies. As it crossed the Amazon Basin into uncharted territories, the unpaved highway brought people, spontaneous settlements, and an array of productive activities into the fragile terrain. Roads always precipitate rapid ecological and social change, and the Amazon was no exception. A major aspect of the first scheme to develop the Amazon involved resettling landless families, particularly from impoverished northeastern Brazil, on plots of 100 hectares. The military regime promised that development of Amazonia would relieve problems of poverty and landlessness. Official propaganda declared that the Transamazon Highway would connect "people with no land to a land with no people" (Schmink 1992:2).

As the road advanced into the jungle, people from all over Brazil settled land on either side. They cut down trees to indicate occupancy and stake claims. Then, to acquire land titles and loans, settlers needed to demonstrate to the government and the banks that they were using the land productively. The quickest and cheapest means of consolidating land claims was to clear the land and graze cattle. Consequently, cattle raising became the favored economic activity. Within a few years large investors and land speculators began crowding out recent settlers. Lured by the tax rebates, subsidies, and credit facilities originally meant to attract small farming families to the region, finance capital from southern Brazil invested in landed property. Land speculation in Amazonia thrived as inflation soared in the 1970s and 1980s, making land and gold valued assets. As large capital entered the region, first-wave settlers either moved to the edge of the frontier and cleared new lands for themselves, sought work as wage laborers on larger ranches, or returned to their former homes, often poorer than before.

The large ranchers who came to dominate the frontier were more success-ful than their predecessors in regularizing private property in land. In the first place, they exerted leverage on bureaucrats and politicians beyond the reach of the small migrant farmers. Also, the earlier populist development model fell from favor in Brasília, and government policy changed in favor of large private enterprise in the modernization of Amazonia. The development of the region sparked the fastest and most extensive enclosure movement in history. It is estimated that from 1970 to 1990, 50 million hectares of com-mon lands were appropriated as private property, most in estates of more than 500 hectares (Hecht and Cockburn 1990:189–216).

This massive expropriation of land brought with it conflict that frequently turned violent. Competing claims to land, eviction, and dispossession cre-ated an unstable social milieu. Yet the underlying order to the violence mir-rored the distribution of power in society. Larger landowners utilized their access to the state to influence the forces of repression. The army and police were generally on their side. When they were not, landowners took law and order into their own hands or, rather, placed it in the hands of their private guards. The result was that the scale of justice decidedly tipped in favor of larger ranchers. Smaller farmers who had been dispossessed organized to as-sert their claims to land. Sometimes they were successful, in part because of the global spotlight on Amazonia.

Cattle grazing created an environmental and a social disaster in Amazonia, as it did in much of Latin America. The infamous burning of the forest, the first step in clearing land, had a global as well as a local impact. There was no scientific consensus that reduction of the tropical rain forest produced global warming, but forest-burning itself added considerable quantities of carbon to the atmosphere that, many contend, contributed to a "greenhouse effect," a heating of the earth's atmosphere. Clearing initiated a rapid process of decline in soil fertility. Tropical forests survive on poor, acidic soils. Without the cov-ering that vegetation provided, runoff from tropical rains reduced nutrients to levels below those necessary to maintain pastureland. In combination with cat-tle grazing, heat and low humidity accentuated by the removal of forest cover reduced grasslands to scrub and further accelerated soil depletion. Ecological degradation condemned land to waste within five to ten years. Nevertheless, the economic and political system promoted the expansion of pastures. Tax re-bates, land concessions, and subsidized credit made it more economical to clear new land than to maintain the fertility of existing pastures. Consequently, pastures were abandoned as more forest was cleared for new ones.

Profits in ranching did not derive primarily from production. The cattle industry became a vehicle for entrepreneurs to acquire land, subsidized credit, and tax reductions. Therefore, destruction of the natural resource base of the industry did not constrain profitability. Rather, it accelerated speculation in land and capital accumulation. For that reason, there were few incentives to use the ecosystem in a sustainable way. Quite the contrary, the economic rationale promoted the wanton and unsustainable use of land. Throughout the opening of the Amazon, financial speculation intensified ecological destruction. The abuse of natural resources in Amazonia was so flagrant that it gave cattle raising a bad name. The disrepute was not the result of a rational appraisal of the economic, social, and ecological costs and benefits of the industry. Rather, criticism of cattle grazing in the rain forest gained worldwide attention after alliances were formed between groups in Amazonia that opposed ranching and international environmental organizations. Together they lobbied to expose the ecological and social consequences of deforestation.

Ranchers and small farmers were joined by others who competed to claim the valuable resources of the forest. Mining was second to cattle in transforming the region. Brazil's Grande Carajás Project, begun in the 1980s, was the largest mining complex in the world. Everything about Carajás was mammoth, including its potential to alter the region's ecosystem. The project converted one-quarter of Amazonia into the world's largest industrial and agrolivestock center (Hall 1989:20). At the hub of the enterprise were massive deposits of iron ore and manganese that reputedly enjoyed the lowest production costs in the world. It was estimated that Carajás alone would produce 10 percent of the world's supply of iron ore.

Grande Carajás became the heart of a vast, integrated development project that included a string of open-cast mines that produced bauxite, copper, chrome, nickel, tungsten, cassiterite, and gold, in addition to iron ore and manganese. Radiating from the mines were processing plants, steel and aluminum mills, agrolivestock enterprises, hydroelectric dams, railroads, and deep-water river ports. Together these covered an area of 900,000 square kilometers—the size of France and Britain combined. The complex was like a giant magnet, drawing farmers, ranchers, gold prospectors, and enterprises of all kinds into Amazonia.

The project had serious ecological implications that, because of its scale, were difficult to predict. Soon after building began at Carajás, however, significant ecological changes became evident. The project involved massive deforestation. In addition to the effects of the mines, farms, and cattle ranches, 1.6 million acres of timber were cut annually to stoke the pig-iron smelters and provide lumber for construction. The state-owned company administering the project paid lip service to conservation and implemented some reforestation. Nevertheless, large areas of the tropical forest were reduced to scrubland because the company bought most of the charcoal for its smelters from loggers who recklessly cut timber. By the time the first iron ore rolled out of Carajás in 1985, rapid deforestation had altered the climate. Less rainfall, combined with soil erosion, siltation and flooding of the region's rivers caused widespread desertification. Extinction of plant and animal species signaled changes in the ecosystem.

Large as they were, Carajás and other corporate ventures did not monopolize mining in Amazonia. After a steep rise in the price of gold in 1979, *garimpeiros,* or small-scale miners, flocked to Amazonia. The roads, railroads, and services installed for Carajás and for the cattle industry facilitated migration. In 1980 discovery of a massive gold deposit at Serra Pelada in southern Pará unleashed a gold rush that dwarfed the California Gold Rush of 1849. It is estimated that almost 1 million *garimpeiros* panning in and around the rivers of Amazonia produced more than 90 percent of Brazil's annual output of gold. Photographs of thousands of mud-covered men at Serra Pelada carrying sacks of gold up rickety ladders on the side of the ravine that formed the pit face focused international attention on the gold rush.

For its size and organization, Serra Pelada was atypical of gold mining in Amazonia. Most gold mining occurred on small sites scattered throughout the zone. Relying on simple machinery and artisanal technologies, *garimpeiros* panned the waterways that crisscross the region. Dredging and sifting the sandy river bottoms, they extracted alluvial gold, which they purified with mercury. Some people argued that *garimpeiros,* the mining industry's informal sector, were more destructive of the environment than Grande Carajás because their activities were unregulated and unplanned (Cleary 1990). They held that the *garimpeiros'* profligate use of mercury contaminated rivers and soil more than would large mining companies. The sheer number of small mining sites, these critics pointed out, left rivers polluted with massive amounts of silt, sewage, and mercury. Finally, the random logging associated with *garimpeiros* caused more serious erosion, they noted, than programmed deforestation/reforestation. Others disagreed. Given the reality that mining will continue, they argued that *garimpeiros* were the lesser of two evils. Despite the damage caused by these miners, they formed an uneasy consort with small farmers, rubber tappers, and indigenous groups to resist the expansion into Amazonia of large capitalist enterprises.

In the 1980s new voices joined the international debate on the Amazon. From the beginning, grazing and mining encroached on lands used by indigenous tribes and rubber tappers. But their demands for recognition of their rights to the resources of the forest were ignored. In the 1970s, politicians had dismissed the Indians and rubber tappers as primitives, soon to be swept away by progress. Fifteen years later the struggle over the fate of the forest appeared, at least on the surface, considerably different. Indigenous groups and tappers were considered legitimate participants in the debate. Their persistent resistance to expropriation and to felling the forest, combined with links to national and international organizations, converted them from pariahs to legitimate actors in the unfolding drama. The story of Chico Mendes was symbolic, for it illustrated both how these groups achieved political recognition and why their victories have been fragile. In 1980 Mendes was an obscure trade union organizer among the rubber tappers in the remote state of Arce in northwestern Amazonia. Nine years later he had become an internationally respected environmentalist murdered by ranchers from the state. His was an unlikely story with an utterly predictable end: a chronicle of a death foretold.

In the mid-twentieth century, rubber was extracted in Arce on large estates called latifundia. Debt peonage bound the tappers—workers who extracted rubber from trees—to the large landowners, a feudal system that broke down as the estates declined and went into bankruptcy in the 1960s (Gross 1989; Hecht and Cockburn 1990:189–216). Just when the tappers were freed from debt servitude and became independent artisanal producers, they faced a new enemy. Land speculators were carving up Arce into cattle ranches, which by 1982 accounted for over 85 percent of land in the state. Ranchers felling the forest as quickly as possible to legitimate their claims clashed with tappers, whose livelihood depended on preserving the trees. It was common practice for ranchers to force tappers at gunpoint to relinquish their claims to lands they had worked all their lives.

Mendes, a tapper from the age of nine, was an organizer for the National Confederation of Rural Workers. The union concentrated on getting tappers a better price for their rubber; Mendes called for a more militant policy of direct action to prevent landowners from clearing the forest. To that end he organized the National Council of Rubber Tappers in 1985 and led tappers to occupy forest sites to prevent burning and clearing. Ranchers resorted to beatings and death threats to persuade tappers to give up their claims. When intimidation failed, murder was common.

Cattle grazing and mining formed the centerpiece of a development model that was antithetical to the interests of people whose livelihood depended on the forest. Tappers realized that to attract international support for their struggle, they needed to elaborate an alternative economic strategy that would safeguard the forest and at the same time promote development. The solution they offered was the extractive reserve. To ensure access to land and to preserve the forest, the local population would have use rights on the reserves, but the land would not be privately owned. Insofar as the tappers advocated common property rights, they provided a radical alternative to private property. International environmental organizations endorsed the extractive reserve as a means of protecting the forest while facilitating exploitation of resources, such as rubber, nuts, and genetic materials. The reserve seemed to be an innovative strategy for conserving strategic ecological zones. It offered an escape from the stalemate of either clearing trees to pave the way for modern enterprises or preserving the forest as a pristine reserve for plants and animals but not for people.

The turning point in struggles over Amazonia came in 1987 when organizations in the United States invited Mendes to speak. This brought him international attention: That an obscure backwoodsman could attract world recognition with proposals to save the forest caused an uproar in Brazil. Mendes skillfully used the limelight to promote the tappers' political agenda. His efforts were successful. The Brazilian congress passed legislation endorsing the legality of extractive reserves and decreeing that lands could be expropriated to create them. Landowners in the state were particularly fearful of the new law because their property titles were of dubious validity. More threatening, however, was the collective action by groups who were formerly quiescent. In the same year, the Indigenous People's Union joined the tappers in forming the Forest People's Alliance. Indians and tappers traditionally had considered each other enemies, even to the point of armed conflict. Despite their past, at the signing ceremony the two groups proclaimed they shared common enemies—ranchers and loggers—and would unite against them. The unity of the subordinate groups intensified ranchers' fears. This was compounded by tappers and Indians making common cause in Brasília and Washington against the model of development that was transforming Amazonia. Together they demanded control over the resources of the forest. The Forest People's Alliance pressed for the creation of an extractive reserve in Arce. National and international pressure moved the governor of the state to create the first reserve in 1988. The decree heightened social tensions; landowners were enraged that poor rubber tappers and primitive Indians could prevent them from clearing the forest. Confronted with the erosion of their political influence, ranchers took the law into their own hands by putting a price on Mendes's life. Notwithstanding the international focus on the struggles of the rubber tappers, Mendes was murdered. Almost immediately he was enshrined as a martyr to the cause of saving the rain forest. In Amazonia Mendes's death had more immediate repercussions: It deterred others from adopting the militant politics that contributed to the tappers' victories.

Like the tappers, indigenous groups in Amazonia combined militant struggles in the forest, skillful negotiations in state and national politics, and leverage in the international development community to achieve their goals (Schmink and Wood 1992:253–272). In the 1980s the Kayapó tribe emerged as leaders of a powerful indigenous movement. Frustrated with the sluggish pace of the bureaucracy in stemming the encroachment on their lands, they took matters into their own hands. On several occasions members of the tribe killed would-be settlers who were clearing lands within the territory that had been set aside for the Kayapó in a 1978 decree. These events called national attention to the unfolding struggle among indigenous tribes, ranchers, and miners.

The resistance of the Kayapó both increased unity among what had been a loose association of villages and heightened intratribal conflicts. Intense differences arose over whether the group should permit logging and mining on the reserve, and if so, how to profit from it. Some individuals who claimed to represent the tribe signed contracts with loggers and mining companies to exploit resources on the reserve in exchange for a percentage of the profits. Others opposed logging and mining altogether. These differences led to intratribal violence.

By 1983 mining posed the greatest threat to tribal unity and territory. Major deposits of gold were discovered on the reserve that mining companies and *garimpeiros* exploited, sometimes under contract with the tribe. Ironically, Kayapó leaders manipulated the government's desire to promote mining within the reserve to finally resolve their territorial claims. Unable to secure official government demarcation of the reserve, Kayapó leaders decided to prohibit mining within their territories until the land issue was resolved. Their strategy succeeded. The Kayapó reserve was officially recognized in 1985.

Notwithstanding that achievement, confidence that the Kayapó would safeguard the forest might be misplaced. The Kayapó were a heterogeneous group incorporating different class interests, some of which conflicted with rational resource use in the past. Individuals within the tribe had promoted logging and destructive forms of mining when the rewards were sufficiently attractive. There was little reason to expect that the same might not happen in the future, especially since in exchange for legal recognition of their territory the Kayapó agreed to allow mining on the reserve, charging a royalty of 5 percent of the profits. Whether the Kayapó would preserve the forest depended on whether conflicts of interest within the tribe over how to exploit resources were resolved in favor of sustainable use. In particular, it depended on whether forest preservation was perceived to be in the interests of powerful groups within the tribe or whether those who were willing to sell off the reserve, or resources on it, could be stopped before they did so. The future of the reserve also turned on whether the Kayapó as a group could defend their territory against outsiders who sought to appropriate its land and resources. In the past Kayapó leaders engaged in financial deals that benefited themselves, not the group. Collective decision-making might check that tendency, but that alone would be no guarantee that the Kayapó would pursue an economic strategy compatible with the sustainable exploitation of the forest. The relative isolation of the Kayapó from the modern world ended abruptly, and their indigenous traditions changed rapidly. The Kayapó's past economic and cultural practices were generally compatible with regeneration of the rain forest. But past practices were no guarantee for the future. The Kayapó's exploitation of the forest will be conditioned primarily by struggles within the Kayapó community.

However the contests might unfold, they altered debate on Amazonia beyond recognition. In 1970 there was no legitimate voice calling for preservation of the forest. In 1990 no group that sought legitimacy could oppose such an aim. Even ranchers and loggers recast their claims in environmental terms. Schmink and Wood call this "the greening of the discourse" (1992:16). In 1970 cattle ranching was promoted as the best way to develop the Amazon: Clearing the forest, pastures, and fences were symbols of progress that few public figures opposed. By 1990 these same practices had become symbols of destruction; cattle grazing was widely condemned as neither economically nor ecologically sustainable. The terms of the development debate shifted because a constellation of forces, led by rubber tappers and indigenous tribes, claimed their rights to the resources of the forest. That those claims were moderately successful reflects the growing influence of environmental movements worldwide. Nevertheless, despite the greening of the discourse and the subsequent creation of extractive and indigenous reserves, Brazilian policy in the Amazon continues to promote large capitalist enterprises for which sustainable resource use is not a high priority.

Central America: Toxification and Deforestation

The expansion of agroexport production after World War II profoundly altered the social and natural fabric of Central America. Cotton, followed by cattle, was the vehicle of that transformation. Until the end of the nineteenth century the Pacific Coast of Central America was a ribbon of mangroves and tropical forests dotted occasionally with farms. European and North American travelers provided vivid descriptions of the region's extraordinary terrain and wildlife (Byam 1849; Scherzer 1857). In Nicaragua until World War II fertile farmland was found in the Pacific lowlands. There, peasants entwined in a matrix of subordinate relations with larger landowners grew food and grazed cattle on small farms and common lands. They produced largely for family consumption, selling their surplus on the small national market. By 1970 what was once the granary of the nation had been transformed into a dust bowl by cotton.

Landowners in Central America experimented with cotton before the war but abandoned it because of the ruinous pests that thrived in the tropical climate. In the 1950s, to promote development, the U.S. government and international agencies financed experimentation with modern methods of cotton cultivation. DDT, a organochlorine pesticide, was at the heart of these new techniques. Landowners evicted peasants to make way for cotton, then hired them as wage laborers to plant, tend, and harvest the crop. But cotton provided work for only several months a year. To survive, families squatted on unoccupied lands, growing corn and beans, the staples of the peasant diet. The interdependence of the capitalist cotton economy and the subsistence peasant economy was socially exploitative and ecologically destructive.

Capitalists in Central America had little leverage in the global economy. The small volume of regional production relative to world supply of cotton, sugar, and beef made them particularly vulnerable to competition. In addition, Central American states were weak internationally, with little power in the global arena to foster local capitalists. As a result, exporters competed in the world market on the basis of low prices. This meant they had to reduce their costs of production relative to costs elsewhere (Weeks 1985:59–60), which they accomplished by paying low wages and using chemicals that had been banned in other countries. In consequence, cotton production in Central America was associated with immiserization of rural laborers and flagrant ecological degradation (Faber 1993:11–43).

Cotton also involved a production process more ecologically destructive than that of any other agricultural commodity. In the 1970s greater quantities of pesticides were used annually in the production of cotton throughout the world than in the cultivation of all other crops combined. Cotton growers unleashed chemical warfare to produce that natural fiber. Copious applications of DDT and other chemicals created pesticide-resistant insects. Like the old woman who swallowed a fly, Central American cotton growers found it necessary to apply greater and greater quantities of increasingly toxic chemicals, setting up a "pesticide treadmill" whereby the more insecticides were used, the more were needed to control increasingly resistant pests.

Crop dusters spraying toxic chemicals on fields full of workers became a familiar sight in Central America. The land, water, air, and people of the region's Pacific Coast were poisoned by the inundation of pesticides. Chemicals, many banned in their countries of origin, entered the food chain. Because DDT decomposes very slowly, by 1970 people of the region showed a higher accumulation of DDT in their tissues than anywhere else in the world; women were advised not to nurse babies because of dangerously high levels of the chemical in their breast milk.

The poisoning of Central America was not a technological response to a biological problem. It evolved out of a particular configuration of social relations. Cotton producers' political power allowed them to virtually ignore mounting evidence of a contaminated environment and laborers' denunciations of intolerable working conditions. The power of landlords to repudiate the demands of the rural poor was woven into the fabric of rural society in Guatemala, El Salvador, and Nicaragua (Weeks 1986:31–53). Since the introduction of coffee in the late nineteenth century, violence was central to the rural labor process: in recruiting workers, in imposing the conditions of labor, and in repressing opposition movements (Dore 1991:1–45). Continuing in that tradition, workers' complaints about the prevalence of toxification, infertility, and death associated with work in the cotton fields failed to move either landowners or governments to alter working conditions.

Cotton producers were particularly prone to douse the Pacific plains with wave upon wave of chemicals because, in many cases, they owned the factories that produced pesticides. Industrialization within the Central American

Common Market in the 1960s was linked closely with the agricultural development of the region. It is hardly surprising that the industrial sector characterized by the fastest growth was the manufacture of the fertilizers, pesticides, and fungicides used to produce cotton. By the mid-1970s more than 1 million hectares on the Pacific plains of Central America were planted in cotton, and each year these fields were inundated with larger volumes of insecticides. So a chemical fix to all of the problems relating to agricultural cultivation was encouraged by industrialists in the region. The use of chemicals was further promoted by government policy. Subsidized credit was available to finance the cotton crop in every country of the region. It was not unusual for larger growers to receive loans of up to 90 percent of their costs of production, repayable after the harvest, a form of financing that provided both the liquidity to purchase huge quantities of chemicals and the need to ensure a large harvest in order to cancel the debt.

Taken together, the social factors favoring chemical use were so great that by 1980 daily aerial spraying of the cotton crop was not unusual. Although it seemed to guarantee large harvests and quick profits each year, in the longer run it contributed to a regional economic and ecological crisis. Ever larger applications of petroleum-based insecticides became increasingly costly and resulted in soil exhaustion and erosion. By the end of the 1980s cotton lands on the Pacific Coast were in a state of ruin. In addition to the human toll, evident from a high incidence of pesticide poisonings, infertility, cancer rates, and deaths, all forms of life on the plains are impregnated with chlorinated compounds. Because these break down slowly and become part of the material composition of plants and animals, they will have unpredictable long-run effects on the ecology of the zone.

The expansion of cotton in the region had other, equally undesirable, social and ecological consequences. Peasants evicted from the Pacific coastal plain resumed small-scale farming wherever possible. In Nicaragua most dispossessed peasants moved to the hilly central region and further eastward to lowland forests, where they cleared trees to plant food. They migrated, first, because their family relations and culture were bound up with small-scale farming and they were attempting to replicate that lifestyle. Second, the cotton estates provided only seasonal work and low wages, so peasants found they had to supplement their cash income by growing food.

Some peasant families thrived in their new surroundings and took up grazing as a means to claim land in somewhat the same way as in Amazonia. For most, however, life on the frontier was precarious and arduous. Since many families in Nicaragua were evicted from the Pacific plains at about the same time, land in the interior that was both unoccupied and suitable for agriculture was in great demand. Consequently, households settled whatever land was available, and often the farm was too small, or the land too poor, to support sustainable agricultural practices. Erosion and decline in soil fertility set in quickly as hillsides were plowed and fallow periods shortened. In addition to the degradation of land, tenancy was precarious, as most settlers lacked titles. At any moment they might be, and were, pushed off the fields they cleared. If lucky, they would locate unoccupied land and begin the process again, and perhaps yet again. Insecure land tenure accentuated the stress on the environment. As peasants expected they might soon be forced to move on, there was little rationale not to overexploit the resources they had access to at the moment. Few of those peasant households survived by direct provisioning alone. Most existed by combining seasonal wage work with small-scale farming. As wages were essential to the reproduction of their peasant economy, some members of the family worked for the cotton barons even if pay was low and conditions unhealthy.

Although not planned, the system as it emerged was advantageous to Nicaragua's capitalist class. Growing cotton required large numbers of workers, but only for short periods each year. If the people who picked cotton had no access to land, then survival throughout the year would depend on wages or other forms of monetary income. If that had been the case, there might have been more pressure than there was for higher wages. The cotton boom in Nicaragua came at a time when there were still unoccupied lands on the agricultural frontier. The capitalists were not averse if the families they evicted settled the interior, as long as their existence remained sufficiently precarious that they returned every year to work in the harvest.

The expansion of cattle raising undermined the interdependence of cotton and the peasant economy. Construction in the 1960s of the Panamerican Highway opened new agricultural zones. Following a scenario that became a leitmotif in Latin America, peasants cleared and cultivated subsistence plots for one or two years, after which time more powerful groups appropriated the land. In Central America ranchers expanded their herds with finance from the U.S. government and multilateral agencies. This established the infamous "hamburger connection": Cheap Central American beef supplied the growing U.S. fast-food industry. The 1970s were the apex of the cattle boom, when more than 25 percent of Central America's land mass was in pasture, two-thirds of it arable land. With 20 million acres of pastures, more land was devoted to cattle grazing than for all other agricultural purposes combined. By 1980, 250 million pounds of Central American beef was exported annually to the United States (Williams 1986:77). Because this was low-quality beef, with pesticide residues exceeding levels permitted for U.S. meat, it entered the U.S. market under special waivers for fast food.

The beef boom intensified the socioecological crisis already under way in the region. It is estimated that two-thirds of all the forests cleared since Central America was settled were felled after 1950. Because most clearing in Latin America occurred in an unplanned and unregulated manner, it is difficult to specify rates of deforestation. Nevertheless, it is generally agreed that in Central America rates of clearing increased every decade between 1950 and 1990 and that 15 percent of the region's forests were felled in the 1970s alone (Leonard 1987:114–127). Soil deterioration was accentuated, in particular in pasture zones. The result was erosion, loss of soil nutrients, compacted soils, declining numbers of plant and animal species—in short, the pasture syndrome.

At the start of the cattle boom, 45 percent of the Central American rural population was already landless or had insufficient land for subsistence farming (Weeks 1985:112). As data on distribution of land fails to take account of fertility and other productive conditions, land shortage was more extreme than even this figure suggests. Peasants who retained access to land tended to overexploit it to survive, and their exhausted fields produced declining yields of corn and beans. Consequently, peasants depended more and more on seasonal wage-earning work. In this context, the cattle boom accentuated landlessness and soil depletion and, unlike cotton, created few jobs in the countryside. As such, it intensified the crisis of the peasantry, a crisis that fed into the revolutionary wars in Nicaragua, El Salvador, and Guatemala in the late 1970s and 1980s (Dore 1990:96–120). Before the 1990s, however, ecological deterioration was not a conscious element of peasant demands in Central America. Peasant forms of production, combined with historical struggles over land, made redistribution of land the objective of peasant movements.

The regional economic crisis of the 1980s undermined the cattle and cotton industries. Wars in the northern countries of the isthmus, aggravated by falling world market prices, marked the end of the cotton and cattle booms. Acreage devoted to cotton in 1990 was one-third of what it had been in 1975. Regional exports of beef in 1987 were 46 percent of what it had been in 1979 (MOPU 1990:207–208). In addition, domestic beef consumption fell markedly throughout the region, a reflection of shrinking per capita incomes. The enigma was that deforestation continued, although at a slower pace. Logic suggested that once land devoted to cotton and cattle became available for other uses, pressure on land would decline and deforestation come to a standstill. However, Central America's forest cover continued to shrink. First, land used for cotton and cattle was so degraded it was often cheaper to clear new land than to rehabilitate the old. Second, pressure for land intensified in the aftermath of war and economic crisis. Falling cotton, coffee, and sugar production resulted in the loss of jobs in the rural sector, while urban unemployment rose because of declining manufacturing output. With wage income reduced, subsistence production became more vital to the survival of many Central Americans. Also, in Nicaragua and El Salvador demobilization of the armies of the Left and the Right and the return of large numbers of people who had fled in the 1980s added to the claims for land. Overall, decline in traditional agroexport production was insufficient to alleviate pressure for land.

In the 1990s, international focus on the environment, as well as critical deterioration of land, gave rise in each country of the region to movements of the rural poor that concentrated on environmental issues. El Centro Salvadoreño de Tecnología Apropiada (CESTA) was the best known of these. Uniting rural and urban ecology groups throughout El Salvador, CESTA, along with other organizations, turned ecology into a major issue in the national political debate. CESTA differed from other groups in that it highlighted the class character of the appropriation of nature. Its practical work centered on immediate issues of environmental protection, complementing a political analysis that sustainable resource use required a fundamental transformation in the class nature of society (Navarro et al. n.d.).

Urban Contamination and Corporatist Mobilization: The Case of Mexico City

At the end of the twentieth century Latin America was overwhelmingly urban. With more than 70 percent of the population of Latin America living in cities, the majority of people of the continent were directly affected by environmental degradation associated with urban concentrations. Yet these pressing urban issues and their human cost tended to be ignored by ecologists in the United States and Europe, who focused on the destruction of trees. Problems of urban sanitation and air pollution do not lend themselves to the simple morality of saving the rain forest.

Although pollution levels made Mexico City infamous, the causes and symptoms of its plight were characteristic of many Latin American cities. At an altitude of some 2,300 meters, sprawling across a valley of 9,600 square meters, surrounded by mountains on two sides and occupying the dry, salty beds of what was once a series of lakes, Mexico City is poorly sited for an industrial metropolis. The zone is prone to thermal inversions, which allows contaminants to accumulate in the atmosphere. But Mexico City's severe environmental problems are caused more by its demographics, its dependence on motor vehicles, and its concentration of heavy industry than by its geographical location.

The capitalist transformation of agriculture in Latin America set in motion a process of rural-to-urban migration. The declining viability of peasant production, combined with the concentration of land holdings, meant peasants either abandoned or were evicted from land. Because machinery, pesticides, and fertilizers had revolutionized agricultural production and processing, only a small proportion of the rural poor found permanent work in the countryside. As a consequence, people migrated to urban centers in search of employment. The capital cities of Latin America, with their concentration of industry, commerce, and government, became magnets for the recently dispossessed rural poor. Mexico City exemplified rural-to-urban migration: Its population doubled each decade from 1940 to 1970. States in Latin

America were unable, and often reluctant, to provide the infrastructure to adequately integrate the waves of poor rural migrants into the fabric of their cities. Arrivals established squatter settlements that sprawled without any measure of planning and that usually lacked legal tenancy. Continuing conflicts over the legality of the settlements and scarce government funds gave rise to the proliferation of vast neighborhoods that lacked basic amenities such as streets, water, sewage, and garbage disposal. Ad hoc means of providing water and disposing of waste created serious environmental problems that were made even worse by the population density in those zones.

The decades that witnessed the urban demographic boom in Latin America were also decades of industrial expansion. Subsidies and tax incentives promoted the concentration of industry in the region's capitals. Transport facilities and the growing urban population, providing workers and consumers, made it attractive for industry to locate in the metropolitan cities. Again, Mexico City presented a pathological case, accounting for 45 percent of the nation's industrial output in 1975 (Schteingart 1989:41). Industrial plants, most with minimal pollution control devices, spewed contaminants into the atmosphere. But as the government sought to promote economic growth, it was averse to imposing environmental regulations that might discourage investment.

The motor vehicle was the major polluter, however, dwarfing damage caused by demographic growth and environmentally unregulated industrial expansion. The size of the urban population, lack of planning, and inadequacy of public transport enforced dependence on motor vehicles for the transport of passengers and cargo. Mexico's "car culture" was particularly pernicious. Gasoline was not heavily taxed and cheap fuel was considered a basic human right. Few vehicles were fitted with pollution control devices, and the lead content of gasoline was high. In addition, as there were no regulations governing the conditions of vehicles, it was common for cars, trucks, and buses to leave great trails of black exhaust. Pollution from carbon monoxide and lead was so great in 1988 and 1989 that the government finally took action: It reduced the lead content of gasoline sold in Mexico City, banned each private vehicle from the road for one day per week, implemented mandatory emissions controls testing, and required pollution control equipment on all new vehicles. Despite these measures, there was little evidence that pollution levels declined (Barkin 1991:93).

Whereas the substance of urban environmental decay in Mexico City was similar to, though greater than, that found in many Latin American cities, the response of the Mexican state was unique. In keeping with its corporatist character, the Partido Revolucionario Institucional (PRI; Institutional Revolutionary Party) created an ecology movement organically linked to the party and the state (Mumme 1992; Barkin 1991). In the 1980s growing political opposition made it evident that the PRI was losing its political hegemony.

One issue that focused discontent, especially among the urban middle classes, was the deplorable quality of air and water in the capital. As the government perceived that opponents might channel this disaffection into a broad movement that could threaten the party's control, the PRI seized on the environment to launch a campaign to reconquer the political initiative. The government perceived that the environment could be a safe and at the same time popular issue that would enhance the PRI's national and international image.

By committing the government to improving the environment, the PRI established the environment as a legitimate area of debate. It created a network of "grassroots" environmental groups and encouraged their activities. The intent was to prevent the emergence of an independent movement that might play a role in destabilizing one-party rule. Also, it used its network of environmental groups to channel rewards, financial and otherwise, to individuals who emerged as leaders. In short, the PRI sought to turn critics into clients of the state, which it had done many times before with other issues. In fact, it had so perfected this corporatist modus operandi of controlling mass organizations and managing dissent that for sixty-five years its one-party rule never had been seriously challenged.

In the 1980s a multitude of environmental groups formed throughout Mexico; most were keyed to the PRI's authoritarian structure. Rather than making demands on the state, these groups related to the government through a process of petition and supplication (Mumme et al. 1988:27–28). To curtail their independence, the PRI linked groups vertically to the party, discouraging horizontal ties forged outside of the party's hierarchy. The PRI recreated in the environmental movement the patron-client relations through which it ruled. The result was an increase in protest and lobbying on environmental issues—almost all coordinated by the government.

In a climate of heightened criticism of the PRI's antidemocratic politics, the government found it could not always control the movement it created. From 1982 the PRI had declared that environmental improvement, especially in the capital, would be a high national priority. That pledge was incompatible with the government's neoliberal economic strategy. In practice, market liberalization and fiscal austerity took precedence over environmental reform. The Mexican government reduced state expenditure and encouraged private investment by removing barriers to profitability. The state was loath to impose environmental regulations that might be viewed negatively by the private sector. In addition, by reducing the government's budget, it curtailed its regulatory capacity. As a result, the state was less able to enforce those environmental standards it legislated. Tensions mounted within the environmental movement because the government reneged on its public commitment to environmental reform. It became apparent to many Mexicans that the PRI's announced policy of environmental improvement was little more than lip service. Nevertheless, the policy had some momentary success. Its politics of mobilizing ecology groups undermined the influence of independent organizations that called attention to the PRI's obeisance to private enterprise at the cost of environmental degradation. In addition, the Mexican ecology movement was highly fragmented at the grassroots level while tightly controlled from above. The government could not ensure, however, that it would continue to control the movement it created. Heightened consciousness and activity on ecological issues produced a growing awareness that, despite its rhetorical commitment, the Mexican government was prepared to undertake only token reforms to alter patterns of natural resource use and abuse, especially when reform implied a cost to capital or to the state.

Conclusion

In most countries of Latin America there was an active and heterogeneous ecology movement in the 1990s. Within the array of organizations, groups devoted to research and lobbying were the most visible. With generous funding from the numerous development agencies for which the environment was a priority, they established close links both with international ecology organizations as well as with government agencies charged with protecting the environment. Alongside those more established centers were many grassroots groups that protested against specific cases of environmental destruction that affected the quality of their lives. Notwithstanding significant funding and the numerous organizations, the Latin American ecology movements remained fragmented, reflecting as much as anything else the global political climate of the era. Crises in the world order marked the end of the millennium. Social and ecological systems changed obviously yet unpredictably, provoking uncertainty about the future of the planet's ecosystems. With the collapse of the Soviet Union emerged an international consensus that socialism was dead and capitalism triumphant. Whereas a critique of the property relations that govern control over natural resources should be at the heart of environmental action and research, with socialism discredited and capitalism ascendant in the 1990s, few ecologists focused on the class politics of environmental change. This reticence undermined the transformative power of the movement.

References

Barkin, David. "State Control of the Environment: Politics and Degradation in Mexico." *Capitalism, Nature, and Socialism* 2 (February 1991):86–108.

Byam, George. *Wild Life in the Interior of Central America*. London: Parker, 1849.

Cleary, David. *Anatomy of the Amazon Gold Rush*. Oxford: Macmillan, 1990.

Dore, Elizabeth. "The Great Grain Dilemma: Peasants and State Policy in Revolutionary Nicaragua." *Peasant Studies* 17, 2 (Winter 1990):96–120.

———. "Coffee, Land, and Class Relations in Nicaragua: 1870–1920." Paper presented at the Annual Meeting of the American Historical Association, Chicago, December 27–30, 1991.

———. "Debt and Ecological Disaster in Latin America." *Race and Class* 34, 1 (1992):73–87.

Faber, Daniel. *Environment Under Fire: Imperialism and the Ecological Crisis in Central America*. New York: Monthly Review Press, 1993.

FAO (Food and Agriculture Organization). *Country Tables 1989: Basic Data on the Agricultural Sector*. Rome: FAO, 1989.

Gross, Anthony. *Fight for the Forest: Chico Mendes in His Own Words*. London: Latin American Bureau, 1989.

Hall, Anthony. *Developing Amazonia: Deforestation and Social Conflict in Brazil's Carajás Programme*. Manchester, England: Manchester University Press, 1989.

Hawkins, Ann P., and Frederick H. Buttel. "The Political Economy of Sustainable Development." N.d., unpublished manuscript.

Hecht, Susanna, and Alexander Cockburn. *The Fate of the Forest*, 2d. ed. London: Penguin Books, 1990.

Kaimowitz, David. "La Economía Política de la Gestión Ambiental en América Latina." 1993, unpublished manuscript.

Leff, Enrique. *Ecologia y Capital: Hacia una Perspectiva Ambiental del Desarrollo*. Mexico: Universidad Nacional Autonoma de Mexico, 1986.

———. "Estudios Sobre Ecologia y Capital." *Estudios Sociales Centroamericanos* 49 (January–April 1989):49–78.

Leonard, H. Jeffrey. *Natural Resources and Economic Development in Central America*. New Brunswick, NJ: Transaction Books, 1987.

Mires, Fernando. *El Discurso de la Naturaleza: Ecología Politica en América Latina*. San José, Costa Rica: DEI, 1990.

MOPU (Ministerio de Obras Públicas y Urbanismo). *Desarrollo y Medio Ambiente en América Latina y el Caribe*. Mexico: MOPU, 1990.

Mumme, Stephen P. "System Maintenance and Environmental Reform in Mexico." *Latin American Perspectives* 19, 1 (Winter 1992):123–143.

Mumme, Stephen P., C. Richard Bath, and Valerie Assetto. "Political Development and Environmental Policy in Mexico." *Latin American Research Review* 23, 1 (1988):7–34.

Navarro, Ricardo, Gabriel Pons, and German E. Amaya. *El Pensamiento Ecologista*. San Salvador, El Salvador: El Centro Salvadoreño de Technología Apropiada, n.d.

Scherzer, Carl. *Travels in the Free States of Central America: Nicaragua, Honduras, and San Salvador*. London: Longman, Brown, Green Longmans and Roberts, 1857.

Schmink, Marianne. *Contested Frontiers in Amazonia*. New York: Columbia University Press, 1992.

Schteingart, Martha. "The Environmental Problems Associated with Urban Development in Mexico City." *Environment and Urbanization* 1, 1 (April 1989):40–50.

Toledo, Víctor. "Utopia y Naturaleza: El Nuevo Movimiento Ecológico de los Campesinos e Indígenas de América Latina." *Nueva Sociedad* 122 (November–December 1992):72–85.

Weeks, John. *Capital and Exploitation*. Princeton, NJ: Princeton University Press, 1981.

———. *The Economies of Central America*. New York: Holmes & Meier, 1985.

———. "An Interpretation of the Central American Crisis." *Latin American Research Review* 21:3 (1986):31–53.

Williams, Robert G. *Export Agriculture and the Crisis in Central America*. Chapel Hill: University of North Carolina Press, 1986.

WCED (World Commission on Environment and Development). *Our Common Future*. New York: Oxford University Press, 1987.

World Bank. *World Development Report 1992*. New York: Oxford University Press, 1992.

11

The Global Context of Contemporary Latin American Affairs

RICHARD L. HARRIS

In this chapter, I will apply a global perspective to the analysis of contemporary Latin American affairs. The concept of globalization will be employed to describe the region's integration into an evolving world system that affects almost every major aspect of contemporary affairs in Latin America. Many of the conditions analyzed in the preceding chapters of this volume will be examined in relation to this global context.

Globalization refers in general to the worldwide integration of humanity and the compression of both the temporal and spatial dimensions of planetwide human interaction. It entails expanding interdependence among the human inhabitants of the planet as well as the increasing awareness of this phenomenon (Robertson 1992:8–31). Latin America's accelerated integration into a rapidly evolving global system of economic, political, and sociocultural relations as well as the development of global consciousness among Latin Americans are important aspects of the contemporary reality of the region. It is important to emphasize that this process of global integration is occurring with increasing intensity *inside* the region's distinct societies as well as between these societies and the rapidly evolving global system (Robertson 1992:104–105).

There is considerable resistance to global conceptualizations of social reality because they threaten Western assumptions about individualism, whereby social life is seen to be little more than the summation of isolated individuals whose interactions with one another are perceived to take place primarily on the basis of the exchange of objects and symbols. Most contemporary

Western philosophy, economic thought, psychology, and literature reflect this minimalist image of social life inherited from eighteenth-century European liberalism. In fact, viewed from this perspective, social reality is largely invisible. The mere suggestion that there may be complex global as well as societal structures undermines the assumptions of autonomous individualism and rational self-interest that underlie this classical liberal view of the world.

Cognitive resistance to global concepts is also evident in postmodernist thinking: According to the conventional postmodernist perspective, the social concepts and theories of the nineteenth and twentieth centuries create a false consciousness of reality and a belief in the myth of modernity. These concepts and theories are therefore seen as invalid and outmoded for the task of understanding the "postmodern" societies of the late twentieth century (Schuurman 1993:23–29).

According to the postmodernist critique of modernist thought, the events of the closing decades of the twentieth century have revealed the erroneousness of the "metatheories" or "grand historical narratives" based on such concepts as social progress, modernization, capitalism, socialism, Westernization, imperialism, development, underdevelopment, industrialization, human emancipation, internationalism, and so forth. For the proponents of postmodernism, the diversity and unpredictability of contemporary life cannot be explained by metatheories and grand historical narratives, nor can contemporary reality be adequately perceived through the use of the universal concepts on which these theories are based.

The postmodernist perspective is difficult to apply to contemporary Latin America because there is scarcely any evidence that the region possesses "postmodern societies" or that it has moved into a "postmodern era" (Schuurman 1993:27). Most of the problems and issues addressed by the supposedly obsolete metatheories of the bygone modern era persist in contemporary Latin America. In fact, many of the region's inhabitants live under conditions more accurately described as premodern.

Globalization has not propelled the Latin American peoples into a new postmodern era. Many old problems and issues continue to be contemporary problems and issues. In fact, globalization has aggravated many of the region's most chronic problems—such as the pronounced degree of economic exploitation and social inequality that have characterized Latin America since it came under European colonial domination in the sixteenth century.

The extreme inequality that exists between the privileged minorities and the impoverished majority in Latin America cannot be adequately explained from a postmodernist perspective. However, viewed through the lens provided by the concept of globalization, it is clear that the region's integration into the evolving global capitalist economy has increased this inequality as well as the relations of exploitation and power that complement it.

A global perspective reveals that the economic, political, and sociocultural effects of capitalism have created extreme inequalities in the region as well as in the entire world. In fact, the globalization process stimulated by the worldwide expansion and development of capitalism has consistently favored only a limited proportion of the Latin American population, while the vast majority have had to suffer the adverse effects. Inequality and unequal development are the natural outcomes of capitalist development. Most of the literature on capitalism concedes this.

Capitalism and Globalization

It is difficult to avoid the conclusion that the primary cause of globalization has been the universal or worldwide expansion of capitalism (see, for example, Wallerstein 1974; Amin 1992). Most orthodox economists as well as their Marxist and neo-Marxist detractors agree that the worldwide spread of capitalism (orthodox economists prefer the term "private" or "free enterprise") has created a single global economic system. They disagree, however, about how this global process of capitalist expansion has taken place, and about its effects. Moreover, many historians and social scientists reject the notion that economic forces per se have been the primary cause of globalization, contending that this distorts interpretations of history with notions of economic determinism and single-factor analysis.

Certainly, other forces (e.g., new communications and transportation technologies, universalistic political ideologies such as liberalism and socialism, modern science, as well as universal religions such as Christianity and Islam) have fostered extensive cross-cultural ties and international relationships. However, as candidates for the principal force of global integration, they all pale in comparison to the expansive global reach of capitalist enterprises, trade, and investments.

The Marxist perspective on this question is convincing: The motive forces associated with the accumulation of and competition for wealth that underlie the capitalist system drive individual capitalists and capitalist ("private") enterprises to expand their operations and overcome all geographic, cultural and political barriers that obstruct their path to accumulating wealth (see Mandel 1975). These same forces are also assumed to motivate individual capitalists and capitalist enterprises to concentrate and centralize their control over the various means whereby wealth is accumulated. As a result, individual capitalists and capitalist enterprises have extended their efforts to accumulate wealth to every corner of the planet, and they have increasingly integrated the world's economies into a single global economic system as a result of their continuing attempts to concentrate and centralize their control over the accumulation process.

According to this perspective, certain sociocultural and political institutions, values, ideas, and worldviews have proven to be, at different historical moments, more compatible with the accumulationist drive of the capitalists than others. As a result, these sociocultural and political forms, values, worldviews, and ideas tend to be combined with and advanced by capitalist economic practices and norms (until they outlive their usefulness). Thus, at one time or another, the nation-state, nationalism, representative democracy, imperialism, liberalism, individualism, militarism, fascism, certain forms of Christianity, and so forth have been promoted by capitalists and capitalist enterprises because they contribute to the private accumulation of wealth and the concentration of private ownership and control over the various forms in which wealth is accumulated (land, machinery, money, stocks, etc.).

Based on this perspective, it is possible to explain how capitalism promoted the development of nation-states and nationalism in Latin America while undermining genuine national economic and political independence in the region (see Torres Rivas 1983). For example, from the mid–eighteenth century to the end of the nineteenth century, the driving forces of capitalism promoted nationalism, economic and political liberalism, the formation of nation-states, and the dismantling of the Spanish and Portuguese colonial empires in Latin America (see Cardoso and Faletto 1979:66–67). However, with the Spanish and Portuguese empires out of the way, these same forces also fostered a new type of imperialism in the region as first the British capitalists and then the North American capitalists, both of whom were protected by their national governments, gained control over the economic life of the new states (see Chilcote and Edelstein 1986:77). By the end of the nineteenth century, the U.S. government and U.S. capitalists had gained control over the economies of many of the Latin American states, and British influence in the region had been marginalized.

It is important to note here that this perspective allows for considerable local variation and does not overlook the importance of internal factors in determining the concrete circumstances and specific course of events in each society and historical conjuncture. As Cardoso and Faletto have pointed out, in the historical development of the Latin American countries both external and internal forces have been closely linked in a dialectical and complex network of "coincident or reconciled interests" (1979:xvi). Consequently, different local or internal conditions have been responsible for considerable variation between the societies of the Latin American region. The internal configuration of power between different classes and social forces has been an important factor in determining the manner in which global influences have affected the individual Latin American states (see also Torres Rivas 1983).

For example, during the Great Depression and World War II, ostensibly national industrial and commercial capitalists in several of the Latin American states (Argentina, Brazil, Chile, and Mexico) entered into political alliances with urban middle-class elements and in certain cases the urban working class (more specifically the trade unions) to form populist governments that sought to promote the industrial development of their economies (Cardoso and Faletto 1979:127–148). Internal social forces, not external capitalists, pursued national industrial development during a historical conjuncture in which the advanced capitalist centers were preoccupied with economic depression and war.

Had the national populist governments succeeded in this project of promoting industrial development through "national capitalism," these countries might have gained more favorable terms of trade and greater national autonomy in the postwar period. However, by the 1960s the various national development projects based on import substitution had reached their political limits, and the global development of capitalism had reached a stage where national capitalism (capitalist accumulation carried out on a strictly national basis) had become incompatible with the global interests of the large transnational corporations that emerged out of the postwar economic recovery in the United States, Western Europe, and Japan.

During the 1960s the local capitalist class in Latin America turned away from national industrial development to join with the transnational banks and corporations in opening up their domestic markets to foreign investments (see Cardoso and Faletto 1979:149–171; Marini 1974; and Evans 1979). This shift in the orientation of capital accumulation in Latin America is analyzed by Weeks in Chapter 4. During the 1960s and 1970s corporations based in the three major geographic centers, or poles, of capitalism increased their trade and investments overseas to the point that they transcended their national characters and became global entities with transnational interests (see Barnet and Muller, 1974; Gilpin, 1975). Since the 1960s "cross-investments" and intrafirm trade among the United States, Western Europe, and Japan have been the major focus of the global activities of these large transnational companies and banks (Henwood 1993; and Magdoff 1992). However, they have also greatly increased their investments and holdings in other parts of the world.

Since Latin America was already within the U.S. sphere of economic influence, it was a convenient area for North American–based transnational corporations to expand their activities following World War II (Jenkins 1984; Henwood 1993; and MacEwan 1994). As they have increased their involvement in the region, they have fostered the denationalization of the economies of the individual Latin American states. They have accomplished this task in the following manner:

- Through loans as well as direct and indirect investments in Latin American banks and financial institutions, they have gained greater control over the finances of the Latin American countries.

- With the backing of the U.S. government and international agencies such as the International Monetary Fund (IMF) and the Inter-American Development Bank (IDB), they have convinced the governments of the region to remove their former restrictions on foreign investments, eliminate their trade tariffs and subsidies that previously protected domestic industries against foreign competition, and give the transnationals open access to their economies.
- Through loans, investments, purchasing agreements, and control over patents and licenses, they have gained dominance over the most important sectors of the economy in most of the Latin American states, including agroexports, mining, petroleum and natural gas, tourism, telecommunications, pharmaceuticals, marketing and advertising, basic consumer goods, and so forth.
- They have purchased or gained controlling interest over many former state enterprises that the Latin American governments have privatized as part of the package of domestic economic reforms they have undertaken to pay the international agencies and banks to whom they are heavily indebted.
- The transnationals have persuaded the local capitalists to join them in promoting export-oriented ventures instead of undertaking economic activities that fulfill the domestic needs and enhance the internal economic development of the Latin American societies.
- They have extracted invaluable, nonrenewable resources from the Latin American countries and diverted these resources to other parts of the globe, thereby denying their use for local development purposes.
- They have transferred the scarce local capital and profits they have accumulated in the Latin American countries to the more developed centers of the global economy rather than investing them in the economies of the region.

The transnational corporations have promoted both the denationalization of the economies of the Latin American states and their consolidation into the larger global capitalist economy as subordinated and marginal elements of the global economic system.

Thus, the contemporary Latin American economies have become integral components of a global economic system dominated not by nation-states but by the large transnational corporations that are the main global actors in this system. Since the end of the postwar economic boom, the global expansion of these transnational corporations has greatly undermined the former "national" organization of economic relations and contributed to the global concentration and centralization of the capital accumulation process. This process has led to the integration of the Latin American economies into the global capitalist economy as captive markets and the source of cheap human and natural resources for the North American–based transnationals, which find themselves increasingly challenged at the global level by the major European- and Asian-based transnational corporations (Henwood 1993; and Magdoff 1992).

Efforts to develop national capitalism (capital accumulation within the territorial confines of a single nation-state) and/or to improve national competitiveness are still possible, but they face enormous difficulties because they run counter to the globalization of the world economy and the global interests and actions of the transnational corporations (Radice 1989:68). Some nation-states such as Japan and Sweden have a capitalist class that is still somewhat committed to a national capitalist project, but the economic and political conditions in these states are quite different from those in contemporary Latin America.

The contemporary capitalist class in Latin America represents a weak bourgeoisie, and their close ties to the global capitalists who control the transnationals make it extremely unlikely they will undertake any kind of national capitalist project. Moreover, the only "competitive advantages" the Latin American capitalists have at their disposal to compete in the world economy are cheap labor (maintained by keeping wages low through high levels of unemployment and political repression) and certain valuable natural resources. They lack the technology, skilled labor, large domestic consumer markets, and financial capital possessed by capitalists in the more developed countries of the world. Since they lack the means to compete on equal terms with the transnational capitalists, they have had little choice but to join with them as their local junior partners. Thus, the local business elites in Latin America have thrown open the doors of their economies to the transnational corporations that are interested in the cheap labor, natural resources, finance capital, and consumer markets of their countries.

It is important to note that the increased integration of the Latin American economies into the global capitalist economy is being accomplished through a close alliance between the Latin American capitalist class and the transnational corporations (Petras and Morley 1992:16–29). Together they have promoted major structural changes in the Latin American countries in order to further integrate the region into the global capitalist economy. These structural changes and the mutual interests of this alliance are cloaked in neoliberal ideology, which has its ideological roots in the eighteenth- and nineteenth-century thought of liberal thinkers such as Adam Smith and John Locke, although it is in fact primarily a product of the contemporary global strategy of the transnationals and the policies of the Reagan-Bush administrations in the United States and the Thatcher-Major governments in the United Kingdom (NACLA 1993:16). As Weeks indicates, neoliberalism has been used to justify the economic restructuring and the adjustment policies followed by most of the Latin American states since the 1980s.

For example, neoliberalism was touted in the IDB's guidelines for economic reform in Latin America during the early 1990s (NACLA 1993:16–17). However, even a cursory examination of Chile, Costa Rica, and Mexico, which faithfully followed the IDB's guidelines, reveals that the macroeconomic growth achieved in these countries was accomplished at the cost of holding down the real wages of the salaried workforce, the deterioration of their public services, the reduction of social benefits, as well as the rapid growth of the informal sector of the economy (NACLA 1993:17). Indeed, neoliberalism's most notable feature is the dispassionate disregard shown by its adherents for the resulting impoverishment of a very large proportion of Latin Americans.

The neoliberal emphasis on the production of exports and the elimination of restrictions on the importation of consumer goods has resulted in (1) government subsidies for the production of so-called nontraditional exports (e.g., fruit, flowers, vegetables, electronic components, etc.) rather than government support for the local production of the basic goods and the essential foodstuffs needed for domestic consumption; and (2) the importation of expensive consumer goods for the upper and upper-middle classes. The latter has aggravated the preexisting dependence on imported goods and the polarization of consumption patterns. Expensive consumer imports have also absorbed scarce foreign exchange obtained from the sale of exports. Many Latin American countries have also been forced to incur additional loans and credits to pay for these imports, which contributes to their foreign indebtedness and their financial dependence on the international lending agencies and banks.

The inability of most of the Latin American countries to finance their imports and pay their foreign loans gave rise to the debt crisis of the early 1980s, which in turn increased their financial dependence on the international lending agencies, such as the IDB and the IMF, as well as the transnational commercial banks. Unable to repay their debts and desperately in need of additional loans and credits to stave off economic collapse, the Latin American countries were forced to restructure their economies according to the terms set by their creditors. Under these conditions, the negotiating position of the Latin American states was extremely weak and they had little choice but to adopt the neoliberal package of monetary, trade, and public sector reforms imposed by the global financial institutions that hold their debts.

Many Latin American countries were thus forced into complete financial dependence on these global financial institutions. In effect, the Latin American governments were forced to place their economies in virtual receivership (as discussed in the chapters by Nef and Weeks in this volume), becoming pawns in the global financial game and vulnerable to the dynamics (e.g., the changing interest rates), dysfunctional practices (e.g., currency speculation), and rules (e.g., removal of restrictions on convertibility of currencies and repatriation of profits) that characterize this game.

Weeks's chapter clearly shows how the Latin American economies are being dragged into a global trading regime that is taking form under the regulatory structure of the General Agreement on Tariffs and Trade (GATT) and the norms and demands of the emerging "dollar trade bloc" (Henwood 1993; and Nader 1993). The latter is emerging under the aegis of the U.S. government and the North American–based transnational corporations involved in Latin America (Nader 1993; and Magdoff 1992:38–39). In order to secure their privileged position in the hemisphere (where they already have dominant influence), and thereby strengthen their position in the highly competitive global economic system, the North American–based transnationals and the U.S. government are developing an exclusive regional trading sphere (encompassing Canada, the United States, Latin America, and the Caribbean) within which North American–based transnationals will be able to exercise unchallenged dominance over trade, finance, and investments. The North American Free Trade Agreement (NAFTA) was the first stage in the formal institutionalization of this regional trading bloc (Henwood 1993:28).

NAFTA will facilitate the integration of the three economies of North America and prepare the framework for integrating the other economies of the Western Hemisphere into what already informally exists as the dollar trade bloc under the control of U.S. transnational capital (Nader 1993). In this scheme, the Latin American economies serve as captive markets for the North American–based transnationals as well as the site for new global production facilities that will take advantage of the low wages, cheap natural resources, weak labor laws, and lax environmental regulations in these countries. In order to guarantee that the advantages of this regional trading bloc are maintained for the transnationals and their local junior partners, the Latin American governments will continue to be expected to accommodate the needs of the transnationals by keeping the wages of their workforces low. They will also have to guarantee a continuing supply of cheap natural resources and maintain their weak labor laws and environmental regulations. In this arrangement, most Latin Americans will have very little to gain, whereas the transnationals and their local business allies will gain a great deal.

The GATT, as expanded by the Uruguay Round of negotiations, concluded in 1994, provides the transnational capitalists with a global regulatory structure for ensuring that the conditions for free trade are maintained throughout the world (Khor 1993). Since most of the countries in the world are members of the GATT, they are bound by the provisions of this elaborate trade treaty to conform to its neoliberal standards of free trade that benefit the transnationals and strip the member countries of their economic sovereignty.

The expansion of the GATT has created a global regulatory structure that undermines national sovereignty and enforces the free trade norms of transnational capital. In the case of Latin America, this global regime for regulating world trade institutionalizes the already-existing subordination of the economies of the Latin American states to the interests of the transnationals. It gives the latter the ability under international law to challenge and potentially overturn domestic laws and regulations that restrict their access to the economies of the Latin American countries (as well as other economies in the world). The GATT ensures the subordination of the Latin American countries to transnational capital and cements their marginal position in the global economy as captive markets within the dollar trade bloc of the North American–based transnational corporations (Kohr 1993).

Although these structures for economic integration are being erected at the global level under the aegis of the GATT, piecemeal efforts at economic integration have been established at the subregional level. In the Western Hemisphere, various subregional arrangements have been established. NAFTA and the MERCOSUR, in the Southern Cone, are the most recent; MERCOSUR member states are Argentina, Brazil, Paraguay, and Uruguay. The MERCOSUR treaty provides for the creation of a free trade zone rather than a common market; in effect, it opens up the Southern Cone to free trade rather than providing a structure for the integrated and balanced development of the countries within this zone (see Alimonda forthcoming). It has created a neoliberal framework that facilitates new forms of association between the entrepreneurial classes of the member states as well as the transnationals that operate in these countries. It also locks the member states into a neoliberal form of macroeconomic coordination controlled by private interests that limit their sovereignty.

The other subregional trade associations in the hemisphere are the Andean Pact (consisting of Bolivia, Colombia, Ecuador, Peru, and Venezuela); the Central American Common Market (Costa Rica, El Salvador, Guatemala, Honduras, and Nicaragua); the Caribbean Community, or CARICOM (composed of twelve Caribbean countries); and the trade association between Mexico, Colombia, and Venezuela. Additional so-called free trade agreements between these various subregional trade associations are being worked out, and the governments of certain countries such as Chile have expressed a desire to be included in NAFTA (Brooke 1994). In fact, it increasingly looks as though these associations will be replaced by an eventual hemispheric trade association dominated by the United States (Henwood 1993:28).

In sum, various forms of regional economic integration are taking place at the same time as global integration. The transnational banks and corporations provide the connecting links between these parallel processes of integration (Henwood 1993), which have been promoted under the slogan of "open regionalism" and with assurances of "legal security for investors" (Brooke 1994).

Experts in the international lending agencies, such as the World Bank, have argued that regional integration involving only Southern Hemisphere countries (e.g., only the Latin American countries) cannot be effective and must include one of the global triad (the United States, the European Union [EU], or Japan) to succeed (Henwood 1993:28). If the contemporary trend of development continues, it seems just a matter of time until this type of regional integration in Latin America culminates in a formal dollar trade bloc that encompasses the entire Western Hemisphere, with the United States as its center.

The Effects of Globalization on Latin America's Nation-States

As the foregoing discussion suggests, the nation-state system that dates back to the nineteenth century is being undermined and transformed by the emerging global structures of the contemporary world capitalist economy (Radice 1989). The nation-states continue to be important structures in the global system, but their position in this system is increasingly subordinate to that of a complex global array of corporations and institutions (such as the IMF, World Bank, the trade blocs, the GATT, etc.) that exercise control over not only the economic but also the political and sociocultural aspects of the global order (even though this order is still not a unified system). In this regard, it is misleading to conceptualize the political domain as an autonomous sphere within the contemporary global order (Slater 1993:106–107); rather, it should be regarded as a fundamental element or integral aspect of the total global system.

Contemporary political thought and action appears to be influenced more and more by the rapidly evolving global system of rules and regulations concerning trade and expanding consciousness about the nature of the global economy (Robertson 1992:26). In fact, the decisions and actions of the main political actors at the national and international levels of this system are clearly influenced by their awareness of the global economy (Brecher 1993). This is certainly the case in Latin America, where the perceived norms and explicit directives of the key international actors in the region tend to shape not only the foreign policies but also many of the domestic policies of the Latin American governments (Petras and Morley 1992). This does not mean, however, that political considerations are always subordinate to economic considerations and that some form of crude economic determinism underlies all political phenomena. To the contrary, the political and economic aspects are clearly intertwined and mutually affect each other.

One of the more important effects of globalization on the region is that it has increased the interconnectedness of political and economic considerations. Consequently, it is often difficult to separate what is specifically political from what is specifically economic, and vice versa. This situation makes a mockery of the claims of neoliberal ideologists and politicians that they are freeing the domain of private economic life from that of government and politics. As one astute observer has noted, the neoliberal rhetoric about limiting the role of the state in the economy is a cover for redirecting the state's role in the economy away from serving the needs of the popular classes in favor of the special interests of the upper classes. In this way, the social and economic inequalities associated with capitalism are legitimized by disinvolvement. Despite this subterfuge, however, there is "a necessary interdependence and complementarity between state and market" in all capitalist societies (Thomas 1989:344).

The political party programs and government policies in the region reflect the interconnectedness of the political and economic domains. They also reflect the global consciousness of the political actors, particularly their awareness of the relationships between national government policies and global economic constraints. In fact, this global consciousness colors and conditions the politics of the region to a striking degree. The deregulation of the economy, the reduction of government expenditures on public services, and the privatization of public enterprises are some of the more obvious examples of national government policies influenced by international economic conditions (NACLA 1993). In a sense, most Latin American government officials and politicians are constantly looking over their shoulders at the powerful global actors, intensely aware that the decisions and actions of the transnationals, the international lending agencies, and the U.S. government often have a direct impact on economic and political conditions in their societies. They also know that their actions can provoke a severe economic and political reaction from these global actors.

A key example of this relationship is what is euphemistically called "policy conditionality." In other words, international lending agencies provide financial assistance to the Latin American governments on the condition that they undertake certain policies that conform to the dictates of these agencies. This practice is explained in the following quote from an IMF publication:

> Use of the IMF's general resources must be in accordance with the provisions of the IMF's Articles and the policies adopted under them. Consequently, the IMF usually approves financial support on the condition that the member make an explicit commitment to a set of policy measures aimed at correcting its economic and financial imbalances within a reasonable period of time. This requirement, known as conditionality, seeks to strike an appropriate balance between the provision of financing and policy changes. (IMF 1993:13)

By conditioning their financial assistance on certain policy changes, the IMF and other international lending agencies are able to shape both the external and domestic economic policies of the Latin American governments.

Since the 1980s the key policy issues for most of the Latin American governments have been the repayment of their countries' external debts and the integration of their economies into the global economic system. Their policy debate has largely been confined to how, rather than whether, they should implement such policies. In this respect, the civilian regimes have largely adopted economic policies pursued by the military regimes that preceded them. As the chapters by Nef and Vilas indicate, the civilian regimes in Latin America have basically assumed that they can compete in the global market and repay their debts only if they hold wages down, continue to make their heavy debt payments, promote the production of exports, and maintain favorable business conditions that will attract foreign investment. This view has involved following the neoliberal policy reforms advocated by the international lending agencies, the U.S. government, and the transnational corporations. As a result, very little has been done to address the basic needs of the majority of their citizens or to combat the conditions responsible for widespread poverty in their countries.

The civilian regimes have also been reluctant to incur the disfavor of the local upper classes and the transnational capitalists who hold investments in their countries. They remember well what happened to the civilian regimes in the 1960s and 1970s that lost the support of the upper classes and their North American allies. They do not want to provoke the kind of repressive reaction from the military and their right-wing allies or the external political and economic pressures that Washington and the transnationals imposed on the earlier generation of civilian regimes. Therefore, they have had little choice but to accommodate their policies to the interests of the transnationals, the local business elites (large producers, bankers, large retailers, and exporters), their middle-class supporters, and the U.S. government.

The U.S. government is often more influential than the transnationals whose interests it largely represents. Washington has a wide variety of means—diplomatic, economic, political, and military—that it can use to influence the Latin American governments (Petras and Morley 1992:47–91). During the 1980s and early 1990s, the U.S. government helped to negotiate the transition from military to civilian rule in many Latin American states while promoting the integration of their economies into the global capitalist economic system. Washington's strategy for the region has been based on the promotion of "free markets," "trade not aid," and support for elected civilian regimes that continue the neoliberal policies of the former military dictatorships (Petras and Morley 1992:47–51). The U.S. government has maintained favorable relations with the Latin American military and continued a visible military presence in the region. Washington has projected its military power in the region through direct military interventions, joint military exercises, and joint military operations (e.g., in Peru, Bolivia, and

Colombia for the announced purpose of stopping the drug trade between these countries and the United States).

A critical analysis of Washington's support for the transition from military to civilian rule in Latin America reveals little evidence of a strong commitment on its part to the cause of political democracy in the region. The "changing of the guard" from military to civilian rulers provided the Latin American states with badly needed political legitimacy at a time when their international image and domestic support had declined to a new low (Petras and Morley 1992:65). The establishment of elected civilian regimes and the return of the military to their barracks has served U.S. interests in the region, since the greater legitimacy of the civilian regimes has enabled them to continue the unpopular neoliberal economic policies initiated under military rule. The restoration of civilian rule has also served U.S. interests by preserving the socioeconomic status quo in Latin America. That is to say, the military's retreat from power has eliminated the focal point for the popular political mobilizations that threatened the status quo in certain countries during the final, extremely unpopular years of military rule.

As Jorge Nef reveals, the authoritarian and classist nature of the Latin American states has remained unchanged despite the transition to civilian rule. The elected civilian leaders have dismantled only the most grievous of the repressive policies and authoritarian state structures they inherited from the military. Their power to transform the states they inherited from the military has been greatly restricted by the terms of the transition. In most cases, the military and the internal security forces remain a state within the state, possessing an informal veto power over any policies that threaten their status and direct interests.

The U.S. government has provided political and ideological support for the civilian regimes in Latin America on the condition that they pursue neoliberal policies and exclude leftist political parties and movements from effective participation in the formulation of government policies. U.S. military support for the armed forces and police has continued in most cases, despite evidence of continuing human rights abuses on the part of the army and internal security forces. For example, military officers from most of the Latin American countries continue to receive training from the U.S. Army at the School of the Americas in Fort Benning, Georgia. However, the deterioration of domestic economic conditions in the United States has limited Washington's ability to provide economic assistance to the civilian regimes in Latin America. In contrast to the copious economic assistance it dispensed throughout Latin America in the 1960s and 1970s, the U.S. government has had few funds to distribute for this purpose in the 1990s. Thus, there is an increasing gap between, on the one hand, the U.S. military and political influence in the region and, on the other, its ability to use financial and economic assistance to shape the policies of the Latin American governments (Petras and Morley 1992:72–74).

Despite differences in style and tone, successive U.S. administrations have evinced a basic continuity of policy toward Latin America during the 1980s and 1990s (Burbach 1993:16–22). The U.S. government has continued to blockade the Castro regime in Cuba, protect and advance the interests of North American–based transnational corporations operating in the region, and make sure that the Latin American governments service the huge foreign debts they owe to the global financial community. Washington has also continued to promote the integration of the Latin American economies into the global economic system and oppose basic political, economic, and social changes in the region that conflict with the national interests of the United States (Henwood 1993:23–28).

Evidence that the U.S. government is not seriously committed to consolidating and promoting political democracy in Latin America is to be found in its reluctance to take a strong stand against (1) the military's insistence in most countries that they be granted immunity from prosecution for the crimes they committed while in power; (2) the assassination of opposition political figures in El Salvador and Guatemala by elements closely associated with the military; (3) the Mexican regime's manipulation of elections and use of the state machinery to prevent the political opposition from gaining office; (4) President Alberto Fujimori's usurpation of political power in Peru with the backing of the military; (5) the human rights abuses committed by the armed forces in Haiti, Colombia, Peru, and Bolivia; and (6) the many other obviously antidemocratic practices that characterize contemporary politics throughout Latin America. Although it gives lip service to the cause of political democracy in Latin America, the U.S. government is primarily committed to promoting free trade, restricting the flow of refugees and unwanted immigrants, and maintaining U.S. political and economic hegemony in the region (Petras and Morley 1992:194–196).

Globalization and the Left in Latin America

The opposition of leftist political parties and movements to the current regimes in Latin America has generally been quite weak in most of the countries of the region since the collapse of the Soviet Union and the Eastern Bloc (Petras and Morley 1992:18–28; Robinson 1992). Global events during the late 1980s and early 1990s profoundly undermined the position of the more progressive forces in Latin American politics. The end of the cold war, the collapse of the Soviet Union and the state capitalist regimes in eastern Europe, the demise of the Sandinistas' revolutionary regime in Nicaragua, the pacification of the revolutionary struggle in El Salvador, as well as China's shift toward capitalism have created a global political environment that has greatly weakened the local appeal and international support for leftist political parties and progressive popular movements in Latin America.

Latin America's more progressive political forces have also been weakened by both the "global retreat of the intellectuals" from leftist parties and movements and the political decline of working-class parties and trade unions throughout the world (Chilcote 1990; and Petras and Morley 1992:151). The retreat of Latin American intellectuals from progressive politics and the political decline of working-class parties in the region began under the repressive military regimes of the 1970s and early 1980s. But post–cold war developments have also led to the massive withdrawal of intellectuals from leftist politics and the greatly diminished appeal of working-class organizations. Some progressive intellectuals and working-class leaders also entered into political compromises with the military to restore civilian rule, which distanced them from the more militant political elements of the popular classes. As a result, they no longer provide political leadership and support to working-class and peasant organizations. They have instead given their support in many cases to the current civilian regimes, whose neoliberal policies are exacting a tremendous toll on the popular classes.

Despite this loss of progressive and working-class leadership, there is continuing popular resistance to the neoliberal policies of the civilian regimes as well as rising popular pressure for major changes in the social order. As the contributions by Hellman, Miller, Vilas, Dore, and Kearney and Varese in this volume reveal, the new social movements that developed during the past two decades represent an important expression of the popular classes and a source of pressure for change. Many of these movements emerged during the period of military rule when the popular classes were forced to survive as best as they could on their own resources. Because the civilian regimes have largely excluded them from meaningful participation in the political process, the popular classes have continued to express their needs in these grassroots movements and community-based organizations.

A complex variety of movements and community-based organizations has been formed by workers, peasants, women, indigenous peoples, the unemployed, urban shantytown residents, gays and lesbians, and other social groups in Latin America. From a global perspective, what is most interesting about these new social movements is the extent to which they represent both a grassroots response to globalization and their internationalization as well. That is to say, many of the environmental, human rights, religious, feminist, and indigenous rights movements in Latin America are connected to and supported by their counterparts in other countries. In addition, even the more isolated and localized movements often receive assistance from international nongovernmental organizations (NGOs). Hellman notes that there were more than two hundred of these organizations operating in the remote Mexican state of Chiapas when the zapatista indigenous movement organized a rebellion there in 1994. In fact, the influence exercised by some of these international NGOs on local social movements through the provision of funds, technical assistance, and ideology has been described as a kind of "NGO imperialism" (Schuurman 1993:203; Petras and Morley 1992:160).

The international connections between social movements in different countries have created the potential for a kind of globalization from below in which the victims of globalization from above organize a concerted international struggle against the inequities of the global capitalist system (Brecher 1993). For example, the struggle against NAFTA gave rise to an international network of environmental, labor, religious, consumer, and political organizations in Canada, the United States, and Mexico. This international and interorganizational network developed a common program not only to oppose NAFTA but also to raise consciousness in the three countries about the need to transform the global economic system. Similar international networks have developed in Central America and the Asia-Pacific region (Brecher 1993:686). These international networks may be the harbingers of transnational social movements that mount an antisystemic challenge to the global capitalist system.

However, if the continued denationalization of the Latin American economies by the transnational corporations and the impoverishment of the popular classes via free market and free trade policies are to be checked by these movements and other progressive political forces in Latin America, they will have to mobilize the popular classes to win control of the state away from the upper classes and their transnational allies. They need a strategy that presents a clear and viable alternative to the prevailing neoliberal policies that now serve transnational capital and their local allies.

To be successful, this strategy will have to offer clear and effective means for rapidly raising the living standards of the majority of the population. This end can be accomplished only through a radical redirection of the economy so that it serves the basic needs of the population rather than the global interests of the transnationals, their local allies, and the international lending agencies. The absence of such a strategy has severely handicapped the progressive forces in Latin America and given the ruling right-wing and centrist parties a clear field to pursue their neoliberal policies at the expense of the general population.

The widespread diffusion of post-Marxist ideas by the international media as well as by North American and European foundations operating in Latin America has persuaded many of the leaders and militants of the more progressive groups in the region that Marxism is not a valid intellectual tool for critical social analysis and political struggle in the contemporary time period (Chilcote 1990; and Petras and Morley 1992:145–164). Influenced by these

ideas, many of these leaders and militants have rejected class analysis at a time
when the relations between those who control capital and those who control
the state, and the unequal distribution of income between the upper classes
and the lower classes, are more obvious than ever before in recent history
(Petras and Morley 1992:146–147). In place of Marxist theory and analysis,
these progressive political leaders and activists have tended to adopt a perspective based on post-Marxist rhetoric and liberal democratic idealism. The
fundamental problem with this perspective is that it does not provide an adequate critical analysis of, or adequate solutions to, the increasing social inequalities in Latin America, the basic authoritarianism of the Latin American
states, and the growing control of transnational capital over their economies.

Opposing the Neoliberal Project: An Alternative Strategy

Most of the progressive parties and movements in Latin America recognize
that they are seriously handicapped by their failure to offer an effective alternative to the reigning neoliberal project. As a result, they have established an
ongoing cross-national dialogue aimed at developing a new identity and
strategy. The main impetus for this dialogue has been the São Paulo Forum,
which was formed in July 1990 by representatives from more than forty leftist political parties and organizations from all over Latin America (Robinson
1992).

The Latin American Left is aware that certain global as well as regional
conditions favor the Left's potential popular appeal. Capitalism has continued to demonstrate that it is incapable of fulfilling the basic needs of the popular classes. Since the 1980s real per capita income and employment have
fallen throughout most of the countries of the region, while these countries
have continued to shoulder the burden of enormous foreign debts. As a result, the levels of poverty and social deprivation suffered by the popular
classes have increased as real spending on education, health, housing, and
other social services has declined. The proponents of capitalism have little evidence that the capitalist system serves the interests of the popular classes.

The end of the cold war and the democratization of the former Eastern
Bloc regimes have permitted the Latin American Left to shed its unwanted association with Soviet totalitarianism and the previous accusations of their
right-wing opponents that they were the local instruments of international
communist subversion. Now free of this political baggage, the Latin American
Left has the opportunity to gain widespread popular support for a new democratic socialist project that addresses the needs of the popular classes and offers
viable policy alternatives to the disastrous economic and social policies of the
pseudodemocratic regimes in power throughout most of the region.

A viable democratic socialist project is needed to advance the economic,
political, and social democratization of the Latin American societies and in

the process fulfill the basic needs of the majority of their populations (Garretón 1989; Harris 1992:205–215). However, socialism cannot be presented to the people as an abstract or a distant future goal but as a concrete program of action practiced on a daily basis. By creating alternative centers of popular power, the Left can build the foundations of a future democratic socialist regime. If this is not done, the Left inadvertently conveys the idea that the existing capitalist order is the only realistic alternative for the present. This false idea reinforces the ideological hegemony of capitalism and undermines the appeal of democratic socialism. Thus the Left must mobilize the popular classes in support of a democratic socialist project that creates alternative centers of popular power at the grassroots level—in the workplace and the community—while it mobilizes sufficient popular support to gain power at the national level.

The neoliberal project pursued by the forces in control of most of the Latin American countries sacrifices the interests of the majority to those of the local business elites and the transnational corporations. It is therefore possible to argue that neoliberalism is the enemy of democracy in Latin America. That is to say, it promotes inequality at both the international and national levels in the name of free markets and free trade, while it extolls the formal institutions, rather than the true spirit and substance, of democracy. As Nef indicates in his chapter, the neoliberal civilian governments in Latin America are only pseudodemocratic regimes characterized by limited political representation, superficial civil rights, and an inherent inability to address the major social problems and needs of Latin Americans.

An effective alternative to the neoliberal project requires the creation of a broad-based political movement in each country as well as regional alliances among such movements. These movements must be united in their commitment to reversing neoliberal policies. At the national level, such action will require the institutionalization of effective popular control over the state and economy; at the international level it will require a system of regional cooperation and integration that serves the interests of the majority of Latin Americans instead of the transnationals and the local business elites. The Latin American states could then negotiate more favorable terms for their participation in the global economy while meeting the needs of their people. This course of development could also contribute to the construction of a new global order based on mutually beneficial, rather than inequitable, relations.

As Elizabeth Dore indicates in her chapter, an alternative economic development strategy is required that both protects the natural environment as well as satisfies the basic needs of the majority of the population. Environmental issues have started to move to center stage of Latin American politics because of local and international concerns about Latin America's environmental degradation. The greening of Latin American politics will probably continue in the coming decades, and visionary leadership will be required if solutions are to be found for the environmental problems that threaten not only Latin America but also the planet as a whole. Such solutions must address the underlying economic and political factors—both local as well as global—that are responsible for the degradation of the natural environment. The solutions must also serve the interests of the indigenous peoples, who inhabit and depend on the ecosystems threatened by global capitalism.

The Sociocultural Effects of Globalization

It is difficult to imagine how anyone could hope to make sense of the world without understanding the many cultural issues associated with the human condition (Robertson 1992:145). This is especially true with Latin America. However, the cultural aspects of Latin American affairs should not be perceived as a separate, self-contained dimension of the larger social reality. The interconnectedness of culture and other major aspects of society is captured by the concept of "commodification," which many believe to be a basic cultural aspect of contemporary capitalist societies (Robertson 1992:42–45; and Thomas 1989:337). With the global expansion of capitalism, social life has increasingly become centered on the sale, purchase, and accumulation of an expanding number of commodities of one kind or another—hence the term *commodification*. There appears to be no limit on what can be bought and sold.

Globalization has intensified the commodification of social life. The global telecommunications media have greatly facilitated the marketing of global commodities throughout the region by the transnational corporations.

Since the 1960s the electronic media have been one of the main conduits for the promotion of values and the lifestyles of the advanced centers of the global capitalist system (Mattelart 1974). A commercial global media network now spans the planet. Through the promotion of global capitalist values, products, and lifestyles, the global media are contributing to the denationalization of the cultures of the individual Latin American countries.

The emphasis on accumulating commodities has changed the lifestyles and values of more and more Latin Americans. The conspicuous consumption of imported commodities of one kind or another has become an important characteristic of the upper and middle classes. Their affluence allows them to purchase many imported as well as locally produced commodities. Through the globalized media, they have been persuaded to adopt the standards of consumption and styles of material existence (dress, entertainment, housing, personal transportation, etc.) of their counterparts in the advanced capitalist countries of North America, western Europe, and to a lesser extent Japan. In the process, global standards and lifestyles have displaced many of the cultural values, beliefs, and customs that were previously particular to a specific national, provincial, or local culture. To a lesser extent, this pattern of global commodification has also affected the members of the lower classes, who often purchase commodities that they can ill afford but have been persuaded by the media to acquire.

Karl Marx used the term "commodity fetishism" to describe the commodification of social life in the capitalist societies of nineteenth-century Europe and North America (Thomas 1984:116). During the twentieth century, commodity fetishism appears to have become an important feature of contemporary culture in Latin America, as well as elsewhere in the world.

The increasing commodification of social life in Latin America has been accompanied, as we have seen, by the denationalization of Latin American cultures. Ironically, in an earlier period of the region's historical development, capitalism favored a certain nationalization of culture. The creation of national states and national cultures (largely reflecting the cultural values of the bourgeoisie) was promoted by the development of the international capitalist system during the period (mid–eighteenth to mid–twentieth centuries) when capital was largely being formed within the territorial confines of national states. To a certain extent, the new states in Latin America were required to develop "national cultures" in order to meet the international standards of statehood at the time, to distinguish themselves from one another, and to control the diverse ethnic communities within their newly formed state boundaries (Torres Rivas 1983:118–127).

However, in the present period of global capitalism, national cultures—like national schemes of economic development and national sovereignty—have become incompatible with the integration of the "national economies" of the Latin American states into the globalized capitalist system. The activities of the transnational corporations, the international financial agencies, and their local allies in Latin America have begun to undermine the national economic structures and national cultures created during the nation-building period of the recent past.

It is important to note, however, that the contemporary globalization does not appear to be creating a single, homogeneous international culture in place of the existing national cultures. To the contrary, globalization seems to be fomenting heterogeneity while promoting the denationalization and partial globalization of cultures (Robertson 1992:130–134). On the one hand, global capitalism has created a series of large 'world cities' in Latin America (Mexico City, Río de Janeiro, São Paulo, and Buenos Aires)—that serve as cosmopolitan nodes of a global network of international communications, transportation, financial transactions, tourism, and commercial trade. On the other hand, globalization is also fomenting cultural differentiation and the resurgence of traditional identities, values, and communities.

By threatening traditional identities and values, globalization has provoked the active resistance of many previously passive ethnic and religious groups who now see the survival of their distinct identities and values increasingly threatened. The global media have fed this resistance by reporting on the political mobilization of traditional ethnic and religious communities in different parts of the world (e.g., the former Soviet Union, Yugoslavia, etc.). This diffusion of information has created a demonstration effect, stimulating the revival of ethnic identities, indigenous communities, and religious practices that were either suppressed or almost eliminated by the forces of cultural nationalization.

Resistance to globalization has tended to take on fundamentalist, communal, and/or utopian forms of cultural and political expression. As John Kirk's analysis reveals, many countries in Latin America have experienced religious revivals in recent years, the main agents of which have been the fundamentalist Pentecostal churches. The fundamentalist Protestant churches have been particularly successful in gaining converts among the more marginalized sectors of the population, although in certain countries (e.g., Guatemala) they have made significant inroads in the middle and upper classes as well. Their skillful use of the media and the financial backing they receive from churches in the United States have greatly facilitated their recruitment of converts throughout Latin America.

Meanwhile, the Catholic Church's traditional support of the status quo has been strengthened by the Vatican's concerted efforts to enforce its conservative religious orthodoxy on both the clergy and laity in Latin America. As Kirk indicates, the ecclesiastical base communities (CEBs) and the progressive "people's church" movement, which were inspired by the universalistic and progressive ideas of liberation theology in the 1970s and early 1980s, have lost considerable ground under the sustained attacks of the conservative hierarchy of the Catholic Church (the oldest global institution in the region).

Countering these conservative trends, other international movements have facilitated progressive and more universalistic developments in Latin American culture and social relations. A variety of women's organizations, for example, are seeking to improve social conditions for women in Latin America, most of whom continue to be the "global victims" of an "international patriarchal system" in which men and masculine values predominate (see Enloe 1990).

Some of the more obvious ways in which Latin American women are victimized by global structures include the exploitative and sexist aspects of international tourism, the patriarchal values and practices of the Catholic Church, the cross-national trade in domestic servants, the exploitation of the largely female workforce in the assembly plants along the Mexican border with the United States, as well as the extensive use of sexism in global advertising and consumer marketing. Yet the expansion of global capitalism has also resulted in the feminization of the workforce in certain industries, the politicization and unionization of women in some of these industries, greater equality for women within the household, and greater autonomy for some women as a result of their increased income through employment (Benería 1989:255–256).

The influence of the international women's movement on Latin American women has been one of the more progressive sociocultural effects of globalization on Latin America. As Miller's analysis indicates, the generation of Latin American feminists that arose in the 1970s was initially influenced by the prevailing views of feminists in North America and western Europe. However, by the 1980s they had begun to challenge the cultural biases in these views and to make an important contribution themselves to the international women's movement.

The proliferation of women's organizations throughout Latin America in the 1980s and 1990s has had an important international effect. Many of these organizations maintain cross-national communications with one another and with women's organizations outside the region. Despite the persistence of patriarchal forms of domination and the victimization of women in Latin America, these organizations have made significant progress in combatting the sexism of Latin American society.

In sum, the sociocultural effects of globalization have permeated Latin America. The proliferation of women's organizations, the growing importance of environmental issues, and the emergence of indigenous people's movements are some of the most progressive examples of the sociocultural effects of the globalization process. The globalization of Latin America has stimulated many groups and communities to defend their identities and confront the more pernicious effects of globalization. As a result, cultural differentiation and resistance are as much a part of globalization as commodification and economic integration.

Conclusion

The foregoing discussion has offered a global perspective on contemporary Latin American affairs. The intent has been to provide the reader with a conceptual framework for viewing in an integrated and global manner the diverse and complex aspects of the contemporary social reality of Latin America. The global context of contemporary Latin American affairs is a primary factor in both the analysis, and the resolution, of the region's major problems.

The globalization of Latin American affairs will likely become a major focus of social theory, empirical analysis, ideological debate, and partisan politics in the coming decades. As public awareness grows about the global conditions responsible for both national and local problems, differences over how to respond to these conditions will become the focal point of the social movements and political struggles of the future (Robertson 1992:76).

Some version of the slogan "think globally and act locally" will most likely become one of the main themes of Latin American politics and economics, just as Latin Americans will likely start to collaborate at the global level. This course of development, which can be called "globalization from below" (Brecher 1993:688), will require widespread recognition of the fact that many intractable Latin American problems—such as extreme economic and social inequality, the degradation of the natural environment, and the breakdown of traditional forms of social solidarity—are embedded in the larger global setting.

The experience of Japan and the newly industrialized countries in Asia during the latter part of the twentieth century has clearly demonstrated that a society's internal conditions as well as its response to global conditions can greatly influence the form of its involvement in the global system (Robertson 1992:96). Although there are global constraints on their options, Latin Americans can clearly exercise choice in determining the forms of social change and the types of global involvement that will best serve their interests over the coming decades. Increasing global consciousness and the formation of strategic alliances among the more progressive forces in the region—such as the many women's organizations, the "New Left" political parties, the mobilized indigenous communities, and the environmentalist movements—could transform Latin America's political, economic, and social conditions as well as the nature of the region's integration with the rest of the world.

References

Aguilar, Alonso. *Pan-Americanism from Monroe to the Present: A View from the Other Side.* New York: Monthly Review Press, 1975.

Alimonda, Héctor. "MERCOSUR, Democracy, and Organized Labor." *Latin American Perspectives* (forthcoming).

Amin, Samir. *Unequal Development: An Essay on the Social Foundations of Peripheral Capitalism.* New York: Monthly Review Press, 1976.

———. *Empire of Chaos.* New York: Monthly Review Press, 1992.

Bambirra, Vania. *El capitalismo dependiente latinoamericano.* Mexico City: Siglo Veintiuno, 1976.

Barnet, Richard, and Ronald Muller. *The Power of the Multinational Corporations.* New York: Simon and Schuster, 1974.

Benería, Lourdes. "Gender and the Global Economy," in Arthur MacEwan and William Tabb, eds., *Instability and Change in the World Economy.* New York: Monthly Review Press, 1989.

Brecher, Jeremy. "Global Village or Global Pillage." *Nation,* December 6, 1993, 685–688.

Brooke, James. "Latins Envision a Single Trade Zone." *New York Times,* June 17, 1994:C2.

Burbach, Roger. "Clinton's Latin American Policy: A Look at Things to Come." *NACLA Report on the Americas* 26 (May 1993):16–34.

Cardoso, Fernando Henrique, and Enzo Falleto. *Dependency and Development in Latin America*. Berkeley: University of California Press, 1979.

Chilcote, Ronald. "The Retreat from Class in Latin America." *Latin American Perspectives* 65 (Spring 1990):3–38.

Chilcote, Ronald, and Joel Edelstein. *Latin America: Capitalist and Socialist Perspectives of Development and Underdevelopment*. Boulder, CO: Westview Press, 1986.

Enloe, Cynthia. *Bananas, Beaches, and Bases: Making Feminist Sense of International Politics*. Berkeley: University of California Press, 1990.

Evans, Peter. *Dependent Development: The Alliance of Multinational, State, and Local Capital in Brazil*. Princeton, NJ: Princeton University Press, 1979.

Frank, André Gunder. *Underdevelopment in Latin America: Historical Studies of Chile and Brazil*. New York: Monthly Review Press, 1967.

Furtado, Celso. *The Economic Development of Latin America: A Survey from Colonial Times to the Cuban Revolution*. London: Cambridge University Press, 1970.

Garretón, Manuel. "The Idea of Socialist Renovation in Chile." *Rethinking Marxism* 2, 2 (1989):8–37.

Gilpin, Robert. *U.S. Power and the Multinational Corporation: The Political Economy of Foreign Direct Investment*. New York: Basic Books, 1975.

Harris, Richard. *Marxism, Socialism, and Democracy in Latin America*. Boulder, CO: Westview Press, 1992.

Henwood, Doug. "Impeccable Logic: Trade, Development, and Free Markets in the Clinton Era." *NACLA Report on the Americas* 26 (May 1993):23–28.

Horowitz, Irving, Josué de Castro, and John Gerassi, eds. *Latin American Radicalism: A Documentary Report on Left and Nationalist Movements*. New York: Vintage Books, 1969.

IMF (International Monetary Fund). "Financial Support for Member Countries Complements Economic Policy Changes." *IMF Survey* (October 1993):13–15.

Jenkins, Rhys. *Transnational Corporations and Industrial Transformation in Latin America*. London: Macmillan, 1984.

Khor, Martin. "Free Trade and the Third World," in Ralph Nader et al., *The Case Against Free Trade: GATT, NAFTA, and the Globalization of Corporate Power*. San Francisco: Earth Island Press, 1993, 97–107.

MacEwan, Arthur. "Notes on U.S. Foreign Investment and Latin America." *Monthly Review* 45 (January 1994):15–26.

Magdoff, Harry. *The Age of Imperialism: The Economics of U.S. Foreign Policy*. New York: Monthly Review Press, 1969.

———. *Globalization: To What End?* New York: Monthly Review Press, 1992.

Mandel, Ernest. *Late Capitalism*. London: New Left Books, 1975.

Marini, Ruy Mauro. *Dialéctica de la dependencia*. Mexico City: Ediciones Era, 1974.

Mattelart, Armand. *La cultura como empresa multinacional*. Mexico City: Ediciones Era, 1974.

NACLA. "A Market Solution for the Americas?" *NACLA Report on the Americas* 26 (February 1993):16–17.

Nader, Ralph. "Free Trade and the Decline of Democracy," in Ralph Nader et al., *The Case Against Free Trade: GATT, NAFTA, and the Globalization of Corporate Power*. San Francisco: Earth Island Press, 1993, 1–12.

Pearce, Jenny. *Under the Eagle*. London: Latin American Bureau, 1981.

Petras, James, and Morris Morley. *Latin America in the Time of Cholera: Electoral Policies, Market Economics, and Permanent Crisis.* New York: Routledge, 1992.

Radice, Hugo. "British Capitalism in a Changing Global Economy," in Arthur MacEwan and William Tabb, eds., *Instability and Change in the World Economy.* New York: Monthly Review Press, 1989, 64–81.

Robertson, Roland. *Globalization: Social Theory and Global Culture.* Newbury Park, CA: Sage Publications, 1992.

Robinson, William. "The São Paulo Forum: Is There a New Latin American Left?" *Monthly Review* 44 (December 1992):1–12.

Schuurman, Frans, ed. *Beyond the Impasse: New Directions in Development Theory.* London: Zed Books, 1993.

Slater, David. "The Political Meanings of Development: In Search of New Horizons," in Frans Schuurman, ed., *Beyond the Impasse: New Directions in Development Theory.* London: Zed Books, 1993, 93–111.

Stein, Stanley Jr., and Barbara Stein. *The Colonial Heritage of Latin America: Essays on Economic Dependence in Perspective.* New York: Oxford University Press, 1970.

Thomas, Clive. *The Rise of the Authoritarian State in Peripheral Societies.* New York: Monthly Review Press, 1984.

———. "Restructuring the World Economy and Its Political Implications for the Third World," in Arthur MacEwan and William Tabb, eds., *Instability and Change in the World Economy.* New York: Monthly Review Press, 1989, 331–348.

Torres Rivas, Edelberto. "La nación: problemas teóricos e históricos," in Norbert Lechner, ed., *Estado y política en América Latina.* Mexico City: Siglo Veintiuno, 1983.

Vasconi, Tomás Amadeo. *Gran capital y militarización en América Latina.* Mexico City: Ediciones Era, 1978.

Wallerstein, Immanuel. *The Modern World System.* New York: Academic Press, 1974.

About the Book and Editors

Over the last two decades, economic, political, and social life in Latin America has been transformed by the region's accelerated integration into the global economy. Although this transformation has tended to exacerbate various inequities, new forms of popular expression and action challenging the contemporary structures of capital and power have also developed.

This volume is a comprehensive, genuinely comparative text on contemporary Latin America. In it, an international group of contributors offer multidimensional analyses of the historical context, contemporary character, and future direction of rural transformation, urbanization, economic restructuring, and the transition to political democracy. In addition, individual essays address the changing role of women, the influence of religion, the growth of new social movements, the struggles of indigenous peoples, and ecological issues. Finally, the book examines the influence of U.S. policy and of regionalization and globalization on the Latin American states.

Sandor Halebsky is professor of sociology at Saint Mary's University in Halifax, Nova Scotia. He coedited *Cuba in Transition: Crisis and Transformation* (Westview, 1992). *Richard L. Harris* is chair of the faculty at Golden Gate University in Monterey, California. He is one of the coordinating editors of the journal *Latin American Perspectives* and the author of *Marxism, Socialism, and Democracy in Latin America* (Westview, 1992).

About the Contributors

Elizabeth W. Dore is senior lecturer in Latin American history at the University of Portsmouth, England, and participating editor of *Latin American Perspectives,* author of *The Peruvian Mining Industry: Growth, Stagnation, and Crisis* (Westview, 1988). Her recent articles on ecology include "Debt and Ecological Disaster in Latin America," in *Race and Class,* 1992, and "Una Interpretación Socio-Ecológica de la Historia Minera Latinoamericana," in *Ecología Política,* 1994.

Judith Adler Hellman is professor of political and social science at York University in Toronto, Canada. She is the author of *Mexico in Crisis* (1978, 1983, 1988), *Journeys Among Women: Feminism in Five Italian Cities* (1987), and *Mexican Lives* (1994), and has written articles on peasant movements, rural development, feminism, ideology, and social movements in Europe and Latin America.

Cristóbal Kay is professor at the Institute of Social Studies, The Hague, Netherlands. He is the author of *Latin American Theories of Development and Underdevelopment* (1989), *New Developments in Cuban Agriculture: Economic Reforms and Collectivization* (1987), and coauthor of *Labour and Development in Rural Cuba* (1988). He has also written numerous articles in professional journals on Latin American affairs.

Michael Kearney is professor of anthropology, University of California, Riverside. He is author of *The Winds of Ixtepeji: World View and Society in a Zapotec Town* (1986) and *World View* (1984); as well as one of the coordinating editors of *Latin American Perspectives.*

John M. Kirk is professor of Latin American studies at Dalhousie University in Canada. He is the author of *José Martí, Mentor of the Cuban Nation* (1983), *Between God and the Party: Religion and Politics in Revolutionary Cuba* (1989), and *The Catholic Church and Politics in Nicaragua* (1992). He has also coedited five anthologies of essays on the Cuban and Central American development models of the 1980s and 1990s.

Francesca Miller was the 1993–1994 Faculty Fellow, University of California, Davis, Washington Center, Washington, D.C., is the author of *Latin American Women and the Search for Social Justice* (1991), and coauthor of *Women, Culture and Politics in Latin America* (1990).

Jorge Nef is professor of political science and Latin American studies at Guelph University in Ontario, Canada. He is the author of *The Political Economy of Inter-American Relations* (1994) and has contributed a number of chapters to books on Latin American politics, including "Governability and the Receiver State in Latin America," in A. Ritter et al, eds., *Latin America and the Caribbean to the Year 2000*

308 About the Contributors

(1992), and "Normalization, Popular Struggles, and the Receiver State," in Jan Kippers Black, ed., *Latin America: Problems and Promise* (Westview, 1991).

Stefano Varese is professor of anthropology, Department of Native Studies, University of California, Davis. The author of *La sal de los cerros: una aproximación al mundo campa,* he has also written articles on ethnicity and ethnopolitics in Latin America.

Carlos M. Vilas is research professor at the Universidad Nacional Autonoma de Mexico, Mexico City. Coauthor of *The Socialist Option in Latin America* (1992), he also wrote *The Sandinista Revolution: National Liberation and Social Transformation in Central America* (1986), *State, Class, and Ethnicity in Nicaragua* (1989), and numerous articles on Latin American affairs that have been published in professional journals in the United States, Latin America, and Europe.

John Weeks is professor of economics and director of the Centre for Development Studies, School of Oriental and African Studies, University of London. He is author or editor of eleven books, including *The Economics of Central America* (1985) and (with Wim Pelupessy) editor of *Maladjustment in Central America* (1993).

Index

and Vatican II, 195, 235–237, 239,
   250
and women, 186, 190–191, 196,
   198, 300
Causa R, 157
CEBs. *See* Ecclesiastical base
   communities
CELAM. *See* Latin American Bishops
   Council
Centro Salvadoreño de Tecnología
   Apropiada (CESTA), 273
CESTA. *See* Centro Salvadoreño de
   Tecnología Apropiada
Cetina Gutierrez, Rita, 191
CGSB. *See* Coordinadora Guerrillera
   Simón Bolívar
Chamorro, Violeta Barrios de, 96
Chance, John K., 62
Chicago School, 88
Chile, 35–36, 55, 58, 84, 145, 187
   activism in, 72, 150, 158, 166, 242
   agriculture in, 23, 28–30, 33
   debt of, 89(table), 91(table), 93,
      122(table), 124(table), 126
   economic reform in, 38, 116,
      117(table), 130, 286
   economy of, 97, 119, 121(table),
      122(table), 129(table), 130,
      144(table), 154(table)
   employment in, 32–33, 142,
      143(table), 144(table), 145(table),
      146(table)
   indigenous peoples in, 207, 217,
      224
   military in, 94, 95(table), 99–100
   politics in, 84, 98–100, 282–283
   poverty in, 38, 61, 67–70, 97, 119
   religion in, 236, 245, 249
   women in, 33, 177, 186, 190–191,
      195–196, 198–199, 203
Chinantecs, 214
Chungara, Domitila Barrios de, 198
Church, Charism and Power (Boff),
   239
CIM. *See* Comisión Interamericana de
   Mujeres
Cities. *See* Urban areas

Class, 8, 81–83, 126–127
   and Catholic Church, 235, 238, 239,
      241
   and the environment, 11, 253, 260,
      269, 271, 273, 276
   and ethnicity, 15, 210, 219
   and globalization, 282–283, 285,
      295–296, 298–299
   and new social movements, 167, 168,
      170–171, 180
   in rural areas, 23, 27, 31, 42, 269
   and women, 188, 194, 198
   See also Working class
Cleary, Edward, 235, 245–247
Cleaver, Harry, 173
Clientalism, 10, 16, 70–71, 178
Clinton, Bill, 99, 103
Club Femenino de Cuba, 193
Coca, 37
Cochibamba, 218
COICA. *See* Coordinating Body of
   Indigenous Peoples' Organizations
   of the Amazon Basin
Collins, Jane, 57
Collor de Mello, Fernando, 98, 157
Colombia, 23, 28, 56, 141
   debt of, 91(table), 122(table),
      124(table)
   economy of, 36, 38, 117(table),
      143(table), 144(table)
   gross domestic product of,
      121(table), 122(table), 144(table)
   human rights abuses in, 100, 293
   income in, 119, 144(table),
      146(table), 154(table)
   indigenous peoples in, 207, 217, 224
   military in, 85, 94, 95(table), 100
   politics in, 71–72, 85, 98, 100, 102
   religion in, 245, 249
   women in, 33, 186, 188, 195
Colonization, 8, 83, 187–188,
   208–210, 213–214, 282
Colorado Party, 100
Colosio, Luis, 101
Comisión Interamericana de Mujeres
   (CIM), 194, 197
Commodification, 298–299, 301